Pennel: April 1974

AN ANNOTATED

SECONDARY BIBLIOGRAPHY SERIES

ON ENGLISH LITERATURE

IN TRANSITION

1880–1920

HELMUT E. GERBER

GENERAL EDITOR

W. SOMERSET MAUGHAM

JOSEPH CONRAD

THOMAS HARDY

E. M. FORSTER

JOHN GALSWORTHY

GEORGE GISSING

D. H. LAWRENCE

H. G. WELLS

# THE CONTRIBUTORS

PIERRE COUSTILLAS
*University of Lille*

PAUL GOETSCH
*University of Freiburg*

JAMES A. ROGERS
*New York Institute of Technology*

JOSEPH WOLFF
*Loyola University of Chicago*

# George Gissing

## AN
## ANNOTATED
## BIBLIOGRAPHY
## OF WRITINGS
## ABOUT HIM

COMPILED AND EDITED BY
### JOSEPH J. WOLFF

NORTHERN ILLINOIS UNIVERSITY PRESS

DE KALB, ILLINOIS

Joseph J. Wolff is a Professor of English at Loyola University of Chicago.

Library of Congress Cataloging in Publication Data

Wolff, Joseph J
  George Gissing: an annotated bibliography of writings
about him.

  (An Annotated secondary bibliography series on English
literature in transition, 1880–1920)
    1.  Gissing, George Robert, 1857–1903—Bibliography.
I.  Series.
Z8346.W65         016.823'8        73–15093
ISBN 0–87580–038–6

# Preface

The writings about George Gissing dating from 1880 to 1970 are here presented as completely as the great breadth of the finding allows. The objective approach in abstracting hundreds of references to Gissing has sought to capture the sense of the original, its content and judgment, while at the same time recognizing its tone and prejudice. The merit, the perceptiveness, perhaps even the ignorance, of the critic at times can only be grasped and appreciated by excerpting from the original; in such instances, I have presented the pertinent quoted matter.

This work purports to be more exhaustive than any previous bibliography of works about George Gissing; the frailty of human endeavor allows for omissions. A bibliography of this magnitude stems from endless sources, particularly now that the modest cost of reproducing and mailing makes articles easily available. As leads to additional entries continue to present themselves, there comes a time when the line must be drawn. I draw it with this presentation, being gratefully aware that "the glory of the imperfect" has its compensations.

I have verified what I have included in this bibliography and thereby trust that erroneous items that have appeared in so many earlier Gissing studies have been eliminated. For the many Gissing bibliographies that have facilitated my task, particularly those noted in the BIBLIOGRAPHY OF BRITISH LITERARY BIBLIOGRAPHIES (Clarendon Press, 1969), I am grateful. Anyone familiar with the partial bibliographies of writings about Gissing in England and America that I prepared through the years for publication in Helmut E. Gerber's ENGLISH FICTION IN TRANSITION and ENGLISH LITERATURE IN TRANSITION will discover that hundreds of these abstracts are given here in greater detail; furthermore, additional abstracts have expanded the total number of entries. The supplemental bibliography of continental references compiled by Pierre Coustillas and Paul Goetsch for EFT have been invaluable. Perhaps the most rewarding discoveries came from Gissing's own notes and letters and from the scholarly articles, books, and annotations derived from them, particularly by Pierre Coustillas, Mabel Collins Donnelly, Jacob Korg, and Arthur C. Young. It is impossible to exaggerate my debt to them not only for the specific articles they have found but also for the yield that their suggestions and clues have produced.

In keeping with the format of the Maugham, Conrad, and Hardy volumes in the Northern Illinois University Press series of annotated secondary bibliographies, all under the general editorship of Helmut E. Gerber, this bibliography concentrates on writings about Gissing. If a critical book about Gissing prompted further reviews, I have listed them in the entry treating the book itself.

Whenever an article reappears, such as an article recast as an introduction to a Gissing reprint, the original reference calls attention to the subsequent use of the same material. This practice is occasionally difficult, particularly when an author like Frank Swinnerton reworks his own memories and opinions with little or no additional information or fresh insights. Doctoral dissertations are included, though seldom abstracted. Where appropriate, I have verified the existence of these dissertations by referring to Lawrence F. McNamee's DISSERTATIONS IN ENGLISH AND AMERICAN LITERATURE (NY & Lond: Bowker, 1968; SUPP I, 1969), or to DISSERTATION ABSTRACTS. If the dissertation has been published in some form, I have included both an abstract and a notation of select reviews.

## ACKNOWLEDGMENTS

Anyone who specializes in English literature in transition, 1880–1920, learns from experience how much the crisp periodicals and newspapers of the period are now flaking away. One wise librarian explained to me that the very quality of the paper used in these publications notably deteriorated in the second half of the nineteenth century. Before it becomes too late, many clumsy volumes of these works ought to be transferred to film. Furthermore, surprisingly few British newspapers of this period are available in any form in America.

Perhaps more than any other scholarly project, an annotated bibliography depends on the resources of research libraries. Fortunately, I have been permitted to use the following libraries and their extensive collections; to their directors and staffs I wish to express my genuine thanks: British Museum Newspaper Library, London; Center for Research Libraries, Chicago; Chicago Public Library; The Newberry Library, Chicago; and the Regenstein Library of the University of Chicago. Sister Rita Stalzer of the Cudahy Library at Loyola University of Chicago has been extremely cooperative, and I wish to offer her my special thanks.

In addition to those already acknowledged as contributors, several other generous admirers of Gissing have helped me. They often reminded me about references that I might well have overlooked, or of annotated articles in their own college or university libraries. While I have imposed upon many others, I am particularly aware of my debt to the following: Philip Armato (Northern Illinois University), Marie Tate Farr (Greenville, N.C.), Helmut E. Gerber (Arizona State University), James Haydock (Wisconsin State University), Shigeru Koike (Tokyo Metropolitan University), Jacob Korg (University of Washington), Edward S. Lauterbach (Purdue University), and Raymond G. Malbone (New York State University College).

Still others in the academic community deserve my personal gratitude, and I wish to extend it warmly to Stuart M. Tave (University of Chicago), George N. Thoma (Indiana University), Rita C. Clarkson and Agnes McN. Donohue of Loyola University of Chicago, and especially to the late Viatorian Father Carl J. Stratman. Each of them at critical times has given me more than words of encouragement.

Loyola University of Chicago has provided me with both a faculty research grant and a sabbatical leave to work in London, thereby enabling me to draw upon the unique holdings of the British Museum. Without this assistance, the present study would never have been completed.

And finally, the success of the behind-the-scenes work of the heart and hands that go to make a work as perfect as man and woman can make it, must be attributed to my family; the cheers go to them. When the work falters, the fault is mine. To Bob, to Alec, but most of all to Mary Ellen, this book in affectionately dedicated.

JOSEPH J. WOLFF

# Contents

Titles of Gissing's books appear in italic type; titles of his stories, in roman capitals and lower case with quotation marks. Titles of books by other authors and names of periodicals and newspapers appear in capitals and small capitals. The translations appearing in parentheses are confined to meanings of the phrases; however, it should be noted that the titles of translations are seldom literal ones.

# George Gissing

## AN ANNOTATED BIBLIOGRAPHY
## OF WRITINGS ABOUT HIM

# A Checklist

## OF THE WORKS OF GEORGE GISSING
## CITED IN THIS BIBLIOGRAPHY

## I. SEPARATE WORKS

*Workers in the Dawn.* London: Remington, 1880
*The Unclassed.* London: Chapman & Hall, 1884
*Demos.* London: Smith, Elder, 1886
*Isabel Clarendon.* London: Chapman & Hall, 1886
*Thyrza.* London: Smith, Elder, 1887
*A Life's Morning.* London: Smith, Elder, 1888
*The Nether World.* London: Smith, Elder, 1889
*The Emancipated.* London: Richard Bentley, 1890
*New Grub Street.* London: Smith, Elder, 1891
*Denzil Quarrier.* London: Lawrence & Bullen, 1892
*Born in Exile.* London: A. & C. Black, 1892
*The Odd Women.* London: Lawrence & Bullen, 1893
*In the Year of Jubilee.* London: Lawrence & Bullen, 1894
*Eve's Ransom.* London: Lawrence & Bullen, 1895
*Sleeping Fires.* London: T. Fisher Unwin, 1895
*The Paying Guest.* London: Cassell, 1895
*The Whirlpool.* London: Lawrence & Bullen, 1897
*Human Odds and Ends.* London: Lawrence & Bullen, 1898
*Charles Dickens: A Critical Study.* London: Blackie, 1898
*The Town Traveller.* London: Methuen, 1898
*The Crown of Life.* London: Methuen, 1899
*Our Friend the Charlatan.* London: Chapman & Hall, 1901.
*By the Ionian Sea.* London: Chapman & Hall, 1901
*The Private Papers of Henry Ryecroft.* London: Archibald Constable, 1903
*Veranilda.* London: Archibald Constable, 1904

GEORGE GISSING

*Will Warburton.* London: Archibald Constable, 1905
*The House of Cobwebs.* London: Archibald Constable, 1906
*The Sins of the Fathers.* Chicago: Covici, 1924
*Critical Studies in the Works of Charles Dickens.* New York: Greenberg, 1924
*The Immortal Dickens.* London: Cecil Palmer, 1925
*A Victim of Circumstances.* London: Constable, 1927
*Selections Autobiographical and Imaginative from the Works of George Gissing.* London: Jonathan Cape, 1929
*Brownie.* New York: Columbia University Press, 1931
*Stories and Sketches.* London: Michael Joseph, 1938
*George Gissing's Commonplace Book.* New York: New York Public Library, 1962
*Notes on Social Democracy.* London: Enitharmon Press, 1968


## II. LETTERS

*Letters of George Gissing to Members of his Family,* ed by Algernon and Ellen Gissing. Lond: Constable, 1927
*George Gissing and H. G. Wells: Their Friendship and Correspondence,* ed with an intro by Royal A. Gettmann. Urbana: University of Illinois Press, 1961
*The Letters of George Gissing to Eduard Bertz,* ed with an intro by Arthur C. Young. New Brunswick: Rutgers University Press; Lond: Constable, 1961
*The Letters of George Gissing to Gabrielle Fleury,* ed by Pierre Coustillas. New York: New York Public Library, 1964

# Introduction

The observation by George Gissing's hero in *The Unclassed* that the "over-powering consciousness of sin is an archaism of our time" found its way in 1884 into the personal notebook of Prime Minister William Ewart Gladstone. This recognition stands as one of many that stamped Gissing as a novelist of ideas. Even in the early years of his career, Gissing's books were sprinkled with such positive assertions, with the result that he became for the reviewers a novelist preoccupied with ideas and attentive to social themes. Seldom pleased with the nature of Gissing's ideas, reviewers repeatedly scolded him for testifying only to the sadness of life. Would the reviewers have treated his novels any differently had they known that the sadness, the suffering, stemmed from his own bouts with life? Gissing's earliest heroes shouted the novelist's own feelings and ideas. To reenforce their arguments, he plunged himself directly into his own books with no pretense at posing as a disinterested observer. He told his friend Eduard Bertz that he never meant to stand at any distance from his fictional characters—"I'm inclined to think that the purely impersonal method of narrative has its advantages. Of course it approximates the dramatic. No English writer that I know (unless it be George Moore) has yet succeeded in adopting this method. Still I shall never try (and you do not wish me) to suppress my own *spirit*. To do that, it seems to me, would be to renounce the specific character of the novelist. Better, in that case, to write plays."

The reviewers, while frequently protesting Gissing's attitudes, never questioned his sincerity. But why did (if indeed he did) so sincere a novelist expect his offensive characters to make interesting reading? Did he intentionally make his penniless characters so sensitive that they perceived their own misery? Gissing's critics apparently were perplexed by what they thought were mistaken judgments; they consequently took many opportunities to recommend such political, social, or religious solutions that were usually endorsed by their publishers.

The reviewers helped little, at first, in expanding the sale of the novels. Gissing's fiction, during the first decade of his career, was usually noted in unsigned, omnibus reviews typically headed "New Novels." Over the years, almost imperceptibly, such omnibus reviews gradually increased

5

the space and improved the position given Gissing's books. When some weekly publications carried a few paragraphs on virtually every work Gissing wrote and frequently witnessed similarities in his previous novels, particularly in *Demos* and *Thyrza,* Gissing was well on his way to becoming a respected novelist, even though the novels actually registered very low sales. Gissing earned respect, not popularity. He did not seek to promote his own work; rather he neglected opportunities to enjoy the hospitality of admiring readers, almost avoiding the dinners honoring the more established writers. Aside from Morley Roberts, W. H. Hudson, and Alfred Hartley, Gissing cultivated few friendships; perhaps he found satisfying his regular and cordial corerspondence with his German friend Eduard Bertz; he did nothing to ingratiate himself with reviewers.

Ready as he was to parade his doom and to blame society for his own misfortunes, Gissing could not possibly lay at the door of his family or society at large his disastrous marriages. Here the choice of the man emerges. Morley Roberts and H. G. Wells leave us with impressions of Gissing's appearance that are probably more reliable than those his sister Ellen projects. Other acquaintances picture him variously, each seeing him differently. W. Robertson Nicoll recalls him as being "well dressed, bland, debonair and communicative"; but Henry James severely describes him as "altogether an extraordinarily ungainly, common, ill-shaped figure; almost knock-kneed, bearing the unmistakable stamp of Wakefield, his birthplace." Are the viewers governed by their own tastes, or did Gissing present himself differently to each? Gissing's letters often suggest that he was conscious of his own awkwardness; however, in view of the flattering portrait drawn by Sir William Rothenstein, that image is difficult for Gissing's admirers to accept.

Despite the fact that Gissing occasionally portrayed characters outside London, he seemed to be at home in the London slums. The verisimilitude and realism that were his methods perhaps needed at this time the drab and the ugly as subjects. In the last ten years of his life this image of Gissing was to change significantly. At first, in *The Emancipated,* the change was slight but forward-looking. In *Sleeping Fires,* Gissing moved his setting to Greece, although his characters remained indisputably English. In *The Town Traveller* he lifted the gray clouds to permit lighter moods and admit laughter; then, with *Charles Dickens: A Critical Study* he achieved success as a literary critic. Perhaps these shifts were related to events in Gissing's personal life—soon after the birth of his younger son in January 1896, Gissing left his second wife; weakened by ill health and discouraged by his writing, he traveled to Italy where he planned to begin the book he had contracted to write about Dickens. He told Bertz that he had to "make a new start, intellectually and commercially." Begun in Siena in 1897, the book on Dickens proved so successful that another publisher soon asked Gissing to write a set of introductory essays for a reprinting of several Dickens novels. Ironically, Dickens, the most popular of all Victorian novelists, was during these years virtually neglected. Gissing had brought Dickens back to the reviewers; they were to reconsider their judgments of Dickens, to draw comparisons between Gissing and Dickens in the representation of the lower classes, and for the most part to praise Gissing's critical achievement.

From Siena, Gissing journeyed to Calabria to indulge himself in the "glorious warmth and colour of the south" and to gather materials for *By the Ionian Sea* and *Veranilda*. In March he received Wells and his wife in Rome and did all he could to reveal the splendors of the past to one who stared into the future. It ought not surprise us that in his anonymous review of *Sleeping Fires,* Wells had had little enthusiasm for Gissing's melancholy. What Wells really thought of Gissing's writings probably best comes to light in the essay originally meant to be Wells's preface to *Veranilda:* "And indeed, for all their merit and value, when one thinks of the middle years of this man's life—of journeys and relationships and hopes and this and that—it all seems to be going on under a sunless sky, across which this grey cloud canopy, this unending, inky succession of words, drives remorselessly forever."

The continent again warmed Gissing in a special way in the last years of his life by providing him Gabrielle Fleury. An unexpected joy embraced him, a trust and ease altogether new to his existence. In Gabrielle was "a mind of rare delicacy, emotional without emotionalism, sensitive to every appeal of art, and rich in womanly perceptiveness." That her mind stimulated Gissing is evident in his remaining books. *The Crown of Life* is a tribute to the love she brought him, and *The Private Papers of Henry Ryecroft* is a sigh of satisfaction unparalleled in any of his other works. A volume of autumnal reflections, the occasional jottings of a man released from the day-to-day urgency of London and comfortably at ease in the English countryside, *Ryecroft* brought Gissing a new public among those who treasured the quiet denunciation of the worry, chase, and futility of city turmoil. Many friendly reviewers cordially greeted the book as proof that Gissing had discarded his glum and haunted hallucination of human life.

*By the Ionian Sea* and *The Private Papers of Henry Ryecroft* seem in retrospect to crown Gissing's literary career and arrange a final impression for his obituaries. Here was a melancholy man who described both the misery which he abhorred and the beauty he treasured. His misfortune was to cherish the classics and to despise the mob when social revolution was elevating the ugly in all that was common.

In contrast to their reaction to Gissing's novels, the reviewers praised *Ryecroft* extravagantly, calling it a masterpiece, a charming and sane spiritual autobiography, although the TIMES LITERARY SUPPLEMENT cautioned that it was a "*tour de force* of authenticity, never of revelation." In death, Gissing was remembered as a true artist, serious and conscientious, whose pessimism was intensified by the great intelligence of his characters.

The details of his private life were withheld from the obituaries, although several sources later confirmed that literary gossip rumored conflicting versions of his life with Gabrielle Fleury. Arnold Bennett recorded in his JOURNALS in July 1904 what Wells had told him of Gissing's last hours: "Wells gave me an account of how he went over to St. Jean de Luz when Gissing was dying. Gissing's mouth had to be sponged over and over with absolute alcohol. Wells did this. The woman was incompetent and stupid." Was this the Gabrielle of "rare delicacy"? Rumor of this sort was probably useful to Morley Roberts when he wrote his fictional biography of Gissing, THE PRIVATE LIFE OF HENRY MAITLAND, and when Frank Swinnerton, a younger writer committed to a newer form of fiction, set out to write his critical study of Gissing's work. Appearing in 1912, these books served Gissing's reputation with little objectivity. Swinnerton's study became the subject of two doctoral dissertations, as the source for Gissing appraisals shifted to the academic community. MAITLAND provoked the curious to ask more questions about Gissing's private life.

Once Gissing's letters to his family became public in 1927 the novelist's past and future passed into the hands of the academic profession. Gissing's social ideas were scrutinized—his representation of women, his classical allusions, his criticism by Swinnerton, and his position in the history of the English novel. But it was several years before Gissing's diary and letters were acquired by Americans, particularly by the Yale University and the New York Public libraries. When they were examined by scholars, the larger questions about Gissing's life were partially answered, and many errors previously held were corrected. Reflecting his beliefs and travels, Gissing's novels could be responsibly assessed in light of his biography. His letters corroborated surmises about his literary allegiances.

Beginning with 1954, for ten extremely important years to Gissing scholarship, Mabel Collins Donnelly, Royal A. Gettmann, John D. Gordan, Jacob Korg, and Arthur C. Young carefully demonstrated the ties between the novelist's life and his writings. While the letters to Wells and Bertz more than compensate for the shortcomings of the family's edition of Gissing correspondence, the full edition of Gissing's letters, now in preparation, will do much to promote his reputation.

Nearly a hundred years after the publication of Gissing's first fiction, his reputation as a literary name seems firmly established. Since 1965, the GISSING NEWSLETTER—initially edited by Jacob Korg and more recently by Pierre Coustillas—has published findings, large or small, concerning

Gissing. Meanwhile, Helmut E. Gerber's ENGLISH LITERATURE IN TRANSITION keeps abreast of Gissing criticism by its annotated bibliography. In the summer of 1971, the National Book League presented an exhibition of Gissing materials in London titled "The Rediscovery of George Gissing." Pierre Coustillas, now in command of all aspects of that rediscovery, has concentrated on clarifying Gissing's biography, a task that is especially appropriate since Gissing's life is always near the surface of his work. Of course Gissing's novels do not tempt serious scholars to superimpose classical myths upon his fictions, simply because they do not lend themselves to such treatment; they suggest no such puzzles. Rather, his books reward scrutiny for new literary dimension in ways that Walter Allen, Irving Howe, George Orwell, William Plomer, V. S. Pritchett, Thomas Seccombe, and Robert Shafer have demonstrated.

If Gissing is a "chip the size of a block," the image to be hacked takes many forms: he is a prose stylist, a conservative recluse, an anti-hero, a protesting liberal, an advocate for women's rights, or a pagan guide to antiquity. Whether Gissing is all or none or just one of these, he is preeminently a writer whose individual works, not yet firmly grasped, demand perceptive assessment. What Pierre Coustillas, John Goode, John Gross, and Robert L. Selig have recently done with *Isabel Clarendon, The Nether World, New Grub Street,* and *In the Year of Jubilee* testifies to the fact that the sensitive reader, is using both an in-depth and an in-breadth approach to a Gissing book, will be amply compensated. A writer whose work, according to Virginia Woolf, merited careful attention because "this man understood," cannot be appraised singly or lightly—his work is many faceted.

# The Bibliography

**1** "New Novels," GRAPHIC (Lond), XXI (19 June 1880), 627.
*Workers in the Dawn* must be "intended as a plea for the necessity of City Missions." The book lacks plot and seemingly wants only to show what "we fain would hide from the gaze of the gentler members of our families," i.e., those savages of our city whose souls must be saved.

**2** "Novels," ILLUSTRATED LONDON NEWS, LXXVII (31 July 1880), 110.
*Workers in the Dawn* has considerable force and undoubtedly shows earnest intention, but the story rambles in various directions resulting in a collection of "squalid and shocking scenes." The hero acts unaccountably, "throwing away many miraculous chances" to choose instead a "drunken drab." The tale is full of "plain, not to say coarse, language, oaths, slang, and questionable company." "It is a very dark and painful story, written in parts with no little power."

**3** "Novels of the Week," ATHENAEUM, No. 2746 (12 June 1880), 758.
In *Workers in the Dawn,* G says that the "social difficulties of over-population and pauperism may be redressed by rousing the passions of the poor." Since G spares no "graphic detail of the miseries of the vicious and the poor," we get a striking picture of the times. G is a partisan, polemical novelist.

**4** "Our Library Table," WHITEHALL REVIEW, 15 July 1880, p. iv.
*Workers in the Dawn* "seems intended to expose the evils of irreligion and drunkenness, but is rather tiresome reading." Seldom have we seen "less amusing puppets."

**5** "Our Wednesday Book-Box," WORLD (Lond), 6 Oct 1880, p. 18.

*Workers in the Dawn* treats of high and low life, rendering the low as "unnecessarily coarse and profane." The work is "as feeble a history of nauseous people and unsavoury things as can well be." [Slight.]

**6** "Recent Novels," DAILY NEWS (Lond), 29 July 1880, p. 6.

*Workers in the Dawn* is an extraordinary book that gives readers "some idea of the depth and extent of depravity which exists in the heart of our social system." The book ends "melodramatically enough in tragic and final disappointment"; its tone is "bitter and resentful"; its "style, often illiterate, is redeemed only by intensity and earnestness."

**7** Saintsbury, George. "New Novels," ACADEMY, XVIII (31 July 1880), 76–77.

*Workers in the Dawn,* despite G's sincerity, is an extravagant novel. G blames the trials of life on the social order. The novel is not for young ladies because in choosing his characters G is "more adventurous than is usual with the English novelist."

**8** [*Workers in the Dawn*], MANCHESTER EXAMINER AND TIMES, 15 Sept 1880, p. 3.

*Workers in the Dawn* is remarkable for its power, its vivid descriptions of London slums, its intense pathos, and its discriminating portrayal of characters. G is earnest and bold, outspoken but not irreverent. His chief characters have dismissed the superstitions of Christianity and have given themselves to reducing human suffering. Which character, if any, are we to positively identify with the novelist and his own views on life? G undoubtedly means to call the reader's attention to serious social inequities. Arthur Golding's early years represent the best passages of the book. G needs more experience in constructing a story, as he learns the "expediency of restraint." *Workers* "emphatically offers a promise of something great."

**9** *"Workers in the Dawn,"* SPECTATOR, LIII (25 Sept 1880), 1226–27.

The novel is powerful despite the "ludicrous ignorance and deep-seated prejudice in the delineation of character and description of life." In Arthur and Carrie, we feel that "we are dealing with real flesh and blood." G is to be congratulated for drawing no moral. G misunderstands Christianity; the novelist ought to have "kept in bounds a cynicism that refuses to see any good in institutions which he does not understand, and with which he has no sympathy." G cannot describe what he has not observed or experienced.

# 1881

[No entries for this year.]

# 1882

[No entries for this year.]

# 1883

[No entries for this year.]

# 1884

**10** Barker, Arthur R. R. "New Novels," ACADEMY, XXV (28 June 1884), 454.
*The Unclassed* must have been written by a woman; the book shows the influence of Zola. Its manner is realistic to "a degree which will shock many readers." Verisimilitude is often sacrificed for effect.

**11** "The Book Market," DAILY TELEGRAPH (Lond), 21 Aug 1884, p. 6.
*The Unclassed* presents "an unpleasant subject, touched upon with considerable force and skill." Through Waymark, G states the cruelty of the solitude of young people without means but with the sensitivity that intensifies their sorrow. With his forcible style, G can hope to gain readers if his next novel exhibits better judgment in choosing materials.

**12** "New Novels," GRAPHIC (Lond), XXX (13 Sept 1884), 286.
*The Unclassed* gives us a glimpse of people usually "excluded from English fiction," athough the author is not "a pioneer of the school of M. Zola." The book cannot accomplish anything; no reader could possibly enjoy it.

**13** "A Novel for Men," EVENING NEWS, 25 June 1884, p. 1.
*The Unclassed* is daring both in character and situation; it treats moral problems seriously and in an unpretentious style. G's representation of the relationship between Ida Starr and Osmond Waymark "is exceedingly fresh and life-like." He also introduces several dwellers of London's slums with such terrible realism as to mark our disgrace. While G knows his sub-

jects thoroughly, his assessment of the problem and its solution—in his evaluation of Christianity—is erroneous.

**14** "Novels of the Week," ATHENAEUM, No. 2957 (28 June 1884), 820–21.
While the subject matter of *The Unclassed* is disagreeable, G's writing deserves our favorable attention. Some passages "show genuine observation at first hand." He succeeds in representing men, but fails with women; "the heroine lives in a moral atmosphere which is certainly dim and perplexed."

**15** "Pages in Waiting," WORLD (Lond), 30 July 1884, p. 22.
*The Unclassed* concerns unsavoury people, but the novel itself is not unsavoury because G takes no pains to "gratify any merely prurient curiosity." *Unclassed* provides a strong and sincere story.

**16** "Recent Novels," MORNING POST (Lond), 7 Aug 1884, p. 6.
*The Unclassed* catches "personages in the lowest depths." While the details of G's novel are "clearly unfit for general perusal," he expresses the material "with great power."

# 1885

**17** "Current Literature," SPECTATOR, LVIII (31 Jan 1885), 158.
*The Unclassed* allows G to use his great powers in delineating realistically the misfits of society. Ida is a "bold, original, careful sketch," but G is fanciful in suggesting that her background can be wiped out. We wish G would learn to solve such problems with Christian tenderness.

**18** "Gissing the Rod," PUNCH, LXXXVIII (3 Jan 1885), 1.
In reference to G's letter on "The New Censorship of Literature" [PALL MALL GAZETTE, XL (15 Dec 1884), 2], "Humbly we own that we never heard his name before, though it seems suggestive of a kind of gutteral German embrace performed by the nationaliser of the Land."

# 1886

**19** "Belles Lettres," WESTMINSTER REVIEW, CXXVI (July 1886), 296.
*Demos* convinces us that its anonymous author is "certainly not a socialist nor even an ardent democrat," but he has given us an "unusually

good novel." Richard Mutimer, the hero, is a "careful and finished study." In representing his famale characters, the author is "singularly successful." The action is the result of clearly given circumstances.

**20** "The Book Market," DAILY TELEGRAPH (Lond), 13 April 1886, p. 2.

*Demos* is an anonymous novel that appears "with a certain grim opportuneness," for the recent riots in the West End of London lend these pages a "pleasantly realistic smack." The outcome of *Demos* suggests that "even a riot may serve some good end, and, secondly, that the profession of a philanthropist is publicly and privately anything but a bed of roses."

**21** "The Book Market," DAILY TELEGRAPH (Lond), 10 June 1886, p. 2.

*Isabel Clarendon* will perhaps find a reading public, for there is "always a sufficiency of dyspeptic and of lacrymose damsels fresh from school to revel in such gracefully presented despondency." G refuses to allow Fortune to smile kindly upon any of his characters, although "it may be realistic in these times of commercial depression" if a great soul tied down by circumstance must sell "cheap stationery to an unappreciative crowd."

**22** "Books to Read, and Others," VANITY FAIR, XXXV (3 April 1886), 196.

*Demos* is a solid contribution to the literature of socialism and deserves to be read with extreme care. "Mrs. Oliphant—if it be she—gives us a picture of a Socialist workman who is suddenly enriched" and able to mix with refined people. She is often cruel and unfair to unhappy workers. Mrs. Oliphant handles youthful louts and refined maidens better than any of her contemporaries. "If we have *not* succeeded in naming the author rightly, then we can only say that England is a very fortunate country, for we have a pair that cannot be matched."

**23** "Books to Read, and Others," VANITY FAIR, XXXVI (10 July 1886), 27.

*Isabel Clarendon* begins with a promise that is never realized. The hero deserves the kind of happiness that Isabel has neither the courage nor the constancy to provide.

**24** "A Conservative Novel: Socialism and Romance," NEW YORK DAILY TRIBUNE, 9 May 1886, p. 10; rptd as "Demos," LITERARY NEWS (NY), VII (June 1886), 174.

*Demos* provides particulars of the "so-called socialism of the working classes"—their tastes, motives, and beliefs. In doing so the novel teaches the futility of the democratic movement because socialists lack an "indefinable superiority of character" attained only through "generations of higher cultures." Through Hubert Eldon and Vicar Wyvern, *Demos* insists that progress cannot help the lower-class people since they are unable to appreciate higher values. Those who suffer most in *Demos* are the educated characters whose financial means are insufficient to provide what they desire and appreciate. Thus, the novel "protests against democratic progress" as well as the socialist movement.

**25** "A Contrast in Novels," SPECTATOR, LIX (23 Oct 1886), 1420.
*Isabel Clarendon* is a book of moral earnestness dealing with socio-religious problems; the characters are types rather than recognizable people. The tone of the book is melancholic. There is "nothing savoring of naturalism" in the novel.

**26** *"Demos,"* SPECTATOR, LIX (10 April 1886), 486-87.
In *Demos,* G uses his knowledge of the working classes. His own bias would appear to be aesthetic and aristocratic, not democratic or scientific. *Demos* reveals a novelist who has "little or no spiritual faith which might have proved a higher motive-power than that of which equality and fraternity are the favorite watch-cries."

**27** "Ethics and Art in Recent Novels," SCOTTISH REVIEW, VII (April 1886), 328-30.
*Demos* "is a thorough exposure of that most transparent of shams," socialism. The anonymous author keeps out of sight and allows us to gather the moral. Mutimer is a sham posing as the champion of oppressed people, a selfish man who is ironically done in by chance. We hope that the full impact of *Demos* comes "home to the class of which it treats."

**28** "Fiction," DAILY CHRONICLE (Lond), 22 May 1886, p. 6.
*Demos* is written by an anonymous author who shows "no particular aptitude for the task he has undertaken." Neither the characters nor the scenes can be considered representative; the author has grasped neither the reality nor the romance of socialism.

**29** "Four Novels," SATURDAY REVIEW (Lond), LXII (21 Aug 1886), 261.
In *Demos,* G handles his characters with "an imperial sternness of purpose." He is "incapable of misdirected enthusiasm." Sparing of commentary and elucidation, G allows his people to explain themselves. *Demos* is unquestionably a first book [it was published anonymously], but intelligent men and women will find the exposition of socialism attractive.

**30** [*Isabel Clarendon*], ST. STEPHEN'S REVIEW, 3 July 1886, p. 23.
*Isabel Clarendon,* a novel that is "thoroughly readable, far beyond the average," convinces us that G admires Meredith. Kingcote's "extreme sensitiveness has rendered him utterly indolent." G makes credible Kingcote's feelings for Isabel, the "perfect woman." But she cannot respond to Kingcote's spiritual appeal.

**31** "The Library," QUEEN, LXXX (31 July 1886), 143.
*Demos,* published anonymously, is apparently "written by a practiced hand"; it deals "incidentally with many of the ideas and topics of the present day." [Outline of story, stressing Mutimer's circumstances.]

**32** "The Library," QUEEN, LXXX (28 Aug 1886), 247.
*Isabel Clarendon* is "fairly well written, but the characters are weak, and, in the case of Kingcote, the supposed hero, contemptible."

**33** "Literature and Literary Gossip," COURT JOURNAL (Lond), No. 2997 (26 June 1886), 753.
*Isabel Clarendon*'s most interesting character is Bernard Kingcote, but his life is fated to be melancholic. The story needs a less depressing close. [Narrative summary.]

**34** "Literature: *Demos,*" PUBLIC OPINION (Lond), XLIX (2 April 1886), 422.
Why *Demos* was published anonymously baffles us, "for it is undoubtedly one of the best of the season," "a novel of remarkable power and finish." Mutimer unexpectedly inherits a fortune and puts his own social theories into practice to benefit the workers. Elevated by his wealth, he abandons the poor Emma Vine for the rich Adela Waltham. In the third volume *Demos* achieves great success when a lost will is found, Mutimer is ruined, and his ambitious nature shows how unworthy he had been. "The closing of the socialist's career is tragic to a degree and forms a great artistic picture."

**35** "New Books," MANCHESTER GUARDIAN, 29 July 1886, p. 8.
*Demos* is another proof that we "are on the eve of a new departure in the literature of fiction," the politico-social novel. The radicals here are "very cheap persons." Fortunately, "all comes right in the end," as the gentleman wins the gentle lady.

**36** "New Novels," GRAPHIC (Lond), XXXIII (1 May 1886), 482.
*Demos* engages people of all social classes, but the book excels in render-

ing members of Mutimer's own class. The types of socialism reflected in the novel "are of a rather antiquated form."

**37** "New Novels," GRAPHIC (Lond), XXXIV (2 Oct 1886), 370. *Isabel Clarendon* shows "the evil results of certain too prevalent mental tendencies of the self-analytic and otherwise morbid and self-tormenting kind." Isabel is a noble-hearted woman, but Bernard is a "miserable invertebrate creature." The contrast is too great to permit them happiness together.

**38** "New Novels," SCOTSMAN, 29 May 1886, p. 12.
*Demos* fails entirely as the story of English socialism. Like the "Cheveley Novels," *Demos* is occasionally clever, sometimes crude; the characters are not realized. All in all, the novel is "far more pretentious than pleasing."

**39** "New Novels," SCOTSMAN, 8 July 1886, p. 7.
*Isabel Clarendon* is, from a dramatic point of view, "one of the freshest and most powerful fictions by a new writer that has appeared for a long time." It is not the sort of fashionable novel that pleases readers with a "nicely rounded off and finished" story. Not all our curiosities are answered. Isabel's passion for Kingcote is developed in such a way as to prove "a master stroke of art."

**40** Noble, James Ashcroft. "New Novels," ACADEMY, XXX (10 July 1886), 24.
*Isabel Clarendon* shows the influence of Henry James; it is a laborious and intelligent study "leaving nearly all the threads of his story hanging loose at the end of the second and last volume." G and James should decide to tell a good story sometime.

**41** "A Novel About Socialism," TIMES (Lond), 3 April 1886, p. 5.
*Demos* is told with such eloquence that it must be "written by one who has a burning sympathy for the toiling poor." Despite the subtitle, *Demos* is "not a Socialistic novel." From the author's representative, Mr. Wyvern, we learn how thoroughly the socialistic ideals have been burned out. Emma Vine and the old Mrs. Mutimer are clearly the author's "most natural creations." Mutimer is so presented as to suggest that the "modern Socialist is insincere," and the whole effect of the book is despair for humanity's future. [Full plot synopsis and lengthy quotations.]

**42** "Novels," GUARDIAN (Lond), XLI (14 April 1886), 544.
*Demos* provides an admirably consistent portrait of Richard Mutimer. The

social creed advanced through the Westlakes is out of place in fiction. Stella Westlake is the "least intelligible character in the book," but the other women redeem the novel from the charge of being too grim.

**43** "Novels," GUARDIAN (Lond), XLI (15 Sept 1886), 1364. *Isabel Clarendon* is dominated by the title figure: charming, intelligent, affectionate, but cowardly. G only half tells us what he intends; the rest depends upon our attentiveness and his suggestiveness. But the book "must stand condemned as a work of art: confusion of purpose" leads to confusion of interpretation and enjoyment. In Ada Warren, G indicates that atheism is "the last word of human wisdom," a matter of despair but not of sin.

**44** "Novels," ILLUSTRATED LONDON NEWS, LXXXIX (10 July 1886), 50.
*Isabel Clarendon* is a romance distinguished by "clever study of character, accompanied by considerable powers of delineation." The type of heroine rendered here has never before been rendered so elaborately. The story consists of very little action; the narrative style is too enigmatic.

**45** "Novels and Stories," SATURDAY REVIEW, LXII (10 July 1886), 58.
In *Isabel Clarendon,* G is "advanced, agnostic, anti-optimist, antagonistic to social conventions." His characters often verge on the preposterous, and his plots are thin enough to satisfy Henry James. The study of character is inconclusive.

**46** "Novels of the Week," ATHENAEUM, No. 3050 (10 April 1886), 485.
*Demos* is a "really able and vigorous romance" weakened because the author chooses unattractive characters to persuade his audience.

**47** "Novels of the Week," ATHENAEUM, No. 3060 (19 June 1886), 808.
*Isabel Clarendon* contains too many improbable events and ends too abruptly.

**48** "Pages in Waiting," WORLD (Lond), 28 April 1886, p. 19.
*Demos,* "which has been so much written and talked about," concerns not our present socialism, rather that of our fathers. So also is the method old-fashioned, as the author labels his characters according to their beliefs— even if the ideas are futile, weak, and vicious. The novelist provides a clever book, containing both literature and humanity.

**49** "Recent Novels," MORNING POST (Lond), 22 April 1886, p. 3.
*Demos* is realistic, exciting, and powerful. The anonymous author "apparently supports no cause, and proposes no remedy." A "purely engrossing story," *Demos* is told "with keen insight into the workings of the human mind." It is a "deeply interesting as well as a remarkable book."

**50** "Recent Novels," MORNING POST (Lond), 28 July 1886, p. 2.
*Isabel Clarendon*'s plot is involved; the characters, "although often gloomy, are lifelike." G paints men and women with extreme pessimism, but "his descriptions of the beauties of landscape are fresh and enthusiastic." [Brief story summary.]

**51** "Recent Novels," NATION (NY), XLIII (1 July 1886), 14.
*Demos,* published anonymously, is "extremely tedious" and only "superficially concerned with socialism."

**52** "Sibylline Leaves," DAILY NEWS (Lond), 1 April 1886, p. 3.
*Demos* treats a subject that is "in" now: socialism. The novel gets off to a slow start, although it proves a readable and certainly opportune work. *Demos* deserves to be recommended, in spite of the amusement with which the author appears to treat the issue at hand.

**53** "A Socialist Novel," LITERARY WORLD (Lond), XXXIII (28 May 1886), 507–8.
*Demos* "depicts with rare power and sympathy the hardships of the working class." The anonymous author "believes that proper culture and due pruning would render" socialism a noble and useful tree. The ideas presented in *Demos* are so interwoven and the story is so interesting that this is "one of the best novels we have seen for some time." The author's own views are expressed less in Mutimer and Adela than in Wyvern. [Several lengthy quotations.]

**54** "Some Books of Reference," BOOKSELLER, CCCXLI (6 April 1886), 321.
*Demos* might well prove "one of the most successful novels of the season." Its anonymous author evidently gathered his details at first hand, so graphic is his description of the inner lives of his working men. [Synopsis of plot given.]

**55** "Some New Novels," ST. JAMES'S GAZETTE, XII (5 June 1886), 7.
*Isabel Clarendon* is "deficient in movement and incident, and it lacks directness and narration." G is given to "affectations of language and high-

flown expressions having more sound than meaning." The title figure represents a woman never before "so carefully, sensibly, truthfully and yet indulgently described."

**56** Wedgwood, Julia. "Contemporary Records: Fiction," CONTEMPORARY REVIEW, L (Aug 1886), 295–96.
In *Demos,* G's one great artistic advantage for treating his subject" is that "his sympathies and his opinions run in different channels." G represents the working classes with understanding, though his own sympathies are apparently conservative. His powers fail him, however, when he most needs them—in representing the chivalric figure who "is a mere flat wash."

---

# 1887

---

**57** "The Book Market," DAILY TELEGRAPH (Lond), 19 May 1887, p. 2.
*Thyrza* presents a heroine fated by the novelist to unhappiness. G is now identified as the author of the very clever *Demos,* and in his new book he plays "much the same tune on new strings." The author's strength lies in his "insight into the hearts of men and women" and in the "facility with which he expresses this knowledge with fine touches."

**58** "Books to Read, and Others," VANITY FAIR, XXXVIII (20 Aug 1887), 126.
*Thyrza,* by "George Gosling," can hardly be recommended; its pictures of the worker "should have been done in stronger colours."

**59** "Contemporary Literature," SCOTTISH REVIEW, X (July 1887), 196–97.
*Thyrza* again realizes the inhabitants of Lambeth; G repeats his success of *Demos.* G employs such subtle irony that one cannot be sure whose voice one is listening to. The novel appeals not to admirers of Ouida, but to the thinkers.

**60** "George Gissing As A Novelist," PALL MALL GAZETTE, XLV (28 July 1887), 3.
*Thyrza,* like G's other novels, provides "dramatic expositions of modern life in all its pathos and often in all its hideousness." Though less unpleasant than his previous books, *Thyrza* will not better G's reputation. G is the best spokesman of the English working class.

**61** "The Library," QUEEN, LXXXII (20 Aug 1887), 246.
*Thyrza* will maintain the "reader's attention" for both its representation of characters and its statement of social themes. Like *Demos, Thyrza* provides "graphic pictures of life" in the poorer sections of London.

**62** "Literature and Literary Gossip," COURT JOURNAL (Lond),
     No. 3042 (7 May 1887), 550.
*Thyrza* deals "principally with scenes in humble life," with insufficient evidence of life's happiness. Thyrza herself resembles no one in real life; her imaginative nature "finds the daily toil unbearable."

**63** "Literature, *Thyrza*," PUBLIC OPINION (Lond), LI (13 May
     1887), 582.
*Thyrza*'s title character is a delicate, sensitive young lady whose heart must choose between a university man of fortune, Walter Egremont, and a candle-maker who has a taste for literature, Gilbert Grail. G describes her struggle in beautiful and simple terms. And his handling of lower-class life is without caricature. *Thyrza* is an "exceptionally good" novel.

**64** "New Books: Novels," ILLUSTRATED LONDON NEWS, XC (14
     May 1887), 561.
*Thyrza* excels in the nobility of its aim, the clarity of characterization, the judicious connection of incidents, and the quiet simplicity of dialogues. We admire the habits and manners of Thyrza, the modest Gilbert Grail, the noble Walter Egremont. When Thyrza must decide on a husband, she unfortunately breaks her engagement to the worthy Grail, following "a natural preference for one nearer her own age." Egremont goes to America, there to subdue his passion by work.

**65** "New Novels," GRAPHIC (Lond), XXXVI (6 Aug 1887), 147.
*Thyrza* "is characterised by all the special merits which have already given its author a high place among an increasing circle of readers." He knows his characters intimately and portrays them convincingly. We wish G would "cultivate a better literary style."

**66** "New Novels," SCOTSMAN, 2 May 1887, p. 4.
*Thyrza* is a "tragedy in the truest sense of the word," for the hero fails despite his noble purposes. The hero, Walter Egremont, loves a girl of the working class, but their marriage is prevented by social conflicts. Her attractiveness also entices Gilbert Grail, an intelligent worker, but he must suffer great sadness for it. They are but three of several very successfully presented characters in a most forceful book. [Some narrative summary.]

**67** "A Novel of the People," WHITEHALL REVIEW, 12 May 1887,
     p. 20.

*Thyrza* tells "of one of the 'people' " who dwell in the East End. The author has also been named as responsible for *Demos,* originally published anonymously. Whoever G is, he—or more likely she—has powers "very far above the average." *Thyrza* is imbued with the despondency of "a thoughtful and cultured mind" and concerns the "attempt to bring two opposite classes of people into more friendly and intimate relations." *Thyrza* does not depend on any "ingenuity of plot or exciting incidents" for its success; the author "writes gracefully and in good taste." Few novelists now writing can rival G in quiet power and intensity.

**68** "Novels," GUARDIAN (Lond), XLII (3 Aug 1887), 1168.
*Thyrza* is vivid and lifelike; the story is interesting throughout. The plot is intricate; the characters are not excessive until we are given Harold Emerson in the third volume. Thyrza herself "is a distinct addition to the heroines of fiction." Bunce's hatred of Christianity is based on "gross ignorance and misconception." [Narrative summary.]

**69** "Novels," SATURDAY REVIEW (Lond), LXIII (11 June 1887), 847–48.
*Thyrza* is powerful and vivid in description; G possesses an unusual ability. He powerfully describes the courtship of the atheist and the "rattle-pated Roman Catholic work girl." G has admitted authorship of *Demos.*

**70** "Novels and Stories," GLASGOW HERALD, 24 May 1887, p. 10.
*Thyrza* is an intensely human story about suffering men and women. The author—very probably a woman—provides characters who are living, loving people, no less recognizable than those represented by great actors. The men are thoroughly acquinted with "subjects of intellectual progress among working-men"; the women are so subtly analytical, so tender that they could only have been drawn by a feminine hand. Thyrza herself is "exquisitely portrayed, and her love story is one of the saddest and most beautiful that ever was penned."

**71** "Novels of the Week," ATHENAEUM, No. 3106 (7 May 1887), 605.
*Thyrza* is a conscientious novel; the plot is consistent and well-proportioned. The book manifests superior power and shows pathetic treatment of character. Thyrza Trent, a child of nature, is "out of her element in the narrow streets of Lambeth." Readers will find some incidents needlessly somber.

**72** "Our Library List," MURRAY'S MAGAZINE, I (June 1887), 864.
*Thyrza*'s great power lies in G's descriptions of the "lives and surroundings

of the hard-working poor." His characters are true to life; his vivid portraits of this gray world are written with earnestness and force.

**73** "Recent Novels," MORNING POST (Lond), 11 May 1887, p. 2.
*Thyrza* is "an able and moving romance." Impartially written, the novel "examines with remarkable frankness some of the social problems" that confront us. Thyrza herself is a "really exquisite figure, as pathetic a figure as can well be imagined." *Thyrza* is "really strong, thought-suggesting, and truthful."

**74** "Recent Novels," SPECTATOR, LX (25 June 1887), 868–69.
*Thyrza* is a "decidedly interesting story"; even the lesser characters are successfully drawn. G's portrait of the "careless, free-spoken, self-reliant, but always respected" Totty Nancarrow is admirable.

**75** "Recent Novels," TIMES (Lond), 21 May 1887, p. 17.
*Thyrza* convinces us that G knows the sordid monotony of the English working classes, but the story is not sufficiently defined in scope. G introduces an excessive number of characters—particularly in the third volume —and thereby obscures the main theme. Thyrza herself would be a miracle among the most refined; she is here "quite out of keeping with her surroundings." Such unreality clashes with G's intentions.

**76** "Trade and Literary Gossip," BOOKSELLER, CCCLV (4 June 1887), 544.
*Thyrza* shows G at home with his characters and scenes; a "more interesting story we have seldom read." Thyrza herself is a charming heroine.

# 1888

**77** "Books of the Week," MANCHESTER GUARDIAN, 10 Dec 1888, p. 6.
*A Life's Morning* is "far above the ordinary novels." It's great charm lies in "subtle and powerful character painting," reminding us of George Eliot and Henry James. It suggests that G "could write a genuinely funny book if he liked."

**78** Gladstone, W. E. "ROBERT ELSMERE and the Battle of Belief," NINETEENTH CENTURY, XXIII (May 1888), 766–88.
[Reviewing Mrs. Humphrey Ward's novel, the Prime Minister mentions G's *The Unclassed*. Gladstone's personal papers contain quotations which he selected and copied from *Unclassed*.]

**79** [*A Life's Morning*], COURT JOURNAL, 29 Dec 1888, p. 1516.
G's *A Life's Morning* will please readers who "prefer a novel which asks for some exercise of their intellectual powers." G tells an interesting story; his characters, while intellectually superior, are nevertheless very human.

**80** *"A Life's Morning,"* PALL MALL GAZETTE, 12 Dec 1888, p. 5.
*A Life's Morning* displays a "far deeper sense of artistic completeness and a far truer conception of human character than is to be found in the average novel of the day." G has dropped the distinctive note of his earlier novels, the social problems of the working classes. The novel's motif lies in "the study of the psychological influences" keeping the lovers apart. G is far more successful in characterizing working men (as in *Workers in the Dawn* and *Demos*) than in gentlemen, though his feminine natures here in Beatrice Redwing and Emily Hood are highly successful.

**81** "Literature: *A Life's Morning,"* PUBLIC OPINION (Lond), LIV (7 Dec 1888), 722.
*A Life's Morning* shows much ability. Wilfrid Athel becomes attached to Emily Hood, though she does not belong to his higher social class; Athel's family would have him choose Beatrice Redwing. The plot consists of "naturally contrived incidents." G excels in describing Emily's struggle in narrow circumstances.

**82** "Literature of the Day," DAILY TELEGRAPH (Lond), 25 Dec 1888, p. 7.
*A Life's Morning* suffers "from a pervading attenuation of expression and a lack of" brevity. G is too much given to hyperbole, though otherwise this book is "graceful and full of life."

**83** "New Novels," SCOTSMAN, 26 Nov 1888, p. 3.
*A Life's Morning* contains many strong scenes, but it will not advance G's reputation. He is too subtle in his speculations about human nature. [Plot outline.]

**84** "New Novels," WHITEHALL REVIEW, 13 Dec 1888, p. 20.
*A Life's Morning* is G's *"chef d'oeuvre."* The story is not well constructed, but the characters are "clearly and graphically drawn." Only "fine writing" contents G. [Brief outline.]

**85** "Novels," SATURDAY REVIEW, LXVI (1 Dec 1888), 650.
*A Life's Morning* seems influenced by George Meredith; its style is tense,

its thinking original. G has lost readers by his pessimism but certainly gained admirers for his "vigour of original thought." The story's value rests on "the noble conceptions of character" given in Emily Hood and Beatrice Redwing. The public will not be sure that G is right in deciding that Wilfrid Athel should choose the "pure womanhood" of Emily over the "beauty, youth, and wealth, genius, and social rank" of Beatrice. G's own sympathies are "intensely with the poor, the weak, and the suffering."

**86** "Novels and Stories," GLASGOW HERALD, 20 Dec 1888, p. 9.
*A Life's Morning* opens with chapters that irritate the reader, for G "seems to subordinate everything to some idea of style." This is a tale of "considerable interest"; it would be admirably told if G would only remember the first rule of fiction: to tell his tale through his characters.

**87** "Novels of the Week," ATHENAEUM, No. 3189 (8 Dec 1888), 770.
*A Life's Morning* is admirable for G's handling of character and incident. G is "loth to say a plain thing in a plain way," having an "unfortunate predilection for ponderous Latinisms."

**88** Sichel, Edith. "Two Philanthropic Novelists: Mr. Walter Besant and Mr. George Gissing," MURRAY'S MAGAZINE, III (April 1888), 506–18.
A comparison of the two novelists suggests that social improvement is more likely to be gained by Besant's optimism than by G's despair. G's characters are interesting in proportion to their "capacity for suffering, and dignity comes of misery nobly borne." G is a "thorough Conservative, who, being powerless to prevent the 'progress' to which he ascribes all the ills of the world, has nothing better left him than sit and bewail them." His hope is with the upper classes because the poor lack imagination. [Stresses G's *Demos* and *Thyrza.*]

**89** "Some New Novels," STANDARD (Lond), 28 Dec 1888, p. 2.
*A Life's Morning* compels us to be interested in Wilfrid Athel's love affairs, although we perhaps disagree with his choice of a partner. The novel shows "imaginative insight, subtle delineation of character, epigrammatic force of style, and gleams of genuine humour."

# 1889

**90** Bertz, Eduard. "George Gissing, ein Real-idealist" (George Gissing, a Realist-Idealist), DEUTSCHE PRESSE, II (3 Nov 1889),

357–59; ibid (10 Nov 1889), 366–67; ibid (17 Nov 1889), 374–75.

G combines social purpose and aesthetic sense. His realism is born of the contrast between reality and his ideal. His pessimism is the purest expression of his idealism. Though not a revolutionist (because of his pessimism and his will to be objective), his writing combines an aristocratic temper, a sense of pity, a keen appreciation of justice, and an extensive classical background both in philosophy and literature. He has a sense of humor, though he is rather bent on the serious. G has probably not yet reached his fullest powers, although he is already the most original and the most important figure of the contemporary English novel. [In German.]

**91** "Books to Read, and Others," VANITY FAIR, XLI (15 June 1889), 454.

*A Life's Morning* is a dish containing "a little philosophy, a little religion, a little personal meditation, but no solid food." The novel's story is not strong enough to carry so much weight, with the result that "much excellent writing" is wasted.

**92** "Books to Read, and Others," VANITY FAIR, XLI (22 June 1889), 474.

*The Nether World* is instructive, telling about London's back alleys "so graphically as to be revolting."

**93** "Contemporary Literature," SCOTTISH REVIEW, XIII (April 1889), 446.

*A Life's Morning* sustains the promise of ability given us in *Demos*. Except for the conclusion of the story, this is an admirable study of human character.

**94** "Contemporary Literature," SCOTTISH REVIEW, XIV (July 1889), 218.

*The Nether World* provides little or no encouragement for noble living. While elaborately planned and carefully written, it is hopelessly pessimistic in the extreme. G portrays Clem in the strongest colors: "a superfluity of naughtiness she certainly has, and it is to be hoped that few such beings exist."

**95** D., M. *"The Nether World,"* PALL MALL GAZETTE, 4 June 1889, p. 3.

*The Nether World* is a "relentless picture of misery and degradation," less attractive than *Thyrza* and not as "disagreeably striking" as *The Unclassed* or *Demos*. "A more pathetic character than Jane Snowden has surely never been drawn." G prevents his most sympathetically drawn hero and heroine from confessing their love for one another. All his characters have some virtue that would flower except for the environment. The result is very depressing—a "feeling of crushing impotence." G provides no hope, no solution; he encourages "the Gospel of Despair."

**96** Farrar, F. W. *"The Nether World,"* CONTEMPORARY REVIEW, LVI (Sept 1889), 370–80.

G's novel is "so sombre and earnest in its terrible realism that it will not easily be forgotten by any serious thinker." The book has not the "leprous naturalism" of Zola. G's characters are typical; his scenes are true to life. G offers no solutions to the problems he describes. [Article also discusses the misery of London's poor.]

**97** "Fiction," DAILY CHRONICLE (Lond), 6 May 1889, p. 6.

*The Nether World* defies the reader who would seek amusement or reality. "Everything is overdone."

**98** "George Gissing's Wholesome Novel," WHITEHALL REVIEW, 4 May 1889, p. 19.

*The Nether World* treats "a world of darkness, of sorrow, of vice, of never-lifting blackest fog, of direst want, and bitterest suffering"—all with the "keenest sympathy." G's representation accomplishes enormous good, for he writes with "no affectation, no prudishness; no glossing over the horrors of whole families penned in one room." His intention is clear—"to bring home to the rich the reality of 'how the poor live.' "

**99** "Library," QUEEN, LXXXV (20 April 1889), 541.

*The Nether World* "depicts with artistic force" the crowded London regions, concentrating on Clerkenwell. It is "likely to excite commiseration for the poor in our over-populated districts."

**100** "Literature: *The Nether World,"* PUBLIC OPINION (Lond), LV (12 April 1889), 455.

In *The Nether World* G "manifestly improves greatly" in the description of the low and industrial phases of London life. He successfully describes the relationships of several characters, particularly between John Hewett and Clara. The charm of the novel lies in the "strong realism and directness of stern purpose to show how the poor of London live, feel, and suffer." While humor is present in the book, G's mark is for representing tragedy. His realism is "on the Dickens plan, but without the perpetual farce."

**101** [*The Nether World*], COURT JOURNAL, 27 April 1889, p. 590.

*The Nether World* brings us to Clerkenwell, "that hive of toiling and moiling human beings" in a condition of "abject poverty, dumb, miserable despair." Rather than just another postal district of London, this world seems one that a modern Dante might imagine as the final punishment of the most degraded types of humanity. G insists, however, that pure lives are also led in this horrible region. The novel "contains a terrible warning, but also more than a grain of hope."

**102** "New Novels," GRAPHIC (Lond), XXXIX (5 Jan 1889), 19.

*A Life's Morning,* compared to other G novels, draws more upon imagination than experience. Emily Hood repudiates the idea of selling herself into an unsatisfactory marriage in a sense of martyrdom. Was this the price she had to pay for brain fever?

**103** "New Novels," GRAPHIC (Lond), XXXIX (15 June 1889), 667.

*The Nether World* "keeps the reader on one deadly level of pessimism," telling us repeatedly how the poor live. The story is neither interesting nor probable.

**104** "New Novels," MANCHESTER GUARDIAN, 30 April 1889, p. 4.

*The Nether World* is a "plain unvarnished tale" showing the "unutterable dullness, the hideous sordidness" haunting London's poor. The result leaves the reader almost in despair, for such promising characters as Sidney Kirkwood and John Hewett drag out lives of unrelieved sadness. [Narrative summary.]

**105** "New Novels," SCOTSMAN, 15 April 1889, p. 3.

*The Nether World* describes the poorer residents of London as "a little darker than the circumstances actually justify." Coarse language is used, language such as is used in our very own streets. There are sensational scenes; drunkenness and misery abound in documented form, contributing to a feeling of helplessness.

**106** "New Publications," NEW YORK DAILY TRIBUNE, 18 June 1889, p. 8.

*The Nether World* reminds us of the patient care of detail of the brothers De Gongourt, but it lacks the radical vice of Zola. Precise and accurate, the novel is "too much in one key," "too destitute of light and relief." Most readers will find the story too melancholy, but it is recommended to thinkers for its power and sincerity.

**107** "Novels," GUARDIAN (Lond), XLIV (23 Jan 1889), 136.

*A Life's Morning,* as we might expect of G, has characters true to human nature, but also much that is grim and despairing. Emily Hood, the governess, is meant to be attractive, but she is not; she "remains a catalogue of imputed qualities." Beatrice Redwing is "kept straight by finer instincts of unselfishness and principles of religion." The novel is both clever and dismal; G wants to teach that "the means of culture are wealth, power, and worldly position." [Summary of narrative included.]

**108** "Novels and Stories," GLASGOW HERALD, 22 April 1889, p. 9.
*The Nether World* constitutes "a distinct advance" on G's previous work, but it probably will not make him a popular novelist. There is "a clearer maturity of thought, and a more assured mastery of expression," but counterbalancing this is an "abundance of unsavoury details incidental to a realistic progress through" the slums of Clerkenwell. Zola himself would probably have condemned G's fidelity to language.

**109** "Novels and Tales," ILLUSTRATED LONDON NEWS, XCIV (1 June 1889), 694.
*The Nether World* compels the reader to view the "unseemly behaviour, drunkenness and brawling" of a bank holiday. Even the most vile creatures —like Clem Peckover—prove credible in all the corruption of their vicious breeding. There are contrasts, however, as in the honest worker, John Hewett, and the high-minded artisan, Sidney Kirkwood. [Brief plot synopsis.]

**110** "Novels of the Week," ATHENAEUM, No. 3222 (27 July 1889), 126.
*The Nether World* is an unconvincing representation of the poor; the novel is episodic. G has failed either "to gain enough superficial knowledge of the poor to draw harrowing pictures of their condition or to dive into their real thoughts and ways."

**111** "Pages in Waiting," WORLD (Lond), 12 June 1889, p. 22.
*The Nether World* is "terrible in its earnestness" in painting the "struggles and bitter misery of the London poor." [Brief.]

**112** "Recent Fiction," CRITIC (NY), XII (6 July 1889), 5.
*The Nether World* leads one to expect information about uncommon life, but that expectation is not rewarded.

**113** "Recent Novels," MORNING POST (Lond), 30 Jan 1889, p. 2.
*A Life's Morning* describes the central characters with "such beauty and purity" that the novel is raised "quite above the level of ordinary romance."

G evidently has a "high idea of the mission of fiction." He permits his characters to "develop themselves under the influence of time and events."

**114** "Recent Novels," MORNING POST (Lond), 27 May 1889, p. 5.

*The Nether World* continues G's "powerfully realistic pictures of life among those with whom toil is a bitter reality." Few writers can match his fidelity in rendering the "tainted atmosphere" of the poor areas of large cities. If there is a solution, G perhaps suggests that human relationships are our only hope.

**115** "Some Recent Novels," STANDARD (Lond), 17 June 1889, p. 2.

*The Nether World* "is not a novel of the 'silver fork' school." Most of the characters are merciless brutes, struggling for survival. If G "runs Zola close as a realist, his thoughts and language are as pure as those of Miss Younge herself." [Plot summary.]

**116** "Three Novels," SPECTATOR, LXII (9 Feb 1889), 204.

*A Life's Morning* lacks humor; it is too somber and laborious. Wilfrid Athel is a "tame, insipid young gentleman" who is unworthy of the love of the two young ladies who award him their affections.

**117** Wendlandt, Wilhelm. "Der literarische Markt" (The Literary Market), DEUTSCHE PRESSE, II (8 Dec 1889), 397.

In G's novels, particularly *Demos,* realism reaches perhaps its highest expression. G pictures contemporary society against a background of universal ideals. [In German.]

## 1890

**118** Badin, Ad. "Bulletin Bibliographique. Publications Étrangeres" (Bibliographical Bulletin. Foreign Publications), NOUVELLE REVUE, LXIV (1 May 1890), 220–21.

*Demos* is a study of manners, with philosophical significance. G shows the dangers of new theories for eager and ill-balanced minds. [French ed. pub. by Hachette, 2 vols, 1890; slight notice.] [In French.]

**119** "Belles Lettres," WESTMINSTER REVIEW, CXXXIV (Sept 1890), 333–34.

In *The Emancipated,* G becomes wearisome in diagnosing character; he fails to pierce beneath the superficial to more profound levels of human nature. Miriam's fierce spiritual pride is conquered only by love.

**120** "Books to Read, and Others," VANITY FAIR, XLIII (19 April 1890), 352–53.
*The Emancipated* is "distinctly a book to read." Mrs. Baske knows enough to build baths rather than chapels, but not enough to marry wisely. Cecily Doran's character is drawn with skill, whereas Miriam Baske is "never sufficiently developed." Why G prevents Ross Mallard from doing what he ought to have done, we cannot understand.

**121** "Current Literature," SPECTATOR, LXIV (21 June 1890), 875.
*The Emancipated* makes one wonder if emancipation is a good thing for women. Miriam becomes detestable when she is freed from "the trammels of her sectarian education." As for Cecily, what did she gain by marrying a reprobate? *Emancipated* is powerfully written, but hardly pleasant reading.

**122** "More Fiction," NATION (NY), L (20 Feb 1890), 160–61.
*The Nether World* provides no happy surprises such as Mr. Besant gives us; instead, the only force operating among G's people is a "tendency to sag." "There is darkness that can be felt, and crime that goes to make statistics, and neither lends itself to a distinctly aesthetic impression." G stresses "literally living troubles" that are "haltingly lived out and established by slow years in bone and nerve." "Our ill-discharged brotherhood" menaces society.

**123** "New Novels," GRAPHIC (Lond), XLI (26 April 1890), 488.
*The Emancipated* purports to prove that "a woman who gets what she wants in life" is happy. This "decidedly stupid story, very cleverly told, has only odious, unconvincing characters."

**124** "New Novels," ST. JAMES'S GAZETTE, XX (8 May 1890), 6.
In *The Emancipated,* Cecily Doran falls hopelessly in love with an unprincipled reprobate, despite the instruction and advice of Mrs. Lessingham. Cecily's emancipation—her knowledge of life—"does not protect her from the saddest of illusions." G writes with "delicacy and good feeling"; the tone is occasionally commonplace and frequently depressing.

**125** "Novels," DAILY NEWS (Lond), 30 May 1890, p. 6.
*The Emancipated* questions the merit of raising women by education "from the simpler conception of life to one where morality becomes a more complex affair." Contrasting positions are taken by the two principal

characters, Miriam Baske and Cecily Doran, and the issue of their circumstances interests us. But the work fails as art, "blurred by the diffuseness of treatment."

**126** "Novels," GUARDIAN (Lond), XLV (28 May 1890), 882.
*The Emancipated,* like so many G novels, fails because the author does not realize that fictional characters must be made lovable. Cecily, the heroine, is the best example of G's failing: she runs off with a man whom she scarcely knows and of whom her friends disapprove. In doing so, she only courts unhappiness in marriage. G has shifted his dreary characters from London to Italy, and they now all belong to the upper middle class.

**127** "Novels," ILLUSTRATED LONDON NEWS, XCVI (19 April 1890), 498.
*The Emancipated* is one of G's best works. It presents a variety of characters who have reacted to traditional religion without thereby determining their moral human worth. Elgar is a sheer blackguard; his sister, Mrs. Baske, outgrows her narrow Puritanism to become "wisely tolerant and gentle." All in all, the title figures exemplify "some likely effects of a recent intellectual movement altering the standards of faith and duty." The most sympathetically drawn characters are marked by conversions that are based on "independent reflection" by which they achieve a high standard of life.

**128** "Novels," SATURDAY REVIEW, LXIX (21 June 1890), 772.
*The Emancipated* deals with the "breaking away of several young people from the creeds, tastes and prejudices of their early training." The subject is, fortunately, "less burdened with miasmatic horrors" than G's earlier novels, like *The Nether World.* But G would do well to endow his heroines with some sweetness, in combination with the light they possess. The emancipation of Cecily Doran is the most "interesting" case in G's examination of the young who renounce their narrow-minded religious heritage of a Puritanic bent. Unfortunately, G does not permit her to realize that Elgar's passions are not as desirable as Mallard's secretly cherished affections.

**129** "Novels of the Week," ATHENAEUM, No. 3259 (12 April 1890), 466.
*The Emancipated* inquires into the plight of the emancipated woman who marries; her husband should be a very strong character. Reuben Elgar, however, "is the weakest man who ever erred along the line of emotions."

**130** "Recent Novels," MORNING POST (Lond), 30 April 1890, p. 2.

*The Emancipated* is a "clever and amusing book." We find it hard to accept Cecily Doran as the ideal for emancipated women. While written for a purpose, *Emancipated* "shows considerable weakness, since no conclusion is distinctly drawn." The work is "full of careful character studies and subtle touches of humour."

**131** Smith, G. Barnett. "New Novels," ACADEMY, XXXVII (19 April 1890), 263.

*The Emancipated* is a powerful and thoughtful novel, but G's pessimism hampers his reputation. All the characters are in the process of being emancipated from false ideas of religion, art, or love. The novel, clever and worth reading, is overcharged with misery. G expresses himself "with unconventional force and freedom."

# 1891

**132** Austin, L. F. "Folios and Footlights," NEW REVIEW, IV (June 1891), 564–65.

G's *New Grub Street* presents a uniformly drab world; there is no sunshine at all. Though "some squalid destiny broods upon every page," *Grub Street* still commands a "sombre fascination." The bookstalls are crowded with the life efforts of countless authors whose struggles are unrewarded.

**133** A[ustin], L.F. "The New Grub Street," ILLUSTRATED LONDON NEWS, XCVIII (2 May 1891), 571.

In *New Grub Street,* G's writers are shown "in extremely sombre colours." Every character is shown "with surprising skill and relentless fidelity to the general scheme of sordid struggle." Everyone is fighting to save his own life. But G's Grub Street might create a grave misconception in the eyes of his readers, for "there is a little sunshine even in Grub Street"; not everyone lives on tea and dripping; not everyone disbelieves in immortality.

**134** Besant, Walter. "Notes and News," AUTHOR, II (June 1891), 15.

G's *New Grub Street* correctly describes ours as a loathsome profession, and he ought "to be publicly thanked for introducing to the world a form of literary life." The profession of letters unfortunately has no "unwritten laws of decency and politeness." G's are "by no means uncommon types," represented in Yule, Jasper, and Edwin: they are portraits of such fidelity that they make me shudder. [Andrew Lang replied to Besant's opinions about G's judgment of the life of letters in "Realism in Grub Street," ibid (July 1891), 43–44. Readers added to the exchange by notes: A Frog, "Correspondence: From Grub Street," ibid (Aug 1891), 95; and Quill Driver, "Correspondence: A Provident Society," ibid (Oct 1891), 151.]

**135** "Books to Read, and Others," VANITY FAIR, XLV (9 May 1891), 408.

*New Grub Street,* "a work of more than common merit," deals with first-hand knowledge of the literary trade. G writes realistically, though "with some little exaggeration." If we were sentimental, we would object to the misfortunes endured by G's unselfish heroine. G employs too much coarse language and constantly uses the word "sexual" in describing love scenes.

**136** "Contemporary Literature," SCOTTISH REVIEW, XVIII (July 1891), 256.

*New Grub Street* recalls *The Nether World* with lurid and painful pictures of London. So intense is its realism that one is convinced it must be drawn from life itself. Not very pleasant reading, *Grub Street* nevertheless demonstrates marked ability.

**137** "Fiction," NATIONAL OBSERVER, V (9 May 1891), 643.

*New Grub Street,* though inferior to *Demos* or *The Nether World,* contains many sordid people. The book lacks "any one individual with practical common sense and good heart." Fortune does not buffet us as it does G's hero.

**138** A Frog. "Correspondence: From Grub Street," AUTHOR, II (Aug 1891), 95.

Lang's "jaunty remark" about the literary profession disturbs a frog who objects to being stoned. For even frogs are hurt by thrown objects and feel their hurt. We may have "objectionable ways," but we do not deserve such irresponsible abuse from Lang. [While this letter never mentions G's *New Grub Street* specifically, both the heading and the contents refer to Andrew Lang's "Realism in Grub Street," ibid (July 1891), 43–44. For further items in this exchange see Walter Besant, "Notes and News," ibid (June 1891), 15; and Quill Driver, "Correspondence: A Provident Society," ibid (Oct 1891), 151.]

**139** Lang, Andrew. "Realism in Grub Street," AUTHOR, II (July 1891), 43–44.

G's *New Grub Street* gives a picture of the literary life that is too bleak, both unrealistic and untrue. The book is blemished by a "perverted idealism, idealism on the seamy side." I cannot share Besant's testimony [Walter Besant, "Notes and News," ibid (June 1891), 15] that G's characters have their originals in London. In "real life the unlucky hero of Mr. Gissing would have had a devoted wife, who believed in her husband's genius; but to give him such a wife would not be Realism." [There followed a slight exchange of letters to the editor: A Frog, "Corespondence: From Grub Street," ibid (Aug 1891), 95; and Quill Driver, "Correspondence: A Provident Society," ibid (Oct 1891), 151.]

**140** "Library," QUEEN, LXXXIX (23 May 1891), 843.
*New Grub Street* "is melancholy reading!" Its "situations are all striking," but the "novel falls short of real success." There is an excess of moral and physical squalor, and an insufficiency of imagination.

**141** "Literature: *New Grub Street,*" PUBLIC OPINION (Lond), LIX (17 April 1891), 486.
*New Grub Street* tells of the struggles of those seeking literary laurels; it is doubtless drawn from experience. While not a brilliant novel, it does show considerable power.

**142** "Literature of the Day," DAILY TELEGRAPH (Lond), 11 April 1891, p. 3.
*New Grub Street* reminds us that the struggles of writers are always with us; G's "poor penmen are delightfully drawn." Still, G has "somewhat over-elaborated the woes of the less fortunate writers of to-day." The book is "exceptionally clever and fascinating."

**143** [*New Grub Street*], COURT JOURNAL, 25 April 1891, p. 710.
*New Grub Street* is both "very clever and very painful." Unfortunately, "much of the author's pessimism and many of his incidents and inferences are only too likely to be true." Particularly will those engaged in the literary world find all the horrors, despairs, and triumphs he describes "an unexaggerated truth of some at least of its sad pictures."

**144** *"New Grub Street,"* PALL MALL GAZETTE, 1 June 1891, p. 3.
*New Grub Street* is not a complete or representative study of the nether world of letters, concentrating rather on only one corner of it. The canvas lacks life, perhaps because of the narrowness of our own experience. Jasper Milvain is hardly a type to be found among contemporary writers; he is ambitious but has neither a "love of literature," nor "hereditary or educational bias towards it," nor even any "special aptitude for it." G is more successful in treating women than men. The book is "not so much a study of literary life as an invective against poverty."

**145** *"New Grub Street,"* SATURDAY REVIEW (Lond), LXXI (2 May 1891), 524–25.

G overdoes the destitution suffered by writers. Perhaps it is a "modern virtue to see everything in black, to abstain from wit, from humour, from gaiety." But the "entire population does not consist of realistic novelists ... and of meanly selfish and treacherous but successful hacks." Even in Grub Street the fog sometimes lifts.

**146** [*New Grub Street*], WHITEHALL REVIEW, 18 April 1891, pp. 19–20.
*New Grub Street* is "a singularly skilful piece of work," proving the prediction of "a great future" for G that we made at the time his first novel appeared. *Grub Street* is a confirmation of "the same masterly and original analysis of character, and the same truth of description." The sadness of the novel is its reality; it is "one long, desolate tragedy." Though critics and public will reject the book for its sad, morbid, gloomy life, *Grub Street* is an "addition to contemporaneous 'literature' which will be appreciated far and wide by readers of culture, refinement and taste." [A glowing review.]

**147** "New Novels," DAILY CHRONICLE (Lond), 13 May 1891, p. 7.
*New Grub Street* sustains G's reputation for "showing a considerable grip on human character." But the work leaves nothing to "impress the imagination." G has "no exalted motive" in *Grub Street*. He knows well the "habitués of the British Museum Reading-room," and we recognize his characters, notably Edwin Reardon, Jasper Milvain, and Marian Yule. But only the "skilful tradesman" succeeds in securing satisfactory employment.

**148** "New Novels," GLOBE (Lond), 23 April 1891, p. 6.
*New Grub Street* is a remarkable novel that will particularly appeal to professional writers. G's characters range through the variety of typical authors, one contrasting another. G's command of dialogue "sounds natural even when unnaturally clever."

**149** "New Novels," GRAPHIC, XLIII (20 June 1891), 707.
*New Grub Street* describes the life of that minority of writers who inhabit the British Museum and work for second-class publishing houses. G is bitter and sincere; his view is "grossly one-sided."

**150** "New Novels," SCOTSMAN, 13 April 1891, p. 3.
*New Grub Street* is "cast in a higher mould" than *The Nether World,* engaging characters of the "shabby genteel" society. But do such people actually exist? While G may not be exaggerating their "difficulties, disap-

pointments, foibles, and freaks," the portraits are perhaps too pretentious and fanciful.

**151** "Novels," Guardian (Lond), XLVI (27 May 1891), 851. *New Grub Street* is G's best book since *Thyrza,* although he errs in thinking that £5000 a year guarantees happiness. Reardon's character shows real pathos, as he witnesses his marriage irretrievably escaping him and knows he must write. Marion Yule "is rather an interesting person," one of the "real living men and women" in the struggle for life drawn by G. Unfortunately, G sees only grief and is unable to "rise to a truer and clearer vision of human life."

**152** "Novels," Manchester Guardian, 14 April 1891, p. 10. *New Grub Street* has for its "immoral moral" the claim that happiness is distributed in "inverse proportions to merit." G's idea of realism is to include or omit what he sees based entirely on his love for dreariness. We wish G would write something pleasant.

**153** "Novels," Saturday Review (Lond), LXXI (9 May 1891), 572.
*New Grub Street* is "terrible in its realism. . .[and] cruelly precise in every detail." G "estimates to a nicety the literary pabulum which the general public enjoys."

**154** "Novels," Saturday Review (Lond), LXXII (17 Oct 1891), 450.
*Thyrza* is "a very wholesome and vivid book, stimulating and picturesque, and full of observations on life and manners." The novel's fault is that "the good characters are all so very virtuous and self-denying, so inherently refined and lovable, while the bad are so mildly bad, and so open to reform."

**155** "Novels and Stories," Glasgow Herald, 23 April 1891, p. 9.
*New Grub Street* will probably strike most readers as repulsive. "Squalor and misery are its prevailing features," as G depicts the scenes with realistic detail. "The degradation of literature is not a pleasant thing to think of, and yet we cannot deny the possibility of persons and incidents such as make up this story." Like *The Nether World, Grub Street* holds the reader's attention with a remarkable power.

**156** "Novels of the Week," Athenaeum, No. 3315 (9 May 1891), 601.
*New Grub Street* deals with the pains of "lower middle class writing folk."

G always gives "something modern" in fiction. There is in this book "a greater diffusiveness" and "a perceptible lightening of touch." G neglects the fascinating times of the glamor of a writer's life.

**157** "Our Library List," MURRAY'S MAGAZINE, IX (June 1891), 855–56.

*New Grub Street* paints in "too sombre colours" the strains of the literary and journalistic competition. G's aim emphasizes the "essentially un-heroic" vast majority of mankind; his ideal characters cannot escape the miseries of "poverty, failure, ineffectual struggle, and ignoble success."

**158** "Pages in Waiting," WORLD, 29 April 1891, p. 28.

*New Grub Street,* G's best novel thus far, is pitched in such a low key of pessimism and poverty that he cannot hope to achieve the popularity he deserves. His depressing and grim subjects endanger his "otherwise in-dubitable claim to rank among the first of rising novelists." [Brief, super-ficial.]

**159** Quill Driver. "Correspondence: A Provident Society," AUTHOR, II (Oct 1891), 151.

Whether or not Andrew Lang believes in a New Grub Street, some writers are struggling to survive. I propose a subscription to fund impoverished authors, a fund arranged like "working men's sick benefit clubs." [Three earlier items in this exchange consist of Walter Besant, "Notes and News," ibid (June 1891), 15; Andrew Lang, "Realism in Grub Street," ibid (July 1891), 43–44; and A Frog, "Correspondence: From Grub Street," ibid (Aug 1891), 95.]

**160** "Recent Fiction," SPEAKER, III (18 April 1891), 473.

*New Grub Street* portrays the "ignobly decent" with exact and merciless truth. G makes all too clear the reviewer's "pet phrases and catchwords," in a study that has not one weak point. He cares nothing for conventional characters; he makes the sordid and dull interesting and affecting. G's "writing is bright and strong, his humour delightful, and his satire is easy and yet restrained."

**161** "Recent Novels," MORNING POST (Lond), 11 May 1891, p. 2.

*New Grub Street* is even more clever than G's previous novels. His pic-tures of literary life are scathing, but the book will probably not gain a wide reading public.

**162** "Recent Novels," SPECTATOR, LXVI (30 May 1891), 764.

*New Grub Street* is vigorous and depressing. Unrelieved melancholy comes from "the persistent dramatic and narrative vigour with which Mr. Gissing embodies his conception of a world in which the man of genius, learning, or fine literary skill is pushed to the wall" while his rival "with nothing but surface cleverness" prospers.

# 1892

**163** "Among the Books," NATIONAL REVIEW, XIX (March 1892), 131–32.
G's *Denzil Quarrier* is a thoroughly modern novel, concerned—as it is—with "matter-of-fact people of the most matter-of-fact order," and modern as well in "its tolerance of all things."

**164** "Belles Lettres," WESTMINSTER REVIEW, CXXXVIII (Nov 1892), 571–72.
In *Born in Exile,* G has put himself to "a disadvantage by choosing an ungrateful theme." Godwin Peak experiences "no generous impulse, no warm-hearted, unselfish emotion." He is not "sufficiently typical" to serve as the central figure of a novel.

**165** "The Books of the Month," REVIEW OF REVIEWS, VI (July 1892), 83.
*Born in Exile* seems "hastily constructed," though much of it is "true to nature and full of noble analysis." We wish G would use more pleasant surroundings for his stories.

**166** *"Born in Exile,"* BOOKSELLER, CDXV (3 June 1892), 515.
*Born in Exile* presents Godwin Peak, an insufferable prig "who possesses an unusual intellectual power." He goes from job to job, even entering holy orders to win the hand of the young girl whom he scarcely loves. The novel illustrates G's "subtle, analytical method."

**167** [*Born in Exile*], MORNING POST, 19 May 1892, p. 2.
*Born in Exile* continues the pattern of G's *Denzil Quarrier* to avoid any kind of emotion. Godwin Peak is subjected to minute observation, so that we learn the painful traits of his nature: "miserably sensitive on the subject of his obscure birth, devoured by ambition, tormented by religious doubt, savagely independent, and yet betrayed by love into the depths of baseness."

**168** *"Born in Exile,"* PALL MALL GAZETTE, 1 July 1892, p. 3.
*Born in Exile* is the tale of Godwin Peak, whose promising life ends dismally. He is a failure both in love and in society. The novel's material, though of the slenderest, is "cleverly worked up."

**169** Cotterell, George. "New Novels," ACADEMY, XLI (9 April 1892), 347.

*Denzil Quarrier,* not G's best work, treats commonplace people. "There is not enough in the incidents of a parliamentary election in a country town to make an agreeable story."

**170** Cotterell, George. "New Novels," ACADEMY, XLII (23 July 1892), 67–68.

*Born in Exile* has a brilliant portrait of Godwin Peak. His ambition was fostered by the passion of love, and G thereby introduces a challenge to all that Peak believed in. The story of *Exile* is melancholy.

**171** "Fiction," SPEAKER, V (14 May 1892), 598–99.

*Born in Exile* poses this problem about G's future: there is no relief from gloom; a "prolonged record of sordid unhappiness is" not necessarily art. Whatever success G achieves in *Exile* comes in delineating Godwin Peak, a brilliant, sensuous young man. Peak suffers in exile, an exile enforced with great irony when he discovers that his hypocritical plan to enter the ministry—for he hoped thereby to win Sidwell's hand—only alienates him. She never wanted a clergyman for her husband. Why does G not break the gloom that smacks of contempt?

**172** "Four New Novels," STANDARD (Lond), 27 July 1892, p. 6.

*Born in Exile* reminds us somewhat of ALTON LOCKE; Godwin Peak is a hypocrite and snob, and his character is developed with unflinching power. *Exile* "is full of suggestion and insight" and leaves us with perplexing social problems.

**173** "Latest New Novels," NEW YORK TIMES, 13 March 1892, p. 19.

*Denzil Quarrier* is well-written and contains scenes possible in real life. The romance of Denzil and Lilian is "clearly and well defined." [Narrative summary.]

**174** "Literature: Mr. Gissing's New Novel," ILLUSTRATED LONDON NEWS, C (28 May 1892), 659.

In *Denzil Quarrier,* G descends to caricature, "one of the poorest tricks of the commonplace novelist." The novel's quality is in character presentation, particularly in "Quarrier himself, in Lilian, in Eustace Glazzard, and above all, in Mrs. Wade." The "original force" of *Quarrier* excuses G for occasional lapses into bathos.

**175** [Logan, Annie R.M.]. "Recent Fiction," NATION (NY), LIV (28 April 1892), 327.

In *Denzil Quarrier,* the hero's decision "to live with another man's wife is a natural enough expression of his arrogance." But will the British public accept this extra-marital union?

**176** "Mr. Gissing's New Book," BOOKMAN (Lond), I (March 1892), 215.
*Denzil Quarrier* is an interesting novel, despite its commonplace moral. The characters are cleverly drawn. The novel is a tragedy of circumstance. Lilian is a victim to Denzil Quarrier's rashness. [Lengthy story summary.]

**177** "New Books and Novels," WHITEHALL REVIEW, 19 March 1892, pp. 18–19.
*Denzil Quarrier* is a well told story about "politics and the varied phases of human nature." [Slight.]

**178** "The New Books of the Month," REVIEW OF REVIEWS, V (March 1892), 308.
*Denzil Quarrier* is "more powerful in conception" but "less finished in execution" than G's previous novels. The setting is for once not near the British Museum. His women characters are more true to life and better drawn than his men.

**179** "New Novels," GRAPHIC, XLV (23 April 1892), 528.
*Denzil Quarrier* does not give us G's constructive skill at its best. The story is hazy, and its meaning challenges our grasp. G has no intention of amusing us in this novel.

**180** "New Novels," GRAPHIC, XLVI (23 July 1892), 102.
*Born in Exile*'s Godwin Peak is a blend of agnosticism and hypocrisy. He is the product of our own generation: the professional examinee. His social ambition is far greater than his ability.

**181** "New Novels," SCOTSMAN, 23 May 1892, p. 3.
*Born in Exile* is a long, intricate, and thoughtful story that is chiefly interesting for "the strength and finish with which the characters of a number of young men are presented." They are clever young people discussing current ideas about literature, philosophy, and religion. It is a novel to "be read with great profit and pleasure."

**182** "News Notes," BOOKMAN (Lond), III (Oct 1892), 6.
"The opinions of novelists on novels are always very interesting, whether one agrees with them or not. Mr. Hardy is known specially to admire the writings of George Gissing." [Slight.]

**183** "Notices of Books," BOOKSELLER, CDXII (4 March 1892), 210*b*.

*Denzil Quarrier* involves a confusion of matings and pseudo-marriages that defy our understanding. *Cui bono?* G himself fails to explain the mix-ups.

**184** "Novels," DAILY NEWS (Lond), 27 June 1892, p. 3.

*Born in Exile* is a blatantly pessimistic view of one side of human nature. We cannot admire the impression that a character is either a member of society or else falls into the abyss, or that poverty condemns one to exile. G is a powerful writer, but the book is "eminently unsatisfactory, because unredeemed by any of the lighter touches and pleasing incidents which give variety to life."

**185** "Novels," GUARDIAN (Lond), XLVII (23 March 1892), 439.

*Denzil Quarrier* professes to deal with politics but instead becomes a story of politicians, particularly of one who takes as his wife a young lady whose husband had been arrested at the church door after their marriage. G develops her "nervous dread of discovery—the simplest reader must know, of course, that discovery is inevitable." G should confine himself to politics.

**186** "Novels," GUARDIAN (Lond), XLVII (20 July 1892), 1098.

*Born in Exile* is a pessimistic book concerning Godwin Peak, who struggles long and painfully for success. Lacking faith, he nevertheless tries to take Christian orders in order "to win the hand of a religious girl." She rejects him for his hypocrisy, though she adopts his skepticism. The "book ends badly."

**187** "Novels," SATURDAY REVIEW (Lond), LXXIII (5 March 1892), 276.

*Denzil Quarrier* is "almost excellent." G always provides "good honest work." The book is "charmingly written, in a clear simple style." "A bolder theme may possibly suit this author better."

**188** "Novels," SATURDAY REVIEW (Lond), LXXIII (11 June 1892), 688.

*Born in Exile* presents Godwin Peak, "part prig, part snob, all egotist." He "appears to us to be the most unlovable creation that ever appealed to the misdirected sympathies of a reader inasmuch as personal advancement is his only goal."

**189** "Novels and Stories," GLASGOW HERALD, 20 Feb 1892, p. 9.

*Denzil Quarrier* argues the "inadequacy of our present social system to meet exceptional social cases." In addition to a strong political tone, the novel addresses itself to "the old question of our marriage laws" as principal characters live in open revolt against traditional practices.

**190** "Novels of the Week," ATHENAEUM, No. 3363 (9 April 1892), 466.

In *Denzil Quarrier,* G's work improves: it has a lighter touch; some scenes are even amusing; the style is less self-conscious. "Electioneering chapters are brisk and amusing." The reader is led to prefer antinomianism to orthodoxy.

**191** "Novels of the Week," ATHENAEUM, No. 3370 (28 May 1892), 693.

*Born in Exile* shows G at his best in recording the progress of Godwin Peak's courtship and the history of his mental development. [Plot summary.]

**192** "Our One English Realist," DAILY CHRONICLE, 26 May 1892, p. 3.

*Born in Exile* is G's best achievement to date; artistically it would be hard to improve upon this work. G long ago mastered the realistic technique; now he is gaining a following. Godwin Peak's ideas could never be realized, and he was forever doomed to exile. G treats him with intellectual analysis, for he cannot love his heroes. Thus the reader is led to pity and sadness. The minor characters are also rendered with convincing realism.

**193** "Pages in Waiting," WORLD (Lond), 24 Feb 1892, p. 24.

*Denzil Quarrier* is more compressed, "less harrowing, more artistic" than either *New Grub Street* or *The Nether World*. It is a powerful, true, and cruel story. [Brief.]

**194** "Pages in Waiting," WORLD (Lond), 8 June 1892, p. 27.

*Born in Exile* is a somber novel, "more pessimistic than realistic," and less bitter than *New Grub Street*. It concerns the reflections of a strong thinker whose judgment is warped. [Brief.]

**195** "A Political Novel," DAILY CHRONICLE, 20 Feb 1892, p. 3.

*Denzil Quarrier* rewards the reader with its seriousness, precision, and unflinching care, for G is never wordy or trivial. Both the major and lesser characters are drawn from actuality. The narrative works drearily, but exactly, to its inevitable conclusion. More than any of his contemporaries G understands the "art of leaving out."

**196** "Recent Novels," SPECTATOR, LXVIII (25 June 1892), 883.

*Born in Exile*'s intellectual interest must be commended. The whole book is "utterly devoid of any feeling for the simple human hopes and enthusiasms and affections which give to life its interest and charm."

**197** "Recent Novels," TIMES (Lond), 1 July 1892, 18.
*Born in Exile,* like all recent G novels, "is a suggestive novel, full of close thought and carefully drawn character." His novels appeal almost exclusively to the head. Godwin Peak is subtly rendered. His actions stem from human fallibility. Can we ever judge probability in such a character?

**198** "Recent Novels and Tales," TIMES (Lond), 12 March 1892, p. 5.
*Denzil Quarrier* is a very effective little satire on electioneering in which G is more interested in the psychological than the political. The central figure hides a secret that is shared by a boyhood friend; the revelation itself makes us wonder why the unexpected disclosure is such a refuge for novelists.

**199** "Reviews," PUBLISHERS' CIRCULAR, LVI (13 Feb 1892), 183.
*Denzil Quarrier* is a powerful, interesting story of a man who marries a prisoner's wife, only to have the circumstance ruin his political career. [Narrative summarized.]

**200** "Reviews," PUBLISHERS' CIRCULAR, LVI (28 May 1892), 621.
*Born in Exile* is more interesting for character study than plot. Godwin Peak is a complex character attending Whitelaw College; we know his "sombre outlines," but the story is too sluggish.

**201** "Reviews," PUBLISHERS' CIRCULAR, LVI (6 Aug 1892), 131.
*New Grub Street,* now coming out in a cheap edition from Smith, Elder, remains "a favourite with the reading public."

**202** Roberts, Morley. "George Gissing," NOVEL REVIEW, I (May 1892), 96–103.
G's novels neither provide the bloodshed that makes for popularity, nor do they show how wretched mortals can be. His characters suffer doggedly, victims of "Circumstance, or, by a pariphrasis, the native malignity of matter." In his early writing, G was "salted by the priests of Positivism," particularly by Harrison. Then he found Dostoevski, so that *The Unclassed* taught "the possibility of redemption by love." In *Isabel Clarendon,* G was influenced by Turgenev. *Thyrza* marked his own independence; it is the

truest "study of the best of the lower classes" that our literature has produced. G is "absolutely honest" in delineating all that he sees. In representing men, G can be faulted because they lack real male strength. His women, thanks to his intuitive creation, are regarded as feminine even by women. All his characters are realized, particularly in their unhappiness: there is a "relentless severity of purpose" in handling man's fate. But G himself must change before his novels can improve inasmuch as he must himself learn that healthy tolerance is preferable to insistent weariness. Before long, G will probably learn to work and to hope, "believing that the only way to teach mankind responsibility is to trust them, and the only hope of doing that is to bid them trust themselves."

**203** "Serious Fiction," LITERARY WORLD (Lond), LXV (27 May 1892), 510–11.
*Born in Exile* involves much conversation about theological subjects and provides a striking picture of social and mental unrest. The theological discourses appear to be a reaction against the religious or quasi-religious novel, although it is not clear where G's own opinions are stated. The novel is very serious, and even lighter passages are bitter in flavor.

**204** "Some New Novels," NEW YORK DAILY TRIBUNE, 27 March 1892, p. 18.
*Denzil Quarrier* has power, but it will not please most readers. The hero is a contemporary man engaged in a situation of ethical flabbiness. Glazzard's action is "so purely malicious" as to be scarcely human. The dialogue is bright, and the interest is sustained by characters who, as social types, "are the reverse of promising."

**205** "Stories to Read," GLOBE (Lond), 10 Feb 1892, p. 3.
*Denzil Quarrier* is occupied with politics, witnessing the history of a couple "who have ventured to live for one another without the formality of a legal tie." The novel is a clever one, and its record of provincial life valid. However unsatisfactory, Lilian's fate is the only choice G had.

**206** "To-Day's Literature: *Denzil Quarrier*," CHICAGO TRIBUNE, 13 Feb 1892, p. 13; rptd as *"Denzil Quarrier,"* LITERARY NEWS (NY), XIII (March 1892), 74.
*Denzil Quarrier,* a "simply and directly told" story, is "strong and impressive," though not a great novel. History might consider this novel "more truly significant and representative" than more famous books because G is "animated by the Time-spirit and receives and transmits the influence that rules the hour." Like Goethe and Arnold, G follows naturalism in asking the clear and straight questions that "get at the root of things."

**207** [*The Town Traveller*], MORNING POST, 8 Sept 1892, p. 2.
*The Town Traveller* is so much less depressing than the previous novels
G has written that we assume he has been influenced by Dickens, although
not in a sense of imitation. While we are inclined to accuse Dickens of
grossly exaggerating his descriptions of London's boarding houses, G's
novels, coming half a century later, give the "broad features of lower
middle-class life" as essentially unchanged. G provides their colloquialisms,
describes their wax-flower ornaments, details their fashions in costume. But
he ought to allow his readers to judge for themselves and not state the
moral so explicitly. *Traveller* is a change for G; amusing passages make
it an "excellent book for holiday reading."

**208** Traill, H. D. "Literature and Drama," NEW REVIEW, VI
(March 1892), 378.
G's *Denzil Quarrier,* recently published by Lawrence & Bullen, exagger-
ates the misery of modern life.

**209** "Women," QUEEN, XCI (5 March 1892), 395.
Clara E. Collet lectured on "George Gissing's Novels" before the London
Ethical Society. G's novels contain more and more realism than theorizing.
In *New Grub Street,* G demonstrates "that the troubles of the relatively
poor are worse than those of the absolutely poor." While G's men are
agnostics, his women are believers.

# 1893

**210** B., N. O. "Novels and Novelists," ECHO, 16 Oct 1893, p. 1.
Directed to the more squalid regions of London, G's vivid descriptions
have brought him "a limited, if enthusiastic, circle of admirers"; and
although he is a "writer of the first rank," the public is scarcely curious
about G's private life. His novels "expose with sympathetic insight" the
failure of the artisan class while simultaneously championing "the cause
of poor professional families." What a variety of memorable characters
he has provided us! In treating social issues, his view is consistently
reactionary. Both *Demos* and *New Grub Street* are unusually effective
condemnations of a system that prospers the unworthy, damages the innocent, and neglects the idealistic worker. And so it is in life itself, for
G's books are "brimful of accurate observation."

**211** Black, Clementina. "Literature," ILLUSTRATED LONDON
NEWS, CIII (5 Aug 1893), 155.
In *The Odd Women,* G treats the problem of the number of surplus mar-
riageable women; he suggests that they ought to be trained for some dig-

nified, independent occupations. G succeeds in providing conversations that both distinguish the speakers and discuss social themes. Rhoda Nunn and Everard Barfoot are especially useful for such purposes, although G plants them in unreasonable circumstances and then prevents their attaining happiness—particularly when he attributes ungenerous conduct to Rhoda.

**212** "Books of the Week," SCOTSMAN, 24 April 1893, p. 3.
*The Odd Women* intends to state a problem so that the reader might consider the solutions possible. The problem, involving the excessive number of marriageable women, and the examination of that problem provide coherence and unity for the book's incidents. G's characters represent the variety of the difficulties involved, with the result that they are insufficiently individualized, or "too typical to be natural."

**213** "Books of the Week," TIMES (Lond), 7 Sept 1893, p. 3.
THE SOCIAL PROBLEM: ITS POSSIBLE SOLUTION, a new book by the Rev. Osborne Jay, gives us a gloomy picture of his poor London parish. Jay contends that soon it will be too late to accomplish any good among these submerged classes. [This review contains a rather long selection taken from Jay's book. G recognized the quotation, supposedly written by Jay, as taken directly from *The Nether World* and accordingly wrote the editor. See "Borrowed Feathers," ibid, 9 Sept 1893, p. 13. W. C. Hunt thereupon wrote a letter ("Mr. Gissing and the Rev. A. O. Jay," ibid 13 Sept 1893, p. 10) that said: "I am responsible for the omission of certain commas of quotation" in THE SOCIAL PROBLEM.]

**214** Cotterell, George. "New Novels," ACADEMY, XLIII (24 June 1893), 542.
*The Odd Women* is a sad book dealing with women who are hardly typical of the unmarried. Style of the novel is forced and flat. The novel is all shadow, showing "scarcely a glimpse of brightness."

**215** "Fiction," SPEAKER, VIII (14 Oct 1893), 417–18.
*The Odd Women* is marked throughout by power and earnestness; it moralizes over the vexed question of the excessive number of marriageable females in England. G assumes a dogmatic and polemical position with an air that is "inconsistent with the true aims of fiction." The book, consequently, becomes more essay than story. G's knowledge of feminine motivation and feeling is admirable. However, his novel is too depressing and dogmatic. [Summarizes the narrative.]

**216** Gosse, Edmund. QUESTIONS AT ISSUE (Lond: Heinemann, 1893), pp. 325–31.

When I wrote "Tennyson—And After?" for the NEW REVIEW, G wrote me a letter (20 Nov 1892) that "confirmed my doubts" about the reading habits of the poor. [G's letter, printed here in an appendix, asserts that the poor, especially in southern England, never read poetry on any occasion. In northern England, where rhythms of speech have verse qualities, some poor read poetry at times.]

**217** "The Library," QUEEN, XCIII (3 June 1893), 941.
*The Odd Women* is another of G's dreary stories about a world of slender purses, and people "bereft of all natural good spirits." Miss Rhoda Nunn and her type are ignorant of the "movement of the world since the question of 'women's rights' was first broached." The men are less life-like, "often repulsive and very often vulgar."

**218** "The Library Table," GLOBE (Lond), 24 April 1893, p. 6.
*The Odd Women* poses a social problem for which G provides no solution. The novel's plot is "thoroughly interesting and the representation of feminine character is especially effective."

**219** "Literature of the Day," DAILY TELEGRAPH (Lond), 22 May 1893, p. 2.
*The Odd Women* is an "ingenious and cleverly constructed story" treating the excessive number of women in proportion to men. The author "displays considerable insight into the idiosyncracies of feminine character." G represents with "masterly force and picturesqueness" a variety of women.

**220** [Logan, Annie R.M.]. "More Fiction," NATION (NY), LVII (13 July 1893), 31–32.
*The Odd Women* is an excellent treatment of unmarried women. These women, as G examines them, carry the hope of the future. His examples of marriage make that institution a failure. G has an admirable intensity of purpose.

**221** "The New Books of the Month," REVIEW OF REVIEWS, VIII (8 July 1893), 99.
*The Odd Women* convinces us that G will have to abandon his gloomy pessimism before "he ever gives us first-rate work." He tells of women committed to spinsterhood unless they prepare wisely for some special occupation. The book warns the serious reader in a convincing though depressing way that parents must provide daughters with rational training.

**222** "New Novels," ATHENAEUM, No. 3422 (27 May 1893), 667.
*The Odd Women* is modern in both theme and treatment. It is a decidedly

"uncheering" novel, even more depressing than *New Grub Street*. The work shows the touch of a reporter more than that of an artist.

**223** "A Novelist on the Woman Question," DAILY CHRONICLE (Lond), 19 April 1893, p. 3.
*The Odd Women* is G's "skilful, cold, impartial diagnosis of a social evil" for which he prescribes no very satisfactory medicament. "Our chief Realist" pictures lives with large patches of gray and leaves the "conviction that life for the most part is futile."

**224** "Novels," GUARDIAN (Lond), XLVIII (24 May 1893), 839.
*The Odd Women* is at least as depressing as G's earlier novels, perhaps his "gloomiest production." If the actual world were as depressing as G describes it, then "the world would have come to an end long ago." He omits Christianity from his universe entirely. "Altogether for grim unhappiness and wretched unsolved problems this book is unsurpassed."

**225** "Novels," MANCHESTER GUARDIAN, 25 April 1893, p. 10.
*The Odd Women* treats marriage "from the point of view of the advanced man and woman." Besides three young ladies who are left to struggle alone after the death of their father, G presents two "very capable young ladies who preside over a type-writing establishment for the encouragement and support of single women." Their independence provides G the opportunity to "indicate a view of marriage which is not the accepted one."

**226** "Novels," SATURDAY REVIEW, LXXV (29 April 1893), 459–60.
In *The Odd Women,* G's women "are far truer to nature than his men." He describes the circumstances of a variety of "surplus females," arguing forcibly in behalf of those who take a more practical view of life, as by "making a comfortable livelihood in the type-writing line." G also inquires into the conventions of the marriage contract, suggesting that a legal and religious arrangement is no guarantee to happiness.

**227** "Novels and Stories," GLASGOW HERALD, 9 March 1893, p. 9.
*Born in Exile* treats of a depressing world. G's hero in *Exile* "is forever checked by his better aspirations, by a morbid sense of his social inferiority, and by the orthodoxy of the family into which he would care to marry." It is a serious book and not meant for anyone "who is afraid of a fit of the blues."

**228** "Novel and Tales," NATIONAL OBSERVER, IX (22 April 1893), 579.

*The Odd Women* constitutes "a real advance" on *New Grub Street*; it keeps G among journalists, not among men of letters. G's "style has no distinction"; his views on people "are not so much the philosopher's as the reporter's." Written for "the public of to-day," *Women* shows both diligence and talent.

**229** [*The Odd Women*], GLASGOW HERALD, 20 April 1893, p. 9. *The Odd Women*, "a genuine work of art," shows a "great advance" in G's art. G's books always possessed thought, "sometimes more thought than action." His odd women "do not belong to the working classes, but are ten times weaker than the women of that class, and pitiably helpless." G never allows any of his characters to become happy.

**230** "Pages in Waiting," WORLD (Lond), 27 Sept 1893, p. 28. *The Odd Women*, like other G novels, makes us think, makes us uncomfortable. This book contains much "fact in fiction" as G wishes to call our attention to the problems of surplus women.

**231** "Recent Novels," MORNING POST (Lond), 12 June 1893, p. 2. *The Odd Women* fortunately never theorizes about the obstacles inherent in our social system. "The mind is not wearied by arguments, the personages are not dragged onto the scene" to become supernumeraries. G treats his issue with "lucid ability."

**232** "Recent Novels," SPECTATOR, LXX (27 May 1893), 707–8. *The Odd Women* is G's most interesting book so far; it is strong, thought-compelling, remarkably clever, but it is also "a good novel to get away from." Unfortunately, "the entire absence of atmosphere gives a feeling of untruthfulness" because distortion (a failure in proportion and perspective) leads one to find that G's world is not the world the reader knows. G's novels have a chilly kind of intellectual interest.

**233** "Reviews: *The Odd Women*," PALL MALL GAZETTE, 29 May 1893, p. 4. *The Odd Women* "represents the Woman question made flesh; his people live it instead of talking it." One risk G makes is to subordinate art to thesis, but his novel does not become a treatise; the other risk is more serious, because characters could easily become "counters in the game of sociology instead of living human beings." G faces the risk: his characters come alive, partly through successful dialogue. While *Women* falls short of genius, it is nevertheless "the most interesting novel of the year."

## 1894

**234** "Books of the Week," MANCHESTER GUARDIAN, 2 Jan 1894, p. 7.

*The Emancipated* originated in observing life and not in reading books. But why do G's characters desire to survive? G's emancipated characters are sometimes trusting, occasionally reckless and self-ruinous. His style is austere and sardonic. The strength of *Emancipated* rests upon Cecily and Miriam, though there is nothing beautiful or buoyant in their lives, tailored as they are to G's dreary spirits.

**235** "Books of the Week: New Novels," SCOTSMAN, 10 Dec 1894, p. 4.

*In the Year of Jubilee* has "undeniable merit as literature," although G's theme will offend many readers. It protests that married partners ought "to live apart as much as possible" and then to "meet as lovers." The principal character, Nancy Lord, is interesting both as maiden and then as wife. Furthermore, G succeeds no less with "a certain humourous force and originality."

**236** *"The Emancipated,"* SPECTATOR, LXXIII (11 Aug 1894), 183–84.

The novel is a treatise on emancipation from old-fashioned ideals, rather than a story. But the emancipation G provides Miriam and Cecily is not attractive. The general reader is "not likely to relish the substitution of mental analysis and reveries for plot and incident."

**237** [*In the Year of Jubilee*], DAILY TELEGRAPH (Lond), 21 Dec 1894, p. 6.

*In the Year of Jubilee* contains characters of no importance, people of "ignorance and frivolity," of "superficiality and narrowmindedness." Into the "inner-selves" of such figures, G brings us; about them he "possesses a clear and comprehensive insight that enables him to depict them with convincing verisimilitude." Like *The Odd Women, Jubilee* is another "thoughtful and introspective contribution to our latter-day fictional literature."

**238** *"In the Year of Jubilee,"* STANDARD (Lond), 28 Dec 1894, p. 2.

*In the Year of Jubilee* tells of the Peachey family; "nothing could be more wretched, morally and intellectually," than their household. One of the most powerful of our realistic writers, G uses naturalistic methods suited to his own manner. The only break in G's pessimism comes with women who break the moral law; thus, Nancy Lord "comes out with flying colours." It seems to be G's theory that married people should live apart. [Several lengthy quotations.]

**239** "The Library Table," GLOBE (Lond), 31 Dec 1894, p. 6
*In the Year of Jubilee* is characteristic of G's study of lower middle-class life, "untinged by anything like romance." The marital arrangement of Tarrant and Nancy "is new to English fiction, and the portrayal of it imparts freshness to Mr. Gissing's work." Contemporary fiction must provide room for "pictures of society dawn from Mr. Gissing's peculiar point of view."

**240** Nicoll, Sir William Robertson. "The News of England," BOOK BUYER, XI (Nov 1894), 480–81.
G's originality and conscientiousness hamper his reputation. While the general reader is coming to know him, "the prevailing sombreness of his work will always stand in the way of a wide popularity." G is scarcely known to London society.

**241** "Novels," DAILY NEWS (Lond), 27 Dec 1894, p. 6.
*In the Year of Jubilee* is, like G's other novels, both "extremely clever and not a little depressing." Through his hero, G expresses some "original ideas about marriage." Character drawing, not story, constitutes the novel's strength. The characters are vital, but hardly amiable. [Narrative outline.]

**242** "Novels and Stories," GLASGOW HERALD, 6 Dec 1894, p. 10.
*In the Year of Jubilee* surprises and gratifies because it relents from the drabness of G's uncompromising realism. At the end of the book there are characters who are "moderately and temperately happy." G is to be congratulated for "this stern and painful novel"; it is not as gross as George Moore's ESTHER WATERS.

**243** "Pages in Waiting," WORLD (Lond), 19 Dec 1894, p. 32.
*In the Year of Jubilee* is more provocative than clever; G achieves the effect of unrelieved unpleasantness by describing the "grovelling vulgarity and base scheming" of low and repulsive characters. G is capable of better work.

**244** "Recent Novels," MORNING POST (Lond), 28 Dec 1894, p. 2.
In *In the Year of Jubilee* "realistic romance attains its legitimate limit." Some portraits are "scathingly severe," but G remains a realist, never striving for excessive effects. The moral evolution of Nancy Lord is perhaps the most remarkable feature of the book.

**245** "Reviews: Novels and Stories," SATURDAY REVIEW, LXXVII (20 Jan 1894), 71.

*The Emancipated* begins sluggishly with the overcrowding of characters. Thereafter, Cecily Doran begins her emancipation, ultimately learning through Miriam Baske's brother, "a conceited young braggart," that excessive freedom can indeed be painful.

# 1895

**246** "Among the Autumn Books," BOOK BUYER, XII (Sept 1895), 452.

*In the Year of Jubilee* is "a strong story" treating people who are "carefully studied."

**247** Austin, L. F. "The Book and Its Story. A Study in Drab," SKETCH, VIII (9 Jan 1895), 517.

*In the Year of Jubilee* selects several dreary inhabitants of Brixton and staggers us with their foulness. G convinces us that there are skeletons all about us, spiteful and unloving figures whose selfishness and degradation strike out everywhere. *Jubilee* is "the honest belief of a skilled observer." G's novels have an "intellectual quality, an austere sincerity in the face of shallow optimism, a moral weight, entirely lacking in the mass of current fiction." For all their grimness, G's characters are not utter scoundrels, but they are certainly not imposing figures. And "to an observer like Mr. Gissing there are infinite possibilities between these two extremes." He argues that married partners should respect one another at least as much as "two friends of the same sex living together."

**248** Besant, Walter. "Notes and News," AUTHOR, V (Jan 1895), 208.

One hopes that G's reputation will improve in keeping with his power as a writer. G's neglect is due to the gloomy themes of his novels.

**249** "Books of the Holiday Season," BOOK BUYER, XII (Dec 1895), 697.

*The Emancipated* is marked by "painstaking workmanship and unquestioned vigor."

**250** "Books of the Week: New Novels," SCOTSMAN, 16 Dec 1895, p. 4.

*Sleeping Fires* is a "slightly built story, but one of considerable human interest." G's lovers are frustrated by the conventions of morality. "Fluently and graphically told," *Fires* contains descriptions of picturesque Athens. [Narrative outline.]

> **251** Cotterell, George. "New Novels," ACADEMY, XLVII (18 May 1895), 422.

*Eve's Ransom* achieves realism without nastiness. The story is more the "history of events and utterances than a record of feelings as they lead up to acts." The love story is told in "the subdued tones of lower middle-class life."

> **252** "Current Literature," SPECTATOR, LXXV (14 Sept 1895), 344–45.

In *Eve's Ransom,* G himself fails to see enough of the natures of the characters he creates; G should choose a higher type of person for representation, preferably the highest type of humanity. Once again G relegates religion to the weaker sex.

> **253** [*Eve's Ransom*], LITERARY WORLD (Lond), LI (26 April 1895), 386.

*Eve's Ransom* is "an unexciting story of middle-class life, and the sole merit aimed at by the author appears to be that of realistic faithfulness." Told from a masculine viewpoint, the novel does not convince the reader because Eve, the heroine, is "devoid of the very common feminine desire to set herself right in the eyes of her associates."

> **254** *"Eve's Ransom,"* SKETCH, IX (24 April 1895), 697.

*Eve's Ransom* repeats the "disappointment, toil, and defeated hopes" of G's previous novels, but it lacks the harshness we associate with his writing. Indeed, the book even ends on "a genial note." We might prefer G to write a fairy tale, but it is better to have stories "austerely and truthfully cut out of hard patches of actual life."

> **255** "Fiction," CRITIC, XXIV (19 Oct 1895), 248.

*Eve's Ransom* is an earlier manuscript which G resurrected to take advantage of the success of *In the Year of Jubilee.* It was written by "one of the younger English realists."

> **256** "Fiction," NATIONAL OBSERVER, XIII (19 Jan 1895), 275.

*In the Year of Jubilee* cannot be recommended to the reader: it is certainly not a work of art, nor does it tell us anything new about G's ability. There is no evidence of "human pity" in this "study of human degradation." The suburbs of London depicted here do not correspond to actuality. "Things cannot be so bad as all that," even for "victims of destiny."

**257** "Fiction," NATIONAL OBSERVER, XIV (18 May 1895), 26.
*Eve's Ransom* can be read without much trouble, though with a great deal of pleasure. G draws upon his own fund of knowledge rather than upon any fresh observation.

**258** "Fiction," SPEAKER, XI (13 April 1895), 416–17.
*Eve's Ransom,* like so many earlier G novels, pictures the "grim irony of fate"; he refuses to see any sunshine in the gloom. Its theme is the effort of a "quixotic young man to save a girl" from wrong. But Eve does not marry her savior; she jilts him to marry one of his friends. Might G not have saved us from this pessimism?

**259** Frederic, Harold. "George Gissing's Works," NEW YORK TIMES, 8 Dec 1895, p. 16.
A dismal cloud of gloom hangs over the novel in England: Meredith is aging; Hardy has fallen from the powerful RETURN OF THE NATIVE to the weaker JUDE THE OBSCURE; the public snaps up huge editions of Grant Allen and Marie Corelli; and it would seem that Mrs. Humphrey Ward would become the "representative British novelist." We welcome, there-fore, "the sign of promise" advancing G's recognition by a thoughtful public: his books are selling; reprints of earlier novels are appearing; and his writing is more and more the topic of literary conversations in which he is named along with Meredith and Hardy. For years his novels were dis-missed as simply "too pessimistic." Perhaps Moore's ESTHER WATERS will help G by making the public realize the importance of "material, strikingly dramatic, terribly human." But Moore's THE CELIBATES hardly gives serious readers cause to praise, whereas G has a long list of important books about London's basements and cellars. *In the Year of Jubilee* is per-haps G's "most important work," following the neglected *New Grub Street, Thyrza, Demos,* and *The Nether World. The Odd Women* "is about as painful a book as I have ever read" and demands rereading. G's first long work, *The Unclassed,* while immature, is perhaps his most interesting. How has this novel lapsed without the notice and attention it deserves?

**260** "A Good Novel," LITERARY WORLD (Lond), LI (4 Jan 1895), 10–11.
*In the Year of Jubilee* is evidence that while novelists are obliged to shift from writing three volume novels to one volume books, G has the strength to survive. Like Norris, G "is above whims," a novelist "not bitten by the flies of transitory modes." G portrays the middle class, allowing his char-acters so much independence that the author is not always explicit about their deeds. *Jubilee* is for "readers who prefer fiction that is simply fiction," and not "a wolf in sheep's clothing, or a parson in tea gown."

**261** "In a Black Country," DAILY CHRONICLE, 9 May 1895, p. 3.
*Eve's Ransom* tells of the unexpected bequest that suddenly releases Maurice Hilliard from a life of drudgery. Similarly, Eve Madeley comes "into possession of a small sum of money." They both crave a full life, and money gives them the opportunity not for waste but for culture. How should the money be spent? Together, they represent "toilers emerging." G's idealism insists that they must suffer a grim repression, as his pessimism prevails.

**262** "The Library," QUEEN, XCVII (2 March 1895), 392.
*In the Year of Jubilee* contains "more of the elements of humanity and feeling" than G's previous novels. He has never compromised his seriousness: the bad are always bad. But here the art remains with G's usual skill, although the characters seem less troubled. [Narrative summary.]

**263** "The Library Table," GLOBE (Lond), 29 April 1895, p. 3.
*Eve's Ransom* is now available in a one-volume edition. Though relatively slight when compared to G's other books, it is no less "thoughtful and provocative of thought."

**264** "A Literary Journal," BOOKMAN (NY), I (May 1895), 226.
G is known only through his work, having thus far "succeeded in evading the wiles of the biographer." A "patient and faithful realist," he has "lately received a good deal of critical attention in France."

**265** "The Literary Lounger," SKETCH, XII (25 Dec 1895), 474.
*Sleeping Fires* shows some brightness in the sordid melancholy one expects from G. Perhaps his new method will bring quality equal to that already sustained.

**266** [Logan, Annie R.M.]. "More Fiction," NATION (NY), LXI (17 Oct 1895), 277.
*In the Year of Jubilee* has for its dreadful subject "The New Woman"; G handles her without gloves. He "hales her forth from the obscurity of the middle class . . . in active revolt against the respectable dullness proudly enjoyed by her mother."

**267** Logan, Annie R. M. "Recent Novels," NATION (NY), LXI (11 July 1895), 32.
In *Eve's Ransom,* G's portrait of Eve Madeley "is indistinct and unsatisfactory," but with Hilliard he is on "surer ground."

**268** "Mr. George Gissing's New Novel," SPECTATOR, LXXIV (9 Feb 1895), 205–6.

*In the Year of Jubilee*'s portrait of the lower middle classes involves too many type characters; G attributes the inadequacies of his characters to their social conditions, and the result is a distorted view of life. G is noteworthy "for vigour and vividness with which he renders his own vision . . . of the vulgarity, sordidness, and ugliness of life."

**269** "Mr. Gissing's New Book," SATURDAY REVIEW (Lond), LXXIX (19 Jan 1895), 99–100.

*In the Year of Jubilee* is another excellent G novel; he deserves serious attention. Quiet humor makes this novel bearable. G excels in depicting "the ignobly respectable." Tarrant is a strange hero: "uninteresting loafer, cur, and prig." Is the treatment of the outcome meant to be ironic? His style is marred by "little whimsicalities and mannerisms plainly traceable to Carlyle and Meredith." It is a remarkable book.

**270** "New Books and New Editions," WHITEHALL REVIEW, 28 Dec 1895, p. 12.

*The Sleeping Fires* shows G "at his best," and we predict its success in the Autonym Series. [Brief summary.]

**271** "New Novels," ATHENAEUM, No. 3507 (12 Jan 1895), 45.

Despite its unpromising materials, *In the Year of Jubilee* convincingly presents human nature. The style is admirable: "always direct, forcible, and free from mannerism." The "squalid squabblings of the Peachey household" make painful reading.

**272** "New Novels," ATHENAEUM, No. 3524 (11 May 1895), 605.

In *Eve's Ransom,* both Eve Madeley and Maurice Hilliard are clearly recognizable types of contemporary humanity; they yearn to know life on a higher plane. Eve's nature is too shallow for Maurice. G renders the relationship with considerable success. [Brief attention to the plot.]

**273** "New Novels," SCOTSMAN, 15 April 1895, p. 3.

*Eve's Ransom* is a clever examination of a woman's conflicting drives. G's representations are not always recognizable, nor is the narrative consistently convincing. The surroundings are of the shadiest. [Eve's dilemma is outlined.]

**274** "New Publications: Powers Under Control," NEW YORK TIMES, 27 April 1895, p. 3.

*Eve's Ransom* is the "farthest remove possible from what is conventional." G leaves the reader entirely alone in any decision about Eve. What marks this novel is the fact that the author's powers "are always kept under control."

**275** "News Notes," BOOKMAN (Lond), VIII (Aug 1895), 129. [Reports G's part in an Omar Khayyam dinner honoring George Meredith.]

**276** "Notices of Books," BOOKSELLER, CDLI (8 June 1895), 509.
*Eve's Ransom* makes one wonder about G's purpose in this novel, even while we realize that he has gained for himself an assured position among contemporary novelists. The plot baffles our understanding; his characters are skillfully drawn.

**277** "Novel Notes," BOOKMAN (NY), I (March 1895), 122–23.
*In the Year of Jubilee* is the most "notable novel that has come to us this year"; it possesses graphic precision and pitiless realism. "The stolid Philistinism of the prosperous members of the lower middle classes" has little humor.

**278** "Novel Notes," BOOKMAN (Lond), VIII (May 1895), 54–55.
G's novels suppress nothing ugly, but he forgets to take account of the sunlight; he "feels too strongly to be simply accurate." The heroine of *In the Year of Jubilee* "is entirely incredible," whereas the hero is artistically a great success. Is the hope that marks the close of *Eve's Ransom* a portent for the future? G is "one of the very few novelists, besides Mr. Hardy, who dares to endow his attractive heroines with real life faults, not only magnificent and interesting vices."

**279** "Novel Notes," BOOKMAN (NY), I (May 1895), 265.
*Eve's Ransom* does not detract from G's reputation, but he might be producing too much for his own good. American critics are waking up to the fact that G is a force in realistic fiction to be reckoned with.

**280** "Novels," DAILY NEWS (Lond), 23 April 1895, p. 6.
*Eve's Ransom,* while not as poignant or powerful as some earlier G books, nevertheless "carries on every page the same imprint of unexaggerated truth." It is less sordid and healthier than his previous books. "Every character in the book bears the stamp of being observed from real life." [Brief narrative outline.]

**281** "Novels," GUARDIAN (Lond), L (3 April 1895), 510.
*In the Year of Jubilee* concerns only uninteresting people participating in a story that has scarcely any originality. The lesser characters are "shadowy and unmeaning." One wonders what G meant to say by this book.

**282** "Novels," GUARDIAN (Lond), L (22 May 1895), 765.

*Eve's Ransom* photographs a very unpleasant bit of life with "realism pure and simple." It does not have even one lovable character, nor does the novel strike any high aim. Eve Madeley behaves meanly yet seems to marry fortunately, leaving a discarded lover who "pretends to rejoice in being free."

**283** "Novels," MANCHESTER GUARDIAN, 22 Jan 1895, p. 10.

*In the Year of Jubilee* presents characters who merit G's severity; he is the "strongest of our most recent novelists." G exposes the suburbs with irony and with a "rigid and penetrating style." The formula for his novels is to treat a world populated with "persons nominally of good considera-tion but living ravenous little reptilian lives." Some escape this world, but G allows them little enjoyment. *Jubilee* is an unusually honest novel marked by "mournful character drawing."

**284** "Novels," MANCHESTER GUARDIAN, 30 April 1895, p. 10.

*Eve's Ransom* disputes the theory that if a poor worker were given a sub-stantial amount of money he would squander it. Maurice Hilliard unex-pectedly receives £400; he quits drinking, and he satisfies his "long-repressed and rational desires." But G's case cannot be considered typical, and the conclusion he reaches is too depressing to accept. *Ransom* has for the first time in G a "subtle power of arresting the attention and arousing the sympathies of the reader."

**285** "Novels and Stories," GLASGOW HERALD, 11 April 1895, p. 9.

*Eve's Ransom* "is pleasantly free both from problems and the bold, bad kind of thing which is at present in fashion." The heroine of the title seems hardly worth the trouble G bestows on her; the chief concern of the nar-rative is her relationship with Hilliard. Not a particularly cheerful tale, *Ransom* "is at least perfectly wholesome."

**286** "Novels and Tales," OUTLOOK (NY), LII (14 Sept 1895), 432.

*In the Year of Jubilee* has not even the slightest moral force. While we recognize G's characters, we ask the value of his presenting them. His talent, therefore, goes to waste in giving us such vulgar people.

**287** "Novels of the Time: The Disorganized 'Middle-Class,'" NEW YORK TIMES, 28 July 1895, p. 27.

*In the Year of Jubilee* presents the reviewer with many of the qualities he would demand of a novelist; it is a "vivacious, yet rather dispiriting book." G has unusual power, industry, and comprehension of life. The presence of some very disagreeable characters among the twenty or so introduced here means that G is "in the fashion." Furthermore, he is thorough, has the "faculty of construction," as well as perspective and verisimilitude. The moral lesson of *Jubilee* is that increased wealth and the diffusion of education in the nineteenth century have not improved the race. G "is quite as frank as Mr. George Moore, but his tendency is toward the wholesome."

**288** "Our Monthly Parcel of Books," REVIEW OF REVIEWS, XI (Jan 1895), 81.

*In the Year of Jubilee* examines sordid and depressing areas of Camberwell. G, always interesting, appears to work from documents.

**289** P., W. *"In the Year of Jubilee,"* TO-DAY, V (12 Jan 1895), 295.

*In the Year of Jubilee* commands interest in "unmistakably real" and often "painfully vulgar" characters. G's "plot seems of small importance" as we attend his interesting people. *Jubilee* is "very easy reading," and G's art deserves our "warmest praise and admiration."

**290** "Pages in Waiting," WORLD (Lond), 1 May 1895, p. 27.

*Eve's Ransom,* "like so many of this clever writer's stories, is distinctly depressing." Yet the book provides "good reading." [Brief summary of story.]

**291** Payn, James. "Our Note Book," ILLLUSTRATED LONDON NEWS, CVI (26 Jan 1895), 98.

G's *In the Year of Jubilee* "is quite as good as anything he has written." We find the characters interesting because of the novelist's genius, not for any qualities they possess. The tone is pessimistic; G's descriptions are like Zola's "but without his uncleanness."

**292** Payne, William Morton. "Recent English Novels," DIAL, XIX (1 Nov 1895), 255.

*The Emancipated* is one of G's best books; it is "untainted by the vulgarity characteristic of so much of his work." An undercurrent of "rather bitter feeling about English Puritanism runs through the book."

**293** Payne, William Morton. "Recent Novels," DIAL, XIX (16 Aug 1895), 92.

*In the Year of Jubilee* contains dull realism that is about "as uninviting as anything that we have lately been called upon to contemplate."

**294** "Recent Literature," DAILY TELEGRAPH (Lond), 19 April 1895, p. 6.

Eve's Ransom is a "dull book by a brilliant writer." G has made us expect "ingenious plots, vivacious dialogue, and convincing delineation of character," but these virtues are absent in Ransom. [Narrative summary.]

**295** "Recent Novels," MORNING POST (Lond), 24 May 1895, p. 7.

Eve's Ransom disappoints those who expect great things from G. His "habitual rigour" is here, but far less human interest than we anticipate. Perhaps the surroundings give G only limited possibilities; at any rate this is merely a clever novel.

**296** "Recent Novels," TIMES (Lond), 9 March 1895, p. 4.

In the Year of Jubilee, like G's first volume Demos, is inspired by plebeian life; he is more cynical than earnest. Nancy Lord's circumstances, painful and complicated, "dwindle in interest towards the close." G obviously "entertains a cordial hatred for the sordidness and vulgarity of the society which he depicts." The novel is "ingenious, realistic in a mild way, and well constructed." [Tale summarized, with selected quotations.]

**297** "Reviews," PUBLISHERS' CIRCULAR, LXII (20 April 1895) 427.

Eve's Ransom is a novel for the discriminating reader. G's characters are well-realized, but the novel itself is weakly constructed. It is not one of G's better novels. [Lengthy summary of the story.]

**298** "Reviews: The Provincial Town," PALL MALL GAZETTE, 14 May 1895, p. 4.

Eve's Ransom comes at a critical time in G's career, just as he approaches "the 'serial rights' stage." "A sort of Zola of the English middle-class," G treats the vulgar and half-educated. Eve Madeley, "a miracle of deceit," fascinates the reader if only because one can scarcely be sure of her; she is the novel's one "distinct success." The other characters hardly deserve G's efforts.

**299** Sharp, William. "New Novels," ACADEMY, XLVII (2 March 1895), 189.

In the Year of Jubilee comes from "one of our most notable novelists." Despite popular taste, G has refused to write romantic tales; he is "the first of our realists." "With conscientious scruple for adequacy of realisable motive," attentive always to his "mission," G has produced a book "much more realistic than anything by that arch-romanticist, M. Emile Zola."

**300** "Some New Novels," NEW YORK DAILY TRIBUNE, 21 July 1895, p. 24.

In Eve's Ransom the hero is weighted down with the vulgarity of brass bedsteads, and Eve herself is not made plausible. She desires the comforts of life and becomes—despite G's efforts—contemptible. The novel traces the development of her soul in all its depressiveness.

**301** "The Wares of Autolycus," PALL MALL GAZETTE, 30 Jan 1895, p. 4.

*In the Year of Jubilee* preaches the gospel of comfort and luxury, for G claims that the middle class, bred of hate as well as love, struggles in depravity. G, like Arthur Morrison, mentions by name all that is ugly, using words that ought never be printed. He makes marriage, his principal theme, possible only for the rich; for the poor it is brutal and defiled. [Outlines G's presentation of marital arrangements.]

**302** Waugh, Arthur. "London Letter," CRITIC, XXIV (3 Aug 1895), 76–77.

[A literary letter reporting an Omar Khayyam dinner in honor of Meredith. As a publisher's reader, Meredith had promoted G's *The Unclassed*.]

**303** [Wells, H. G.]. "The Depressed School," SATURDAY REVIEW (Supplement) (Lond), LXXIX (27 April 1895), 531

In *Eve's Ransom,* G fails to give sufficient play to the humorous. The novel is marked by minute observation and finished workmanship—characteristic of G. But his figures refuse to take advantage of their opportunities. Given a windfall, Hilliard "lacks nervous energy" and cannot escape. His is "one of the dismallest raids upon pleasure that ever man made." We commend G for his photographic fidelity, but "is it absolute veracity"? Why do his people never laugh? No "social stratum is so dull as this melancholy world" of G's. Since happiness is "mainly a question of physical constitution," one need only take advantage of one's opportunities. True realism "looks both on the happy and on the unhappy, interweaves some flash of joy or humour into its gloomiest tragedy. Weighed by that standard, Mr. Gissing falls short." It is all remarkably well done, but the coloring isn't true. [Wells identified by Gordon N. Ray, "H. G. Wells's Contributions to the SATURDAY REVIEW," 5th ser, XVI (March 1961), 29–36.]

# 1896

**304** Addleshaw, Percy. "New Novels," ACADEMY, XLIX (29 Feb 1896), 173.

*The Paying Guest* is a subtle study of human nature that will surprise G readers because it is not as long and somber as his earlier novels. *Guest* is an excellent bit of writing and composition; G will not easily write its equal.

**305** "Among Newest Books," BOOK BUYER, XIII (March 1896), 88–89.
*The Paying Guest* is a dull book. [Summary of plot.]

**306** "Belles Lettres," OUTLOOK (NY), CXLV (April 1896), 472.
*Sleeping Fires* fails to convince us that Warboys and Louis Reed are life-like representations.

**307** "The Bookery," GODEY'S MAGAZINE, CXXXIII (Aug 1896), 208.
In *Sleeping Fires,* modern thought clashes with stilted diction. The characters are recognizable, the story weak.

**308** "Briefer Notice," OVERLAND MONTHLY, XXVII (April 1896), 468.
*The Paying Guest* is not worth reading; fortunately, the vulgar middle-class girl described by G is not an American.

**309** "Chronicle and Comment," BOOKMAN (NY), IV (Sept 1896), 18.
G's first novel, *The Unclassed,* has just been reissued in America by R. F. Fenno. The novel is too somber to be popular.

**310** Cotterell, George. "New Novels," ACADEMY, XLIX (22 Feb 1896), 154.
*Sleeping Fires* proclaims the gospel of joy; it is a remarkable contrast to previous G themes. "G gives every thought its fitting word, every motive its appropriate act, and every act its inevitable consequences."

**311** "Current Fiction," GLOBE (Lond), 22 Jan 1896, p. 3.
*The Paying Guest* and *Sleeping Fires* are further examples of G's talent. *Guest* chronicles the troubles of a young suburban couple and with relentless truth records the consequent wrecking of their home. *Fires* contains characters of a wholly different sort. Langley, a mild egoist, experiences the sleeping fires of passion when in middle life. The work is an "excellent example of Mr. Gissing's talent."

**312** "The Diary of a Bookseller," TO-DAY, IX (1 Feb 1896), 409.
*The Paying Guest* is impressive for the charm with which G makes uninteresting people fascinating. He selects characteristics to make his people memorable.

**313** *"The Emancipated,"* CRITIC, XXVIII (22 Feb 1896), 123.

The novel is self-conscious and earnest, but the author is not yet an artist; the work needs condensation and design. G is a "perpetual chorus, telling what is meant by the developments of the story." Overladen with detail, the novel relies on astute observation. The relationship between Reuben Elgar and Cecily Doran is the most successful aspect of *The Emancipated*.

**314** "Fiction," SPEAKER, XIII (4 Jan 1896), 23.
*The Unclassed* descends to depths "better left unsounded" by the average reader, though the book has no trace of "uncleanness of thought and suggestion." Ida Starr is probably an exaggerated portrait, though she proves to be a noble character. Like other G novels, *Unclassed* deals with the sad side of life where necessity is most cruel.

**315** "Fiction," SPEAKER, XIII (18 Jan 1896), 81.
*Sleeping Fires* provides evidence of greater versatility and strength than G's studies of dingy London life led us to expect. Langley's awakening from "his dream of hopeless intellectual sterility" is the most touching thing G has ever written. The novel combines "all the essential features of a true romance and a real tragedy." [Summary of story.]

**316** *"In the Year of Jubilee,"* CRITIC, XXVIII (4 Jan 1896), 5.
The book is "an annal of unrelieved sordidness"; the outcome of the novel is a concession to romantic readers. G's figures are not typical of their class. [Partial review of Nancy Lord's role. Not significant.]

**317** "Libraries of Fiction," ATHENAEUM, No. 3561 (25 Jan 1896), 116.
*Sleeping Fires* is a "brave venture in a new style" for G; it brings "more attractive characters" than we ever expected from him. *The Paying Guest* takes us to G's more familiar haunt where gentility and vulgarity blend. The story, lacking in sufficient plot, is almost jocose.

**318** "Library Table: Glimpses of New Books," CURRENT LITERATURE, XX (Aug 1896), 185.
*Sleeping Fires* is a "carefully studied story, well told." [Brief summary of narrative.]

**319** "Literature," CRITIC (NY), XXV (22 Feb 1896), 123.
*The Emancipated* allows the reader little surmise, as G gives us great detail, little suggestion; he is "observant, earnest, and astute," but not yet an artist. The slight plot needs design and condensation; his characters are sometimes held too severely to himself and appear puppets. The most successful part of the story comes in the collapse of Reuben Elgar's relationship with Cecily Doran.

**320** [Logan, Annie R.M.]. "Two Novels," NATION (NY), LXII (6 Feb 1896), 124–25.

*The Emancipated* again explores G's pessimistic temperament. While he has shifted from England to Italy for his setting, he cannot express the "charm of a southern landscape." How can we accept Cecily Doran's eloping with Reuben Elgar?

**321** Meyer, Annie Nathan. "Neglected Books," BOOKMAN (NY), III (March 1896), 48–50.

*The Odd Women* should help G gain a reputation as a serious writer, though he has been slow in achieving fame. [Slight.]

**322** Michaelis, Kate Woodbridge. "Who Is George Gissing?" BOSTON EVENING TRANSCRIPT, 21 Feb 1896, p. 11.

G is "one of the strongest and most thoughtful of presentday novelists." While we can formulate a tentative description of G from his books, his novels command our interest even if we know nothing of his private life. He appears to lack agreeable companionship, to be destitute of humor, and to be ignorant of real Christianity. *Workers in the Dawn, Demos,* and *The Unclassed*—in that order—helped start the "Gissing boom." He repeatedly exploits the tragedy of marriage; *In the Year of Jubilee* argued that joy is found only in mutual independence and tolerance. G respects honest labor and poverty, learning and refinement. Now that *The Paying Guest* has appeared, we can anticipate the publication of *Sleeping Fires.*

**323** "Minor Books," SCOTSMAN, 13 Jan 1896, p. 3.

*The Paying Guest* has been published in Cassell's Pocket Library series; it is a "brightly told" but "somewhat inconclusive" story.

**324** "Mr. Gissing's Latest Suburbia," DAILY CHRONICLE (Lond), 21 Jan 1896, p. 3.

*The Paying Guest* provides "an admirable subject for Mr. Gissing's pen, cunning in suburban life and lore." We scarcely expected him to perform so well in this cramped, short space. G preserves lower life with cameo-cut clearness, "but he must reckon with the larger humanity—which is not a matter of locality—at the same time."

**325** "New Novels," GRAPHIC, LIII (22 Feb 1896), 224.

G's *Sleeping Fires* is set in Greece, but its "characters are as English as his readers." He denies love to the young but permits it to the middle-aged.

**326** "New Publications: George Gissing's New Romance," NEW YORK TIMES, 5 April 1896, p. 31.

In *Sleeping Fires,* the idea is not complex though its treatment is. Once Agnes's scruples are over and she can forgive Langley his early mistake, G permits them some happiness. He treats the topic delicately "with much special pleading" for Langley's mistake.

**327** "New Publications: A Middle-Class Heroine," NEW YORK TIMES, 25 Jan 1896, p. 10.

*The Paying Guest,* a mere sketch, contains further studies of English middle-class life and character. Louise Derrick, finding her home circumstances unattractive, becomes the "paying guest" with a respectable family. She hopes in this way to meet "nice people." The situation enables G to expose human nature among "reasonably well-educated middle-class folk."

**328** "Notes on Books," ILLUSTRATED LONDON NEWS, CVIII (7 March 1896), 302.

*The Paying Guest* is another of G's "mordant studies." There is some irony, though it is not as grim as that of *In the Year of Jubilee.* Touches of pure comedy enable one to read this novel "with something like pleasure."

**329** "Novel Notes," BOOKMAN (Lond), IX (Jan 1896), 130.

Instead of a' sordid London setting, *Sleeping Fires* gives us Athens and a beautiful English countryside. The wronged hero insists on joining his life to another's so that he can secure the most good for both of them.

**330** "Novel Notes," BOOKMAN (NY), III (June 1896), 367.

The "spontaneous humor" that distinguishes *The Paying Guest* shows a light touch hitherto rare in G. *Sleeping Fires* should not have been published; it "lacks movement, spontaneity, force, and point."

**331** "Novels and Stories," GLASGOW HERALD, 2 Jan 1896, p. 2.

*Sleeping Fires* shows that G can be "tolerably cheerful when he likes." We are transported from London to Greece where we breathe a freer air. Moreover, the story ends happily. Not a remarkable story, *Fires* is still "pleasantly told."

**332** "Novels and Stories," GLASGOW HERALD, 16 Jan 1896, p. 7.

*The Paying Guest* suggests that G would have us read this as a humorous trifle, since it is as humorous as anything G has ever written. But the book will not add significantly to G's reputation.

**333** "Novels and Tales," OUTLOOK (NY), LIII (25 April 1896), 772.

*Sleeping Fires* is less hopeless and oppressing that G's earlier books.

**334** O., O. "The Literary Lounger," SKETCH, XIII (29 Jan 1896), 44.

*The Paying Guest* is a disappointing and tediously dull story relieved only briefly by the scenes of "love-making by the heroine and the man she marries." G's besetting sin is diffusiveness. His setting has moved from London, but he still finds "imperfectly suppressed vulgarity" everywhere.

**335** [*The Paying Guest*], DAILY NEWS (Lond), 10 Jan 1896, p. 6.

*The Paying Guest* is a cleverly executed novel written in an admirable style, a book that depicts "with convincing and unexaggerated truthfulness" the "dulness and vulgarities" of genteel suburban life. G is the "English Balzac of middle-class suburban life." [Short narrative outline.]

**336** "Recent Novels," TIMES (Lond), 22 Feb 1896, p. 10.

In *Sleeping Fires,* G gives us real scenes and not scenic paintings of Athens. His characters are long in dialogue and short in action. The plot turns upon the always moving topic of love. [Story summarized.]

**337** "Reviews," PUBLISHERS' CIRCULAR, LXIV (11 Jan 1896), 53.

*Sleeping Fires* is a charming and interesting addition to the Autonym Library of T. Fisher Unwin. [Narrative outlined.]

**338** "Reviews," PUBLISHERS' CIRCULAR, LXIV (1 Feb 1896), 130.

*The Paying Guest* is "just the book to slip into the pocket for a railway journey." It is bright, vivacious, and humorous, and not the gloomy tale we expected from G. [Story summary.]

**339** "Reviews: Ephemera," PALL MALL GAZETTE, 17 Feb 1896, p. 4.

*Sleeping Fires* is a departure for G from "photographing with painful detail the toiling failures of the middle class." This fairly cheerful romance is "a new line indeed for" G, and "he must need it."

**340** "Reviews of Books," PUBLIC OPINION, LXIX (24 Jan 1896), 112.

*The Paying Guest* is a homily warning young wives against "troublesome additions to the family circle," and the plotless story merely recounts the difficulties of the Mumford family. The novel is a "poor specimen" of G's literary workmanship.

**341** "Short Notices," BOOKSELLER, CDLIX (7 Feb 1896), 125.

*The Paying Guest* tells of a middle-class family in a London suburb; it sketches the quiet Mumford home and describes their paying guest, Miss Derek. This new edition ought to sell well, although the novel is probably not quite a work of art.

342 "Short Notices," BOOKSELLER, CDLX (6 March 1896), 296.

*Sleeping Fires* shows G's skill in character representation, particularly in Lady Revill.

343 [*Sleeping Fires*], LITERARY WORLD (Lond), LIII (17 Jan 1896), 47.

*Sleeping Fires* "strikes us as proof of Mr. Gissing's fatigue," since the novel appears forced by need and not prompted by any of the signs of the marked ability that has given G "an important position among living novelists." Even G's admirers will find the work disappointing.

344 *"Sleeping Fires,"* LITERARY WORLD (Boston), XXVII (18 April 1896), 117.

*Sleeping Fires* has four "strongly differentiated" principal characters. G's work is "original, artistic, and dramatic," managing "disagreeable themes with unusual refinement."

345 "Some New Fiction," NEW YORK TIMES, 13 March 1896, p. 27.

In *The Unclassed,* Osmond Waymark classifies his own writings among "the unsavory productions of the so-called naturalist school," and G himself would resent such a judgment. G uses his literary art to represent the saddest inhabitants of a big city. He treats the careers of unfortunate women; if such subjects must be used, the "romantic form" of portraying them is becoming more common both in England and in the United States.

346 *"The Unclassed,"* LITERARY NEWS (NY), XVII (July 1896), 205; rptd from BUFFALO COURIER [not seen].

*The Unclassed* is a "dispassionate statement on the woman question," written "with a fine skill." Its theme asserts that a man risks no more in marrying a "fallen woman" than a woman does in marrying a man "who has repeatedly yielded to temptation." G appears to be saying that "the debased and exalted have like longings, like aspirations, like souls."

347 [Wells, H.G.]. "Fiction," SATURDAY REVIEW (Lond), LXXXI (11 Jan 1896), 48–49.

*Sleeping Fires* is "a grammatical novelette" whose characters move "on the strings of principle" and not inevitably out of their own nature. The book may be "more than an artistic lapse; it may be the indication of a change of attitude." The possibility of a novel celebrating the delights of Greece "from this minute and melancholy observer of the lower middle-class fills us with anything but agreeable anticipation." [Wells identified by Gordon N. Ray, "H.G. Wells's Contributions to the SATURDAY REVIEW," LIBRARY, 5th ser, XVI (March 1961), 29–36.]

**348** [Wells, H.G.]. "Fiction," SATURDAY REVIEW (Lond), LXXXI (18 April 1896), 405–6.

In *The Paying Guest,* G is at his best, dealing with the middle class. G and George Moore are exponents of the "colourless" theory of fiction. But this shorter than usual book is entertaining, for here G has broken with a too severely limiting realism. It is a good book because of many "faint flashes of ironical comment in the phrasing." [Wells identified by Gordon N. Ray, "H.G. Wells's Contributions to the SATURDAY REVIEW," LIBRARY, 5th ser, XVI (March 1961), 29–36.]

## 1897

**349** "Books of the Day," MORNING POST (Lond), 22 April 1897, p. 2.

*The Whirlpool* reminds us that G expects fiction to entertain us, believing as he does that "drabs of various dulness" are rarely relieved, and then only by gray. His books, nevertheless, have both power and originality, though *Whirlpool* does not display his great talent. He retains his doctrine of pessimism, claiming that the "motives governing the actions of civilised humanity" are only forebodings of disaster. [Lengthy narrative summary.]

**350** "Books of the Week: Novels," MANCHESTER GUARDIAN, 13 April 1897, p. 4.

*The Whirlpool* is not for the reader who enjoys only conventional love stories; it gives a "thoughtful presentment in dramatic form" of modern social issues. This book covers a wider canvas than G used earlier. Its real unity takes shape only gradually in treating the "relentless clutch of Mammon" upon everyone. Harvey and Alma are "finished studies," blending good and evil. Their development is illustrated with subtle situations.

**351** "Books of the Week: Novels," MANCHESTER GUARDIAN, 9 Nov 1897, p. 9.

*Human Odds and Ends* is another example of G's relentless realism in studying "the more sordid aspects of life." Has G forgotten the literary canon that obliges the artist to please? His observation is true, the effect somber, and his insights sympathetic. But while these "bits of ignoble life" are cleverly drawn, we have had enough instruction in ugliness.

**352** "Current Fiction," GLOBE (Lond), 7 May 1897, p. 6.
*The Whirlpool* takes us "fathoms deep in pessimism." The men are weak, but their wives are worthless. Patiently, G brings his tale to a tragic close. [Plot outline.]

**353** Davray, Henry-D. "Lettres Anglaises" (English Letters), MERCURE DE FRANCE, XXII (June 1897), 584–85.
G's *The Whirlpool* reminds one of Zola (e.g., LA DEBACLE, L'ARGENT) by its title, its proportions, and the aims to which it testifies. But G lacks Zola's power and shows himself provokingly biased towards womankind. Yet *Whirlpool* is a considerable book which reveals an enormous effort and great literary power. [Davray did not yet know G personally. His reviews of G's later novels were much more enthusiastic.] [In French.]

**354** Dolman, Frederick. "George Gissing's Novels," NATIONAL REVIEW, XXX (Oct 1897), 258–66.
G's best known books, *Demos* and *The Nether World,* examine the conditions of contemporary society. Even the chief figures of *Nether World* are actually far removed from the very lowest stages of existence. The heroine of *Thyrza* is both real and interesting. The pessimism of *New Grub Street* is almost morbid; the career of writing is not the bleak thing G portrays. With the reprinting of *The Unclassed,* we have a convincing portrait of the relations of the sexes. No one can deny G's conscientiousness. [Not a very sensitive article.]

**355** "Fiction," LITERATURE, I (11 Dec 1897), 243.
*Human Odds and Ends* contains "extremely light sketches" of people everyone knows well. Some of these characters might have served G for a full novel. The book will "serve admirably for a railway companion."

**356** "Fiction," SCOTSMAN, 12 April 1897, p. 3.
*The Whirlpool* shows great "power and skill in the evolution of a drama" involving characters "unrestrained by religion or morality." G's "social puppets" are interesting, although their behavior is erratic. Prejudices of morality still linger in shadows, but the central figures earnestly search for happiness without the aid of "clear faith or fixed purpose." Meant to be realistic, *Whirlpool* proves pessimistic; its society is grim and revolting. [Story summary.]

**357** "Fiction," SCOTSMAN, 1 Nov 1897, p. 3.

*Human Odds and Ends* is a "collection of sketches, such as an artist might make in the course of his work," dealing with the "less taking types of character" in sordid circumstances. A London fog and gloom pervades all these tales; they are presented in "truthful and realistic fashion."

**358** [Frederic, Harold]. "Mr. Gissing's Latest Novel," SATURDAY
  REVIEW (Supplement) (Lond), LXXXIII (10 April 1897), 363.
In *The Whirlpool* G subscribes to methods alien to his own talents. He subordinates his characters and plot to the image marked by the title. G's snarl at women, the entire sex, grows "a shade wearisome, not to say vexatious." Yet G shows great promise as a novelist, since even his poorest work has "a curious indefinable suggestion of individual capacity" that appeals to our imagination. *Whirlpool* appears conceived in the spirit of Zola, treating London's middle-class society as a "gigantic maelstrom." But he is actually a realist; his talent does not permit his characters to be mere puppets. "He has too profound a sense of the individuality of his people"; they take over and "proceed about their own affairs in their own fashion."

**359** "George Gissing's Novel," LITERARY WORLD (Lond), LV
  (28 May 1897), 506–7.
*The Whirlpool* proves once more that G's aim is "to write of life as it has to be lived." He refuses to "tickle the ribs of the populace" in order to win a following. While "a kind of moderated cynicism" leads him to pick characters "in a somewhat uncompromising fashion," it is still real life that he yields, and we respect him for this. *Whirlpool* is "admirably written and admirably conceived." [Lengthy quotations; plot outline.]

**360** Hilliard, John Northern. "The Lounger," CRITIC (NY),
  XXXI (25 Sept 1897), 174; rptd from the ROCHESTER UNION
  AND ADVERTISER [not seen].
G is a "conscientious student of social conditions and a painstaking writer." He is "perhaps the ablest English novelist of his day." He lives at Epsom, a busy recluse, profiting from the increased income of magazine work. But for reasons of health, G has quit London to enjoy the fresh air and splendid downs of Epsom. G told me in a note: "I like to be left alone to do my work as best I can." [The material from this article appeared later as "The Author of *The Whirlpool*," BOOK BUYER, XVI (Feb 1898), 40–42; "Mr. Gissing At Home," ACADEMY (Supplement), LIII (5 March 1898), 258. When the ACADEMY printed this material, G himself replied (ACADEMY, LIII [19 March 1898], 334) in a letter, calling the tone offensive and the information contrary to fact.]

**361** [*Human Odds and Ends*], GLASGOW HERALD, 4 Nov 1897,
  p. 10.

*Human Odds and Ends* dwells less than G ordinarily does on the "prosaic and gray aspects of life." The collection includes tales that are well written and well imagined; "the narrative is invariably terse and to the point."

**362** James, Henry. "London, July 1, 1897," HARPER'S WEEKLY, XLI (31 July 1897), 754; rptd with very slight changes as "London Notes, July 1897," in NOTES ON NOVELISTS (Lond: Dent, 1914), pp. 346–51.

*The Whirlpool,* like *In the Year of Jubilee* and *New Grub Street,* excites "a persistent taste," although G seems to neglect "the whole business of distribution and composition." G represents "above all a case of saturation, and it is mainly his saturation that makes him interesting." He is "the authority" on the lowest middle class of contemporary England. Dickens also told us of the vulgar, but "he escaped the predicament of showing them as vulgar by showing them only as prodigiously droll." G, on the other hand, "is serious—almost imperturbably—about them, and, as it turns out, even quite manfully and admirably sad." However, while G possesses saturation, he lacks form, "the whole question of composition, of foreshadowing, of the proportion and relation of parts." He "overdoes the ostensible report of spoken words." But his dialogue segments fail to give the sense of duration, and his characters do not always "talk with the needful differences." Frankness and straightness distinguish G. In giving us the real, "he gives us, in the great welter of the savourless, an individual manly strain." [These critical judgments contain James's artistic tenets later applied to the fiction of Wells and Bennett.]

**363** "The Library Table," GLOBE (Lond), 1 Nov 1897, p. 6.
*Human Odds and Ends* contains more of G's conscientious pictures of humanity. [Slight.]

**364** "Literature: Mr. George Gissing's New Novel," ILLUSTRATED LONDON NEWS, CX (1 May 1897), 600.
*The Whirlpool* is assembled, part by part, with such care that the satire perhaps loses its effectiveness. G is "probably the most careful observer of shady society now writing the English language." His stories are earnest, powerful, and somewhat bitter. "An artist without question," G drives his satire without mercy. [Accompanied by a photograph of G, this article constitutes No. XXVI in a series entitled "Writers of the Day."]

**365** M., A. "Mr. Gissing's New Story," BOOKMAN (Lond), XII (May 1897), 38–39.
*The Whirlpool,* in a realistic manner, represents weak and vulgar people. G "has a conscience for the next generation, to whom he thinks we are not

playing fair." "No novelist has taken more pains to understand the condition of the average woman's life today . . . to mete out to her an austere kind of justice."

**366** "Mr. Gissing's New Novel," DAILY CHRONICLE (Lond), 10 April 1897, p. 3.

*The Whirlpool,* like all G's novels, assumes the "supreme importance of life's trivial things." G alerts us most of all to the "gadflies of life," and he bases his theories on the "rock of experience." As an artist, G's "most remarkable characteristic is his skilful use of small detail," and his giving "apparently inessential revelations" actually yields "life itself." One could not better be introduced to G than through *Whirlpool.*

**367** "New Books: Mr. Gissing's Odds and Ends," ST. JAMES'S GAZETTE, XXXV (26 Nov 1897), 5.

*Human Odds and Ends* contains some of G's best and most representative stories, tinctured by his peculiar, resigned pessimism. In these sketches ordinary men in drab circumstances labor amid the sordid. "Nearly all the stories are worth reading, and some of them pre-eminently so, to anybody not afflicted with nervous depression."

**368** "New Novels," ATHENAEUM, No. 3626 (24 April 1897), 536.

In *The Whirlpool,* G's characters, faithfully represented, act according to their tense natures. The reader can always "perceive how closely and faithfully" G reproduces the phenomena of life and "how conscientiously he strives to place upon his canvas the figures and expressions which attract him."

**369** "New Novels," DAILY TELEGRAPH (Lond), 29 April 1897, p. 9.

*The Whirlpool* is a clever book that photographs men and women with the accuracy of a camera's lens. But although G has Zola's capacity for keen observation, he "lacks the French sense of 'mise-en-scène,' the French gift of investing the commonplace with charm and magnetism." When we reach the end of this exactly reproduced history, "the movement is that of a coroner's inquest and the police news." G gives us arid realism, obviously refusing to provide "simple, unaffected, innocent pleasure."

**370** "New Novels," GRAPHIC, LVI (11 Dec 1897), 776

*Human Odds and Ends* seems to consist of "very rough notes for possible stories" that are published only because of G's "high reputation" and not for their merit.

**371** "Notices of Books," BOOKSELLER, CDLXXIV (7 May 1897), 446.

*The Whirlpool* is a great novel, even if G confines himself to somber views of life. A study of character, rather than of plot, it shows how incompatible Harvey Rolfe and his wife are. We wish he had given more attention to such a pleasant figure as Morton.

**372** "A Novel by an English Realist," NATIONAL OBSERVER AND BRITISH REVIEW, XVIII (24 April 1897), 140–41.

*The Whirlpool* is realistic in the best sense; G provides what he has seen and nothing that he has not seen. There is no effort to invest his characters with any of "the atmosphere of romance, tradition, and refinement" that one erroneously attaches to society. Realism is achieved without one word of vulgarity. He captures the competitive spirit of the middle-class English, with the result that the story interests us not so much for plot as for the delineation of character. Alma Rolfe is both conceived and drawn with "extraordinary skill" so that "nothing in George Eliot could be finer" than the one scene, both sinister and comic, where Alma overlooks her unfaithfulness to her husband even while asking one last favor of him. G spots the dreary and incongruous, but not the absurd.

**373** "Novel Notes," BOOKMAN (Lond), XIII (Dec 1897), 106.

*Human Odds and Ends,* a representative collection of G's short stories, shows neither waste nor preamble as he tells the fate of those in the shadows of poverty. He continues to examine the sordid, but more and more he "cannot bear the thought of help being withheld in so much curable human misfortune."

**374** "Novels," GUARDIAN (Lond), LII (4 Aug 1897), 1217.

*The Whirlpool* is another novel from that school "which appears content to look on human life from no higher point of view than as a series of 'dark and mournful enigmas.' " Alma Frothingham is a singularly interesting heroine: lazy, unprincipled, selfish, unloving, and willful.

**375** "Novels," MANCHESTER GUARDIAN, 9 Nov 1897, p. 9.

*Human Odds and Ends* shows G to be "relentless in his realism." While G's observation is extraordinarily minute and true," has he forgotten entirely the old canon that "the function of art is to please"? His bits of ignoble life are cleverly drawn, but they are also ugly and unpleasant.

**376** "Novels and Stories," GLASGOW HERALD, 15 April 1897, p. 9.

*The Whirlpool* "is a very powerful study of certain aspects of London society," concentrating on two households threatened by the vortex of the social whirlpool. G admirably contrasts the flightly Alma and the enigmatic Sybil.

**377** O., O. "The Literary Lounger," SKETCH, XVIII (5 May 1897), 66.

*The Whirlpool* is even more "depressed and hopeless" than *New Grub Street*. G's style is to give us the details, "crowded patches of vision." His outlook, while unfair and unsympathetic, also has "too much truth." His picture of an average person identifies our own wrongs; we are frivolous and restless and lack lofty ideals.

**378** O., O. "The Literary Lounger," SKETCH, XX (24 Nov 1897), 206.

*Human Odds and Ends* carries a bleak moral, although it is not as black as G has been. Some tales are "so obviously bent on showing the brighter chances of life that they are distinctly unfashionable." G is now almost in the class of Hardy and Kipling for "condensed farce and fitting effectiveness."

**379** "Pages in Waiting," WORLD (Lond), 5 May 1897, p. 38.

*The Whirlpool* is a disappointing book. While there are "passages of keen analysis and occasionally striking realism," the lives of G's characters are dreary and do not "excite curiosity or justify interest." *Whirlpool* is a "special pleader of everything for the worst in the worst of all possible worlds."

**380** "Pages in Waiting," WORLD (Lond), 1 Dec 1897, p. 34.

*Human Odds and Ends* is a collection of gloom, bitterness, and sordidness. Its "to-be-assumed realism is repulsive, not impressive." [Brief.]

**381** Paul, Herbert. "The Apotheosis of the Novel Under Queen Victoria," NINETEENTH CENTURY, XLI (May 1897), 790–91.

G's novels, though cynical and gloomy, possess original power and unvarnished truth. But to become a very great writer, he needs a little more romance, poetry, and humor.

**382** "Recent Fiction: Mr. Gissing's Powerful Study of London Life," NEW YORK TRIBUNE ILLUSTRATED SUPPLEMENT, 27 June 1897, p. 13; rptd as *"The Whirlpool,"* LITERARY NEWS (NY), XVIII (Nov 1897), 327.

*The Whirlpool* draws from unpromising materials "a certain human and spiritual significance which is in its way beautiful and romantic." Though vivid in detailing the drab and sordid, the novel still achieves "subtleties of feeling and power" that a lesser novelist could never have suggested. G's portrayal of Mrs. Rolfe is consistently absorbing, though she is herself weak, malicious, and vulgar. G gains realism in *Whirlpool;* he "has not written a better book."

**383** "Recent Novels," SPECTATOR, LXXVIII (24 April 1897), 596.

*The Whirlpool* is marked by its terse style. G is too uncompromising a delineator of man to be popular. "Sobriety of method is essentially a strong point with Mr. Gissing." His "characters are human but undistinguished."

**384** "Recent Short Stories," SPECTATOR, LXXIX (11 Dec 1897), 863.

*Human Odds and Ends* contains stories that consistently invert the convention of a happy ending. G is a "dry-eyed pessimist who sees life steadily but sees it foul." As works of art, these pieces are inferior to G's novels.

**385** "Reviews," ACADEMY (Supplement), LII (18 Dec 1897), 125–26.

*Human Odds and Ends* contains the "raw material of fiction, sketches and studies, mere scraps and suggestions." While sordidness is removed from scenes by the "impersonal reticence" of narration, G is "as remorseless, as deliberate, as logical a pessimist as ever."

**386** "Reviews," PUBLISHERS' CIRCULAR, LXVI (22 May 1897), 619.

*The Whirlpool* will enhance G's reputation as a conspicuous member of the new generation of novelists. Though he works with somber materials, the effect is natural and convincing. Had he humor, G "would come near being a great novelist." [Plot condensed.]

**387** "Reviews: Mr. Gissing's New Novel," PALL MALL GAZETTE, 27 April 1897, p. 4.

*The Whirlpool* is a sincere and pessimistic novel saying that "everything is certain to turn out badly." But life isn't really like this, for there are some good moments afforded us. "When the sun shines, Mr. Gissing shuts his eyes." Life is so arranged, says G, that "you may as well be thoroughly wicked," for "it is better to be wicked than silly, and much less perilous." The characters are made "distinct and definite." Fortunately, G's drawings of the middle class are distinguished by their avoidance of cheap satire and sentiment.

**388** "Some Younger Reputations," ACADEMY, LII (4 Dec 1897), 489.

G is an excellent craftsman, but not popular. He writes "solid, honest, patient novels" that are full of ideas. His portrait of slum life, in *The*

*Nether World,* "anticipated alike Mr. Morrison and Mr. Maugham."

**389** "Two Contrasting Volumes," DAILY NEWS (Lond), 26 Nov 1897, p. 9.
*Human Odds and Ends* closely and intensely observes the middle class, its trials and aims. The result is at once "depressing to the emotions and intellectually stimulating." The stories often read like "notes and jottings to be further amplified."

**390** Wells, H. G. "The Novels of Mr. George Gissing," CONTEMPORARY REVIEW, LXXII (Aug 1897), 192–201.
*The Whirlpool* "has for its structural theme the fatal excitement and extravagance of the social life of London." As in other G novels, one favored character, an "exponent personage," plays the most sympathetic part. "If he errs he errs with elaborate conscientiousness." Struck with unconventional ideals, such characters are "created to serve the author rather than his readers." Whatever their names, they are variations on Waymark of *The Unclassed,* marked by "an attitude of mind essentially idealistic, hedonistic, and polite, a mind coming from culture to the study of life, trying life," itself sad, terrible, brutal, and tenderly beautiful. Ultimately, such idealists discover "the insufficiency of the cultivated life and its necessary insincerities," and are obliged to return to struggle. As for the idealized "noble" women, they disappear entirely from G's more recent novels, leaving the exponent personages a tarnishing nobility. Unlike the novels of persons written by Hardy and Meredith, *Whirlpool* is typical of the G novels that are "deliberate attempts to present in typical groupings distinct phrases of our social order."

**391** *"The Whirlpool,"* ACADEMY, LI (15 May 1897), 516–17.
The plot is not arresting, but characterization is brilliant. G "dwells on the demoralising influence of the supposed need for costly superfluities of civilisation, upon the wretched and demoralising crime that comes of it, the squalid frauds and ugly intrigue and paltry ambitions." The tragic note of the novel is struck "in the obscurer colloquies and debates of the will, . . . in the sense of life as a thing tangled, involved, perplexed."

**392** *"The Whirlpool,"* GRAPHIC, LVI (21 Aug 1897), 259.
*The Whirlpool* is powerfully interesting. Its pessimism "is only too powerfully convincing." Alma Rolfe needs the "excitement of trying to gratify her own restless vanity," and thereby becomes a victim of the whirlpool.

**393** "The Whirlpool of Society," REVIEW OF REVIEWS, XV (May 1897), 498–99.
In *The Whirlpool,* the absence of light hardly makes the picture inspiring.

The novel tells of "an unsuccessful struggle to obtain liberation from the fatal fascinations of the whirlpool." [Plot summary.]

## 1898

**394** [Archer, William]. "Mr. Gissing on Dickens," DAILY CHRONICLE, 23 Feb 1898, p. 3; rptd in William Archer, STUDY AND STAGE: A YEAR BOOK OF CRITICISM (Lond: Grant Richards, 1899), pp. 28–32.

*Charles Dickens: A Critical Study* attempts a very difficult task, for Dickens defies any critic who would judge his work by any set of formal criticism. G's success is commendable particularly because of the great challenge and risk in making such a study; he "shows that the keenest sense of a man's limitations is not inconsistent with the most ardent appreciation of his unique and beneficent genius." Perhaps G would have been wise to treat Dickens's novels chronologically, rather than under various headings that inevitably overlap. Would it not have been better to approach Dickens from a psychological instead of a sociological point of view? G correctly recognizes that one of Dickens's great strengths was his sense of human kindness. Furthermore, G notes that what would have been limitations in conventional novelists became instead advantages to Dickens. But G is wrong in claiming that Dickens has never been popular with women readers, for while some female characters are made foolish or even offensive, Dickens graces them with humor, so that they become irresistible.

**395** "Belles Lettres," WESTMINSTER REVIEW, CXLIX (May 1898), 591.
*Charles Dickens: A Critical Study* overrates Dickens. "The truth is that Dickens wrote no *great* work." [Brief.]

**396** Besant, Walter. "The Voice of the Flying Day," QUEEN, CIII (7 May 1898), 793.
For *Charles Dickens: A Critical Study*, "I desire to express my gratitude" to G. It gives us G's own personality, as G is himself a novelist whose reputation is most deserving. G tells us more about Dickens than we have ever known and tells us more ably than any previous critic. I "very honestly and heartily" recommend this critical study.

**397** "Book Reviews," CRITIC (NY), XXXIII (Dec 1898), 509–10.
*The Town Traveller*'s mirth is boisterousness that degenerates into horseplay. G is incapable of being cheerful in a convincing way.

**398** "Books and Authors," OUTLOOK (NY), LVIII (9 April 1898), 929.

*Charles Dickens: A Critical Study* is "eminently discriminating." G's "knowledge of the technique of fiction is large."

**399** "Books and Authors: Novels and Tales," OUTLOOK (NY), LVIII (19 Feb 1898), 488.

In *The Whirlpool,* G is "strongly influenced by a too keen sense of the fatality of environment." His power in character representation is strong; he analyzes individuals slowly and carefully. If G lacks the analytical subtlety of Henry James or the humor of W. D. Howells, he in some ways reminds us of them for his realism.

**400** "Books and Authors: Novels and Tales," OUTLOOK (NY), LX (15 Oct 1898), 446.

In *The Town Traveller,* G enters George Moore's province of low-class London life, displaying a liveliness and joviality absent in his earlier novels.

**401** "Books of the Week," MANCHESTER GUARDIAN, 1 March 1898, p. 4.

*Charles Dickens: A Critical Study* shows that W. D. Howells is wrong when he proclaims that "Dickens has had his day." G, the "distinguished writer," has contributed a "sympathetic, careful, and admirably written study" for the promising Victorian Era Series. This volume is especially valuable for its "estimate of Dickens's relationships to the times in which he wrote and lived." No one has "yet come so near to saying 'the last word' about Dickens."

**402** "Books of the Week," TIMES (Lond), 4 April 1898, p. 9.

*Charles Dickens: A Critical Study* shows G "to be almost enthusiastic in his admiration for the great humorist—an admiration which his own novels have never suggested." G notes the evidence of realism in his eminent predecessor. At times, G fails to realize how much Dickens's audience differed from our present reading public; Dickens believed that "what did not please could not be good work!" Only indiscriminate enthusiasts of Dickens will fail to approve G's criticism.

**403** "Charles Dickens," LITERARY WORLD (Lond), LVII (6 May 1898), 405–6.

*Charles Dickens: A Critical Study* is a "sensible and valuable book." "Dickens's work is curiously unequal in merit," so that he has both detractors and admirers. G helps us distinguish the superior from the inferior, marks the true fictional character from the type, even while he assumes that the reader is familiar with the novels of Dickens.

**404** "Charles Dickens," LITERARY WORLD (Bost), XXIX (11 June 1898), 186.

*Charles Dickens: A Critical Study* is an indispensable work marked by "a warmth of feeling, a gentleness, though complete fairness, in adverse criticism." Women will find G's "diatribe against womankind" offensive.

**405** *"Charles Dickens: A Critical Study,"* LITERARY NEWS, XIX (May 1898), 148.

G's study is a brilliant, interesting, extremely sensitive monograph. [Sample quotations from G's book. Comments from the NEW YORK SUN.]

**406** "Current Fiction," GLOBE (Lond), 7 Sept 1898, p. 6.

*The Town Traveller* has been advertised as a mirthful book, but this is true only if considered in relation to G's other novels. G's characters are "vulgarly lifelike," and the "story is quite entertaining enough for the ordinary reader." [Plot outline.]

**407** "Current Literature," SPECTATOR (Supplement), LXXX (30 April 1898), 603.

*Charles Dickens: A Critical Study* comes at a time when Dickens's writings are in decline. G's "generous eulogy" allows that without humor, Dickens would not have achieved great popularity.

**408** Davray, Henry-D. "Lettres Anglaises" (English Letters), MERCURE DE FRANCE, XXVI (June 1898), 909–10.

*Charles Dickens: A Critical Study* is an excellent critical study, based on a thorough knowledge of Dickens's life and works. G proves as good a critic as a novelist. His book is one of the best studies ever written on Dickens. [In French.]

**409** "Dickens," LITERATURE, II (19 March 1898), 311.

*Charles Dickens: A Critical Study* gives us the criticism of "a distinguished novelist" who is intimately acquainted with his subject. It is the best book on Dickens we have ever read, "brightly and vigorously written, stimulating, sympathetic in tone, keen in judgment." G forms strong judgments and supports them, even if he "proves too much" by citing evidence and illustration.

**410** "Dickens: A Valuable Study of His Works," NEW YORK TRIBUNE ILLUSTRATED SUPPLEMENT, 3 April 1898, p. 16.

*Charles Dickens: A Critical Study* fills a "great need" in our knowledge of Dickens; it complements Forster's life admirably. At a time when there is great prejudice about Dickens, this volume, written with "ingratiating good temper," achieves remarkable balance. Judged in cold blood by G's method, Dickens stands pre-eminent in his own field. G notes the "tremendous moral force" wrought by Dickens in his own time. The immortals he created have counterparts in our own world now. G convinces us that Dickens had a "definite literary plan" that obligated him to make such mistakes as melodrama and artificiality. But while Dickens concentrated on his own times, his novels have a breadth present only in great works. G recognizes that the fantastic in Dickens does not blemish the total achievement. G's style, while never graceful, is always "clear and forcible."

**411** "Dickens To-Day," Court Journal (Lond), No. 3607 (5 March 1898), 350.

*Charles Dickens: A Critical Study* proves that the Dickens theme is still not exhausted. G gives the impression "of having read the stories with you," and of all criticism of Dickens, this certainly is the best. G "treats of Dickens on a higher plane, because he takes the outlook of to-day in reviewing his subject."

**412** Droch. "Bookishness: A New Novel by George Gissing," Life (NY), XXXII (22 Dec 1898), 526.

*The Town Traveller,* an "ingenious tale," presents characters who bicker and quarrel and "move about in their little world of commonplace vulgarities." Compared to G's other writings, this book is a "cheerful story."

**413** "Fiction," Literature, III (17 Sept 1898), 255–56.

In *The Town Traveller* G gives us "no starveling genius" but a happy-go-lucky salesman. In his heroine, Polly Sparkes, G resorts to the vulgar shrew, "niggardly of soul, mercenary, unintellectual." The title character and Polly are among the best portraits in this year's fiction.

**414** "Fiction," Manchester Guardian, 27 Sept 1898, p. 7.

*The Town Traveller* gives us admirable characters, particularly Mr. Gammon himself who is "almost the true Dickens." But G's "realistic handling gives him the advantage in some respects," for Dickens would likely have carried the traveler beyond the range of credibility. The plot is not important; it is "somewhat carelessly handled."

**415** "Fiction," New York Tribune Illustrated Supplement, 20 March 1898, pp. 17–18.

*New Grub Street,* now published for the first time in the United States, should prosper, thanks to the success of *The Whirlpool.* Though on the tragic side, *Grub Street* "pierces to the core of human things." G is a writer of "indubitable power," and his "sincerity is unquestionable." This is a brilliant novel clearly presenting the pettiness, pretense, and vulgarity of his characters.

**416** "Fiction," NEW YORK TRIBUNE ILLUSTRATED SUPPLEMENT, 2 Oct 1898, p. 15.

*The Town Traveller* is an "unmixed pleasure" and would probably make a "rattling comedy of the slightly farcical sort." G tells a "plain, straightforward tale," and the novel ends happily—"which must have caused the author a pang." *Traveller* reveals G in a new light, treating "with the liveliest relish" all that is "quaint and amiable" in Cockney life. Did Dickens teach G that even slum dwellers laugh?

**417** "Fiction," SATURDAY REVIEW, LXXXVI (17 Sept 1898), 387.

In *The Town Traveller,* G finds a more cheerful note among his lower middle-class figures than he has previously, with the result that G "shows a suppleness and freedom." We recognize his characters, particularly Mr. Gammon and Polly Sparkes; "the plot though light is ingenious." The tone of the whole work is "curiously and pleasantly genial."

**418** "Fiction," SCOTSMAN, 1 Sept 1898, p. 7.

*The Town Traveller* is an "amusing story about a number of odd characters in London." The hero, Mr. Gammon, a commercial traveler, appears "a little unsettled and unstable, though free from vice"; he is searching for a missing uncle, and that search constitutes G's story. Light and clever, *Traveller* is "full of humorous and whimsical situations."

**419** Garland, Hamlin. "George Gissing's Whirlpool," BOOK BUYER, XVI (Feb 1898), 38–40.

In *The Whirlpool* there is a "reality which many English novels utterly lack." *Whirlpool* is not always fresh in expression; its tone is unattractive in color. [Garland had read nothing of G's earlier writings.]

**420** "George Gissing Grown Gay," DAILY CHRONICLE (Lond), 13 Sept 1898, p. 3.

*The Town Traveller* at first strikes us as an anachronism. Having a great reputation for catching the dark, G here gives a "scarlet venture." We prefer the "sober style." In this book G shrugs his shoulders and jests about "squalid ineptitudes and bad tempers." *Traveller* has only the meager equivalent of tragedy, pathos, and passion.

**421** "A Good, Gray Novelist," CRITIC (NY), XXIX (5 March 1898), 159.

*The Whirlpool* proves that G's attitude, not his subject matter, leads him to find everything blurred and black. His characters are "intelligent, cultured, well-to-do" and have no reason to be unhappy. Perhaps the fault lies with Sibyl or Alma in not allowing the men to escape London; more likely it is G himself who commits them to "stumble heavily along a miry road" never hearing "the master-words of life." But G is not the "pestilential type of novelist." He is earnest, sincere, patient, accurate—but since his characters have no spirit, they are not alive.

**422** Hale, Edward E. "A Latter-Day Novelist on Dickens," DIAL (Chicago), XXV (1 Nov 1898), 297–99.
*Charles Dickens: A Critical Study* proves that the "sad-faced and sad-minded" G appreciated Dickens's humor. G is interested in Dickens's social issues and plot constructions. Both Dickens and G provide readers with photographic realism.

**423** Henley, W. E. "Charles Dickens," OUTLOOK (Lond), 5 March 1898, pp. 134–35.
G's *Charles Dickens: A Critical Study* makes us think of how the century has treated Dickens's reputation. While I think of him as one of the "three or four who at their best" might vie with Shakespeare, certain other readers have tired of Dickens. Now G, "an ardent seeker after Truth," has written a book on Dickens which brings our "warmest commendations." I think G is wrong in some of his judgments, in his belief that the American scenes in MARTIN CHUZZLEWIT are exaggerated, for example. Nevertheless, "I have read nothing about Dickens which has pleased half so well as this bookling." G has most of the qualities of a critic: "sanity, clarity of thought and style, a point of view, the capacity for appreciation, and the excellent sense" that a critic need not bring his subject down to his own level.

**424** [*Human Odds and Ends*], LITERARY WORLD (Lond), LVII (7 Jan 1898), 8.
*Human Odds and Ends* contains several stories whose moods are "at variance with the usual tone" of G's books. The writing lacks the "fulness and importance" that we expect from G. Knowing the quality of his novels, readers have been willing to accept his "disclosures of mischance, sordidness, and wretchedness," even though we usually prefer a sunny tale to a shadowy one. "An Inspiration" is probably the best story in this collection.

**425** Hutton, Laurence. "Literary Notes," HARPER'S MONTHLY (Supplement), XCVII (June 1898), 3–4.
As a realist, G may be pardoned for not accepting as real some of Dickens's characters. G's *Charles Dickens: A Critical Study* is a thorough, unprejudiced, and exhaustive study.

**426** Lang, Andrew. "At the Sign of the Ship," LONGMAN'S

MAGAZINE, XXXII (Sept 1898), 467–71.
While Dickens and G differ in approach, in *Charles Dickens: A Critical Study,* G is more than fair when one would expect him to be severe with Dickens; G should write similar books on Thackeray, Fielding, Scott.

**427** "The Library Table," GLOBE (Lond), 14 March 1898, p. 3.
*Charles Dickens: A Critical Study* demonstrates that G "knows the middle and lower-middle classes of to-day" as well as Dickens knew those of his time. G supplies a picture of Dickens "marked by firmness in drawing and moderation in colour." Both a defender and apologist for his predecessor, G was a wise choice by the publishers in arranging for this "Victorian Era Series" volume.

**428** "Library Table: Glimpses of New Books," CURRENT LITERATURE, XXIV (Sept 1898), 217.
G's *Charles Dickens: A Critical Study* "cannot be too highly commended." Though G apparently never knew Dickens personally, it is clear that he has an intimate acquaintance with his writings. In America, G is known as a novelist who treats the seamy side of life. Yet he proves here that he appreciates even the lighter figures from Dickens and has wisely placed Dickens in the history of English fiction.

**429** "Literary Bulletin," COSMOPOLIS, IX (March 1898), 705.
*Charles Dickens: A Critical Study* shows that G realizes that criticism is not indiscriminate praise. He properly compares Dickens not with Thackeray but with Balzac, Hugo, Dostoevski, and Daudet. His study is well-planned and clear.

**430** "Literary Bulletin," COSMOPOLIS, XII (Oct 1898), 84.
*The Town Traveller* is a "welcome and interesting respite from the weary sadness" pervading G's writings. The subjects are still London's lower middle class, but the tone is cheerful, almost boisterous.

**431** "Literary Notes," MORNING POST (Lond), 3 March 1898, p. 2.
*Charles Dickens: A Critical Study* deserves to be read by those who need guidance in reading Dickens, and by those who admire and know his novels. G endeavors to vindicate Dickens from the charge that his characters are fantastic, but he is "by no means a partial eulogist." G, like Dickens, draws upon the strong and gloomy aspects of life.

**432** "Literature," CRITIC (NY), XXXII (7 May 1898), 313.
*Charles Dickens: A Critical Study* fails to achieve the "breadth of view, serenity and detachment" necessary for true criticism. While G and Dick-

ens treated similar subjects in fiction, G could not appreciate Dickens's humor or optimism.

**433** "Literature," ILLUSTRATED LONDON NEWS, CXIII (8 Oct 1898), 514.

*The Town Traveller* is another of G's "hard and true" pictures of London. The title figure is vulgar, genial, and honest; Polly Sparkes is absolutely realized.

**434** [Logan, Annie R.M.]. "Recent Novels," NATION (NY), LXVI (26 May 1898), 408.

In *The Whirlpool,* G cares less for effect than for character representation; he is unrealistic in his understanding of women. G falls into the most common error of pessimists: he fails to see relationships of individual characters.

**435** Matthews, Brander. "New Trials for Old Favorites," FORUM (NY), XXV (Aug 1898), 758–59.

*Charles Dickens: A Critical Study* is significant for the strange frankness with which G concedes Dickens's failures and for the ingenuity with which G shows that Dickens's "power is indisputable and his genius transcendent." This study "reveals genuine insight into the principles of the novelist's art"—it is modest and moderate; it is convincing. G even ventures "to compare Dickens with Balzac," Hugo, Dostoevski, and Daudet. This volume obliges us to revise our estimate of Dickens, so "cogent is this plea of confession and avoidance."

**436** "Miscellaneous Books," GLASGOW HERALD, 26 Feb 1898, p. 9.

*Charles Dickens: A Critical Study* discusses Dickens's defects—his abuse of coincidences, the faulty construction of some plots—as well as his excellences. G treats several aspects of Dickens, "his art, veracity, and moral purpose, his characterisation, his satiric portraiture, his humour and pathos, and his style." The study is written with tact and skill, "with originality of thought and independence of judgment."

**437** "Mr. George Gissing In a New Light," DAILY NEWS (Lond), 9 Sept 1898, p. 6.

In *The Town Traveller* G trades his somber monotone of darkness for "the comedy of life" of the lower middle class. He retains "the same vitality of characterisation, the same power of presentation and grasp of subject" that we associate with his earlier work. G's style is admirable for its simplicity, directness, and absence of self-consciousness. Perhaps his new attitude makes his observations more true to life.

**438** "Mr. Gissing on Dickens," ACADEMY, LIII (12 March 1898), 280–81.
*Charles Dickens: A Critical Study* shows that G and Dickens have much in common, especially in subject matter. This is good criticism, despite the fact that G's style is "somewhat jerky and rough-hewn." The study is remarkable, as a whole, "for its sympathetic and tolerant attitude."

**439** "Mr. Gissing's Mirth," ST. JAMES'S GAZETTE, XXXVII (1 Sept 1898), 12.
*The Town Traveller* is "well-written, interesting, and eminently readable, but also sardonically farcical." We scarcely expected to find the robust humor of Dickens in a G novel. G's criticism of life is ironic; his stories are sound and stimulating. The plot entanglements are "ingeniously and attractively dealt with."

**440** "Mr. Gissing's New Story," BOOKMAN (Lond), XV (Oct 1898), 19; rptd as "Novel Notes," BOOKMAN (NY), VIII (Nov 1898), 256–57.
*The Town Traveller* proves that G can laugh heartily. Will he continue to do so? It deals with the vulgar people living in sordid streets, but the ugliness we associate with G has thinned.

**441** "New Books," SCOTSMAN, 21 Feb 1898, p. 3.
*Charles Dickens: A Critical Study* "may be warmly commended to admirers" of Dickens. "Tempered by a clear-visioned appreciation of the weak points" of Dickens, this study does not lapse "into mere panegyric." It is a literary study, not a biography.

**442** "A New George Gissing," OUTLOOK (Lond), II (24 Sept 1898), 242.
*The Town Traveller* presents G in a "New Humour." Entirely absent here is G's "intensity of angry and bitter emotion." Are we to call the new rollicking feeling melodrama? The result is not less faithful to life than G's earlier transcripts, but those who relished his earlier treatment will not take kindly to the new attitude. Here, however, is a new microcosm of England. [Plot outline.]

**443** "New Novels," ATHENAEUM, No. 3698 (10 Sept 1898), 346.
*The Town Traveller* is "interesting, but not exciting, mainly by reason of a clever analysis of character." Like other G novels, this is never "scamped or careless." G reveals the "selfishness of human motive."

**444** "Notices," GUARDIAN (Lond), LIII (20 July 1898), 1134.

*Charles Dickens: A Critical Study* attends too little to Dickens's humor, too much to "art, veracity, and moral purpose." The study is a "searching and sympathetic and withal generally judicious examination" of Dickens.

**445** "Novels," GUARDIAN (Lond), LIII (19 Jan 1898), 98.
*Human Odds and Ends* may be realistic according to G, but these clever stories are without atmosphere—and that is a "fault in a work of art." Nevertheless, "we like some of these stories much better than anything else" from G thus far (though "Lord Dunfield" is an "impertinently odious" story). "The Beggar's Nurse" contains grating conditions of life that can only be redeemed by "the idealising touch of an imagination fed by faith and hope."

**446** "Novels," GUARDIAN (Lond), LIII (12 Oct 1898), 1594.
*The Town Traveller* is much more cheerful than G's earlier works, though the story gets confused, and the reader gets lost in the chase. We are reminded of Dickens by the novel's briskness and veracity, its good-humored tolerance of weakness, and its rough-and-ready reward of honesty.

**447** "Novels and Stories," GLASGOW HERALD, 10 Sept 1898, p. 7.
*The Town Traveller* is as admirable a study of lower London life as we have had since Dickens. G's rendering of essentially vulgar people constitutes "the great merit and one of the main charms of the book." Mr. Gammon is one of the most "likeable figures in recent fiction," and we are grateful for G's introduction of Gammon to "the dingy, yet cheerful, world of lodging-houses, music-halls, public-house bars, and lamplit pavement."

**448** "Novels of the Period: Gissing's *Whirlpool,*" NEW YORK TIMES SATURDAY REVIEW OF BOOKS AND ARTS, 23 April 1898, p. 268.
*The Whirlpool* reminds us of George Moore's ESTHER WATERS for its dreariness but without the "inexorable style" that dignified the latter. We do not complain about G's choice of subject matter but about his "solemn perplexity" and "uncourageous pessimism." In the psychological study of Rolfe, G comes closest to "conquering his mediocrity of craftsmanship" and to "showing the serious quality of his very limited inspiration." The life that G provides is "not life as the great writers have shown it." G is superficial and ineffective; the result is sluggish and depressing.

**449** "Novels of the Week," SPECTATOR, LXXXIII (4 Nov 1898), 661–62.

*The Crown of Life* introduces a trace of optimism into a G novel, but G has lost none of his artistic sincerity. The portraits of the middle-class emancipated women are excellent.

**450** O., O. "George Gissing on Charles Dickens," SKETCH, XXI (16 March 1898), 342.

*Charles Dickens: A Critical Study* is neither as penetrating nor complete as it ought to be; G is not well-qualified to appreciate Dickens. They share a knowledge of London, but G is pessimistic, Dickens optimistic. And while G is "serious, thoughtful, and truthful," he is hampered in his judgment and opinions because his own beliefs about life and art are too fixed to allow him to understand Dickens. How can one expect G to fairly judge Dickens's humor? G's worst chapter considers Dickens's women. G's own prejudices blind him, for G believes "that the coming wife will be the intellectual equal of her husband, and that she will besides be able to do without servants." Can he expect women to be able "to turn from a page of Sophocles to the boiling of a potato or even the scrubbing of a floor"? G could never really understand Mrs. Nickleby or Dora. All in all, the study has "too much of the schoolmaster tone."

**451** O., O. "The Literary Lounger," SKETCH, XXIII (19 Oct 1898), 566.

In *The Town Traveller,* G "hob-nobs with the most ordinary, vulgar people, and finds them excellent company." Gone is G's satire, though the subject might well have served his satire. Gammon "is a masterpiece," the sort one hardly expects from G.

**452** O'Brien, Desmond. "Letters on Books," TRUTH, XLIV (22 Sept 1898), 736.

*The Town Traveller*'s characters walk directly "out of the London streets and slums." The sordid, selfish Polly Sparkes "is life itself."

**453** "Our Library Table," ATHENAEUM, No. 3676 (9 April 1898), 467.

*Charles Dickens: A Critical Study* is lucidly written. G's study abounds in insights; there is no better book on Dickens. Perhaps at times G is "too severe on an optimism which his own work does not favour."

**454** "Pages in Waiting," WORLD (Lond), 14 Sept 1898, p. 29.

*The Town Traveller* "tells of a peer who led a double life." This book by G is "more lively than is his wont." [Slight.]

**455** Payne, William Morton. "Recent Fiction," DIAL (Chicago), XXV (Aug 1898), 78.

*The Whirlpool*'s title suggests the restlessness and dull cynicism that pervades the book; it is a random chapter from the annals of everyday life. G is committed to a school of "austere fiction that does not allow a story to get anywhere in particular."

**456** Peck, Harry Thurston. *"The Whirlpool,"* BOOKMAN (NY), VII (March 1898), 64–66.
The novel is less pessimistic than G's earlier books, but it is bewildering in detail. Alma Frothingham, who deliberately chooses to become an artist, does not convince us of her passion for art. *The Whirlpool* falls below the highest level of G's achievement. [Careful attention is given to particulars of plot, character, etc.]

**457** "Recent Novels," SPECTATOR, LXXXI (3 Sept 1898), 312–13.
*The Town Traveller* brings the unexpected from G: a happy ending. It is a successful experiment G should repeat with more cheerfulness. G remains the interpreter of middle-class life

**458** "Recent Novels," TIMES (Lond), 14 Feb 1898, p. 10.
In *Human Odds and Ends,* G is perhaps less depressed than he has been in his earlier biographies of the unfortunate. When G treats a vagabond, he is a sad fellow; Stevenson would make him cheery. Many of the stories seem to reach no end, though they give us abundant detail of unfortunate lives.

**459** "Recent Novels," TIMES (Lond), 23 Nov 1898, p. 13.
*The Town Traveller* is a "pleasant variation" from the misery and pessimism of G's other novels. Gammon's "imperturbable good nature" brightens the entire book. [Summary of the narrative.]

**460** "Reviews," ACADEMY (Supplement), LIV (10 Sept 1898), 245.
*The Town Traveller,* touching on the lighter aspects of the middle class that G knows so well, provides a good study of temperament. G is expert in recreating dialogue. [Several quotations.]

**461** "Reviews," PUBLISHERS' CIRCULAR, LXVIII (5 March 1898), 282.
*Charles Dickens: A Critical Study* is "an excellent and appreciative study." G recognizes Dickens's faults and distinguishes his qualities; he convinces us of his wide knowledge of the subject.

**462** "Reviews: Dickens," SATURDAY REVIEW, LXXXV (5 March 1898), 330.

*Charles Dickens: A Critical Study* demonstrates both how thoroughly G is acquainted with Dickens's novels as well as how much keener G's literary conscience is and how much larger his literary endowment. Consequently, G is here "too honest to conceal his accurate knowledge of Dickens's narrow intellectual range, and of the technical weaknesses which deform nearly all his work." Finally, G realizes that these matters are insignificant "because Dickens was a genius." The greater part of G's criticism "is occupied with very generous, and usually discriminating, praise of those qualities in Dickens which no one has ever sought to minimise." [Lengthy samplings from G's study.]

**463** "Reviews: Missing Words and Husbands," PALL MALL GAZETTE, 2 Sept 1898, p. 4.

*The Town Traveller* seems to have originated in a missing word competition. G's treatment, popular and contemporary, is decidedly his own. Though we can be sure that G draws from a real London, that world is still removed from the average reader. The story is witty and bright and seems to serve no "purpose." *Traveller* ought to aid G's reputation.

**464** "Reviews: A Novelist on a Novelist," PALL MALL GAZETTE, 7 March 1898, p. 10.

*Charles Dickens: A Critical Study* is a "complete and careful study," one of the best any novelist has ever written on another novelist. Furthermore, G presents Dickens when the subject has been "fiercely and contemptuously depreciated." G studies Dickens in due perspective, praising and criticizing judiciously. The fact that G treats characters of a class similar to those chosen by Dickens—though with a different realism—adds a significant dimension to our reading this book.

**465** "Reviews of Books: Gissing's *Town Traveller*," NEW YORK TIMES SATURDAY REVIEW OF BOOKS AND ARTS, 15 Oct 1898, p. 686.

*The Town Traveller* tells us of Mr. Gammon and others like him occupying a cheap boarding house. The book lacks refinement; the language is inelegant, and the people are coarse.

**466** "Short Notices," BOOKSELLER, CDLXXXIV (4 March 1898), 251.

*Charles Dickens: A Critical Study* emphasizes the truthfulness with which Dickens chronicled national life and sentiment. The volume deserves "unstinted admiration."

**467** "Short Stories," BOOKSELLER, CDXCI (12 Oct 1898), 949.

*The Town Traveller* allows a little relief from the gloom of G's earlier work. The plot is far-fetched, but G excels in its evolution and in the delineation of characters.

**468** "Short Stories," ATHENAEUM, No. 3665 (22 Jan 1898), 116. *Human Odds and Ends* is a volume of well-told stories marred by the oppressiveness of contents. G's theme is "painfully one-sided: the meanness . . . of the half-alive existence which is all that is attained by the masses of Londoners."

**469** "Some Recent Novels," WESTMINSTER GAZETTE, 30 Aug 1898, p. 3.
*The Town Traveller* turns from the melancholy of earlier books to pure farce. The result is far out of G's beat and "does not strike us as a very happy or successful idea." G's characters, evidently drawn from "real observation and knowledge," include some "queer and interesting" people. [Plot outline.]

**470** Stevenson, E. Iraneus. "Dickens," NEW YORK TIMES SATURDAY REVIEW OF BOOKS AND ARTS, 14 May 1898, p. 326.
*Charles Dickens: A Critical Study* again calls to our attention what the great sales of Dickens's novels have proved for decades: much as subsequent generations of novelists sought to ignore Dickens, he has still been the hero and model for a vast number of appreciative readers. G's study is affectionate, perceptive, and discriminating, particularly in discussing Dickens's theatricalism, his realism and idealism, and his occasional fine writing.

**471** [*The Town Traveller*], LITERARY WORLD (Lond), LVIII (7 Oct 1898), 233; rptd as "Reviews: *The Town Traveller,*" LITERARY ERA (Phila), V (Nov 1898), 319.
With *The Town Traveller* G appears to turn a "summer-sault" from his pessimistic tone, and he is ill at ease in his new style. This book will not advance G's reputation; it is "wildly improbable, and somewhat noisy" in plot presentation.

**472** "The Trail of the Bookworm," NEW CENTURY REVIEW, April 1898, pp. 325–26.
G's *Charles Dickens: A Critical Study* appreciates the charm and warmth of Dickens's delicious optimism, although G's own novels are pessimistic in tone.

**473** White, Grennough. "A Novelist of the Hour," SEWANEE REVIEW, VI (July 1898), 360–70; rptd in COLLECTED ARTICLES ON GEORGE GISSING, ed by Pierre Coustillas (Lond: Frank Cass, 1968), pp. 142–51.

*The Whirlpool,* like other G novels, provides an accurate picture of the times. G is "too dispassionate to be called a pessimist." In G the realistic movement reaches its goal.

**474** "The World of Books," WHITEHALL REVIEW, 3 Sept 1898, p. 25.

*The Town Traveller* "is a story of lower-middle-class life in London, seen from a mirthful point of view." We witness the love of Gammon and Polly Sparkes. [Slight.]

**475** [Wright, Wilmer C.F.]. *"Charles Dickens: A Critical Study,"* NATION (NY), LXVI (19 May 1898), 388.

G's criticism is praiseworthy for judging with both head and heart. [Very slight.]

**476** Zangwill, Louis. "In the World of Arts and Letters," COSMOPOLITAN, XXVI (Dec 1898), 238.

*The Town Traveller* amazes us because it was apparently "written in a rollicking spirit," although G's characteristic bitterness remains. Gammon, G's traveler, is "astonishingly vitalized." Most of all, one is struck by G's "general want of flexibility, a fault hard to associate with unquestionable artistic gift."

## 1899

**477** Alden, William L. "London Literary Letter," NEW YORK TIMES SATURDAY REVIEW OF BOOKS AND ARTS, 23 Dec 1899, p. 898.

*The Crown of Life* is not a book I can enjoy; for while I saw promise in his first book, *The Unclassed,* and G has continued to gather respect as a novelist, still a great number of people find no pleasure in his books.

**478** B[ennett], E[noch] A[rnold]. "Mr. George Gissing: An Inquiry," ACADEMY, LVII (16 Dec 1899), 724–26; rptd in FAME AND FICTION: AN INQUIRY INTO CERTAIN POPULARITIES (Lond: Richards, 1901), pp. 197–210.

The "grey" quality of G's novels, "so repellent to the public, . . . specially recommends" them to critics, to serious artists and readers. G provides us with the beauty of shade, even as others give the beauty of light. G's weakness is that "he seems never to be able to centralise his interest." *Demos,* G's "best book," is an "unqualified success." Rather than a study of socialism, *Demos* is the story of Adela, G's "finest and loveliest creation." G is not a pessimist; rather he is "a man who can gaze without blinking." [An important appraisal of G's literary promise.]

**479** "Books and Reviews," AUTHOR, X (1 Dec 1899), 164.
*The Crown of Life,* according to the DAILY NEWS, "is rich in the interest so conspicuous in Mr. Gissing's work, which springs" from the notion that we are watching life itself. This novel may be described "as a study of the various sorts of love that make for marriage."

**480** "Books of the Week: Fiction," MANCHESTER GUARDIAN, 7 Nov 1899, p. 4.
*The Crown of Life* frequently discusses "the new Imperialism and its conflict with other traditions of our race," so that it might well be described as a *roman à clef.* The success of *Crown* depends less on the representation of Piers Otway and Irene Derwent than it does upon "its strong interest in underplots and secondary characters." Dialogue is sometimes brilliant, though perhaps "unnaturally philosophical " A capable, thoughtful book, totally absorbing, *Crown* is worthy of G's "reputation as a serious artist."

**481** [*The Crown of Life*], LITERARY WORLD (Lond), LX (17 Nov 1899), 377.
*The Crown of Life,* a "novel of uncommon merit," is "rather over-burdened by incidents." The book demonstrates G's "fertility of invention" and his strength in managing characterization. [Narrative outline.]

**482** *"The Crown of Life,"* WESTMINSTER GAZETTE, 30 Dec 1899, p. 3.
*The Crown of Life* combines careful workmanship, original observation, and genuine imagination. There is no suspicion of scamping in G's book; indeed, perhaps he is too conscientious. What remains is the need for some "impressionist art"; he is "already one of the most conscientious and careful" of our novelists. [Plot summary.]

**483** *"The Crown of Life* and Other Novels," SATURDAY REVIEW, LXXXVIII (2 Dec 1899), 712.
*The Crown of Life* will hardly please those who relished G's earlier books, those studies of melancholy about souls that have known the ironies of life. In Piers Otway and Irene Derwent, G examines the prospects for happiness in marriage, learning "that some people may love more than is necessary for [a] happy marriage." G provides a strong story, a profusion of secondary characters, distinct, clear-cut types. [Summary of story.]

**484** "Current Fiction," LITERARY WORLD (Bost), XXX (18 Feb 1899), 54.

*The Town Traveller* is not an example of G's best work. Its characters belong to a class disposed between the "depths of *The Unclassed* and the heights of *The Whirlpool.*" The plot ends by solving all the mysteries and by pairing off the happy couples.

**485** "Fiction," LITERATURE, V (24 Nov 1899), 469.

*The Crown of Life* was announced as an optimistic novel, but that is hardly true. It is the sort of story one expects from women novelists, a love story of the older school. The romance of the book is destroyed by G's analysis, by "too accurate observation, too careful description, and too acute analysis." G is not familiar with members of Parliament, and this shows. His knowledge is of the lower social stratum.

**486** "Fiction," SCOTSMAN, 9 Nov 1899, p. 3.

*The Crown of Life* is a "well varied love tale" whose merit is more "in its method of narration than in the construction of its plot." Piers Otway is "an exceedingly good study." If the novel lacks sensation, it is nevertheless a probable story of middle-class London society, of joyous home life and pretty loves.

**487** "Fiction," SPEAKER, I (11 Nov 1899), 153.

*The Crown of Life* unfortunately leaves the lower middle class, where G is so knowing, and enters the West-End; the result is weakness and confusion. The histories of his characters are rendered "by a multitude of details which seldom fail to produce the illusion of life." G's future is promising: he is serious, he observes acutely, but his style lacks distinction.

**488** Johnson, Lionel. "About Dickens," ACADEMY, LVI (22 April 1899), 461.

*Charles Dickens: A Critical Study* is "by far the finest and truest elaborate piece of criticism that has yet been written on Dickens." However, it is spoiled by infinitesimal slips of memory involving specific details in Dickens's work. [Select errors of fact concerning events and characters are itemized.]

**489** "The Library," QUEEN, CVI (9 Dec 1899), 1006.

*The Crown of Life* "transports us to no dreary and squalid suburban refuge," but has characters who "dress for dinner in the evening without protest." What a concession this is for G! Altogether less dreary than G's previous novels, this book is more true to life "and therefore more artistic."

**490** "The Lounger," CRITIC (NY), XXXIV (Jan 1899), 20.
[Literary column briefly summarizes G's career as author of realistic fiction.]

**491** "Mr. Gissing's Art," OUTLOOK (Lond), IV (9 Dec 1899), 626.
*The Crown of Life* is more of G's art, "dreary and confused and mediocre"; but for the setting he gives us a new outlying suburb instead of a London street. It is still wet November, and his style is neither penetrating nor clear. Yet G's value is the tone of "freezing self-consciousness, the unnecessary restraint, the awkward stiffness of the English temperament" that documents our lives. He catches the faint snobbery of belief in "duty," "character," and "spirituality"—all indescribably English.

**492** "New Novels," ATHENAEUM, No. 3760 (18 Nov 1899), 683.
In *The Crown of Life,* G shows how men act without showing why they act as they do; the reader lacks sympathy for the characters because of the novelist's aloofness from his creations. "This want of sympathy . . . is illustrated by the hero, and is apparent throughout the book." The most interesting character is Arnold Jacks, a person with very little warm blood.

**493** "Notes on Novels," ACADEMY, LVII (28 Oct 1899), 485.
G's *The Crown of Life* "is probably the most optimistic book" he has ever written; it excels in the representation of "love scenes, the rough as well as the smooth."

**494** "Novel Notes," BOOKMAN (Lond), XVII (Dec 1899), 89.
*The Crown of Life* reflects a calmer G, a writer capable of "conventional romance." The novel is free from social and political prejudices; the portraits of characters are painstaking.

**495** "Novels and Stories," GLASGOW HERALD, 17 Nov 1899, p. 4.
*The Crown of Life* "deserves welcome as one of the author's happiest efforts." It concerns "a very charming heroine, and a hero who contrives to be an estimable and amiable young man without becoming altogether insipid." The main characters are well chosen and well drawn, although there are some superfluous people also.

**496** "Our Library Table," ATHENAEUM, No. 3718 (28 Jan 1899), 111.
*Eve's Ransom,* now appearing in a French translation (*La Rançon d'Eve* [Paris: Calmann Lévy, 1899]), is not G's "best work, it is rather dull,

and it deals with most unconventional characters." Moreover, this translation loses the clarity and precision of the original and becomes "very funny literature."

**497** "Pages in Waiting," WORLD (Lond), 22 Nov 1899, p. 31.
*The Crown of Life* contains some of G's best writing, though it is his "least satisfactory work." The sentiment is sincere and sound; G's weakness is in narrative.

**498** "Recent Fiction," MORNING POST (Lond), 16 Nov 1899, p. 3.
*The Crown of Life* has "less uncompromising pessimism" than G's earlier books. He is "perhaps the most distinctive writer of the day" in subject and treatment. His thoroughness is "almost uncanny." But he will never be a popular author. [Brief story outline.]

**499** "Reviews," PUBLISHERS' CIRCULAR, LXXI (4 Nov 1899), 498.
*The Crown of Life* has none of G's usual squalor. The theme asserts that love is the crown of life, and G demonstrates this in several lives. Perhaps the novel attempts to render too many characters, and the reader is likely to become confused. [Narrative summary.]

**500** "Reviews: Mr. Gissing Off Colour," PALL MALL GAZETTE, 11 Nov 1899, p. 4.
In *The Crown of Life,* G renounces the amusing matter of *The Town Traveller* to return to depressing situations and characters. Piers Otway exists to "have a soul above Imperialism and British self-conceit." He temporarily attracts Irene Derwent, but she later marries an "earnest cosmopolitan." The result is an exceedingly "dull story" told chiefly to attack imperialism.

**501** Sphinx. "Literary Chat," ENGLISH ILLUSTRATED MAGAZINE, XX (Jan 1899), 460.
In *The Town Traveller,* G has evidently "emerged from the depths of melancholy." After the "dreary novels with a purpose," here is a refreshing picture of real life, "full of sly psychology and delicate lights and shades."

**502** "Three of Our Novelists," DAILY CHRONICLE (Lond), 10 Nov 1899, p. 4.
*The Crown of Life* really fails to tell a story, although it does contain 229 pages of the inessential. The book is not badly constructed, for it is not constructed at all. He gives us the details of our lives; however, this book does nothing to keep G's hold on "a front rank place among modern writers of fiction."

**503** "An Unexpectedly Cheerful Book by Mr. Gissing," NEW
YORK TRIBUNE ILLUSTRATED SUPPLEMENT, 5 Nov 1899, p. 13.
*The Crown of Life* will increase G's reputation; it possesses mature thoughts
"temperately set forth." He skillfully and powerfully states his theme, the
story of a friendship carefully detailed and gradually developed. Restraint
and sobriety are the key to his narration.

# 1900

**504** "The Book Buyer's Guide," CRITIC (NY), XXXVI (Jan
1900), 91.
*The Crown of Life* arrived from Paris in manuscript form "water-soaked
on the rocks"; its publication was consequently delayed by Stokes.

**505** "Books of the Week," OUTLOOK (NY), LXVIII (22 June
1900), 460.
*Our Friend the Charlatan* contains characters ably worked out; their natures unfold with "measure, force, and ease."

**506** Davray, Henry-D. "Lettres Anglaises" (English Letters),
MERCURE DE FRANCE, XXXIII (Feb 1900), 551.
In *The Crown of Life,* G passes from the lower to the upper middle
classes. *Crown* shows the same qualities as his former novels—accuracy of
observation and description, psychological insight, and subtlety. The rather
cool reception at the hands of British critics is due to the author's stand
against imperialism. The book shows no set-back of G's power. [In
French.]

**507** Findlater, Jane. "The Slum Movement in Fiction," NATION-
AL REVIEW, XXXV (May 1900), 447–54; rptd in STONES FROM
A GLASS HOUSE (Lond: James Nisbet, 1904), pp. 65–88.
G treats the slums in the tradition of Dickens with a significant difference:
G has no gospel of hope. The pedigree of the slum novel extends from
OLIVER TWIST through Kingsley's ALTON LOCKE to G's *The Nether
World,* and then on to Kipling's "Badalia Herodsfoot," Morrison's TALES
FROM MEAN STREETS, Maugham's LIZA OF LAMBETH, Pett Ridge's MORD
EM'LY and finally Rook's THE HOOLIGAN NIGHTS. *Nether World* maintains
a level of "almost insane depression." A "tragedy of want," it is "not
written with brutality, and that is why it is so terrible and undeniable."

**508** "The Literary Week," ACADEMY, LVIII (12 May 1900),
400.
G's novels have never been sufficiently praised. Now the American BOOK-

MAN and Miss Jane Findlater in the NATIONAL REVIEW, XXXV (May 1900), 447–54, have written enthusiastically about *New Grub Street* and *The Nether World*. Findlater ought to have included Moore's ESTHER WATERS in her list of slum novels.

**509** "The Literary Week," ACADEMY, LIX (8 Dec 1900), 541. G's introduction to Dickens's BLEAK HOUSE, in the Rochester Edition, is "a sound piece of criticism." G is right in saying that Dickens too often resorted to arbitrary coincidence. Ingenuity and complexity are present, but they are not good in art.

**510** "Novels," GUARDIAN (Lond), LV (17 Jan 1900), 103. *The Crown of Life* analyzes a young woman who contemplates one marriage, reconsiders, and then chooses instead "the man she loves with her whole heart and soul." The views on marriage advanced by G are not ours. There is nothing ugly in the novel; it lacks "fulness of tone, vitality, and the dramatic accent."

**511** "Reviews: Bio-Sociological," PALL MALL GAZETTE, 6 June 1900, p. 4. *Our Friend the Charlatan* gives us "a nearly perfect example 'of finished portraiture," displaying G "at his best." Dyce Lashmar parades as his own the theories he has stolen from another; he is ambitious, superficially clever, lazy, and conceited. G is "thoroughly original and even amazingly skilful" in deftly combining these traits to examine Lashmar's moral disease.

---

# 1901

---

**512** Bertz, Eduard. "Gissing," GOLDENES BUCH DER WELTLIT-TERATUR (Golden Book of World Literature), ed by Wilhelm Spemann (Berlin: Spemann, 1901), p. 362. The social novel in England is carried forward after 1880 by G, whose works stressed, with realistic if pessimistic attitudes, the laboring class. His principal books thus far include *Demos, The Nether World, New Grub Street,* and *The Odd Women.* [In German.]

**513** "Books and Authors," MORNING POST (Lond), 7 June 1901, p. 2. *Our Friend the Charlatan* is a character study of a clever young man who is "only permanently successful with himself." But his deception is not shared by others, and his doom is inevitable. We regret to hear that G is unwell, and we hope he soon recovers.

**514** "Books of Travel," ATHENAEUM, No. 3848 (27 July 1901), 121.

With *By the Ionian Sea,* G joins the guides to Calabria. As such he is a worthy follower of Edward Lear, "though less robustly jolly"; still he is a "genial traveller." The illustrations are ugly.

**515** *"By the Ionian Sea,"* WESTMINSTER GAZETTE, 27 June 1901, p. 3.

*By the Ionian Sea* takes us to the hot, dusty road from Naples to Sicily, a dead and haunted region. G captures with charm and color the sadness of that landscape. This is not a guide book but an inspired vision of antiquity.

**516** Courtney, W. L. "Books of the Day: *Our Friend the Charlatan,"* DAILY TELEGRAPH (Lond), 31 May 1901, p. 11.

*Our Friend the Charlatan* is composed about a set of contrasting characters, as G provides a counter-hero for every hero, an opposing idea for every theme. This is a work of the mind, scarcely of the heart. G is more psychologist than storyteller. In the "management and construction" of the story, G is deficient. His strength lies in "acute analysis, quick perceptiveness, clever psychological insight." Dyce Lashmar, the charlatan, is a "characteristic modern type, born of a civilisation very materialistic," where charlatanism is "not precisely of a vulgar sort." G is "head and shoulders above the majority of his novelistic contemporaries." [Elaborate summary of narrative concentrating on Lashmar and Constance Bride.]

**517** Davray, Henry-D. "Lettres Anglaises" (English Letters), MERCURE DE FRANCE, XXXVIII (May 1901), 557–59.

*New Grub Street* and *Born in Exile* show how G excels in rendering impartially the pitiful and overwhelming struggle of his middle-class characters. At times, however, the action drags with pointless dialogue. G differentiates the various characters with impressive ability. In France, novelists too often present human depravity under the pretext of realism or naturalism. With considerable veracity G presents such diverse characters as the cynical Jasper Milvain and the tormented Edwin Reardon. The highly sensitive and sympathetically portrayed Godwin Peak dominates *Exile;* the horrors of his life are gradually unfolded. [In French.]

**518** "Fiction in the Light of Travel," ACADEMY, LX (22 June 1901), 535–36.

*By the Ionian Sea* is an excellent account of travel in southern Italy. G loves Italy, but he never idealizes; his sensibility is mature; he instinctively selects the telling detail. "G has the rare faculty of loving without illusions." *Ionian Sea* convinces us that while his novels concentrated on sordid and insular aspects of London, his "aesthetic and moral pre-occupations are of the widest." Combined with *Our Friend the Charlatan,* this new work "indicates a kind of second spring" in G's talents.

**519** "Fiction: The Portrait of a Man 'Excelling in Speciousness,' " NEW YORK TRIBUNE ILLUSTRATED SUPPLEMENT, 14 July 1901, pp. 11–12.

*Our Friend the Charlatan* has an exceptionally well-chosen title; it fits the hero perfectly. Dyce Lashmar is examined "with a kind of robust impartiality" and with great accuracy. An acute student of human nature, G reviews Lashmar's character, providing us pictures of his parents and his gradual relaxation to indifference and laziness. The novel presents life "truthfully and vividly."

**520** "Great Greece," DAILY CHRONICLE (Lond), 13 June 1901, p. 3.

*By the Ionian Sea* collects G's essays from the FORTNIGHTLY REVIEW into a volume that echoes his love for Horace and Vergil, Troy and Rome. He describes his travels in Calabria, recording his experiences, occasionally amusing, sometimes wretched, always with shrewd observation. Eventually we know this land as the "promised land of our youth," here described in "limpid prose inspired by a true love of classical scenery and literature."

**521** Gwynn, Stephen. "Some Recent Books," FORTNIGHTLY REVIEW, LXXVI (July 1901), 166–67.

*Our Friend the Charlatan* has sardonic humor but becomes a depressing study of unattractive characters. A cold passion of hate dominates G's figures: Lady Ogram is tempestuous, tenacious of her authority and vigor. Lashmar, the charlatan, is "coldness personified." G can never be popular: the public demands "heart rather than intelligence."

**522** Harland, Henry. [*Our Friend the Charlatan*], DAILY CHRONICLE, 10 June 1901, p. 3.

*Our Friend the Charlatan*'s hero, Dyce Lashmar, is really "the average man of a certain class," a vain and ambitious man who greatly wants admiration. "Moreover, he is vaguely, feebly unscrupulous," although G allows him to prosper, even to become a member of Parliament. Every detail is authentic, every movement motivated, every feeling well-wrought. G has extraordinary ability, such that no reader will want to part with his copy of this book.

**523** Irwin, Grace Luce. "The Biography of a Pretender," OVERLAND MONTHLY, XXXVIII (Oct 1901), 314–15.

*Our Friend the Charlatan* presents a new fictional type: a hero "who has brains and sensibility, but who lacks principle." Characters are conceived with psychological thoroughness. It is an entertaining novel but not a sensational adventure story. [Long narrative summary.]

**524** Lee, Elizabeth. "Englischer Brief" (Letter from England), DAS LITTERARISCHE ECHO, III (July 1901), 1430.
G's *Our Friend the Charlatan* is well worth reading. Its hero, a modern type, considers women as his fellow-workers and friends. [In German.]

**525** "The Library," QUEEN, CX (24 Aug 1901), 306–7.
*Our Friend the Charlatan* is a satire that must be taken seriously. The book is far above the ordinary run of romances. [Summary of narrative.]

**526** "Literature," ILLUSTRATED LONDON NEWS, 29 June 1901, p. 942.
*Our Friend the Charlatan* presents another side of G's outlook on modern London: he satirizes society as all but barbaric. The rot he offers makes us uncomfortable. Dyce Lashmar, G's version of "pushing manhood," is a politician who gains position by presenting as original ideas stolen from a French book. Does G expect us to believe that such pretense can bring success?

**527** MacDonnell, A. "Mr. Gissing's New Novel," BOOKMAN (Lond), XX (Aug 1901), 152.
*Our Friend the Charlatan* leaves a "vague sense of lost opportunities." G's hand must have shaken in portraying Dyce Lashmar: Does an author like or dislike such a hero? G ought to have been more sure of his intentions, of planning the effect of the novel.

**528** "Mr. Gissing and Some Others," ST. JAMES'S GAZETTE, XLII (19 June 1901), 5.
In *Our Friend the Charlatan* G returns "to his relentless study of mankind through smoke-coloured spectacles." Lady Ogram is perhaps the "best thing" in the novel, an indomitable spirit who inspires respect from a sordid crew. From Lashmar we cannot hope for any lasting good.

**529** "Mr. Gissing 'Egoist,'" OUTLOOK (Lond), VII (13 July 1901), 762.
In *Our Friend the Charlatan,* the title character is an "intellectual hypocrite" who deceives himself. Lashmar reminds us of Sir Willoughby Patterne or George Meredith, and he forms an admirable portrait. The novel has "the well-knit sobriety of the true workman."

**530** "New Books," SCOTSMAN, 17 June 1901, p. 2.

*By the Ionian Sea* introduces us to that part of Calabria as yet "undesecrated by the tourist." G inspects the beauty of this poor and desolate region during the winter, ignoring the texts of history, and providing "delightful reading" about these celebrated areas.

**531** "New Books: Fiction," SCOTSMAN, 6 June 1901, p. 2.
*Our Friend the Charlatan* is a clever story of that all too common figure who is supplied with what "vulgar people call cheek." Lashmar steals a French bio-sociological theory and promotes it as his own, advancing to Parliament on this fraud. His secret revealed by a childhood friend, the charlatan is reduced to failure. While a departure from G's "usual kind of work," *Charlatan* makes interesting and pleasurable reading.

**532** "New Novels," ATHENAEUM, No. 3843 (22 June 1901), 783–84.
*Our Friend the Charlatan* proves once more that G never creates a character he intends us to admire. At the same time, G is "unable to write a book which is not powerful." The progress and failure of Dyce Lashmar are "brilliantly displayed." All his figures "are moved by motives of material advantage." Faith has died among educated people.

**533** "New Novels," MANCHESTER GUARDIAN, 5 June 1901, p. 3.
*Our Friend the Charlatan* interests us not for its drama but for its "study of life from the intellectual standpoint." G sets forth a "protest for right and humanity." Lashmar combines genius and vulgarity, trying to achieve a career by advancing borrowed opinions as his own. In him, most honest people recognize something of their own ambitions. Lesser characters are worked out with equal care and sometimes with greater success.

**534** "Notes on Novels," ACADEMY, LX (1 June 1901), 466.
It is profitable to compare the political interests of Dyce Lashmar in G's *Our Friend the Charlatan* with those of M. Jean Izoulet's LA CITÉ MODERNE.

**535** "Novel Notes," BOOKMAN (NY), XIV (Sept 1901), 95–96.
In *Our Friend the Charlatan,* the representation of Dyce Lashmar will inevitably trouble G's readers, for while G "evidently dislikes Dyce cordially," he nevertheless "shuffles in unmasking" the charlatan. It is clear that G never intended to subject Lashmar to unsparing analysis.

**536** "Novels," GUARDIAN (Lond), LVI (12 June 1901), 806.
*Our Friend the Charlatan* is "a very clever book." G is shrewd and observant in collecting typical characters, but he distorts them so that they

become unamiable. While only the old clergyman "perceives that Christianity is the best and greatest thing," G denies him happiness.

**537** "Novels," Saturday Review, XCII (6 July 1901), 20.
*Our Friend the Charlatan* is principally interesting for its character study of sordid persons. Some relief from the misery of these characters would "make a pleasanter, though possibly not truer story." In presenting his characters G is clever and subtle, but the book has little charm.

**538** "Novels and Stories," Glasgow Herald, 6 June 1901, p. 9.
*Our Friend the Charlatan* shows us G at his best. He has assured us that he writes only about what he knows best, and if there is much sadness that is because his life has contained much grief. *Charlatan* is brighter than any earlier work by G; the title character "is a really first-rate study of egotism and self-conceit ending in failure and disappointment." G is a "realist studying life attentively, while crowds of pseudo-realists are performing literary stage tricks to please the public."

**539** "Novels of the Week," Spectator, LXXXVI (1 June 1901), 809.
*Our Friend the Charlatan* is one more example of G's uncompromising method. While the title identifies the central character, "Dyce Lashmar is not irrevocably branded": let the reader arrive at a judgment. The book holds the reader's sustained interest. All the strong characters are women.

**540** O'Brien, Desmond. "Letters on Books," Truth (Lond), L (15 Aug 1901), 446.
*Our Friend the Charlatan* is as clever and cynically sour as G's other novels. His characters are most believable.

**541** "Our Bookself," Graphic, LXIV (27 July 1901), 128–30.
*Our Friend the Charlatan* contains several portraits of successfully drawn characters in a "rather bitter comedy of modern life."

**542** *"Our Friend the Charlatan,"* Literary News, XXII (Sept 1901), 260.
G's *Our Friend the Charlatan* belongs in a permanent library, on a shelf above Zola, not far from Turgenev.

**543** *"Our Friend the Charlatan,"* Literary World (Bost), XXXII (1 Aug 1901), 115.
*Our Friend the Charlatan* is a "study of character distinctly conceived and

sharply defined." Dyce Lashmar is a "downright immoral adventurer," but he carries our sympathy. Lady Ogram is the book's "most forceful and striking figure," and the reader will find meeting her "an experience worth having."

**544** [*Our Friend the Charlatan*], LITERARY WORLD (Lond), LXIV (23 Aug 1901), 127.
*Our Friend the Charlatan* is a "wilfully pessimistic" novel in which G reverts "to blue devils, the dumps, and pessimism." One ought to read the story if only to watch G "evolutionise the character of Dyce Lashmar."

**545** "Pages in Waiting," WORLD (Lond), 3 July 1901, pp. 31–32.
*Our Friend the .Charlatan* is "not merely entertaining and clever," but it also impresses on us some vital truths about life. Its literary workmanship commends itself; the "women are well drawn."

**546** "Recent Literature," DAILY TELEGRAPH (Lond), 21 June 1901, p. 6.
*By the Ionian Sea* is G's charming account of his rambles in Calabria. Even readers not devoted to the classics will be "galvanised into responsive warmth" by G's enthusiasm and glow of poetic feelings that marks his sensuous preception of the Ionian shores. The same "incisive dissection" that distinguishes G's earlier descriptions of the slums helps him to record his intimate fascination and acquaintance with the loveliness of antiquity.

**547** "Recent Novels," TIMES (Lond), 29 June 1901, p. 5.
*Our Friend the Charlatan* continues G's earlier barrage of satire, ridiculing the "peculiar vices and absurdities of the hour." But his tone has changed; his satire "is amused and not indignant." His characters are remembered less as people than as ideas. Dyce Lashmar, for example, "represents the idea of a man of shallow ability who would sacrifice everything to material success." But we must wait, for G has still an even better novel in him to express his genius.

**548** "Reviews of Books," TIMES (Lond), 15 July 1901, p. 8.
*By the Ionian Sea* is a pleasant and surprising departure from G's London to Calabria; the book is lively and scholarly. If the places described are noble and historic, they are also squalid, and their sordid conditions are fully detailed. Perhaps the best passage in the book is G's account of his own fever at Cotrone, and the incredible vision that the illness caused him. Would other travelers experience such dreams, or are they actuated by G's readings and his imagination?

**549** "Revue des derniers livres Anglais" (Review of the Latest English Books), LA REVUE, XXXVIII (15 Aug 1901), 421–23.

*Our Friend the Charlatan* is especially remarkable for its creation of Dyce Lashmar, Lady Ogram, and Constance Bride. Constance is so absolutely charming that one trembles when the charlatan, Lashmar, exerts his clever and egotistic powers over her. With G, the psychology of character is more subtle than sharp; his characters are patiently analyzed and not just superficially observed. Too often the characters themselves are shallow in heart, strong in intelligence. [In French.]

**550** Roberts, Morley. "George Gissing," LITERATURE, 20 July 1901, pp. 52–53; rptd in part as "Morley Roberts on George Gissing," BOOKMAN (NY), XIV (Sept 1901), 13–14.

G, who belongs to no school of English fiction, resembles Turgenev, certainly not Zola. *Born in Exile* is his masterpiece. Serious readers will find his work a "form of art" which diagnoses a disordered civilization.

**551** S[horter], C. K. "A Literary Letter," SPHERE, VI (24 Aug 1901), 226.

*Our Friend the Charlatan* is not G at his best, such as we did have in *New Grub Street*. But *Charlatan* does add "one more egotist of fiction" to the select list that includes George Eliot's Melema and George Meredith's Sir Willoughby Patterne. The portrait of Dyce Lashmar has many Dickensian touches.

**552** "Southern Italy," GUARDIAN (Lond), LVI (31 July 1901), 1056.

*By the Ionian Sea* is a delightful surprise for those who know G as "a student of the dreary streets of outer London." The classical style of the "epigrammatic manner" and the literary allusion distinguish this volume. We come to know the author as an intimate friend, so much does he reveal himself. And he relishes the sonorous Latin and Greek as few others can.

**553** "Travel: *By the Ionian Sea,*" LITERATURE, VIII (29 June 1901), 557.

*By the Ionian Sea* invites comparison to Bourget's SENSATIONS D'ITALIE, with the result that we acknowledge G's surpassing charm. G's book excels in comprehensible insight, motivated by his impetuous desire to visit the settings of ancient lore. We profit from his pleasures and his great inconveniences in travel, for he provides "graphic and living pictures" caught with his subtle perception and exquisite literary gift. The book is "simply a delight."

# 1902

**554** B[ennett], E[noch] A[rnold]. "English and French Fiction in the 19th Century," ACADEMY, LXII (15 Feb 1902), 173–74.

G is among six [Conrad, Kipling, George Moore, Wells, and Eden Phillpotts] English novelists whose work will survive.

**555** de Wyzewa, T. "A propos d'une nouvelle biographe de Dickens" (Concerning a New Biography of Dickens), REVUE DES DEUS MONDES, CCCLXXXIX (15 Nov 1902), 458–68.

Forster's LIFE OF DICKENS, though cut down to half its original length by G, now seems fuller; it is more carefully written, better composed, and infinitely more pleasant to read. Forster and G present a false picture of Dickens. They show him as an unmannered, boisterous, vainglorious upstart, proud of his worldly acquaintances and his fortune. They have overlooked the salient feature of his life and works: the spontaneously— and often unwillingly—Christian character. Forster and G have seen only the exterior features of Dickens's character. [A spirited attack against the famous biography by a biased, old-fashioned critic.] [In French.]

**556** "Dickens in Memory," ACADEMY, LXII (11 Jan 1902), 665.

Both Dickens and G followed a heavy work schedule. [Slight.]

**557** "Forster's DICKENS—Abridged," LITERARY WORLD (Lond), LXVI (7 Nov 1902), 365.

Because John Forster's LIFE OF DICKENS is inordinately long for contemporary readers, G's abridged version is "distinctly a volume to attract admirers of Dickens" who are pressed for time. G has "jealously preserved the autobiographic matter" upon which Forster drew. [Some quotations fill out this review.]

**558** [Forster's LIFE OF DICKENS], DAILY CHRONICLE, 20 Oct 1902, p. 3.

John Forster's LIFE OF DICKENS has been reduced to about one-third of its original length by G, and the task cost G "incessant pangs." His judgment must be questioned in some of the reductions because proportion and sense are not easily kept. Yet even when G abbreviates, he retains the attitude and tone of the original, so close is his own sympathy with Dickens akin to Forster's. At times G provides more factual material, giving information that his predecessor had the discretion to withhold.

**559** "List of New Books and Reprints," TIMES LITERARY SUP-
PLEMENT (Lond), 17 Oct 1902, p. 310.
Forster's LIFE OF DICKENS has been revised by G. [Very slight.]

**560** "The Literary Week," ACADEMY AND LITERATURE, LXIII
(18 Oct 1902), 407.
Forster's LIFE OF DICKENS, abbreviated by G, deserves particular attention among the many new books recently received for review. It
retains most of the biographical material of the first edition, though it is
not written in the first person.

**561** M., A. "Les Livres" (The Books), NOUVELLE REVUE,
XVIII (1 Sept 1902), 142.
*La rue des meurt-de-faim* (*New Grub Street*) is a well-made novel,
true to life, pitiless in the extreme, as long as a year of misery and as
compact as brown bread. The book should be a lesson to the middle-class
youths who mean to give themselves to a literary career and to old, em-
bittered professional circles. [In French.]

**562** "New Editions," GUARDIAN (Lond), LVII (29 Oct 1902),
1552.
Forster's LIFE OF CHARLES DICKENS, as abridged by G, provides the best
possible version we could have. G "has also introduced corrections of fact,
and occasionally substitutes criticism of his own on the novels for Forster's."

**563** "The Nobodies," ACADEMY AND LITERATURE, LXII (8
March 1902), 247–48.
G's *New Grub Street* introduces us to one segment of the vast multitude of
nameless common people; but, unlike Dickens, who "went into the crowd
a great emotional interpreter of its surface oddities, pathos and variety,"
G has "gone into it as a keenly interested but merciless searcher into its
mind, habits and tastes." Harold Biffen's treatment of the "ignobly decent" best represents G's own method, taking as his subjects London's nobodies. One notch above the nobodies are the "undistinguished decent"—
another stratum of existence. G's spirit is totally lacking in the gusto of
H. G. Wells.

**564** "Notices of Books," PUBLISHERS' CIRCULAR, LXXVII (27
Dec 1902), 690.
G's abridgement of Forster's LIFE OF DICKENS adulterates the original
and becomes an "unhallowed interference with our old favourites." Instead
of grafting himself on Forster, let G do his own biography of Dickens.

**565** "The Novel of Misery," QUARTERLY REVIEW, CXCVI (Oct 1902), 391–414.

While G is very sensitive to the influences of continental literature, never has he submitted to the French realistic school. His strength is in using fiction to criticize social wrongs; he excels in the complexity and individuality of his characterization. His most noble creature to date is Emma Vine of *Demos*. *The Nether World* is "one of the most depressing and powerful novels of misery . . . [composed] in a spirit of despondency which affects one more keenly than all the outrageousness of the realistic school." [Valuable observations on contemporary French and British novels.]

**566** [O'Connor], T.P. "The Book of the Week: The Youth of Charles Dickens," T. P.'s WEEKLY, I (26 Dec 1902), 193–94.

Forster's LIFE OF DICKENS, abridged by G, enables us to examine Dickens's early life. We find there not only the originals for Dickens's many characters but also the causes of the "abiding hatred and terror" that led him to "years of slow suicide through very eagerness and overwork." [A lengthy survey of the squalid youth of Dickens, as drawn from Forster's LIFE. G is not mentioned except as co-author of the new edition.]

**567** "Our Library Table," ATHENAEUM, No. 3914 (1 Nov 1902), p. 585.

Forster's LIFE OF DICKENS, abridged and revised by G, is the skilled work of an expert, wholly commendable.

**568** "Pages in Waiting," WORLD (Lond), 22 Oct 1902, p. 665.

Forster's LIFE OF DICKENS has been carefully edited by G to preserve the autobiographical quality while removing some blemishes from the original. [Slight.]

**569** Rachilde. "Revue du Mois" (Review of the Month), MER-CURE DE FRANCE, XLIII (Sept 1902), 748.

*La rue des meurt-de-faim* (*New Grub Street*) is a restrained piece of work with a fine repressed emotion. [Very slight. The translation is wrongly attributed to Claire Ducreux; the French version is actually the work of Gabrielle Fleury. The absence of her name on the title page of the book led some English critics to state in obituary articles that G himself had translated *Grub Street* into French. He merely helped Gabrielle Fleury with some difficult points.] [In French.]

**570** "Some Books of the Week," SPECTATOR, LXXXIX (18 Oct 1902), 576.

The publication of Forster's LIFE OF DICKENS, abridged and revised by George Gissing, results from "a good idea well carried out." However, G might have added an account of Dickens's income, including a record of the sales of his literary works. [Several comments on Dickens's biography and writings.]

---

# 1903

**571** Adcock, A. St. John. *"New Grub Street*—And After," BOOK-MAN (Lond), XXIII (March 1903), 245–46.
Once we read the meditations and reveries of *The Private Papers of Henry Ryecroft* we are led to a greater regard for G. [Summary; long quotations.]

**572** "An Author at Grass," ACADEMY, LXIV (7 March 1903), 228.
*The Private Papers of Henry Ryecroft* particularly appeals to serious readers and critics. [Effusive, but not very perceptive.]

**573** "An Author at Grass," WESTMINSTER GAZETTE, 20 Feb 1903, p. 4.
*The Private Papers of Henry Ryecroft* provides a happy escape from the sordid things that G wrote of in *Demos* and *New Grub Street*. It is an idyll of well-deserved rest. [Quotations.]

**574** "Autobiography," WORLD'S WORK, I (April 1903), 582–83.
*The Private Papers of Henry Ryecroft* undoubtedly contains G's own "idea and ideals put into the mouth of an imaginary character." A curious and interesting book, *Ryecroft* is a detached brooding in tranquillity. [Several quotations.]

**575** "The Book Mart," BOOKMAN (NY), XVII (April 1903), 198.
*The Private Papers of Henry Ryecroft* provides the writings left G by a friend who died about a year ago. G has himself provided a preface that includes considerable information about Ryecroft.

**576** "A Book of To-Day: The Common Life of Man," TO-DAY, XXXVIII (4 Feb 1903), 51–52.
*The Private Papers of Henry Ryecroft* initially caught my eye because "no living British novelist" more deserves my profound affection and respect. These contemplative pieces form a human document, partly fiction, partly autobiography. The author makes the homeliest things beautiful. [Lengthy quotations.]

**577** "Books and Their Writers: An Uncommon Book," T. P.'s WEEKLY, I (27 Feb 1903), 489.

*The Private Papers of Henry Ryecroft* consists of the "disjecta membra of a writing man's life" as he sighs in relief, escaping from the literary arena. While it is not pure autobiography, it cannot be read as the supposed papers of a real Ryecroft. [Several lengthy quotations nearly fill the page.]

578 "Books Worth Reading," MORNING POST (Lond), 5 March 1903, p. 2.

*The Private Papers of Henry Ryecroft* is a soliloquy, a collection of reflections containing many well-phrased observations on life. G lacks enough originality to appeal to those who demand "flashy fiction"; there is plenty here for those seeking a restful hour or two. [Occasional quotations from *Ryecroft.*]

579 Courtney, W. L. "George Gissing," ENGLISH ILLUSTRATED MAGAZINE, XXX (Nov 1903), 188–92.

G has never gained the recognition that he deserves because the bitterness of his attitude "militates against his success." If life had been easier on G, would we not have had more books like *By the Ionian Sea* and *The Private Papers of Henry Ryecroft?* Instead, we know him for pessimism and satire. G clearly dislikes his middle-class subjects, and he turns upon them rather like a psychologist than a novelist, showing more brain than heart. Not until *Ryecroft* do we get the charm of reflection that is closer to the real G, amiable and tender-hearted. [One of a series on contemporary writers, this article is accompanied by a portrait of G by Elliott and Fry, and a bibliography.]

580 "A Daniel Among the Hollyhocks," OUTLOOK (Lond), X (31 Jan 1903), 763.

*The Private Papers of Henry Ryecroft* presents "the hack after twenty years' struggle and more, suddenly and unexpectedly transformed into a man of independent means." Ryecroft is a wan, sensitive figure, "shrinking from argument and self-assertion." This "old war-horse of the British Museum Reading Room," this "man of reveries, exhibits no bitterness." G takes us to the hollyhocks and sunflowers.

581 Davray, Henry-D. "Lettres Anglaises" (English Letters), MERCURE DE FRANCE, XLVI (June 1903), 843–44.

*The Private Papers of Henry Ryecroft* is a charming piece of autobiography full of moving sincerity. [In French.]

582 "Dickens, Forster, and Mr. Gissing," MANCHESTER GUARDIAN, 1 Jan 1903, p. 4.

Forster's LIFE OF DICKENS remains a masterpiece, and G is admirably suited to prepare this outstanding biography in a new edition. Dickens "remains deeply interesting to a vast multitude of comparatively unleisured persons." Forster had remarkable opportunities to know the relationship between Dickens and his work, and he made the most of them. [Sample quotations from Forster's biography.]

**583** "From Grub Street to Arcadia," DAILY CHRONICLE (Lond), 7 Feb 1903, p. 3.

*The Private Papers of Henry Ryecroft* extends two revelations of G's art: he is capable of depth and originality in asides that are rare in other writers, and he includes autobiography in his fiction. The book is a great treat, for G is an able writer of beautiful prose. The subjects here are immensely various, treated with much grace. From G we have learned to expect fiction of a high order, consistently marked by honesty. He is neither brutal realist, cynic, nor satirist. His novels are always "strongly and honestly built," like foursquare towers.

**584** "Gentle Melancholy," NEW YORK DAILY TRIBUNE, 4 April 1903, p. 8.

*The Private Papers of Henry Ryecroft* is one of G's most melancholy books, "containing the reflections of a man of letters." It is autobiographical and painful but also peaceful and interesting. G repeatedly draws upon his classical tastes and his fascination with travel.

**585** "George Gissing," TIMES LITERARY SUPPLEMENT (Lond), 6 Feb 1903, pp. 38–39.

*The Private Papers of Henry Ryecroft* is destined to command a small, but very ardent, following. In its way, G "has never written anything more remarkable." He has steadily documented the dreadful, dull, hopeless lives of London's very poor. G's pictures of the "brotherhood of our bewildered humanity," rendered with "impeccable honesty," provide "the most masculine expression of pathos to be found in any contemporary English novelist." Without Balzac's vitality or imagination, G "reminds us of Balzac in his methods of cumulative power" and in his "disregard of the charm of words." Even when G's personages escape the London slums, their lives in small villages are deprived of intellectual nourishment. In *Ryecroft* he relents, permitting his hero release from labor, to rest during the last, emancipated years in an autumn exile in Devon. But though Ryecroft is released from the misery of London, his memory is too full of that wretchedness, and G presents this character study of joyless reminiscences. "But great art has never yet sprung from negation or suppression." *Ryecroft* is documented, sincere, and convincing as a study, but the hero never comes alive; the book "in many ways is his best work," but a "*tour de force* of authenticity never of revelation." [An illuminating, carefully argued, and sensitive survey of G's writings and *Ryecroft's* virtues.]

**586** Lee, Elizabeth. "Englischer Brief" (Letter from England), DAS LITTERARISCHE ECHO (Stuttgart), V (1 March 1903), 771. In many ways *The Private Papers of Henry Ryecroft* is G's most remarkable work. It differs from most of G's novels because it contains a touch of poetry. A quiet, peaceful book, it mirrors clearly an Englishman's ideas about man and life. [In German.]

**587** "The Library Table," GLOBE (Lond), 16 Feb 1903, p. 8. *The Private Papers of Henry Ryecroft* will probably be more attractive to many readers than G's novels have been. It contains an element of autobiography, enabling G to discuss numerous subjects with great frankness. *Ryecroft* is a book for leisure and pleasure.

**588** "Library Table: Glimpses of New Books," CURRENT LITERATURE, XXXIV (Feb 1903), 244. G's abridgement of Forster's LIFE OF DICKENS is thoroughly well-done, bringing up to date our knowledge of Dickens.

**589** "Literature," ATHENAEUM, No. 3930 (21 Feb 1903), 234. *The Private Papers of Henry Ryecroft,* essentially G's autobiography, betrays "a man who is at heart a recluse and a student, . . . probably more at home as a don than as a writer of realistic fiction." G's book reveals "a man of letters, yes, but not a novelist." [Knowledgeable review.]

**590** "Literature," ILLUSTRATED LONDON NEWS, CXXII (14 Feb 1903), 236. *The Private Papers of Henry Ryecroft* collects reminiscences, reveries, and feelings of a London journalist who is unexpectedly released from toil and permitted a peaceful independence in Devon. The pages are delightful and suggestive, often tinged with sadness, and always expressed "with a right choice of words and phrases."

**591** [Logan, Annie R. M.]. "Five Novels," NATION (NY), LXXVI (11 June 1903), 478. *The Private Papers of Henry Ryecroft* contains a "frank expression of unpopular truths"; it is a "naive revelation of abysmal selfishness" which Ryecroft himself does not realize. He does not perceive life around him. [Concentrates on self-centeredness of Ryecroft.]

**592** M., V. E. "Of the Fascination of the Life of Letters," AUTHOR (Lond), XIII (1 April 1903), 188–90.

G's *The Private Papers of Henry Ryecroft* shows him "tenderly compassionate," and—for him—relatively optimistic. Though G has been temperamentally out of the world, he has acquired a resignation, perhaps forced by circumstance, that enables him to see many things on the bitter side. [Article assembles quotations from G and W. D. Howells's LITERATURE AND LIFE.]

593 McCarthy, Justin. "The Prospects of the Ministry in England," INDEPENDENT (NY), LV (9 April 1903), 853–54.
*The Private Papers of Henry Ryecroft* is a study of the human soul, based both on imagination and autobiography. *Ryecroft* contains much of G's best writing. [Transparent article.]

594 Martin, Grace E. "Not the Real Thing," CRITIC (NY), XLIII (July 1903), 87.
*The Private Papers of Henry Ryecroft* is a fascinating diary composed in a scholarly style. Only English cooking brings any enthusiasm into *Ryecroft*. *Ryecroft* is meant for thoughtful people who have abundant leisure.

595 "Miscellaneous," SPEAKER, VII (10 Jan 1903), 381.
Forster's LIFE OF DICKENS, as abridged by G, disappoints us because we know how much is left out. Yet "no better editor |than G| could have been found." Would it not have been better if G had prepared an entirely new biography?

596 "Mr. George Gissing," MANCHESTER GUARDIAN, 30 Dec 1903, p. 4.
G was "little tied by theory, and belonged to no school, while his choice of scene and method sometimes ally him with Mr. George Moore." G delighted in the "bitterness of truth." His theme caught the "conscience, the pretensions, and the frustrations of the English middle class," exploring "the mental squalor of a truly bad suburban interior." G's study of Dickens "is far the best in the language, as well for style as for equity and sagacity." G's work "and its example should last long." [Obit that is full of usual errors.]

597 "New Books," SCOTSMAN, 5 Feb 1903, p. 2.
*The Private Papers of Henry Ryecroft* describes the relief of a Londoner who is able to spend his declining years in the quiet of Devon. The book is reflective, shrewd, and subtle. Ryecroft himself is at his best in telling of his favorite books and the pleasures of the countryside, even though in leisure moments the author's mood is frequently depressing. [Lengthy quotations.]

**598** "Notices of Books," PUBLISHERS' CIRCULAR, LXXVIII (28 March 1903), 360.

*The Private Papers of Henry Ryecroft,* while very well received by the reviewers, is "a trifle mawkish, and not a little boring." While G's style is good, the work in dull; "we are tired of tired people and the lazy life of sentimentalists."

**599** "Nouvelles de l'Etranger" (Foreign News), TEMPS, 31 Dec 1903, p. 2.

G was a faithful disciple and admirer of Dickens. [Slight obit paragraph.] [In French.]

**600** "Novels," SPECTATOR, XC (14 March 1903), 418.

In *The Private Papers of Henry Ryecroft,* G's pessimism reappears. Even democracy holds no hope for the future. [Brief; several quotations.]

**601** "Novels and Stories," GLASGOW HERALD, 12 Feb 1903, pp. 9–10.

*The Private Papers of Henry Ryecroft* "is in many respects the saddest and most depressing book Mr. Gissing has written." Like *New Grub Street, Ryecroft* is "evidently to some extent autobiographical." Like Grant Allen and Robert Buchanan, Ryecroft insists that writing is a miserable career. The relief of Devon can never eliminate the memory of Ryecroft's dismal London existence; the book, like life, is often excessively saddening.

**602** "Obituary: Mr. George Gissing," TIMES (Lond), 29 Dec 1903, p. 4; rptd in *The Letters of George Gissing to Members of His Family,* ed by Algernon and Ellen Gissing (Lond: Constable, 1927), App. B, pp. 400–402.

G's sad outlook on life approached hopelessness, but he was determined to tell what he believed the truth. G was a "man of the highest literary ideals." Like Balzac, he was a "conscientious literary artist" who wished to picture the truth of life by the enumeration of small and accurate details. His "purity and solidity may win him a better chance of being read a hundred years hence than many writers of greater grace and more deliberately sought charm." All of his books show the despair of modern life, but they are written in a style marked by the lucidity of his thoughts. G's pessimism "was no wilful maundering, and his 'realism' no prurient probing into unsavoury things for the fun of it." [Perceptive, balanced, sympathetic.]

**603** O'Brien, Desmond. "Letters on Books," TRUTH, LIII (26 March 1903), 833.

While *The Private Papers of Henry Ryecroft* is a "great and exceeding bitter cry" against publishers, it "rises high above the other groans from Grub-street [*sic*]." The work is "by far the best thing" G has ever done.

**604** "Pages in Waiting," WORLD (Lond), 24 Feb 1903, p. 322.
*The Private Papers of Henry Ryecroft* comes with the statement that G received these papers and merely edited them. In any event, the writing is "distinguished by a graceful literary style, a habit of moralising at large in a somewhat peevish vein" about matters of greater or lesser importance. But there is so little of life's joy here that the passages become "more than a little oppressive."

**605** "The Personal Note," PILOT, 7 March 1903, p. 238.
*The Private Papers of Henry Ryecroft* is conveniently put forward as the diary of a dead friend, providing thereby a disguise for G's own ideas and personality. Ryecroft is given the opportunity to retire early and to relish the wisdom allowed by quiet. A "note of deep indignation" condemns the waste of youthful energy and idealism. Is G right in warning young people against making literature a career? He examines the aristocratic, undemocratic nature of the English national mind. Ryecroft's own dominant note merges love of Nature, of home, and of country.

**606** [*The Private Papers of Henry Ryecroft*], MANCHESTER
   GUARDIAN, 20 Feb 1903, p. 4.
*The Private Papers of Henry Ryecroft* reminds one of Charles Lamb's quitting the hectic life of London to record his emancipation in eloquent and romantic essays. G's book catches both the mood and technique of Lamb. *Ryecroft* charms us into submission: we listen to G's ideas about a variety of subjects. The traditional British grumble is transformed into an exultation, for Ryecroft is himself enthusiastic about the quiet of Devon, its food, its expression, its style of life, and its scenic remoteness.

**607** "Random Reflections of a Recluse," DIAL, XXXV (July
   1903), 16.
*The Private Papers of Henry Ryecroft* displays a tendency to materialism and selfishness; G abhors conventions of polite society and dwells too much upon hunger and weariness. The book is somber and introspective; Ryecroft himself has a passionate love for literature and learning, for painting and music.

**608** "A Real Book," LITERARY WORLD (Lond), LXVII (20
   Feb 1903), 166–67.
*The Private Papers of Henry Ryecroft,* while not a novel, is "the best book he [G] has given us." *Ryecroft* is a spiritual autobiography, reminding us of books by Thoreau, James Thomson, De Quincey, and Richard

Jefferies. It contains descriptive passages of natural beauty and London slums, as well as deep thought about life and death. [Considerable praise is augmented by liberal quotations from *Ryecroft*.]

609 "Reviews: Mr. Gissing's Latest," SPEAKER, VII (7 March 1903), 559.

*The Private Papers of Henry Ryecroft* tells us everything about G himself, yet nothing could ever gain him thousands of Mrs. Mudie's readers. *Ryecroft* gives us peace and reflection after a life of suffering and poverty. If it lacks the "tragic force" of the Mark Rutherford series, it nevertheless compels our respect. Its tone is reflective; its conclusion is resignation.

610 "Reviews: The Solitary Life," PALL MALL GAZETTE, 4 March 1903, p. 4.

*The Private Papers of Henry Ryecroft* is G's masterpiece. It defends physical, emotional, and intellectual solitude; with amazing reality it describes the gentle quietism that comes to Ryecroft upon his escape to the calm of the West Country. For Ryecroft the problems of wealth and poverty cause no further worry.

611 "Reviews: Two Lives in One," PALL MALL GAZETTE, 20 Feb 1903, p. 4.

Forster's LIFE OF DICKENS has been reduced to "about one-third, roughly speaking," and we hope that G does not intend to do the same with Boswell. G did extremely well in his own critical study of Dickens, but here he fails. For example, when he omits letters by Dickens "swayed by a love of humour," he is not moved as he ought "by any sense of proportion."

612 "Short Notices," BOOKSELLER, DXLV (8 April 1903), 330.

*The Private Papers of Henry Ryecroft* details the quiet relief enjoyed by a former drudge of Grub Street: he savors the beauties and delicacies of Devon and relishes his Horace.

613 "Some Recent Books," CONTEMPORARY REVIEW, LXXXIII (April 1903), 599–601.

*The Private Papers of Henry Ryecroft* is a spiritual autobiography, an irresistible book for those who love literature. All that G wrote, from *New Grub Street* to *The Whirlpool,* "bears the stamp of artistic sincerity." *Ryecroft* contains "exquisite feeling for the poetry of English landscape." Yet the opinions expressed in the book will prove distinctly unpopular. As the world grows noisier, G "extols the virtues of quietism."

614 "Until the Evening," DAILY NEWS (Lond), 27 Feb 1903, p. 8.

*The Private Papers of Henry Ryecroft* "is quite the best thing" G has ever written and "occupies a unique position amongst the books of the year." The pattern of the book allows G to "range over many of the subjects of human misery"; and although the hero himself is released from the day-to-day drudgery of poverty in London, he still grieves for the degeneration that surrounds his fellow creatures. About the entire work there is a mood, tender and sad, "as of late afternoon," marked by "benignity, peace, and a certain pleasing sense of rest and acquiesence." But above all there hovers "the sense of the futility of all human life." [A sympathetic and careful reading of *Ryecroft*.]

**615** W[ilkins], A[ugustus] S[amuel]. "Letter to the Editor," MANCHESTER GUARDIAN, 31 Dec 1903, p. 10.
The obituary of the previous day is a "just and sympathetic notice," but it errs in saying that G had not gained academic distinction. In July 1875, G "placed first in the first class both in Latin and English . . . taking the University exhibition in both subjects." "A paper written by him about the same time still lives in my memory as the most flawless paper which I ever received in a college examination."

**616** "A Wise Book," WEEK'S SURVEY, 4 July 1903, p. 619.
*The Private Papers of Henry Ryecroft* reflects G sincerely and spontaneously on every page; it is such a rare book as one buys "for the pleasure of reading it again and again," for its charm, sanity, and wisdom. It is G's spirit more than his intelligence that emerges in the wisdom signaling great literature. [Laced with several quotations from *Ryecroft*.]

# 1904

**617** Barry, William. "Mr. Gissing's Last Book," BOOKMAN (Lond), XXVII (Nov 1904), 81.
*Veranilda* is too bookish, too "steeped in classical phrases." *Veranilda* shows fine workmanship; "it belongs, emphatically, to literature." The true heroine is Rome, fascinating and unconquerable. Descriptions are marked by grace and sobriety.

**618** Bateson, Margaret (Mrs. W. E. Heitland). "Mr. George Gissing," GUARDIAN (Lond), 6 Jan 1904, pp. 34–35.
G's death causes us to realize that a whole epoch has passed, an epoch chronicled in such bitter works as *Born in Exile, New Grub Street,* and *The Odd Women.* Almost all of G's characters were in fact born in exile, forming a population clouded with melancholy, and grimly headed by the educated poor. The specimens he provides in his novels are distinguished

by intelligence and ambition, but particularly by the crowding at the doors of opportunity where so many perished. G was "pre-eminently a woman's novelist." He sensed the helpless, spiritless condition of ladies in the closing quarter of the century, diagnosing the petty maladies of such hapless women as the Misses Maddens. From such characters as Miss Barfoot we must learn to "turn the faculties of human beings to more varied account." The educated odd-woman must not feel that her opportunities are restricted to teaching or to clerking. But liberty remains "the hidden princess in the impenetrable wood," as riches are overcoming class after class.

**619** Beswick, Harry. "In the Library," CLARION (Lond), 8 Jan 1904, p. 3.
G's death at forty-six years leaves literature the poorer. The poverty of his own life is constantly mirrored in his books, though it is hard to assess how much of his pessimism was natural and how much induced by mental and bodily suffering.

**620** Bjorkman, Edwin. "The Works of George Gissing," BOOKMAN (NY), XVIII (Feb 1904), 600–603; rptd in VOICES OF TOMORROW (NY & Lond: Mitchell Kennerley, 1913), pp. 224–39.
G's books were marked by sincerity of purpose, "shrewdness of observation, depth of sympathy and command of form." G's admirers will increase. Every G novel "is a piece of life, terrible at times in its reality, but never loathsome." His pessimistic outlook on life reminds one of Strindberg, though G was "braver as a man, less given to make his art the vehicle of personal grievances." Ultimately, G's success "lies in the sympathy which he gave to all his figures." *The Nether World, New Grub Street, In the Year of Jubilee,* and *The Whirlpool* "must be counted among the strongest pieces of imaginative" modern English literature. [A comment on this item appeared in REVIEW OF REVIEWS, XXIX (1905), 353–54.]

**621** "Books in Brief," PALL MALL GAZETTE, 1 Oct 1904, p. 5.
*Veranilda* is G's posthumously published historical novel. Frederic Harrison's preface recalls that he met G when *Workers in the Dawn* appeared and that he recommended G to John Morley, editor of the PALL MALL GAZETTE. G refused to engage in any miscellaneous journalistic work at that time.

**622** The Bookworm. "Bibliographical," ACADEMY, LXVI (9 Jan 1904), 30.
[Provides a requested list of G's publications.]

**623** Colles, W. Morris. "George Gissing," ACADEMY, LXVI (9 Jan 1904), 40.

G is a "true artist, a fine scholar, and a most capable workman in letters."
Reviewers misrepresented both the man ("one of the most loveable of
men and the brightest of companions") and his choice of subject in fiction
("the vulgar and the sordid were to him an abomination"). [Colles was
G's literary agent.]

**624** Courtney, W. L. [*Veranilda*], DAILY TELEGRAPH (Lond),
28 Sept 1904, p. 6.

"*Veranilda* is an historical romance such as we rarely see in our modern
time." G is not a pedant but a "scholar who has a dramatic joy in life, a
man who can describe character" so that we feel the impulses of his characters. During his life, G was a curious failure who "never could express
his real essence." Books like *Demos, New Grub Street, The Crown of
Life, The Unclassed, The Nether World,* and *The Whirlpool* were deliberately painted on "a dull and squalid canvas in the spirit of those melancholy realists that were once, both in France and England, a transitory and
melancholy fashion." But the real G showed slightly in *By the Ionian Sea*
and *The Private Papers of Henry Ryecroft*. Then, just before he died, G
started the book "for which he was eminently fitted by his tastes and pre-
dilections." [Elaborate and appreciative résumé of *Veranilda*.]

**625** "Fiction," ACADEMY, LXVII (8 Oct 1904), 311–12.

*Veranilda* expresses G's emancipation from the somber London settings.
But G has not escaped the atmosphere of Grub Street: his "methods of
minute observation and analysis" do not belong to this fictional form.
Over-elaboration results. *Veranilda* is "scholarly, earnest work, seldom
attaining to beauty and never to spiritual unity." *Veranilda* is "exquisite
evidence of G's own search for peace," the peace of *The Private Papers
of Henry Ryecroft.*

**626** "Fiction," GUARDIAN (Lond), LIX (16 Nov 1904), 1931.

*Veranilda* is less interesting for its story than for its vivid picture of Roman
times, "a picture which could only have been drawn by one who was
steeped in the subject." While it is full of interest and beauty, G will rather
be remembered for his "studies of contemporary life in London."

**627** "Fiction," SCOTSMAN, 6 Oct 1904, p. 2.

*Veranilda* is "entirely unlike the studies of 'contemporary life' which readers will always associate" with G. Frederic Harrison says that only G's
view is changed, but it goes far deeper than that: the dreary, drab London
gives way to romantic antiquity, as G makes history realistically present.
[Content of story surveyed.]

**628** Findlater, Jane H. "The Spokesman of Despair," NATIONAL

REVIEW, LXIV (Nov 1904), 511–22; rptd in LIVING AGE, CCXLIII (17 Dec 1904), 733–41.

G's characters lived between misery and despair. "The special problem which G sets forth in his books is that of poverty as it affects morality." Degradation sets in when effort stops; G cannot see that people survive want. But privation and starvation are not the same. In *New Grub Street,* G describes the suffering of Edward Reardon to prove that "high ideals of artistic work will not buy bread." G never inquires into the situation of the artist who has bread nor does he show the bliss of artistic creation. The picture of *The Odd Women* is "appallingly true and unexaggerated." G seems to think that business training will free such women. "Character, not circumstance, creates the odd women." *The Nether World* is a "nightmare book," a statement of despair; it ranks next to *Grub Street* among G's best. Like *Women, The Whirlpool* is amazing proof of G's artistic intuition. *Veranilda* was too great a strain for G's imagination. [Important critical survey of G's works.]

**629** "From the Novelists' Workshop," ILLUSTRATED LONDON NEWS, CXXV (15 Oct 1904), 540.

*Veranilda* has been praised by Frederic Harrison and H. G. Wells, but the public will scarcely be enthusiastic with the novel. *The Private Papers of Henry Ryecroft* showed flesh and blood, but *Veranilda* cannot stir us. The narrative drags; nothing happens. G's picture of sixth-century Rome is blurred.

**630** "George Gissing," ACADEMY, LXVI (2 Jan 1904), 4–5.

G's death is a great loss to readers of serious fiction. G's world was a sad, rather hopeless dwelling place. His criticism of Dickens is excellent.

**631** "George Gissing," ATHENAEUM, No. 3977 (2 Jan 1904), 18.

Gloom and scholarship marked G's novels; *The Private Papers of Henry Ryecroft* deserved the success it achieved. Having fixed G as a pessimist, the public "hardly appreciated" *The Town Traveller* and neglected *Our Friend the Charlatan,* a novel touching "cultivated ranks of society" who were not the subjects of his earlier works. [Obit.]

**632** "George Gissing," OUTLOOK (Lond), XII (2 Jan 1904), 649.

G was "the made as distinct from the born artist in letters." A scholar and booklover, G's memorable *New Grub Street* is "pre-eminently a novel for writers." [Obit.]

**633** Hallam, J.H. "Correspondence," MANCHESTER GUARDIAN, 5 Jan 1904, p. 12.

G's novels have "considerable historical value for their faithful pictures of certain aspects of the life of our times." [Letter suggests a memorial for G.]

**634** Harrison, Frederic. "Preface," *Veranilda* (Lond: Constable, 1904), pp. v–vii.

This novel, here published posthumously, was never completed by G. It deals "with real historic personages and actual historical events." G has a sense of history in finding a parallel between the decline of his own society and the fall of Rome. It is "by far the most important book" G ever wrote, "composed in a new vein of genius." *Veranilda* especially represents G's "really fine scholarship and classical learning." [Displeased with the preface H. G. Weils wrote for G's unfinished work, G's literary executors asked Harrison to write this substitute. See H. G. Wells, "George Gissing: An Impression," MONTHLY REVIEW, XVI (Aug 1904), 160–72.]

**635** Harrison, Frederic. *"Veranilda,"* POSITIVIST REVIEW, XII (Nov 1904), 261–62.

*Veranilda* is a conscientious and elaborate study of Imperial Rome, entirely without fire and pomp. More than any other book, *Veranilda* captures "this vast cataclysm, the contrasts of race, of creed, of ideals of life." The story "is meditative rather than exciting." The characters are often pathetic failures. G is "an old friend," a "scholar of rare and curious learning, something of a poet, and something of a philosopher."

**636** Hubert. "A Note on George Gissing," SUNDAY CHRONICLE (Lond), 3 Jan 1904, p. 2.

G never achieved popularity in his lifetime, although he ranks just after Meredith and Hardy as the greatest of our contemporary novelists. Meredith and Hardy were blessed with a genius denied G. His subjects hampered his popularity because the ordinary reader wants to be amused, and G scarcely amused. G's first books gave us the facts about the poorest classes, novels like *The Unclassed, The Nether World,* and *Demos.* These novels were not sentimental; their characters were drawn from countless people in the real world. Aloofness "was the strongest note" of G's method. "Gissing came much nearer to being a realist than any other writer of our day, nearer than Zola." In *The Whirlpool* ("his highest literary achievement"), G allows us a "glimpse of a deeper, fuller, ah, even of a higher life." Perhaps his most characteristic and autobiographic novel is *Born in Exile.* G's study of Dickens is "one of the very best pieces of contemporary criticism extant"; it helped Dickens's reputation at a time when "superfine literary folk were beginning to depreciate if not actually to sneer at Dickens."

**637** "An Idealistic Realist," ATLANTIC MONTHLY, XCIII (Feb 1904), 280–82.

"G was a realist controlled by an ideal," so that although he dwelt upon the sordid, his comparisons with the beautiful led him to idealize. He was neither morbid nor indecent. Compared to Zola, Flaubert, and Moore, G was never indifferent: he had the "keen sympathy of the artist." After his first novels, G concentrated more and more on significant things, like the "unequal bond of wedlock" between incompatible people, as in *New Grub Street,* or the plight of the unmarried woman, as in *The Odd Women.* His fame is secure. [Thoughtful article.]

**638** "In Memoriam: George Robert Gissing," CHURCH TIMES (Lond), LI (8 Jan 1904), 33.

G was "always groping for the light." His search, "we are glad to record," was satisfied at his death, "in the fear of God's Holy Name, and with the comfort and strength of the Catholic Faith." [See reply by Morley Roberts, "The Late George Gissing," ibid (15 Jan 1904), 61.]

**639** K[leary], C.F. "George Gissing," ATHENAEUM, No. 3977 (16 Jan 1904), 82.

G is sincere; he was not influenced by Zola. "The special characteristic of Gissing is that by a natural development his art went on improving, until, towards the end, it came to be a remarkable, and for our country almost unique, example of real realism and natural naturalism working in their own surroundings and drawing from legitimate sources." G best understood "a particular section of the lower middle class." He "was a writer of highest talent, who described sincerely and most forcibly the world he knew." G rose to be his best in *The Whirlpool* and *In the Year of Jubilee.*

**640** Lee, Elizabeth. "Englischer Brief" (Letter from England), DAS LITTERARISCHE ECHO, VI (1 Feb 1904), 642.

G's death is a loss to English letters. The author of twenty novels, a book of travels, and a volume examining his own philosophy (*The Private Papers of Henry Ryecroft*), G is partly indebted to Dickens and to Zola for his literary ideals. [In German.]

**641** Lee, Elizabeth. "Englischer Brief" (Letter from England), DAS LITTERARISCHE ECHO, VII (15 Nov 1904), 273.

*Veranilda* provides a valuable picture of ancient Rome, but the action is rather lifeless. G's reputation will be based on his realistic novels. [In German.]

**642** "Literature," ATHENAEUM, No. 4017 (22 Oct 1904), 544.

For *Veranilda,* G has "soaked himself in his period, and is imbued with the spirit of it." It does not seem that G's "finest qualities have here the suitable material." G's genius was characterized by fidelity to fact, in his finest achievements like *New Grub Street* and *Demos*. Such sincerity and accuracy are not felicitous gifts for romantic history. Though written with care and skill, "it has all the trappings of romance—but it is Gissing in disguise."

**643** "Literature: Two Novels," SPEAKER, XI (22 Oct 1904), 88. *Veranilda* may have claims as historical research, but as a work of art it is feeble. Basil and Marcian seem almost "patently transmogrified Londoners." *Veranilda* is an "honestly painstaking effort to picture an epoch," but the characters are transparent and papery. *The Private Papers of Henry Ryecroft* failed because it did not set forth plainly G's "true spiritual autobiography." The significance of G's place in literature is that in his novels "we could feel and taste just those grim, prosaic facts of the life of our big cities . . . concerning which the public and its writers are in a conspiracy of silence."

**644** "The Lounger," CRITIC (NY), LXIV (March 1904), 197. G lacks popular appeal; he was too gruesome and too relentless. But his few admirers are enthusiastic.

**645** McCarthy, D. *"Veranilda,"* INDEPENDENT REVIEW, IV (Dec 1904), 479–80.
*Veranilda,* G's last novel, is an unfortunate book because while it probably allowed him comfort and delight, it does not take advantage of his chief merits. His merits actually result from "an extreme sensitiveness to points of individual character, to gesture, movement, and inflections of voice," and particularly from "describing the gradual effect of prolonged trial." In *Veranilda,* the plot is simple and the conversations unnatural, so that the effect is of a waxwork.

**646** McCarthy, Justin. "Politics and Literature in England," INDEPENDENT (NY), LVI (18 Feb 1904), 379–81.
[McCarthy had met G in London and shared an enthusiasm for Athens. Brief character sketch.]

**647** Meyerfeld, Max. "Neue Englische Bücher" (New English Books), DAS LITTERARISCHE ECHO, VI (1 Feb 1904), 614–15.
*The Private Papers of Henry Ryecroft* displays a hard-won resignation. As an expression of G's longing for a life without bitterness, the book is anticipated by *Demos* and *New Grub Street*. G neither made concessions to the reading public, nor did he shy away from the gloomy side of life. He was influenced by Dickens but had not the latter's humor and didactic attitude. He also learned much from Zola but avoided showing his figures

in heroic situations inconsistent with the usual drab monotony of their lives. G suffered from being labeled a representative of thorough-going naturalism. [In German.]

**648** "Misdirected Patronage," OUTLOOK (Lond), 22 Oct 1904, p. 352.

*Veranilda* is not, as Frederic Harrison would have us believe, G's "best and most original work." How can Harrison say this, and in the same breath confess that he has not read all G's books? G's strength was in depicting "certain phases of the real life of his own time," not in attempting in a scholarly way to revitalize musty details of Byzantine Rome. Now G's early novels, those on which his " 'fame' will certainly rest," should gain better appreciation, such books as contain "living, breathing, human creatures,"—*Demos, Thyrza, The Nether World, A Life's Morning,* and *New Grub Street.*

**649** "Mr. Gissing's *Veranilda*," TIMES LITERARY SUPPLEMENT (Lond), 7 Oct 1904, p. 303.

In *Veranilda,* G hoped to leave the restricted, embattled, degraded world of the hideous edge of the abyss, to gain the kingdom of culture and scholarship. G had "made himself into the scholar" and preferred research into the ancients to research into the misery abundantly near at hand. Having paid the price for entering the promised land by writing many novels about mental and moral deterioration, he allowed himself the pleasure of writing *By the Ionian Sea* and *The Private Papers of Henry Ryecroft,* and, even as death overtook him, *Veranilda.* However, because a novelist does his best writing about "what he has felt and known," this book of scholarship, "mellow and serene," has none of the bitterness that urged his earlier books. *Veranilda* parades none of G's ideas; it is full of his knowledge of Rome, "as if he had lived in it in a previous incarnation." For us, G makes the period live, although his characters do not.

**650** "New Novels: Gissing's Posthumous *Veranilda*," MANCHESTER GUARDIAN, 5 Oct 1904, p. 3.

*Veranilda,* though unfinished at G's death, "leaves no sense of incompletion." G's characters are rather conventional and are of secondary interest. Prompted by historical investigations, G writes of Roman days with enthusiasm and grace. But his earlier books set in modern times, like *The Nether World* and *New Grub Street,* are superior to *Veranilda* for their "expression of fortitude in poverty and privation." This marked his most vital phase; *The Town Traveller* was a "brilliant success in a new vein."

**651** "Notes of the Week," SATURDAY REVIEW, CXVII (2 Jan 1904), 4.

G is a second rank novelist like Trollope and perhaps Jane Austen.

**652** "Notices of Books," PUBLISHERS' CIRCULAR, LXXXI (10 Dec 1904), 660.

*Veranilda* contains some of G's most earnest and studied work, but it is probably not as exceptional as Harrison's introduction claims. The historical subject is congenial to G, and he delineates his Roman characters with subtlety.

**653** "Novels," SPECTATOR, XCIII (3 Dec 1904), 903–4.

While *Veranilda* is the result of considerable study, G has "suppressed all parade of his learning." The subject matter does surprise us. The warm Italian skies have mellowed G, and they have revealed a new vein of his genius. *Veranilda* contains a wealth of circumstantial detail and follows the best historical authorities.

**654** "Novels and Stories," GLASGOW HERALD, 15 Oct 1904, p. 11

*Veranilda* is an historical novel left unfinished at G's death. It displays G's "intimate knowledge of the history of the period and of the condition of Italy in the sixth century." In *Veranilda,* the "desolation of the country and towns and the corruption of society in Italy are vividly but not naturalistically described." It must be one of the "best historical novels lately produced."

**655** "Our English Realist," DAILY CHRONICLE (Lond), 28 Sept 1904, p. 3.

*Veranilda,* written at the close of G's life and not completed at his death, is an escape in fancy to a world of imagination removed from the actual world that surrounded him and forced him to become a realist. Despite Frederic Harrison's judgment, *Veranilda* will not affect G's reputation, since "for depth and sincerity of effect it does not seem to compare even remotely with *New Grub Street* or *In the Year of Jubilee.*" Whereas accumulated details are essential for the "realistic treatment of contemporary life," such accumulation is contrary to the imagination necessary for the historical novel. While this story is "finely constrained and elaborately poised," it unfortunately "lacks the breath of life," and has scarcely any charm. Indeed, a lack of charm was G's most significant shortcoming.

**656** "Pages in Waiting," WORLD (Lond), 18 Oct 1904, p. 636.

*Veranilda* evidences for the first time G's taste for classical studies of city life. Unlike his sordid and sorrowful studies of city life, here is a grand, beautiful story, so scholarly, "without one disconcerting suggestion of pedantry," that will transport the reader "into that vanished era of the old world." "We know where to place Gissing now."

**657** Ransome, Arthur. "George Gissing," WEEK'S SURVEY
(Lond), 9 Jan 1904, pp. 173–74.

G's death ends the life of a writer who wrote for writing's sake. He sought
to see, and to describe clearly what he saw. He was a great man, an earnest man. If what he saw was mournful, that was what he committed to
paper, "hopelessly and defiantly."

**658** "Recent Fiction," GLOBE (Lond), 7 Oct 1904, p. 8.

*Veranilda* is far different from such works as *Demos* that created G's reputation. It reveals his "purely classical sympathies," as G recreates a dying
epoch. Perhaps this posthumous work is also G's most satisfying.

**659** Roberts, Morley. "The Late George Gissing," CHURCH
TIMES (Lond), LI (15 Jan 1904), 61.

In his "delerious and unconscious" last days G never changed his religious
views. "He not only accepted none of the dogmas formulated in the
Creeds and Articles of the Church of England, but he considered it impossible than any Church's definition of the indefinable could have any
significance for any intelligent men." [Reply to "In Memoriam: George
Robert Gissing," ibid (8 Jan 1904), 35.]

**660** S., A. L. "In the Library: A New 'Story of My Heart,'"
CLARION, 25 March 1904, p. 3.

With *The Private Papers of Henry Ryecroft,* G, that "clever, relentless
chronicler of the ugly fact of life," reminds us of Jefferies and THE STORY
OF MY HEART. Here is an unusual book deserving very high praise. While
Ryecroft is undoubtedly G himself, there is nothing of the misery of so
many of his novels in the delicacy and humor of this book. [Long quotations from *Ryecroft.*]

**661** S[horter], C. K. "A Literary Letter," SPHERE, XVI (9 Jan
1904), 48.

G was a sad, complex, but not bitter person; he had a "grip on the realities
of life that left him unequalled among recent English writers of fiction."
One editor repeatedly published his work although there was "practically
no public appreciation of his work." [Sketch drawn from life by Mrs.
Clarence Rook, also signed in jest by H. G. Wells, accompanies letter.]
[Obit.]

**662** Sturmer, Herbert. "George Gissing," WEEK'S SURVEY
(Lond), 9 Jan 1904, p. 173.

Now that G is dead we can survey his achievement as an author and as
a person. "At heart an idealist," G was misjudged by those who thought
him misanthropic, by those who challenged him to deal with those social

and political evils noted in his novels. He produced books "for thinking men to treasure," especially books like *The Nether World* and *Demos,* containing "imperishable English prose" sympathetically marking the sorrow and suffering of real life. His best writing has "something massive, majestic" in its marshalled power. He observed in human events the helpless trials of the poor; if he sought to avoid poor people themselves it was that he might express their misery with the least waste of involvement.

**663** "An Unfinished Novel," LITERARY WORLD (Lond), LXX (28 Oct 1904), 326.
*Veranilda* is an attempt to make dry and ancient bones live; but despite G's great learning, enthusiasm, and effort, the magic did not work. The achievement is not as great as Frederic Harrison's superlative praise leads us to expect. *Veranilda* is a "delighting, but not a really great, novel." [Plot outline and quotations.]

**664** *"Veranilda,"* MORNING POST (Lond), 28 Sept 1904, p. 6.
*Veranilda* is quite unlike anything else G ever wrote and will undoubtedly appeal to "lovers of good literature" for its quiet charm. Perhaps G's own attention to the setting has caused him occasionally to forget his narrative, so immersed is he in Gibbon. The style is "generally simple and appropriate," with an "occasional tendency to preciosity." [Story outline.]

**665** von Ende, A. "Amerikanischer Brief" (Letter from America), DAS LITTERARISCHE ECHO, VI (15 June 1904), 1287.
The novels of the late G resemble those of Israel Zangwill for their knowledge of English life. [In German.]

**666** Waugh, Arthur. "George Gissing," FORTNIGHTLY REVIEW, LXXXI (Feb 1904), 244–56; rptd in LIVING AGE, CCXL (March 1904), 714–23; RETICENCE IN LITERATURE AND OTHER PAPERS (Lond: J. G. Wilson, 1915), pp. 161–82.
Popularity always evaded G in his lifetime; a "truer artist, a more conscientious and sincere workman" never lived. His early death a month ago reminds us how much he deserves respect. G's characters lived in "the limbo external to society," as he said in a preface to *The Unclassed,* "one of the soundest of" his books. Though G entered Dickens's world, he viewed it through his own eyes—for all realistic writing is tempered by the personality of the author. And G had bitter memories, as his friend Noel Ainslie recalls, that haunted him and influenced all his work. His novels are overwhelming in details that "confuse the fancy." Unlike Zola, G wrote not "to illustrate a theory, but simply to picture life." His greatest attribute is the steadiness with which he viewed life—always with a mild indignation. [Important article.]

**667** Wedd, Nathaniel. "George Gissing," INDEPENDENT RE-
VIEW, II (Feb 1904), 101–6.

G's death closes out a life dedicated to writing great fiction, books "scarcely
less skilled in adapting fiction to interpret life" than the work of Dickens
and Meredith. G's books stressed the vital importance of culture, itself an
outgrowth of education devoted to the beautiful. G's chief theme was the
"degrading effects of poverty on all above a certain low level of spiritual
development." G's characters had a greater capacity for suffering from
meanness and hypocrisy than Dickens's characters had, because of their
greater thirst for culture. G examined London with intuition and fidelity,
"becoming her second great interpreter after Dickens."

**668** Wells, H. G. "George Gissing: An Impression," MONTHLY
REVIEW, XVI (Aug 1904), 160–72; rptd in LIVING AGE, CCXLIII
(Oct 1904), 38–45; ECLECTIC MAGAZINE (Bost), CXLIII (Nov
1904), 580–87; GEORGE GISSING AND H. G. WELLS: A RECORD
OF THEIR FRIENDSHIP AND CORRESPONDENCE, ed with an introduction by Royal A. Gettmann (Lond: Rupert Hart-Davis; Urbana: University of Illinois P, 1961), pp. 260–77.

G "exhausted the resources of a very fine irony upon the narrowness and
sordidness of contemporary life." The public never appreciated him; he
could not accept the realities of life. G "never entirely grasped the spirit
of everyday life." "He irritated others and thwarted himself." He could
hardly be popular for works that rejected journalism; in folly he rejected
an academic life, resenting tasks that kept him from the classics. G wrote
"about people he did not understand." He lacked inspiration and confidence. When he finally escaped to Rome and Athens, he wrote of them,
but "he wrote nothing of the realities of his sensations then." In private,
as a friend, he revealed his treasures, showing "the empty cover of his
railway tickets home, a flattened blossom from Hadrian's villa, a ticket
for the Vatican Library." He spoke of them "as one speaks of a lost
paradise." Though unfinished, *Veranilda* is unified, "the picture of a
magnificent decay." It shows G's learning, saturated with classical tradition. The book has permanent, if not contemporary, fame. [Essay
originally intended as a preface to G's *Veranilda*. See Frederic Harrison,
"Preface," *Veranilda* (1904). Quotes G's last letters about *Veranilda*.
Valuable appraisal of G.]

**669** Williamson, George C. "George Gissing," ACADEMY, LXVI
(9 Jan 1904), 46.

G is a shy, sensitive, fastidious man. Unfortunately G too often suffered
from unfair judgments. [Letter to ed.]

**670** Zangwill, Israel. "Without Prejudice," To-Day, XLI (3 Feb 1904), 433–34.

There was a time when I considered G "Shakespearean in his psychologic range," and now that he has died I scarcely feel less admiration for his books. He wrote an excellent study of Dickens, although no writer was more foreign to his temperament. G's work has never been sufficiently applauded. His novels changed in scope and attitude as he developed; *The Whirlpool* is probably the best example of his later manner. The narrowness of his vision allowed the concentrated impression of life that his novels provide.

# 1905

**671** Adcock, A. St. John. "Gissing's Last Novel," BOOKMAN (Lond), XXVIII (Aug 1905), 162.

*Will Warburton* is skillfully contrived and admirably written; G's last works deserve to be popular. While it yields to the cry for a lighter vein and a happy ending, it possesses none of the strength, the dark but vital earnestness that distinguished *New Grub Street*.

**672** Benson, A. C. THE UPTON LETTERS (NY: Putnam, 1905), p 209.

G's characters are "not so much vulgar as underbred." As long as G stayed within his *milieu,* his characters were real; however, *By the Ionian Sea* and *The Private Papers of Henry Ryecroft* brought G into a new province of "exquisitely beautiful and poetic idealistic literature."

**673** "The Book Buyer's Guide," CRITIC (NY), XLVI (May 1905), 478.

*Veranilda* was motivated not by the novelist's impulse but by the historian's. G's posthumous novel does not match in "strength, penetration, sympathy, and humor" the work that made him "so conspicuously able a writer."

**674** "The Book Buyer's Guide," CRITIC (NY), XLVII (Aug 1905), 190.

*By the Ionian Sea,* just released in an American edition, is the expression of a "highly cultivated intelligence." The book does not enchant. [Slight.]

**675** "The Book Buyer's Guide," CRITIC (NY), XLVII (Sept 1905), 284–85.

*Will Warburton* is further evidence of the "fluctuating and insecure quality" of G's ability. The range of characters is not extensive. The book has possibilities which Meredith could have handled well; G is too often pre-occupied with "self-deceiving social criminals."

**676** "The Book Mart," BOOKMAN (NY), XXI (Aug 1905), 654.
*Will Warburton* is the second of G's books to be published posthumously. The story of the novel is said to be pathetic and humorous. [Slight outline of plot.]

**677** "A Book of the Day: Gissing's Latest Novel," DAILY NEWS (Lond), 5 July 1905, p. 4.
*Will Warburton* is not one of G's greatest books. He returns from the antiquity of *Veranilda* to the ignobility of London's suburbs to follow Balzac in interpreting the wretchedness of life. Absent are the poor of Lambeth, as in *Thyrza* ("perhaps the finest of all his works"); instead we have some humor, some moderation in G's disgust with the modern world.

**678** "Books of the Week," OUTLOOK (NY), LXXIX (4 March 1905), 606.
*Veranilda* is a dignified and careful work containing a charming love story. Frederic Harrison's introductory essay is commendable. [See Harrison, "Preface," *Veranilda* (Lond: Constable, 1904), pp. v-vii.]

**679** "Books of the Week," OUTLOOK (NY), LXXX (13 May 1905), 137–38.
*By the Ionian Sea* details G's personal reactions in a journey from Naples to Reggio. Veiled with melancholy, his feelings are deeply moved by what he knows of the history of Calabria.

**680** "Books of the Week," OUTLOOK (NY), LXXX (8 July 1905), 644.
*Will Warburton* leaves the critic with a warmer personal feeling towards G. The book provides "one true man—placid in misfortune, generous to all the world."

**681** "Books of To-Day and Yesterday," ILLUSTRATED LONDON NEWS, CXXVII (22 July 1905), 128.
In *Will Warburton* G is far more at ease than he was in *Veranilda;* it is light, sportive comedy. We cannot charge G here with "too sordid fidelity." But while the novel is readable, it cannot be classed with his best work.

**682** "Current Fiction," LITERARY WORLD (Lond), LXXII (15 July 1905), 250.
In *Will Warburton,* G reverts to present-day London to satirize "middle-class snobbery, particularly of the feminine variety." [Full narrative outline with quotations.]

**683** Davray, Henry-D. "Lettres Anglaises" (English Letters), MERCURE DE FRANCE, LIII (15 Jan 1905), 304–6.
Contrary to Frederic Harrison's opinion in the "Preface" that *Veranilda* is G's most important book, with all its great merits, this historical novel does not outdo G's excellent novels of manners. [This article is followed by a review of the French trans of H. G. Wells's THE FOOD OF THE GODS; Davray compares G and Wells, espec *Born in Exile* and LOVE AND MR. LEWISHAM.] [In French.]

**684** "Fiction," GUARDIAN (Lond), LX (19 July 1905), 1224.
*Will Warburton* promises to be liked by many readers who did not appreciate *Thyrza* or *The Nether World*. It provides "ultimate victory" for characters who would have suffered shame and defeat in earlier G novels. The "tragic intensity of former years has disappeared."

**685** "Fiction," SCOTSMAN, 26 June 1905, p. 2.
*Will Warburton* is probably not G's most brilliant achievement. Not since Dickens has any novelist so happily translated the streets of London into fiction, although G's humor is less ripe and his comparisons less sharp than those of Dickens. Yet his pictures, "restful and suggestive," capture "the commonplace of the commonplace."

**686** "Fiction: George Gissing's Last Book," OUTLOOK (Lond), XV (1 July 1905), 951–52.
In *Will Warburton* G seems to have abandoned all his theories about art and life. We have known his "immense and insistent gloom," his sincerity concerning "theories about life" and not life itself, his preoccupation with mediocrity, his fascination with the middle class, his admiration for Dickens, and his following Zola as a realist. Only *By the Ionian Sea* and *The Private Papers of Henry Ryecroft* convince us that he was really an artist and craftsman. But no one can grow passionate about the people in *Warburton*.

**687** "Fiction: *Will Warburton,*" TIMES LITERARY SUPPLEMENT (Lond), 30 June 1905, p. 209.
*Will Warburton* "must take a lower place among" G's novels, for it says feebly what others say forcibly. G's "ineradicable impression" on readers came from novels like *New Grub Street,* for the "hideous nightmare" that was undoubtedly his own experience. G was great only when gloomy, when his "helpless hedonist" was in exile even as G himself. Release from suffering came too late for him to achieve a new truth. Like earlier heroines, Rosamund Elvan states G's "favourite theory about women—to wit, that those of them whom successful men find charming are in reality self-seeking, blind to ideals, and incapable of sacrifice."

**688** Garnett, Edward. "Fiction," SPEAKER, XII (8 July 1905), 352–53.

*Will Warburton*'s hero resembles G himself: "modest, but timidly self-conscious, high-principled, generously self-sacrificing, but morbidly reserved and full of self-distrust." If the satire of the novel arouses "uneasy suspicions" in the reader, G certainly prefers the ideals of Warburton to the artificial success of the artist Norbert Franks, who prostituted his soul to gain "position, a nice house, a handsome wife, heaps of friends." G's reputation as a novelist is secure because he alone recognized that life was monotonous, drab, and vulgar. It "was his distinction as an artist to stamp in literature with an insistence and scrupulous patience" the dreary, "anaemic, joyless growth of London lower middle-class existence." How fortunate for him that he was saved from becoming a tranquil, scholarly university professor of classics.

**689** "George Gissing: A Realistic Novelist's Posthumous Historical Romance," NEW YORK TIMES SATURDAY REVIEW OF BOOKS, 25 Feb 1905, p. 118.

*Veranilda,* an effort at historical romance, surprises us, coming from one of the "strongest of the latter day novelists." G's perfection of style and conscientious attention to detail are here. Frederic Harrison assures us that *Veranilda* is G's most important book. But it hardly strikes us as the work of the author of *In the Year of Jubilee* or *The Paying Guest.* Did G intend this "flying off upon such a tangent" as a grim joke? Besides the immense effort in research to document the ancient times here narrated, G brought to *Veranilda* the knowledge, power, and insight that distinguished his previous novels.

**690** "George Gissing's Last Novel," WESTMINSTER GAZETTE, 15 July 1905, p. 14.

*Will Warburton* must have been written in a time of stress and agony, although G's own delight and interest can always be read between the lines. While most modern in his writings, G fell prey to no impressionistic doctrines. It is regrettable that this book must represent the vanished hand of G.

**691** "Gissing's Last Novel," NEW YORK TRIBUNE ILLUSTRATED SUPPLEMENT, 19 Feb 1905, pp. 6–7.

*Veranilda* further justifies G's "claim to be ranked as one of the most finely imaginative men of his time." It interests us keenly even though he was unable to complete the work with an "impressive climax." The story glows with old-fashioned dignity and quiet fervor and proves how much G immersed himself in ancient Roman history. It is a masterly and lovable book. [Narrative outlined.]

**692** "Gissing's Last Story," NEW YORK TIMES SATURDAY RE-
VIEW OF BOOKS, 22 July 1905, p. 487.

*Will Warburton* is a quiet, sincere, infinitely refreshing story of a warm-
hearted man defrauded by his best friend. Deprived of his resources, Warburton opens a grocery rather than have his mother and sister suffer the
loss. Other characters can be gauged by their response to his circumstances.
G has never written a "more healthful and human" book. As a posthumously published novel, it gives us a final glimpse of G's own personality
as well.

**693** L., C. E. "Love and the Grocer," DAILY CHRONICLE (Lond),
28 June 1905, p. 3.

*Will Warburton,* G's second posthumous work, gives the "true Gissing,
not the Gissing of depression and gloom." The characters are human—
the very people we meet daily. No man is a villain. [Plot summary.]

**694** Lee, Elizabeth. "Englischer Brief" (Letter from England),
DAS LITTERARISCHE ECHO, VII (15 Aug 1905), 1645–46.

*Will Warburton* is one of G's best novels. The difficulties Warburton has
to face are skillfully revealed. G succeeds in avoiding melodrama. [In
German.]

**695** "The Library Table," GLOBE (Lond), 10 July 1905, p. 4.

*Will Warburton* recalls something of both *Demos* and *New Grub Street*
although it is closer to *The Town Traveller* in style. While well written
and well imagined, it might have been written by somebody else, so un-
characteristic is it of G. [Brief outline.]

**696** [Logan, Annie R.M.] "More Fiction," NATION (NY),
LXXX (1 June 1905), 441.

*Veranilda* is too much the product of the mind. "No novelist was ever
more the slave of his temperament than was the late George Gissing." G
knew his characters but could not identify with them. *Veranilda's* best
parts describe the desperate conditions of Rome, starving and fallen.

**697** Masterman, C.F.G. "George Gissing," IN PERIL OF CHANGE
(NY: Huebsch, 1905), pp. 68–73; selections rptd in "Victim of
Nineteenth Century Grub Street," CURRENT LITERATURE, XL
(May 1906), 509–10.

G's death comes just as he "escaped this insistent and hideous dream" of
the futility of life in London's slums. *The Private Papers of Henry Ryecroft* signaled a "benigner look, a softer, kindlier vision." His bitterness
and protest, his "indignation had yielded to perplexity as of a suffering

child." Perhaps posterity will compensate for public neglect and allow him some fame as "the painter, with a cold and mordant accuracy, of certain phases of city life."

**698** Meyerfeld, Max. "Englischer Bücher" (English Books), DAS LITTERARISCHE ECHO, VII (1 Jan 1905), 475.

*Veranilda* is a mild disappointment. It is faithful to the historical background, but the whole is colorless, lacking the personal touch except in the chapters dealing with Basil's crisis on Monte Cassino and reminiscent of the motif of resignation in *The Private Papers of Henry Ryecroft*. [In German.]

**699** Monkhouse, Allan. "George Gissing," MANCHESTER QUARTERLY, April 1905, pp. 106–23.

Although G's most memorable books lack the form and imagination present in the work of his greatest contemporaries, novels like *New Grub Street* and *The Nether World* expressed fortitude in poverty and privation with such force as to make them historically significant. G's record of his own era stressed the conditions of the unclassed, the intellectually isolated figure, constantly struggling to survive. No artificer, G "lives intensely in his books." His own personal suffering provided the material for his novels. The "squalid and brutal surroundings" are magnificently translated in *Nether World*. Even people whose lives appear promising are destroyed by "arbitrary and disastrous antipathies" that separate them. Clara Hewett and Sidney Kirkwood are denied happiness; our interest is in the moral quality of their struggle. Kirkwood's martyrdom reconciles us to this world. *In the Year of Jubilee* pictures the "most unlovely household in literature" with bitter irony. G's motive is not sociological interest. Still, he engages us with man's struggle to escape the base, the sensual "through self-betrayal or pressure of circumstance." Godwin Peak of *Born in Exile* is blocked by intellectual honesty from accepting Christianity, but he surrenders his integrity in the frustrated hope of securing a happy marriage. *Our Friend the Charlatan* attempts real comedy but becomes only clever. Allowed a moment of tranquillity, G turned out his most literary book, *The Private Papers of Henry Ryecroft,* but it unfortunately lacks the "zest for life" that it defines as the goal of art. *The Town Traveller,* "a masterp'ece of genial humour," suggests that G was turning in a new direction; Gammon is his most successful creation. *Veranilda* might be called G's ROMOLA; however, G's great historical novels are *Grub Street* and *Jubilee*. Like Ryecroft, G was unable to reconcile his own ideas with those of London's middle class, so that his novels are not essentially political in motivation. He belonged to an earlier generation of novelists, though he was able to sympathize with those contemporaries who suffered with no hope of salvation. He captured certain modes of feeling—vulgar marriages, the conflicts of ideals and traditions—with exceptional clarity. He often wrote of failure and compromise, but his writings are neither failures nor compromises; they are "our enduring possession."

**700** "Mr. Gissing's Last Book," MORNING POST (Lond), 23 June 1905, p. 9.

*Will Warburton* is the work of a "sturdy and an honest craftsman." G never sought popularity, preferring to abide by his "austere and unalterable tenets" whereby he presented the "material which lay nearest to him." His novels, however, "suggest that he never liked the material in which he worked—that the people and the circumstances about him oppressed his soul with pity and horror." It is clear that the real G appears in *The Private Papers of Henry Ryecroft*. [An appreciative judgment of G's literary values.]

**701** "Mr. Gissing's Last Novel," T. P.'s WEEKLY, VI (7 July 1905), 17.

*Will Warburton* "shows us that a gentleman may remain a gentleman even with the handicap of a grocer's apron." Warburton himself is "the lonely and fastidious dreamer, swamped by the energetic mediocrity of the modern hurly-burly." When the heroine wins Norbert Franks, the artist, she in fact picks "the real grocer, the eternal épicier, the rich, triumphant enemy of art."

**702** "New Books: The Aftermath," EVENING STANDARD AND ST. JAMES'S GAZETTE, 23 June 1905, p. 13.

*Will Warburton* leaves a more popular impression of G than his other posthumously published novel, *Veranilda*. An entertaining novel, without the unrelieved melancholy that distinguished G's characteristic mood, *Warburton* might have been the first of several humorous stories if death had not ended G's career. [Rather long outline of the story.]

**703** "New Editions," LITERARY WORLD (Lond), LXXI (15 June 1905), 214.

*By the Ionian Sea* gives us G the idealist and dreamer, enjoying the enchantment of Italy. He is far removed from the British "nether world" that so troubled him.

**704** "New Novels," ATHENAEUM, No. 4054 (8 July 1905), 41.

In *Will Warburton,* pessimism has given way to the amiable and friendly; the style remains clear and efficient. The book shows "a vast difference in treatment and spirit" when compared to *New Grub Street* and *Demos*. *Warburton* is a realistic romance, genial, friendly, eased by lighter effects.

It shows both humor and irony. It is in some respects G's best work; it is a balanced narrative peopled with real characters, "firmly endued with flesh and blood, not painted shadows."

**705** "A Notable Book of the Week: Gissing's Last Novel," PALL MALL GAZETTE, 8 July 1905, p. 4.

*Will Warburton,* G's "last novel," marks a "progress in temperament— of elevation to a broader and juster view of the balance between human happiness and misery." G's novels "failed to gain in popularity, in spite of their sensitive observation and brilliant technique," because he was unable to recognize that the poor find "satisfaction with modest rewards of effort, with the daily conquest over want and toil, with the sweetness of family affection, and with the exhilaration of sacrifice." But G was too detached to realize their true feelings. *Warburton* brings a "distinctly mellower tone of feeling." The hero survives a blow of bad luck; he opens a grocery store and faces reality to "become a stronger man and one with a more assumed basis of happiness." G's realism fails him in suggesting that Warburton should prosper in an occupation that he detested. Had G survived to write more novels, he would undoubtedly have presented less dismal pictures, "grasping the human problem in its true relations."

**706** "Notices of Books," BOOKSELLER, DLXXII (6 July 1905), 576.

*Will Warburton* again depicts the dull, gray side of life, G's staple theme. Perhaps the book belongs among the best by G because the sarcasm is so subtle that most readers will miss it. Will Warburton, a wholesale sugar merchant, is reduced to becoming a grocer. But the partner who had defrauded him, Norbert Franks, abandons his ideals and prospers as a fashionable painter of ladies' portraits.

**707** "Notices of Books," PUBLISHERS' CIRCULAR, LXXXIII (9 Dec 1905), 669.

*Will Warburton* leaves the usual realistic pessimism that we expect from G. The brighter novel is pleasing, a positive advance over his previous novels.

**708** "Novels," SATURDAY REVIEW (Lond), C (19 Aug 1905), 251.

*Will Warburton* is "mellower, more hopeful, more amiable in tone and conception" than G's earlier works. "Strength and sincerity characterised all he did." While *Warburton* does not rank with *The Nether World* and *Demos,* it "shows no failure in power." The materials of the novel are commonplace materials and people, but his "art lies in the elements of distraction with which he endows them."

**709** "Novels," SPECTATOR, No. 4018 (1 July 1905), 19–20.
*Will Warburton*'s characters grew during "the brief Indian summer of contentment" that G enjoyed at the close of his life. Engaging and friendly, they are "so unlike G's usual creations." Even the strugglers of *Warburton* are more hopeful and buoyant than the depressing figures of G's earlier novels. It is pleasant to think that G's own circumstances led him to be more amiable at the end of his career.

**710** "Novels and Stories," GLASGOW HERALD, 5 July 1905, p. 10.
*Will Warburton* examines the circumstances of a young man when misfortune reduces him to a lower plane than that of his birth. In the experience Warburton discovers his true self. G takes great care in exposing Warburton's motivation and "the elementary forces that sharply separate between social assumption and a stern sense of duty." *Warburton* is a "work of genuine insight and power."

**711** "Our Bookshelf," GRAPHIC, LXXII (1 July 1905), 806.
*Will Warburton* again convinces us that G was at his best among the middle and lower classes, rather than among the characters of *Veranilda*. The title figure loses a fortune through no fault of his own; reduced to becoming a grocer, he reaps "in peace of mind the reward of his courage." The characters are skillfully sketched.

**712** "Portrait," CRITIC (NY), XLVI (March 1905), 208.
Dutton is to publish the American edition of *Veranilda*. It is just as well that no one else has tried to provide an ending for the novel.

**713** "Recent Literature," DAILY TELEGRAPH (Lond), 5 July
1905, p. 12.
*Will Warburton* is not up to the level of G's earlier books. "A tolerably simple story," *Warburton* is not striking or original; it contains too little soul. [Brief narrative summary.]

**714** "The Review's Bookshop," REVIEW OF REVIEWS, XXXII
(Aug 1905), 208.
In *Will Warburton* G is again "occupied with the analysis of the sordid pettiness of English middle-class life." It tells of a man who loses his fortune and has to become a grocer.

**715** Rice, Wallace. "Wanderers in Many Lands," DIAL, XXXVIII
(1 June 1905), 385.
*By the Ionian Sea* illustrates the fact that novelists can write fine travel essays. G shows a real love for antiquity. Neither illness nor bad food dissuades G. [Some quotations.]

**716** [Stillman, Marie S.]. *"By the Ionian Sea,"* NATION (NY), LXXX (8 June 1905), 464–65.

A pattern is evident in G's travel account: the glory of the South, the hospitality of the Italians, the character of small villages. *By the Ionian Sea* makes delightful reading; it provides convincing evidence of the poverty of Calabria. [Lengthy quotations; wordy.]

**717** [Thomas, Edward]. "Fiction," ACADEMY, LXIX (8 July 1905), 710.

*Will Warburton* shows tenderness in love, even scorn; no melodrama. "There is consistent and most patient creation of characters moving . . . in studied surroundings." But the characters became, at best, "a good likeness." [Narrative summary; attribution by Pierre Coustillas.]

**718** [*Will Warburton*], MORNING LEADER, 23 June 1905, p. 3.

*Will Warburton* makes one wonder how G himself could have thought that *Veranilda* "represented his true bent and his highest achievement." For *Warburton,* also written shortly before his death, "is more mature, more generous, more human than anything else Gissing wrote." *Warburton* shows G "as a great literary artist, master of his medium, but never playing tricks for the sake of effect." This book makes us realize "the abiding loss English literature has sustained" in G's death.

# 1906

**719** [Ainslie, Noel]. "Recollections of George Gissing," GENTLEMAN'S MAGAZINE, CCC (Feb 1906), 11–18; rptd in LIVING AGE, CCXLIX (28 April 1906), 238–42.

An acquaintance recalls a conversation with G about an experience in Troy, N. Y. The use of episodes did not serve G's style of story.

**720** [Ainslie, Noel]. "Review," GENTLEMAN'S MAGAZINE, CCC (June 1906), 527–28.

In *The House of Cobwebs,* G's power is less than it had been in his earlier work. G knew those poor who will never improve. Seccombe's introductory essay is sympathetic and readable. [Not significant.]

**721** Barry, William. "George Gissing: In Memoriam," BOOKMAN (Lond), XXX (July 1906), 141.

In *The House of Cobwebs* are the quiet half-tones discovered by a solitary observer. Why did Seccombe not attend more to G's religious beliefs?

**722** Chesterton, G.K. CHARLES DICKENS (Lond: Methuen, 1906;

NY: Dodd, Mead, 1906); rptd as CHARLES DICKENS: THE LAST OF THE GREAT MEN (NY: Reader's Club, 1942), pp. 5ff., 229, 253–54, 276–77.

The soundest of Dickens's critics, G failed to realize that his own novels pictured a world infinitely more hard and cruel than his predecessor's. G's novels possess none of Dickens's hope. While G complained that the workers in Dickens's novels were never highly intellectual, he did not observe that Dickens "seldom made any character what we call intellectual." G was sure that prisons were full of only dead souls, but Dickens found them full of living souls.

723 "Comment on Current Books," OUTLOOK (NY), LXXXIV (1 Sept 1906), 44.

The House of Cobwebs is more valuable for Thomas Seccombe's introductory survey than for the stories by G in the collection itself. G's tales "are hardly entertaining enough" to hold the reader's interest.

724 "Current Literature," DAILY TELEGRAPH (Lond), 18 May 1906, p. 14.

The House of Cobwebs is a "most interesting and remarkable volume of short stories," accompanied by an "admirable appreciation" by Thomas Seccombe. G's stories contain an element that reminds us of Charles Lamb; they are "beautiful stories, told with consummate art," told in "a way that Lamb might have liked to have written" them. There is something here of Ryecroft's personality, as well as something of the technique of Henry James.

725 Davray, Henry-D. "Lettres Anglaises" (English Letters), MERCURE DE FRANCE, LXII (15 July 1906), 295–97.

The stories in The House of Cobwebs are realistic slices of life. G is closer to his fellow English novelists than to French realists, but he does not obey the dictates of the non-conformist conscience. In his short stories he keeps close to the real, and often to the reality of his own life. "The Scrupulous Father" is a little masterpiece, and this volume will be counted among G's best. [In French.]

726 "Fiction," ACADEMY, LXX (19 May 1906), 479.

Stories in The House of Cobwebs make one wonder what manner of man would write of characters he so detests. How much of G's life do we need to read his tales? Reading "these often exquisite grey and mauve studies in semi-autobiography" may lead others to examine G's early novels, particularly Born in Exile, The Odd Women, and In the Year of Jubilee. Seccombe should expand his excellent introduction. [See Seccombe, Thomas. "The Works of George Gissing: An Introductory Survey," The

*House of Cobwebs* (Lond: Constable, 1906; NY: Dutton, 1906), pp. vii–liv.] [Outlines G's life.]

**727** "Fiction," SCOTSMAN, 17 May 1906, p. 2.

*The House of Cobwebs* contains "chips from the workshop of a writer of some distinction who died in his prime." Seccombe's introduction makes a strong case for a difficult position, to claim for G a place among the great masters of fiction; it also helps explain G's historical position and his attitude toward life. The tales are illuminative in a biographical sense and are typical of G's carefully wrought stories; they will not, however, significantly affect his reputation.

**728** Garnett, Edward. "Fiction," SPEAKER, XIV (26 May 1906), 190–91.

*The House of Cobwebs* is introduced by a sympathetic survey of G's fiction written by Thomas Seccombe. Will G's reputation finally be assessed for the truth of his observations on life or for his literary style as a detached novelist? Undoubtedly his present claim rests upon his singular achievement in portraying "the grayness, the sordid ugliness, the petty mean vulgarity of the life of the London crowd." Seccombe notes G's subjectivity but fails to stress the fact that G's style "is too lacking in distinction and beauty." If G fails it is because he fails "to fuse and harmonize the two men within him—the realist and the idealist." The "idealist has his fling in *Ryecroft*," the realist in *New Grub Street*. In *Cobwebs* G details the "spiritual imprisonment" of so many Englishmen whose restrictions, cautions, and reserve sterilize life. "The Scrupulous Father," "A Capitalist," "A Lodger in Maze Pond," and "A Charming Family" are perhaps the best pieces in his collection.

**729** "George Gissing," TIMES LITERARY SUPPLEMENT (Lond), 8 June 1906, pp. 208–9.

*The House of Cobwebs* is prefaced by a "careful and judicious essay" by Thomas Seccombe surveying G's struggle for existence, his failure to achieve recognition, and his prospects for a future reputation. During his lifetime, G failed to gain any enthusiasm from publishers and reviewers, nor will this posthumous collection of tales improve his name. G's characteristic writing at its best—"clear, restrained, modern, full of observation" but without "frills"—was sustained in nine or ten books like *Demos, Thyrza, The Nether World, New Grub Street,* and *The Whirlpool.* Such works were "filled in the half lights and shadows of a phase of life, psychologically obscure" but clear to G from his own contact. His ultimate disposition will be determined by his "grasp of the problem of the rising proletarian and the 'educated' degenerate of both sexes," combining details with his own criticism of life.

**730** Harrison, Austin. "George Gissing," NINETEENTH CENTURY, XL (Sept 1906), 453–63; rptd in LIVING AGE, CCLI (27 Oct 1906), 216–25.

G "made his own poverty; he could not be practical." He "gloried in the vanity of self-compassion." By nature, G was "an idealist, a dreamer, an impressionist, a scholar." [Biographical details; some inaccuracies.]

**731** [*The House of Cobwebs*], GLASGOW HERALD, 31 May 1906, p. 11.

*The House of Cobwebs* contains stories by "one of the greatest and, within his strictly defined limits, most perfect of English stylists." G's tales "bear the searing impress of those unhappy early struggles" of his youth, so that this collection holds "not a page which is not pure Gissing, and not a story but would have been utterly spoiled by another hand." G presents the downward career of "some picturesque dead-beat or under dog, some hapless round peg in a square hole." Using a "terse, mature, yet exquisitely unusual style," G has, by "hewing at the sodden dough of London proletarian existence with the chisel of a great craftsman, raised English fiction higher into the region of pure literature than any writer since Thackeray."

**732** [*The House of Cobwebs*], LITERARY WORLD (Lond), LXXIV (15 Sept 1906), 395.

*The House of Cobwebs* contains stories that "are good examples of Gissing's style." The collection is prefaced by Thomas Seccombe, who describes G's circumstances and accounts for some of his attitudes towards life.

**733** Ley, J.W.T. "Mr. G. K. Chesterton on Dickens," DICKENSIAN, II (Oct 1906), 267–69.

G's work on Dickens is superior to Chesterton's.

**734** "Literary Notes and Criticism," NEW YORK DAILY TRIBUNE, 4 Aug 1906, p. 5.

*The House of Cobwebs* has obvious autobiographical touches in the hardships of London existence. These stories, souvenirs of an interesting author, treat the squalid circumstances of life with some relief. For G finally did learn to smile. Seccombe's introduction perhaps takes G a little too seriously.

**735** "Literary Notes: The Work of George Gissing," ARGONAUT (San Francisco), LIX (25 Aug 1906), 28.

*The House of Cobwebs* is marked by G's "always scrupulous and artistic workmanship." G is known for "highly finished novels," particularly *New*

*Grub Street, Thyrza, The Nether World,* and *The Private Papers of Henry Ryecroft,* which won him "an admiring group of discriminating readers." His "passionate idolatry of Dickens" is especially noticeable in *Thyrza.*

**736** Matz, B.W. "When Found—," DICKENSIAN, II (Dec 1906), 323.
G misunderstood Dickens's political and social positions. [Brief.]

**737** M[onkhouse], A.N. "New Novels: Gissing's Short Stories," MANCHESTER GUARDIAN, 23 May 1906, p. 5.
*The House of Cobwebs* contains interesting stories corresponding in quality to *Will Warburton.* G's "own strong personality" speaks in several characters. G should be judged principally by *New Grub Street, The Nether World,* and *In the Year of Jubilee.* Seccombe's introduction [see Seccombe, Thomas. "The Works of George Gissing: An Introductory Survey," *The House of Cobwebs* (Lond: Constable, 1906; NY: Dutton, 1906), pp. vii–liv] is distinguished for both its moderation and its "cordially appreciative spirit."

**738** "Novels," SPECTATOR, XCVI (26 May 1906), 835–36.
Stories in *The House of Cobwebs* represent G at his best and sanest; there is less of the merciless cruelty present in his novels. His figures are chiefly small lodging-house keepers, petty tradesmen, impecunious authors, governesses—people rarely portrayed in fiction. "The solidarity of the unsuccessful is one of the most striking features of these sketches and studies." [Salutes Thomas Seccombe's "The Works of George Gissing: An Introductory Survey" (1906), while not sharing all its claims for G.]

**739** "Recent Fiction," NATION (NY), LXXXIII (20 Sept 1906), 246.
*The House of Cobwebs* is a remarkable survey of the narrow world of obscurity and penury; G's characters are invested with a curious dignity. Though impoverished, they stand in "damning contrast with the children of worldly success." G's work combines "the eager humanitarian curiosity that he learned from Dickens and the austere restraint of phrase and feeling imposed by his life-long classical studies." No writer is G's superior in tracing the hidden lives of London. He writes with "great purity and incisiveness."

**740** "The Review's Bookshop," REVIEW OF REVIEWS, XXXIII (June 1906), 651.
*The House of Cobwebs* contains "some of the best short stories I have read for months." G succeeds in drawing the "independent woman worker without making her hard or unattractive."

**741** Rice, M. Gordon Pryor. "Gissing's Last Stories," NEW YORK TIMES SATURDAY REVIEW OF BOOKS, 25 Aug 1906, p. 519.

*The House of Cobwebs* is a collection of delicately tender stories, spotting the "wincing of a refined nature under the yoke of poverty." Helped by Thomas Seccombe's introduction, our generation should come to know G's characters "as those of Dickens were known by the preceding generation." G came to know poverty as the greatest secluder. Apart from G's novels, these stories have an interest of their own. "Dickens was the novelist of the recognized poor," and G of the poorer poor.

**742** Rzewuski, Stanislas. "La vie littéraire à l'étranger: Georges Gissing" (The Literary Life Abroad: George Gissing), FIGARO (Supplément Littéraire), 13 Oct 1906, p. 4.

It is high time for the French to get acquainted with G's work because he is one of the most perfect artists and is most likely to please them. His love for France has been ill-requited. Though he did not possess the genius of Tolstoy, Dickens, Poe, Fielding, or George Eliot, his work does not betray the defects of construction to be found in their works. Nor are his novels marred by pedantry, a preaching tone, or tedious digressions. He is the best storyteller since Maupassant, and his best novels should be translated into French. [This highly eulogistic article seems to be based on only two translations: *La rue des meurt-de-faim* (*New Grub Street*) and *La Rançon d'Eve* (*Eve's Ransom.*)] [In French.]

**743** Scott-James, R. A. [*The House of Cobwebs*], DAILY NEWS (Lond), 17 May 1906, p. 4.

*The House of Cobwebs* is a collection of "profound, searching, movingly realistic pictures of mean and petty life," stories infused by G's genius for suggestion. While everyone hears about the envy of those who aspire to the social level of those directly above themselves, G reverses this to examine the people "who have been driven down to the class below them" where "the only idealising element left is the desire for the insignificant things which they have ceased to possess." Most of *Cobwebs* treats of "lost caste and cherished respectability." The collection returns to the dismal scenes of G's own life and thought; he sounds the "note of tragi-comedy rather than that of unalterable gloom."

**744** Seccombe, Thomas. "The Works of George Gissing: An Introductory Survey," *The House of Cobwebs* (Lond: Constable, 1906; NY: Dutton, 1906), pp. vii–liv.

From the "cumbrous and grandiose paraphernalia" of the Victorian novel, G emerged writing "highly finished novels" in a scholarly style. His early writings were "rather fastidious." If his books have not been popular, it is because his novels show a "failure in humour, a remoteness from actual life, . . . a shortcoming in emotional power." Knowing little of the world, he wrote himself into his novels (e.g. Osmond Waymark in *The Unclassed* and Bernard Kingcote in *Isabel Clarendon*). His best novels, *New Grub Street, Born in Exile,* and *The Nether World* date from 1889–1892; all are excessively somber. His next works show how well his power of satire had grown; he applied it most successfully in a few problem novels, notably *The Odd Women.* His pictures of the London scene are detached, remorseless, and photographic. Even now his characters from *Grub Street* people the British Museum. [Accurate and sensitive, Seccombe's essay is the most perceptive of the early biographical-critical studies of G.]

**745** "Short Notices," BOOKSELLER, DLXXXIV (10 July 1906), 546–47.
*The House of Cobwebs* contains more carefully written, sad, occasionally humorous tales by G. The introduction by Thomas Seccombe constitutes an appreciation rather than a biography of G.

**746** "Short Stories," ATHENAEUM, No. 4106 (7 July 1906), 10.
*The House of Cobwebs* contains an admirable introduction by Thomas Seccombe. The tales have little artistic sense; rather they are studies of atmosphere. No one can doubt that G's "sincerity, his sympathetic observation, his extreme patience and relevancy have made for him a place in modern fiction." Had he lived, G's canvas would have been broader. His novels lack the "dramatic."

**747** "Some Stories by George Gissing," GUARDIAN (Lond), LXI (25 July 1906), 1253.
*The House of Cobwebs* has several stories that are perhaps less appealing than Thomas Seccombe's introduction. The shadow of G lingers in the shadows of gray places, writing novels in garrets and cellars. G's novels had no romance or chivalry and hardly appealed to potential buyers seeking relief from their own depression. The same can be said for these short stories.

**748** Waugh, Arthur. [*The House of Cobwebs*], DAILY CHRONICLE, 26 May 1906, p. 3.
*The House of Cobwebs* is "a thoroughly characteristic volume, full of the ripest and most impressive" of G's work. Almost entirely lacking in imagination, G relied on what he had seen or felt; these stories contain further pictures of life, "almost all veiled in his inevitable atmosphere of drab." Seccombe's introduction "cheers one up in the cause of one's own generation" so excellent is his sympathetic study. The collection helps prove A. H. Bullen's belief that G's "genius was seen to peculiar advantage in the short story."

# 1907

**749** [More, Paul Elmer]. "George Gissing," NATION (NY), LXXXIV (17 Jan 1907), 53–55; rptd in SHELBOURNE ESSAYS (NY: Putnam, 1908; Fifth Series), pp. 45–65.

G's literary career consists of three phases, the first culminating in *Born in Exile*. During the second period (1892–1899), G wrote books of undeniable power, comparable in some ways to JUDE THE OBSCURE. The best known books of this phase are *In the Year of Jubilee* and *The Whirlpool*. G's most characteristic writing represents the poor of London as he told the Epic of Poverty. Only G could have written *New Grub Street,* especially about Reardon and the others who dwell in the valley of books. Defeat and consternation form the chorus of *The Nether World,* as G makes art the "mouthpiece of misery." G could never have understood Dickens's zest for life, because G could not rise above his own misery. Yet his characters have a will to survive; they are victims of circumstance who are conscious all the time of their moral responsibility. In G's late novels, his characters suffer from new miseries, from tedium and vanity. Throughout G's books we are aware of continental and classical influences. Towards the end of his life, a gentle and amusing irony replaces his earlier satire. *The Private Papers of Henry Ryecroft* has no companion in the volumes of English literature; if G saw any hope, it was in the superiority of the aristocracy over the spread of science and "half-education." [Important and sympathetic reading of G's social and artistic values. The occasion for the article was Seccombe's edition (1906) of *The House of Cobwebs.*]

# 1908

**750** Schaefer, August. GEORGE GISSING: SEIN LEBEN UND SEINE ROMANE (George Gissing: His Life and His Novels) (Marburg: Pvtly ptd, 1908); University of Marburg dissertation.

In his private life, G was a solitary novelist greatly influenced by the classics and by Dickens. *Demos, Thyrza,* and *The Nether World* are all excellent psychological studies of the proletariat, but they are burdened by excessive detail and subplots. *The Whirlpool,* an impressive portrait of society, glorifies the simple life. *The Private Papers of Henry Ryecroft* carries great personal appeal and presents the key themes to all of G's writings. G's early novels cried out against his own fate and moaned the writer's distance from the beauty of antiquity. *Demos, The Unclassed,* and *Thyrza* exhibited his bitterness, and the gloom of these early novels persisted throughout *New Grub Street* and *The Odd Women*. By 1898, G reached a state of voluntary resignation and self-control. [Marburg Inaugural Thesis; old-fashioned; of little value.] [In German.]

## 1909

**751** Hirata, Kiichi (Tokuboku). "George Gissing," SHIN-SHOSETSU, XIV (June 1909), 184–91; (Sept 1909), 177–83.
[First article serially in Japanese on G. The first part gives a brief account of G's life, the second of his work, mainly *The Private Papers of Henry Ryecroft*.] [In Japanese.]

**752** M[artin], F. H. *"Born in Exile*: A Social Difficulty Considered," T. P.'s WEEKLY, XIV (23 July 1909), 113–14.
*Born in Exile,* while not a new book, studies "the conflict arising from the contradiction of the pride of intellect and genius with mean circumstances." From the start, Godwin Peak is noted by "his hawk-like scrutiny of aristocratic dames," by his "humble make and origin." He is intensely proud and self-conscious, qualities that are to deepen his eventual exile. All the professions have such figures: men educated for positions by distinguished academic work, but men also "irrevocably barred because of the social or personal" circumstances of their origin. Natural gifts, their enormous pluck notwithstanding, forever mark both their manners and appearance. Ought they never seek to become "gentlemen"? Perhaps "the students of Ruskin College are most wise" in remaining among their own so as "to leaven it with their own culture and education." Whatever his decision, the Godwin Peaks are shunned forever: "He dies as he is born, like another hero of fiction, Mr. Hardy's Jude, 'in exile, poor fellow.' "

**753** Matz, B. W. "George Meredith as Publisher's Reader," FORTNIGHTLY REVIEW, LXXXVI (Aug 1909), 282–98.
[Mentions Meredith's handling of G's *The Unclassed* for Chapman & Hall.]

## 1910

**754** Chapman, Edward Mortimer. ENGLISH LITERATURE IN ACCOUNT WITH RELIGION, 1800–1900 (Boston: Houghton Mifflin, 1910), pp. 526–32.
*The Nether World* best represents G's work. G was a master of tragedy, not a spokesman of despair.

## 1911

**755** Chesterton, G. K. APPRECIATIONS AND CRITICISMS OF THE WORKS OF CHARLES DICKENS (Lond: Dent, 1911), pp. xix, 182. Because G and his contemporaries thought Dickens "all the worse for the optimism" of Micawber, they naturally praised him for the pessimism of LITTLE DORRIT, which G came close to calling Dickens's best novel.

**756** Douglas, Norman. SIREN LAND (Lond: Dent, 1911), p. 238.
G surely relished the leisure of Neapolitan Italy and savored its wine. *By the Ionian Sea* provides us with G's mood of introspection; *The Private Papers of Henry Ryecroft* shows the limitation of his outlook. [Index erroneously lists Algernon Gissing as the author of these titles.]

**757** Harrison, Frederic. AUTOBIOGRAPHIC MEMOIRS (Lond: Macmillan, 1911), II, 116.
My introduction to *Veranilda* gives "all that need be said of the short sad life" of G. [See Harrison, Frederic. "Preface," *Veranilda* (Lond: Constable, 1904), pp. v-vii.]

## 1912

**758** Fehr, Bernhard. STREIFZÜGE DURCH DIE NEUESTE ENGLISCHE LITERATUR (Patterns in Modern English Literature) (Strassburg: Teubner, 1912), pp. 98, 114–20, 170.
G's works move from comprehensive realism to a kind of philosophical impressionism that toys with the ideas of Nietzsche, Spencer, Mill, and especially Meredith (the emancipation of women). [In German.]

**759** Kennedy, J. M. "George Gissing," ENGLISH LITERATURE: 1880 1905 (Lond: Stephen Swift, 1912), pp. 253–78.
G's main theme is "the life of a man of culture spent amid uncongenial surroundings." G's best work deals with "men and women of the lower middle class, and when he left these people, as in *Our Friend the Charlatan,* he failed." Rather than yield to friends or publishers and perhaps thereby please the public, G "deliberately endured poverty at its worst."

**760** Pugh, Edwin. "An Inverted Idealist," BOOKMAN (Lond), XLIII (Dec 1912), 173.
There was always a "look of ineffable tragedy" about G. Morley Roberts called him an "inverted idealist," because he always looked back. G him-

self scorned the title *Realist;* no realist can be an idealist. Swinnerton's GEORGE GISSING: A CRITICAL STUDY (1912) provides "quantities of sympathy and insight and imagination" that provide "food for thought." Swinnerton's concluding judgment of G is particularly sound. But the public could never appreciate G, even as he hated the average reader.

**761** Roberts, Morley. THE PRIVATE LIFE OF HENRY MAITLAND (Lond: Nash; NY: Doran, 1912); rptd with an introduction by Morchard Bishop (Lond: Richards, 1958).

Although this book is meant to provide only an impression of Maitland and not be an ordinary biography, some circumstances of his life must be set forth. Discovered in a theft at school, Maitland left in disgrace for America, where he supported himself, in part, by writing stories for the Chicago TRIBUNE. Later, as a novelist in England, Maitland attacked conventional notions of morality. He successfully portrayed the impoverished worker and the single woman. He never believed his novels would accomplish any good; he possessed no hope. Unlike Wells, Maitland never enjoyed metaphysical thinking or speculation. He lived in the past like a "non-combative Tory." Of all his books, *By the Ionian Sea* is the purest representation of himself. *The Private Papers of Henry Ryecroft* falsifies, in the literary sense. The novels of Maitland's middle period are all "pot-boilers," as he sought to gain a public; they also kept him in exile. His strength consisted in "deep and accurate knowledge and keen observation." He chose figures who were most repulsive to him. [MAITLAND pretends to be a far more sympathetic treatment of G than it proves to be; Roberts shows both some hostility and some envy. Nor does the guise of fiction relieve Roberts of his guilt as a biographer. As criticism, MAITLAND is more interesting for what it reveals about Roberts's own books than of G's.] [Reviews: "The Candid Friend," NATION (Lond), XII (16 Nov 1912), 323–24. (Was MAITLAND occasioned by a simple love of truth or "the writer's own itch for literary fame"? Roberts finally tells us what everyone has been curious about concerning G's youthful indiscretions. Roberts's patronizing tone in representing G's "wounded and often sickly spirit" is distressing.); Frank Swinnerton, "Roberts' THE PRIVATE LIFE OF HENRY MAITLAND," BOOKMAN (Lond), XLIII (Dec 1912), 173–74. (Only Roberts could have written this biography; G appears "with the warmth of life, a lovable and engaging figure."); ENGLISH REVIEW, XIII (Dec 1912), 162. (Roberts's book is excessively bitter. Why does G's body have to be thus snatched from the grave?); "Body-Snatching in Fiction," LITERARY DIGEST, XLV (21 Dec 1912), 1180–81; E. F. E., BOSTON TRANSCRIPT, 11 Jan 1913, p. 8; "Was George Gissing a Distinguished Failure?" CURRENT OPINION, LIV (Feb 1913), 143–44; SPECTATOR, CX (1 Feb 1913), 199; "George Gissing," INDEPENDENT, LXXIV

(20 March 1913), 655; LITERARY DIGEST, LXXVI (17 May 1913), 1136–37; Virginia Woolf, "An Impression of George Gissing," NEW STATESMAN, 30 June 1923, pp. 371–72. (Author's identity established by B. J. Kirkpatrick's bibliography of Virginia Woolf's works.).]

762 Seccombe, Thomas. "George Gissing," DICTIONARY OF NA-TIONAL BIOGRAPHY (Second Supplement) (Lond: Smith, Elder, 1912), II, 116.

G gradually lost his "extraordinary power of intensifying the misery of the world's finer spirits who are thrown among 'the herd that fed and bred.' " His sad outlook prevented his becoming popular while he lived; now there are signs that more people are appreciating his work. [Important biography.]

763 Swinnerton, Frank. GEORGE GISSING: A CRITICAL STUDY (Lond: Martin Secker, 1912; rptd, NY: Kennerley, 1923).

Among G's early novels, *Thyrza* is the best. His fiction reaches a high point in the early 1890s with *New Grub Street, Born in Exile,* and *The Odd Women.* Even then, G was still laboring to escape the Victorian traditions; his fiction lost spontaneity as he sought maturity. G's men are given to excessive thought: as characters they are preoccupied with self-analysis, and they are entirely the product of G's mind. But the women stand forth both in variety and credibility; they must escape the domination of overbearing dogma. G's criticism of Dickens is the best yet produced; it is admirable and creditable. *The Private Papers of Henry Rye-croft* will appeal only to bookish men who lack a zest for life, because it expresses G's own personality so perfectly. G's fame as a writer rests securely on *Thyrza, Grub Street, Women, Exile,* and *Eve's Ransom.* His strength lies "primarily in the judgment he displayed in his analyses of situation, in his portraits of women, and in his resolute defiance of low standards of work." [The first competent book-length study of G; a most able treatment of G's characters and craft. It calls attention to Swinnerton's own theories of fiction. Unsigned reviews appear in the ENGLISH REVIEW, XII (Nov 1912), 660 61 (probably written by Austin Harrison, editor of the periodical between 1910 and 1923 and G's former pupil); SPECTA-TOR, CIX (23 Nov 1912), 861; and SATURDAY REVIEW, CXV (29 March 1913), 402.]

764 Wells, H.G. "The Truth about George Gissing," RHYTHM (Literary Supplement), Dec 1912, pp. i–iii.

Morley Roberts's unfavorable judgment of *Veranilda* expressed in THE PRIVATE LIFE OF HENRY MAITLAND (1912) is unwarranted. G was "a humourless prig, a snob, most shamefully timid, addicted to indulgence in 'scorn,' . . . yet he was most attractive."

**765** [Woolf, Virginia]. "The Novels of George Gissing," TIMES LITERARY SUPPLEMENT (Lond), 11 Jan 1912, pp. 9–10; rptd in LITTELL'S LIVING AGE, CCLXXII (March 1912), 675–80.

A few years before he died, G wrote Edward Clodd that "there is a curious blending of respect and contempt in the publishers' mind towards me," and it is the word *respect* that now represents the reading public's attitude. It is rather a minority that respects him, but perhaps an increasing minority. G, a "born writer," had one great theme: "the life of a man of fine character and intelligence who is absolutely penniless and is therefore the sport of all that is most sordid and brutal in modern life." That he is penniless is important, because G knows that poverty inevitably degrades; one falls into the nether world where there is "no room for the soul." Others have written ably about the poor, like Mrs. Gaskell and Dickens, but "the impressive part about Gissing is that knowing them as he did he makes no secret of the fact that he hated them." The hate made G bitter and harsh, though "the measure of his bitterness is the measure of his love of good." The people G loved are allowed pleasures of reading, of companionship, of the glow of redhot coals. Above all, "his men and women think," and that in itself makes them unpopular. The advantage of using people who think "is that you can describe other relationships besides the great one between the lover and the beloved." His best work describes miseries and sufferings; his world is a struggling world, and once he quit that world and showed people at ease "he lost his grip." His world, a small world, remained absolutely his own; the misery he portrays is truth. In making us see that misery, that truth, G is convincing; he gives the essential qualities of art, life, and completeness. Because they have these qualities, G's books will not perish.

# 1913

**766** Adcock, A. St. John. THE BOOKLOVER'S LONDON (Lond: Methuen, 1913), pp. 44, 63, 80, 92–97, 98, 121, 122–24, 167, 176, 189, 191–210, 211, 235, 236, 247–48, 251–52, 266–67, 269, 284, 288, 289, 292, 299–308.

One can still identify the buildings and streets named by G, particularly the Lambeth of *Thyrza,* Liverpool Street Station and the haunts of Sidney Kirkwood and the Snowdens, Holburn Viaduct Station and Clerkenwell Green of Clem Peckover and Bob Hewett of *The Nether World,* and the British Museum region of *New Grub Street.* Other places named in *The Unclassed* and *In the Year of Jubilee* can also readily be found.

**767** Eagle, Solomon [pseud of J. C. Squire]. "Books in General," NEW STATESMAN, I (14 June 1913), 310.
Rather than contribute money to endow a "Gissing Memorial Scholarship at Owens College," Manchester, admirers of the late novelist think it would be more appropriate to help G's aged mother, or his sisters, or his son, all of whom need financial help. "It is certainly ludicrous" to collect money "to provide for the education of total strangers at Owens College rather than to assist the education" of G's own son. [An exchange followed with a representative for the scholarship committee that appeared in the same literary column for 28 June 1913.]

**768** Eagle, Solomon [pseud of J. C. Squire]. "Books in General," NEW STATESMAN, I (28 June 1913), 375.
In response to my remarks in this column (14 June 1913, p. 310), Percy Withers, Secretary of the "Gissing Memorial Scholarship" fund, Owens College, has objected by insisting that the collection has the "warm approval" of G's family. Withers claims that my remarks have molested the privacy of G's survivors. But how could any members of the family object? It remains a fact that G's best friends know that neither G nor his heirs owed the institution anything; the greater need for help rests with the family.

**769** Grünbaum, David. "George Gissing," NORDISK TIDSKRIFT (Stockholm), LXXX (1913), 568–86.
[A study of G's life and works. The biographical sketch is based on Morley Roberts's THE PRIVATE LIFE OF HENRY MAITLAND.] [In Swedish.]

**770** Middleton, George. "New Lights on Gissing," BOOKMAN (NY), XXXVI (Feb 1913), 655–57.
One almost suspects Roberts of sensationalism "for having thus written Gissing's biography." [Middleton recalls G while reviewing the recent books about G by Roberts and Swinnerton.]

**771** [More, Paul Elmer]. "George Gissing," NATION (NY), XCVI (13 March 1913), 256–57.
"To the present writer Gissing seems likely in the end to take a place by the side of Hardy and above Meredith, but never by the side of Fielding or Thackeray or Dickens." G does not deserve to join the first rank of novelists "for the good and simple reason that his genius was not quite of the highest order." That he enjoyed Roman history ought not affect our judgment of his fiction. [Reviews the Swinnerton (1912) and Roberts (1912) books on G.]

**772** Nicoll, Sir William Robertson. "George Gissing," A BOOK-

MAN'S LETTERS (Lond: Hodder & Stoughton, 1913), pp. 288–96. [A biographical sketch with some comments on the Roberts–Gissing friendship.]

**773** Schüddekopf, A. W. "Englischer Brief" (Letter from England), DAS LITTERARISCHE ECHO, XVI (15 April 1913), 1006. Owens College, the school G attended, is collecting a memorial fund for a scholarship to be named after the novelist. [In German.]

**774** [Scott-James, R.A.]. "A Frustrate Talent," NATION (Lond), XII (18 Jan 1913), 674–75.

"If Gissing had any supreme claim upon our attention, it is just this, that with unfaltering devotion he was true to his own vision of life, however perverted that vision may be; it is of value only insofar as it gives us a picture of lower and middle class life, as seen through the eyes of an 'inverted idealist.'" [Occasioned by Swinnerton's book.]

**775** Wells, H. G. "Truth About George Gissing," NEW YORK TIMES BOOK REVIEW, 12 Jan 1913, pp. 9–10.

Swinnerton's book (GEORGE GISSING: A CRITICAL STUDY [1912]) is a model for such monographs; it is a distinguished and admirable book. G was one of the most perplexing people one could meet. Morley Roberts's THE PRIVATE LIFE OF HENRY MAITLAND (1912) is "downright bad, careless in statement, squalid in effect, poor as criticism, weakly planned and entirely without any literary distinction." Though Roberts would have us believe that G was a repellent person, he was actually "most attractive. He had devoted friends upon whom he could rely." Roberts failed to appreciate G's books, especially *Veranilda,* because his own values were in error. The well-made novel has bored us to death with "machine-chopped fare." [Wells obviously carries his own disagreement with Roberts concerning theories of fiction into his appraisal of this fictional biography; he accuses Roberts of shaping the end of MAITLAND to satisfy his "craving for a happy ending."]

# 1914

**776** B., W. R. "Foreword," BOOKS AND THE QUIET LIFE: BEING SOME PAGES FROM *The Private Papers of Henry Ryecroft* BY GEORGE GISSING CHOSEN BY W R B (Portland, Maine: Thomas B. Mosher, 1914), pp. v–vii.

The "choicest and most characteristic specimens" of spiritual autobiography have been written by the French. But G's *The Private Papers of Henry Ryecroft* deserves a place with "the journals of Amiel and de Guérin and the 'Obermann' of de Sénancour." [Possibly by William R. Benet.]

**777** "Gissing the Extraordinary," BOOKMAN (NY), XXXIX (March 1914), 16–19.
[Drawn from Nicoll's A BOOKMAN'S LETTERS (1913); outlines G's life. Not significant.]

**778** "The Trail of George Gissing," BOOKMAN (NY), XXXVIII (Feb 1914), 590–91.
[Ink sketches of Lambeth with notes about G's book which are set there; prompted by Adcock's THE BOOK LOVER'S LONDON (Lond: Methuen, 1913).]

---

# 1915

---

**779** Benson, A.C. "The Reader," BOOKMAN (Lond), XLVII (Jan 1915), 119.
A gentle and courteous man, G did his best work in *The Whirlpool* and *New Grub Street*. His characters affect one as real people, notably Alma Rolfe of *Whirlpool* and Mrs. Edmund Yule of *Grub Street*. The books retain their "harsh life unabated," touched as they are with "an essential dreariness."

**780** Burgin, G.B. "The Reader," BOOKMAN (Lond), XLVII (Jan 1915), 120.
G said that his work was ground out with "infinite pain and labour." The truth present in his novels will sustain them.

**781** Clodd, Edward. "The Reader," BOOKMAN (Lond), XLVII (Jan 1915), 118–19.
G deeply craved sympathy. The real G is best expressed in *By the Ionian Sea, The Private Papers of Henry Ryecroft,* and *Veranilda,* rather than in *Born in Exile* or *New Grub Street*. Meredith tried to persuade G not to write *Veranilda*.

**782** Douglas, Norman. "Memories of Gissing," OLD CALABRIA (NY: Dodd, 1915), pp. 296–302.
G's shade haunts the chambers and passages of Cotrone. Dr. Sculco, who treated G as a patient, is reticent about discussing the author's ailments. Other inhabitants of the town found their way into *By the Ionian Sea,* such as the "amicable guardian at the cemetery."

**783** Findlater, Jane H. "The Reader," BOOKMAN (Lond), XLVII (Jan 1915), 119.

G's "whole attitude to life is too abject, too cringing," for him to gain immortality. *The Odd Women* shows marvelous insight into the mind of a woman.

**784** Kernahan, Coulson. "The Reader," BOOKMAN (Lond), XLVII (Jan 1915), 120.

Even if one knew G only slightly, he had "the look of a man who felt great pain."

**785** Locke, W. J. "The Reader," BOOKMAN (Lond), XLVII (Jan 1915), 119.

*The Private Papers of Henry Ryecroft* compels my admiration.

**786** Marriott, Charles. "The Reader," BOOKMAN (Lond), XLVII (Jan 1915), 121.

*New Grub Street, Born in Exile,* and *The Whirlpool* are G's best books. Like all fine imaginative work, these books are "distinguishable by truth rather than by accuracy."

**787** "The Reader," BOOKMAN (Lond), XLVII (Jan 1915), 117–25.

["Some Personal Impressions and Opinions" about G by Edward Clodd, A. C. Benson, Coulson Kernahan, W. J. Locke, Jane H. Findlater, G. B. Burgin, Charles Marriott, Frank Swinnerton, and Constance Smedley are printed in addition to pictures of G and a letter to Morley Roberts written by G on 10 Feb 1895 concerning *In the Year of Jubilee.* This G number of the BOOKMAN was occasioned by Secker's reprinting Swinnerton's GEORGE GISSING: A CRITICAL STUDY (see 1912). A synopsis of the remarks of each of these contributors appears under the writer's name for this year.]

**788** Smedley, Constance. "The Reader," BOOKMAN (Lond), XLVII (Jan 1915), 122.

There is no denying G's fidelity to facts, yet his horizons were too narrow. As a realist, G's power lay in his recording the conditions of existence; great writers need more vision of judgment.

**789** Swinnerton, Frank. "The Reader," BOOKMAN (Lond), XLVII (Jan 1915), 122.

G's "uncompromising and pathetic sincerity" as a writer led him bravely to describe life as he saw it. Lacking detachment and humor, wanting a passionate imagination, G wrote novels that give us a "sense of unrelieved apprehensiveness without producing tenseness or intensity." We admire him for his "intellectual and artistic integrity."

**790** Walker, Hugh. THE ENGLISH ESSAY AND ESSAYIST (Lond: Dent, 1915), pp. 323–27.

Chiefly for *The Private Papers of Henry Ryecroft,* G has a reputation as an essayist. His fame is greater than that of any other recent essayist except Stevenson.

## 1916

**791** Anderson, Melville B. "Chat About George Gissing," DIAL, LXI (June 1916), 3–7.

[Anderson, in Florence, recalls G's *By the Ionian Sea*: general comments about G's fiction.] [Very informal.]

**792** Clodd, Edward. "George Gissing," MEMORIES (Lond: Chapman & Hall, 1916), pp. 165–95.

G's character is best represented by Waymark of *The Unclassed*. G's letters [several of which, addressed to Clodd, form the principal part of this chapter] show how much his head and heart craved sympathy. His acquaintances (e.g. James Payn as John Glass, or H. G. Wells as G. H. Rivers) are easily recognized and identified in Morley Roberts's THE PRIVATE LIFE OF HENRY MAITLAND (1912).

**793** Dibelius, Wilhelm. CHARLES DICKENS (Leipzig, Berlin: Teubner, 1916), p. 450.

Dickens did not found a literary school. G's radical realism is due to French and Norwegian influence. [In German.]

**794** Ellis, S. M. GEORGE MEREDITH (Lond: Grant Richards, 1916), pp. 210, 308.

As reader for Chapman and Hall, Meredith advised G in his revisions of *The Unclassed* and *Isabel Clarendon*.

**795** Goodspeed, Edgar J. "A Letter of Gissing," NATION (NY), CIII (17 Aug 1916), 154.

[Prints a letter from G concerning Italian regions described in *By the Ionian Sea*.]

## 1917

**796** E[dgett], E[dwin] F[rancis]. "Writers and Books," BOSTON EVENING TRANSCRIPT, 24 Jan 1917, p. 9.

The last chapter of THE CAMBRIDGE HISTORY OF ENGLISH LITERATURE, by W. T. Young, groups Meredith, Butler, and G together. Meredith's fame was established before the century had ended; Butler was nearly seventy when he died; G died early. However, G probably "accomplished as much for English literature as either of the other two." He is among the first English novelists "to probe deeply into the psychology of sex." Preoccupied with environment, G was little concerned with heredity. He wrote with "rare rhythmical grace and variety."

**797** Wells, H. G. "Introduction," NOCTURNE, by Frank Swinnerton (NY: Doran, 1917), p. xiii.
Swinnerton's early books were strongly influenced by the novels of G; "they have something of the same fatigued greyness of texture." But Swinnerton has nothing of G's "almost perverse gloom and despondency."

**798** Young, W. T. "George Gissing," CAMBRIDGE HISTORY OF ENGLISH LITERATURE (Lond: Cambridge UP; NY: Macmillan, 1917), XIII, pp. 505–14.
G's novels are saturated with detail; they are desolate and mirthless; dialogue is likely to be bookish. In style, G adds "to the worth of words by the care with which they are used, and his best writing has a rare rhythmical grace and variety." Historically, G's novels are transitional in that they are "sentimental, capacious, benevolently admonitory, plot-ridden"; they are Victorian. They are also modern because they picture a "slice of life" and analyze the inner world of thought and feeling.

# 1918

**799** Adcock, A. St. John. "The Book in London," BOSTON EVENING TRANSCRIPT, 1 June 1918, p. 7.
One of G's early publishers told me that G failed to gain a larger audience "largely through his own fault," because G's stories are too drab. But could G write happy stories and remain true to himself? The inferior artist can produce sensational yarns, but fine artists have no heart for mediocrity. G resembles Leonard Merrick, an author greatly admired by his fellow writers, "a novelist's novelist," but his tales are sad and wistful though not gloomy and despondent like G's.

**800** Follett, Helen T., and Wilson Follett. "George Gissing," SOME MODERN NOVELISTS (NY: Holt, 1918), pp. 50–74.
G was a novelist, not an artist; the reader is too conscious of his efforts, of

his craft, of his documentation. All his characters are climbers, eager to improve. The idealism of his fiction prevented his becoming popular during his life; now he is over-praised for the same idealism. G is an important figure in the history of the sociological novel in England. However, G presents no solutions to the problems he presents. His dull characters are offered no hope; poverty makes all his men "sickeningly alike." *The Whirlpool* is G's only success in portraying lives more prosperous than his own; color mixes with the usual black and white extremes in his best book. [Important survey; draws heavily upon James's critical essay on G.]

**801** Follett, Wilson. THE MODERN NOVEL (NY: Knopf, 1918), pp. 172–74.

[A concise statement of G's achievements largely drawn from SOME MODERN NOVELISTS (1918).]

**802** Horn, Wilhelm. "George Gissing über das dichterische Schaffen" (George Gissing on Poetic Creation), ARCHIV FUR DAS STUDIUM DER NEUEREN SPRACHEN, CXXXVII (ns XXXVII) (1918), 25–33.

*The Private Papers of Henry Ryecroft* may be considered as G's personal confession. Ryecroft's comments on art are illuminating for anyone desiring to learn about the nature of the creative process. G stresses the role of the subconscious and the power of inspiration of music. [In German.]

**803** Williams, Harold H. MODERN ENGLISH WRITERS: 1890–1914 (Lond: Sidgwick & Jackson, 1918; 3rd rvd ed, 1925), pp. 294–99.

G's long, drab passages are the result not of purposive realism but of a failure to write; G is a man laboring under a sense of the injustice of circumstances.

## 1919

**804** Cunliffe, John W. "George Gissing," ENGLISH LITERATURE DURING THE LAST HALF CENTURY (NY: Macmillan, 1919), pp. 97–118.

Since his death, G's literary reputation has been enhanced, particularly among serious students of literature. While the popular impression of G pictures him as a realistic and sympathetic student of English working-class life, he actually loathed the worker. G was really an aristocratic scholar with a great affection for Greek meters. His novels treat the London slums, which he came to know by roaming the streets and recording what he saw. "In general G had a low estimate of women and no real acquaintance with them." His book on Dickens "is one of the finest works of its kind in the English language." G's best novel is *New Grub Street*. [In this chapter, Cunliffe also summarizes G's life.]

# 1920

**805** Cazamian, Louis. L'ÉVOLUTION PSYCHOLOGIQUE ET LA LITTÉRATURE EN ANGLETERRE: 1660–1914 (The Psychological Evolution and Literature in England: 1660–1914) (Paris: Felix Alcan, 1920), p. 255.

G stands alongside Stevenson for his stern realism. In G's works, the renascent romantic atmosphere is felt only through the bitterness of his avowed pessimism. [In French.]

**806** Danielson, Henry. "Bibliographies of Modern Authors," BOOKMAN'S JOURNAL, II (21 May 1920), 52; (28 May 1920), 69; (4 June 1920), 86; (11 June 1920), 101; (18 June 1920), 116; (25 June 1920), 134; (2 July 1920), 150; (9 July 1920), 166.

[This sequence gives a full description of each G first edition published before 1921.]

**807** Goldring, Douglas. "An Outburst on Gissing," REPUTATIONS: ESSAYS IN CRITICISM (NY: Thomas Seltzer, 1920), pp. 125–32.

G's books document lower-class life during "one of the darkest ages of English social history. They are statements by one who actually lived the life" detailed in the novels. But G himself could not escape the horrors. Above all, he lacked imaginative insight, so that like his fictional characters he could not pull himself together so as to free himself. His style is pretentious: he enjoys big words. *The Private Papers of Henry Ryecroft* reeks of corruption and decay and cannot appeal to readers who seek stimulation and refreshment.

**808** Van Maanen, W. "George Gissing: A Short Sketch," ENGLISH STUDIES (Amsterdam), II (Aug 1920), 104–10.

Frank Swinnerton has said that to write of G is to write of one who failed, but if G cannot claim rank equal to that of Balzac, Meredith, or Dostoevski, his works will still live. With the exception of Meredith, he was the greatest writer of his time. G's strong personality, his hostility to the lower classes, and his hatred of poverty influenced his fiction. G was influenced by Meredith in *A Life's Morning*, and the notions and methods of Zola and Turgenev are echoed in his novels, though the decadent movement had not affected them.

**809** Villard, Léonie. LA FEMME ANGLAISE AU XIX SIÈCLE ET SON ÉVOLUTION D'APRÈS LE ROMAN ANGLAIS CONTEMPORAIN (The English Woman in the 19th Century and Her Development Afterwards in the Contemporary English Novel) (Paris: Didier, 1920), pp. 37–42, 104–6, 109, 157–61, 196–99, 324.

Alice and Virginia Madden of *The Odd Women* are the victims of their education and prejudices. After Dickens and Thackeray, G gives the last portrait of the governess with moving sincerity and truthfulness. Pennyloaf Candy of *The Nether World* illustrates the working conditions of women. The type of female philanthropist belonging to the people has never been so touchingly described as by G in Jane Snowden. [In French.]

# 1921

**810** "Autobiography in *The Private Papers of Henry Ryecroft*," NOTES AND QUERIES, IX (1921), 371, 435, 477–78.

[A question about the autobiographical nature of *Ryecroft*, asked by A. Edgerton, ibid (5 Nov 1921), p. 371, is answered by Arthur Bowes, ibid (26 Nov 1921), p. 435 and by H. Tapley-Soper, ibid (10 Dec 1921), pp. 477–78.] [Not significant.]

**811** Kellner, Leon. DIE ENGLISCHE LITERATUR DER NEUSTEN ZEIT: VON DICKENS BIS SHAW (Modern English Literature: From Dickens to Shaw) (Leipzig: Tauchnitz, 1921), pp. 27, 28, 337–38.

G is generally considered to be the best among those writers who, from 1885 to 1895, dealt with men devoted to art and suffering from their temperaments as well as from a hostile environment. [Unimportant.] [In German.]

# 1922

**812** Alden, Stanley. "George Gissing: Humanist," NORTH AMERICAN REVIEW, CCXVI (Sept 1922), 364–77; rptd in COLLECTED ARTICLES ON GEORGE GISSING, ed by Pierre Coustillas (Lond: Frank Cass, 1968), pp. 14–26.

There are evidences of romantic, humanistic, and unrealistic qualities in G's writings. G is indebted to Dostoevski, Zola, and Balzac, rather than to Fielding or Eliot. G has a mystical reverence for womanhood. In interpreting life, G provides a perfected individual, one poised between freedom and restraint. This individual cannot rise from the inarticulate lower classes but must be a figure like Ryecroft who makes himself the center of the universe. The complexity of life is bearable only if one finds solace in nature. [Alden also shows his familiarity with the writings of Bennett, Wells, Swinnerton, Seccombe, and others.] [Important.]

**813** Allen, Margaret. *"The Odd Women* and The Girls," North American Review, CCXVI (Nov 1922), 691–94.
These novels by G and Edna Ferber describe the condition of unmarried women in society.

**814** Hind, C. Lewis. More Authors and I (NY: Dodd, Mead, 1922), pp. 129–34.
G led a sad life. [Personal reminiscences; recalls the appearance of *The Private Papers of Henry Ryecroft.*]

**815** Osborne, E. B. "A Dismal Dickens," Morning Post (Lond), 6 Oct 1922, p. 5; rptd in Living Age, CCCXV (11 Nov 1922), 361–63.
In George Gissing: An Appreciation (1922), May Yates proves that there is "idealism to spare" in G's gloomy novels. G lacked Dickens's ability to "turn vulgarity to a magical merriment." G loved beauty rather than truth. His women are a civilizing but conservative force.

**816** Priestley, J. B. "Belles-Lettres," Mercury (Lond), VII (Dec 1922), 214–15.
May Yates's book (1922) on G is "not sufficiently penetrating to be of very great service." She fails to follow the clue to G's weakness as a novelist, namely, that he "looked at life through books and never saw it for himself."

**817** Yates, May. George Gissing: An Appreciation (Manchester: Manchester UP, 1922).
Realistic rendering of slums is moderated by a "certain fastidiousness of touch" that distinguishes G from continental novelists. G's travel in Italy made him conscious of setting: *The Emancipated* best reflects this new awareness. G's male characters, his greatest achievement, are largely auto-biographical. They carry his basic theme of man's revolt against circumstances. G's heroes idealize women; his women are types, not individuals. G's allusions reveal the depth and range of his readings; his prose style, scholarly and polished, appeals to academic people. [Hardly a thorough, perceptive criticism; the subtitle, "An Appreciation," is fitting. Perhaps most curious for her remarks about G's emancipated women. Reviews: Karl Arns, "Besprechungen," Englische Studien, LX (1925), 390–95; "George Gissing," Saturday Review, CXXXIV (14 Oct 1922), 550; S[amuel] C. C[hew], "Brief Mention," Modern Language Notes,

XXXVIII (April 1923), 256; V., NEW STATESMAN, XXI (30 June 1923), 371–72 (attributed to Virginia Woolf in B. J. Kirkpatrick's bibliography of her works); J. B. Priestley, LONDON MERCURY, VII (Dec 1922), 214–15; J. Macy, NATION (NY), XCV (6 Dec 1922), 620.]

## 1923

**818** Beer, Thomas. "Frank Swinnerton," BOOKMAN (NY), LVIII (Dec 1923), 404–9.

"Mr. Swinnerton's earlier work, visibly, was influenced by Gissing, but the hold of the unhappy Victorian was not sufficient to break his apologist's detachment." In a conversation, Henry James once compared G's style to "thick soup."

**819** Buchan, John. A HISTORY OF ENGLISH LITERATURE (Lond: Nelson, 1923), pp. 564–66.

[Summary of G's position as a pioneer in English realism.]

**820** Cazamian, Madeleine L. "L'Influence de la Science" (The Influence of Science), LE ROMAN ET LES IDÉES EN ANGLETERRE (Strasbourg: Librairie Istra, 1923), pp. 302–71.

G's earliest novels underscore the pessimism of his own outlook on life. With *Demos,* he sought to treat the effects of economics on the impoverished. Despair also dominates the dismal lives of the characters in *Thyrza.* In *New Grub Street,* G, as the realistic observer, focuses on the circumstances of various writers in all phases of their occupation. *Born in Exile* contrasts the lives of churchmen and scientists. The sad, suffering hero of *The Private Papers of Henry Ryecroft* reminds one of Hale White's Mark Rutherford. [In French.]

**821** E[dgett], E[dwin] F[rancis]. "Writers and Books," BOSTON EVENING TRANSCRIPT, 1 Dec 1923.

A new edition of Swinnerton's study of G reminds us of the legendary novelist. His early troubles convinced G of the prevalence of human unkindness. Back in London he converted whatever he saw into a series of reflections. "He was an essayist, a writer upon moral themes" who wrote novels about the depressed. But even *The Unclassed* is "puny when it is compared with a single work of Balzac." It is as a lover of nature that G stands forth. "A great rambler," G caught details in lengthy walks in the country, and he leaves us the pictures he found there in his happiest moods.

**822** Fehr, Bernhard. "Gissing," DIE ENGLISCHE LITERATUR DES

19 UND 20 JAHRHUNDERTS (English Literature of the 19th and 20th Centuries) (Berlin: Neubabelsberg, 1923), pp. 376–78.
Treating G's underworld with the philosophy of Schopenhauer's pessimism, G's early novels give evidence of his preoccupation with social, political, and psychological matters. His debts to Zola are evident in several respects; his realistic devices are clearly Dickensian. G's attention to the inner feelings of his heroes emphasizes the psychological aspects of his analysis, stressing the backgrounds and temperaments of character study. *New Grub Street* and *Born in Exile* particularly mark his psycho-realism, so that if we are to appreciate G we would be wise to concentrate on his representation of Godwin Peak. [Biographical content repeats many errors from Morley Roberts's THE PRIVATE LIFE OF HENRY MAITLAND.] [In German.]

**823** Forman, Henry James. "Two Old Favorites Critically Undone," NEW YORK TIMES BOOK REVIEW, 30 Dec 1923, p. 5.
Frank Swinnerton corrects the general belief that G was a realist; G's books actually lacked a "certain warm vitality" in his characters. [Also reviews the reissue of ROBERT LOUIS STEVENSON: A CRITICAL STUDY.]

**824** Hudson, W. H. LETTERS FROM W. H. HUDSON TO EDWARD GARNETT, intro and notes by Edward Garnett (Lond: Nonesuch P, 1923; Dent, 1925), pp. 59–62; 71.
Morley Roberts is a "good deal cut up at" G's death; G's widow has come to visit his family at Wakefield. During his life G probably suffered because of some dreadful religious ideas imbibed in his youth.

**825** Whitcombe, Charles. " 'Henry Maitland,' George Gissing, and Dickens," DICKENSIAN, XIX (Oct 1923), 225–27.
G's study of Dickens was a potboiler; G was incapable of appreciating Dickens.

# 1924

**826** Cazamian, Louis. "Les Pessimistes: Thomson, Hardy, Gissing," in Emile Legouis's and Cazamian's HISTORIE DE LA LITTÉRATURE ANGLAISE (Paris: Hachette, 1924), pp. 1182–86; A HISTORY OF ENGLISH LITERATURE, trans by Helen D. Irvine, W. D. MacInnes, and Louis Cazamian (Lond: Dent, 1927), pp. 1252–57; (NY: Macmillan, 1927), II, 428–31; subsequently rvd, reset, and rptd several times.
Besides the great differences in their personalities, Dickens and G were

representatives of contrasting periods of literature. G had bitterness at "the core of his nature," whereas Dickens was sustained by "courageous cheerfulness." In Dickens's period there was hope for reform; G's period was dominated by the doctrine of Schopenhauer and the beliefs of the French naturalists. In G's realism there is evidence of a controlled youthful Romanticism. His realism is courageous; however, because it is not wholly natural to him, it is also labored. G is "no dissenter from traditional values." G never hopes to cure the social diseases he describes. His best novels, *Demos, The Nether World,* and *New Grub Street,* focus attention on the horrors of slum life. G's characters are "studied patiently, conscientiously, from the outside, with uneven penetration." G's style is vigorous and rich in suggestiveness. [Original in French.]

**827** Horrox, Lewis. "Gissing and Mr. Swinnerton," NATION AND ATHENAEUM, XXXIV (1 March 1924), 770–72.

Swinnerton's GEORGE GISSING: A CRITICAL STUDY has been reprinted. Swinnerton failed to understand G because he could not sympathize with the beauty of G's soul and knew nothing of the social and political movements of the last century.

**828** Roberts, Morley. W. H. HUDSON: A PORTRAIT (NY: Dutton, 1924), pp. 37–38, 52, 213.

The "Quadrilateral," the group so named by G, joined him with Roberts, Hudson, and Hartley. "Though two more different beings never perhaps existed," G and Hudson shared a love of books.

**829** Scott, Temple. "Introduction," *Critical Studies in the Works of Charles Dickens* (NY: Greenberg, 1924), pp. 1–13.

"There is not in English literature a more fulfilling estimate of the writings of Dickens than Gissing's critical study of him, which is at once finely judicious and delicately appreciative." G was not a novelist, and the public realized this. He was rather a scholar, a man of letters, and this is proved by *The Private Papers of Henry Ryecroft, By the Ionian Sea,* and his essays of Dickens. G lacked the temperament, imagination, and the abounding sympathy for people necessary to tell a good tale. [Scott's selections for this volume include the nine prefaces that G wrote for the "Rochester Edition" of Dickens, and an essay called "Dickens in Memory." Reviews: BOOKMAN (NY), LX (Jan 1925), 485–86; NATION (NY), CXIX (19 Nov 1924), 550; NEW YORK TIMES BOOK REVIEW, 30 Nov 1924, p. 2; NEW YORK TRIBUNE, 11 Jan 1925, p. 12.]

**830** Spielman, Mabel H. "A Coincidence: Striking and Peculiar," DICKENSIAN, XX (April 1924), 98–99.

[A letter to the editor claims that G thought Dickens paid too much attention to trivial things.] [Worthless.]

**831** Starrett, Vincent. "Introduction," *Sins of the Fathers and Other Tales* (Chicago: Pascal Covici, 1924), pp. [vii–xviii].

G's admirers have carefully searched the Chicago TRIBUNE files to find these tales and to share them with "other Gissing 'fans.'" G's early work is often "of considerable biographical and bibliographical interest."

## 1925

**832** Chevalley, Abel. THE MODERN ENGLISH NOVEL (NY: Knopf, 1925), pp. 84–89.

G's conscientious and autobiographical novels describe suffering more than poverty. G feared the harlot and pitied intellectual women. His heroes, like their creator, are depressing.

**833** Frierson, William C. L'INFLUENCE DU NATURALISME FRANÇAIS SUR LES ROMANCIERS ANGLAIS DE 1885 À 1900 (The Influence of French Naturalism on the English Novelists From 1885 to 1900) (Paris: M. Giard, 1925), pp. 205–18.

G was intimately acquainted with the French realists and naturalists— Balzac, Flaubert, the Goncourt Brothers, and Zola. *The Nether World* recalls the manner of Zola, especially by the description of misery and the moral vices it entails. Already in *Workers in the Dawn, The Unclassed,* and *Demos,* similar devices and intentions are present. Yet, unlike his French inspirers, G is mainly interested in character drawing, and as Thomas Seccombe has shown in his introduction to *The House of Cobwebs,* G's novels perpetuate the distinguishing features of the Victorian novel. His unhappy endings, his stress on the tragic elements of human life are reminiscent of French realism. G may have been influenced by Zola in his theme of the brutality of the masses (*Born in Exile* and *The Odd Women* are almost experimental novels after the manner of the French master). With Flaubert he shares his distrust of the people. No English writer has more powerfully described the sordid lives of the poor. He has sapped the authority of Dickens and disturbed the complacent optimism of his admirers. [A very useful article which nevertheless suffers from its having been written before the publication of G's letters to his family (1927); also, Frierson has overlooked G's important article on realism (HUMANITARIAN, VII [July 1895], 14–16.)] [In French.]

**834** Harrison, Austin. "Signposts of Fiction," CONTEMPORARY REVIEW, CXXVIII (July 1925), 82–89.

Important to the history of the English reform novel, G's novels on the freedom of women are predecessors of Fanny Hurst's LUMMOX.

**835** Hudson, W. H. MEN, BOOKS AND BIRDS, with notes, some letters, and an intro by Morley Roberts (Lond: Nash & Grayson, 1925), pp. 65, 72, 90–91, 115, 143, 193, 249.

[Hudson had written Roberts on more than one occasion encouraging him to prepare a book on G. Roberts's THE PRIVATE LIFE OF HENRY MAITLAND (1912) convinced Hudson that the details of G's sad life best served his reputation. Thomas Seccombe had learned about G's disgrace at Owens College from Dr. Greenwood. It is well that MAITLAND was published before G's biography, which Bertz was reportedly writing for Constable, was finished. Henry James had carefully questioned Roberts about G.]

**836** Matz, B. W. "Introduction," *The Immortal Dickens* (Lond: Cecil Palmer, 1925), pp. vii–ix.

In these essays on Dickens, G concentrated on individual novels rather than scattering his comments; G is "trenchant in his criticism of Dickens's bad methods, and seizes on his failures as quickly and justifiably as he does on his inimitable powers and finest work." G establishes "the genius which has made Dickens immortal." [*Immortal Dickens* contains several introductory essays G wrote for the "Rochester Edition." Reviews: NEW STATESMAN, XXVI (7 Nov 1925), 122; *"The Immortal Dickens,"* SPECTATOR, CXXXV (26 Dec 1925), 1911; TIMES LITERARY SUPPLEMENT (Lond), 5 Nov 1925, p. 742.]

**837** Priestley, J. B. "The Secret of Dickens," SATURDAY REVIEW (Lond), CXL (26 Sept 1925), 342.

*The Immortal Dickens* is inferior to the criticism of Chesterton or Forster. Dickens did not gain popularity by his position on social matters. G is wrong in insisting that Dickens gained readers by presenting an essentially unrealistic picture of life. Dickens's popularity, rather, comes from his memories of childhood.

**838** Pugh, Edwin. "Gissing on Dickens," BOOKMAN (Lond), LXIX (Dec 1925), 187.

*The Immortal Dickens* shows that G "appreciates unreservedly" the creativity of the Victorian genius, so that the reader derives "nothing but profit and pleasure from reading this tribute of a star to a sun."

**839** Quiller-Couch, Sir Arthur. CHARLES DICKENS AND OTHER VICTORIANS (Cambridge: Cambridge UP, 1925), pp. 10, 11, 98, 99.

G, "a genuine genius," deserves a "heaven of recognition in which all true artists meet." His studies of Dickens cry out for reprinting.

# 1926

**840** Hansen, Harry. "Introduction," *New Grub Street* (NY: Modern Library, 1926), pp. v–xii.
G is a "capable stylist, a keen analyst of motives, and an extraordinary literary figure whose inexplicable hardships and distressing failure stir the imagination of an age surfeited with material things." As in several other novels by G, *New Grub Street* has much autobiography.

**841** Harrison, Austin. FREDERIC HARRISON: THOUGHTS AND MEMORIES (Lond: Heinemann, 1926), pp. 80–84, 89, 110–12.
As a tutor, G made study a joy; however, he was no disciplinarian. G was a "voluptuary in pessimism." He had no religion, refused to adopt any moral discipline, and disdained politics. Although the life of the poor all but drove him to despair, he nevertheless claimed that one must know the poor before one could help them.

**842** Stearns, George A. "George Gissing in America," BOOKMAN (NY), LXIII (Aug 1926), 683–86.
[Reminiscence of a former student of G's in America.]

**843** Waterlow, Sidney. "Memories of Henry James," NEW STATESMAN, 6 Feb 1926, p. 514.
The quality of James's integrity shines clearly in his remarks about fellow authors, such as in his memory of G's appearance: "The front face was not bad . . . [but] one side of the face [was] disfigured by a great expanse of purple scar, the mouth and chin were uncommonly feeble. Altogether an extraordinarily ungainly, common, ill-shaped figure; almost knock-kneed, bearing the unmistakable stamp of Wakefield, his birthplace. And how queer that such a being should speak French so well—with a precise affectation that made it almost *too* well."

# 1927

**844** Aiken, Conrad. "George Gissing," DIAL (NY), LXXXIII (Dec 1927), 512–14; rptd in A REVIEWER's ABC (NY: Meridian, 1958), pp. 217–19.
G's *A Victim of Circumstances* contains tales that are reports of life,

aesthetic rather than moral in describing London life, and thoroughly honest pieces of observation. The story or plot amounts to very little. One is astonished at G's modernity; he is more modern than Hardy or James. G tells his story "with a clear eye and a fine gravity of spirit."

**845** Ashdown, Ella. "A Study of the Work of Henry James, George Gissing, Samuel Butler, and George Moore, More Particularly in Its Relation to the Development of the Theory of the Novel in the Late Nineteenth Century." Unpublished dissertation, University of London, 1927.

[Listed in Lawrence F. McNamee, DISSERTATIONS IN ENGLISH AND AMERICAN LITERATURE (NY & Lond: Bowker, 1968).]

**846** Biron, [Sir Henry] Chartres. "Biography and Memoirs," MERCURY (Lond), XV (March 1927), pp. 555–56.

*The Letters of George Gissing to Members of His Family* is convincing evidence that G had the knack to write good letters. Born a generation too soon, G still regarded the novel "as a sort of fairy tale for those riper years." *Demos* proved to be the turning point in G's career. As a person, G was essentially fastidious.

**847** "The Bookman's Diary," BOOKMAN (Lond), LXXII (Sept 1927), 309–10.

The prediction made by Thomas Seccombe that G's public would increase seems to be coming true with the variety of reprints of G's brought out by T. Fisher Unwin, Methuen, Constable, and Nash & Grayson.

**848** Boyd, Ernest. "Readers and Writer," INDEPENDENT, CXVIII (9 April 1927), 391.

The collection of *The Letters of George Gissing to Members of His Family,* ed by Algernon and Ellen Gissing (1927), shows him to be extremely conscientious and always troubled by poverty.

**849** Burrell, Angus. "Gissing the Reticent," NATION (NY), CXXIV (8 June 1927), 648–49.

The volume of *The Letters of George Gissing to Members of His Family,* ed by Algernon and Ellen Gissing (1927) shows that the novelist "lived with the morbid consciousness of lost honor."

**850** "George Gissing," SATURDAY REVIEW (Lond), CXLIII (29 Jan 1927), 159.

*The Letters of George Gissing to Members of His Family,* ed by Algernon and Ellen Gissing (1927) reinforces the image of G as a loyal man guided by simple family affections. G should be remembered for his novels, not for the adversity that this "plain straightforward workman" suffered in life.

**851** "George Gissing in His Letters," NEW YORK TIMES BOOK REVIEW, 27 March 1927, p. 7.

As a volume, *The Letters of George Gissing to Members of His Family*, ed by Algernon and Ellen Gissing (1927) tells us that G was a prig, a precocious child. But critics err when they call him a pessimist. Actually he was an overly serious sort of person who found that realism was the only literary mode available to him. In trying to improve living conditions in London, G undertook a moral purpose.

**852** Gissing, Alfred C. "Preface," *The Letters of George Gissing to Members of His Family*, ed by Algernon and Ellen Gissing (Lond: Constable, 1927), pp. v–vi.

During his life, G gradually learned to find the heart more reliable than the intellect. What has been omitted from these letters would scarcely interest the public. Some passages from G's diary have been included principally to record his travels.

**853** Gissing, Alfred C. "Preface," *A Victim of Circumstances* (NY: Houghton Mifflin, 1927), pp. vii–xii.

G was uncompromising in his "efforts to paint the sordid realities of life in their exact shades, and hence arose those sombre studies in grey, which are unique in literature." Some of G's best writing (e.g. "The Fate of Humphrey Snell") was in short fiction. The author must be permitted his choice of subject, however severe or extreme it might seem to the reader.

**854** Gissing, Ellen. "George Gissing: A Character Sketch," NINETEENTH CENTURY, CII (Sept 1927), 417–24.

G was born "with a strong tendency to depression." When in school, G often lacked discernment in choosing his friends.

**855** "Gissing's Letters," TIMES LITERARY SUPPLEMENT (Lond), 27 Jan 1927, p. 57.

*The Letters of George Gissing to Members of His Family*, ed by Algernon and Ellen Gissing (1927) gives us part of G's life, "if not the whole of it." The sincerity of his novels and the human zest of *The Private Papers of Henry Ryecroft* are reflected in his correspondence. Writing to his family, G was "unfailing in sympathy, unwearying in counsel." If "his sensitive consciousness also barred him from the world," he possessed a "strong affection to his family" that persisted throughout his life. "In his struggle he created his novels, which were unhappy, pale, and, save for one or two, imperfect; but Gissing was justified—they have a curious distinction, and he succeeded in drawing certain quandries, certain types of characters never presented so searchingly elsewhere."

**856** Gosse, Edmund. "Gissing," LEAVES AND FRUIT (Lond: Heinemann, 1927), pp. 275–81.

*The Letters of George Gissing to Members of His Family* throws "considerable sidelight on the intellectual character of Gissing, and on his essential aims." He was a novelist made, not born. Unlike Balzac and Zola, who gathered their materials from the outside, G stimulated "a keen intuition by means of intense and unmitigated self-contemplation." The advance of democracy terrified as it fascinated him. Finally, in Calabria, he found relief; these letters tell us that far from bitter he was childlike in his appreciation of life's faint pleasures. "His was, in fact, a very gentle, sensitive, and appreciative mind, tied fast to a temperament the most unfortunate that could have been devised."

**857** LaLou, René. PANORAMA DE LA LITTÉRATURE ANGLAISE CONTEMPORAINE (Panorama of Contemporary English Literature) (Paris: Kra, 1927), pp. 117–20.

With G, pessimism assumes the form of the realistic novel. Frank Swinnerton has restored a truer picture of him and divested him of the legend of poverty. His master was Dickens, and he dreamt of becoming the English Balzac; he also deeply admired the Russians, but he was devoid of the vitality of them all. His message is obscure: he was the painstaking analyst of confused discontent. He has rightly been called "the historian of the middle classes," and *Born in Exile* contains the most genuine of his heroes —Godwin Peak—who stands between revolt and concern for respectability. His *Demos* is anti-democratic. His novels are unrelieved by poetry or humour. Besides the novelist we find the traveler (*By the Ionian Sea*) and the essayist (*The Private Papers of Henry Ryecroft*) who called forth the "infinite pathos of human resignation." [In French.]

**858** Lappin, Henry A. "George Gissing's Letters," BOOKMAN (NY), LXV (May 1927), 345–47.

Four years after G's death, Constable planned to bring out a biography of G to be written by his friend Eduard Bertz. At the time, Thomas Seccombe was an editor for Constable.

**859** McFee, William. "A Superior Person," SATURDAY REVIEW OF LITERATURE (NY), III (11 June 1927), 894.

*The Letters of George Gissing to Members of His Family,* ed by Algernon and Ellen Gissing (1927) tells us "how not to become a novelist." G's reputation must rest upon the historical value of *New Grub Street,* "the quiet excellence" of *By the Ionian Sea,* and the appeal to cultured people made by *The Private Papers of Henry Ryecroft.* G's short stories, written at the suggestion of Clement Shorter, are the work of "a literary man flogging his brain to produce mediocre fiction."

> **860** McKay, Ruth Capers. "George Gissing and His Critic Frank Swinnerton." University of Pennsylvania dissertation, 1927. [Listed in Lawrence F. McNamee, DISSERTATIONS IN ENGLISH AND AMERICAN LITERATURE (NY & Lond: Bowker, 1968)]; pub as GEORGE GISSING AND HIS CRITIC FRANK SWINNERTON (Phila: Pennsylvania U, 1933); a selection from pp. 52-67 of the original study has been rptd as "Gissing as a Portrayer of Society," in COLLECTED ARTICLES ON GEORGE GISSING, ed by Pierre Coustillas (Lond: Frank Cass, 1968), pp. 27–42.

A critic should have a "desire to do well by" his subject, but Swinnerton constantly condemned G, looking always for weaknesses. Other early critics of G, like Harrison, Wells, and Seccombe, while admirable in what they did say, neglected to say enough. Roberts wrote a sensational biography, not just a critical study. As a consequence, the real G is obscured in a sentimental haze, becoming "poor Gissing," a legend caused in part by G's own "tendency to self-depreciation," by his ill-advised marriages, and by the impression that he was a better essayist than a novelist. Historically, G is transitional, as Young sets forth in his article in the CAMBRIDGE HISTORY OF ENGLISH LITERATURE, coming between such Victorians as Dickens, Thackeray, and George Eliot, and in advance of Bennett, Beresford, and Swinnerton himself. His central fictional characters provide us with the spirit and form of late nineteenth-century life, and these characters appear in rich variety. Swinnerton thought of G as essentially an egotist, unfit to be a great novelist; he said that G "displayed his greatest strength in the study of abnormal temperaments" and that G "had a frustrated career." Both G and Swinnerton wrote of London subjects, and Swinnerton was very likely influenced by his readings in G. We can discover resemblances among their heroes; both writers were pre-eminently concerned with portraying the lower middle classes. G employed a wider canvas and stands out as one of the "Victorian giants of fiction."

> **861** Morley, Christopher. "A Note on George Gissing," SATURDAY REVIEW OF LITERATURE (NY), III (14 May 1927), 821.

Mournful, prosy, and ironic as G's novels were, they still command readers, even when these attributes are out of fashion. The opening thirty pages of *The Odd Women* are "perversely grotesque," and they arouse "the wanton nerves of merriment" to such a degree that one is scarcely fit for the "really fine stuff that follows." Now that "the footing of woman seems so much more secure," it is remarkable that G felt these "speculations about his emancipated ladies" so long ago. While G's "passion for human happiness and decency" led him to "bedevil his characters for the sake of his high-minded theories," it is the attitude that now "makes him the ideal novelist for moments of depression."

**862** O'Sullivan, Vincent. "More About Gissing," SATURDAY REVIEW OF LITERATURE (NY), IV (6 Aug 1927), 26.
McFee's article of 11 June 1927, claiming that G's non-fiction is superior to his novels, fails to appreciate their excellence. *The Whirlpool* ranks with TESS OF THE D'URBERVILLES and is superior to A MUMMER'S WIFE.

**863** Pure, Simon [pseud of Frank Swinnerton]. "The Londoner," BOOKMAN (NY), LXV (April 1927), 189-90.
*The Letters of George Gissing to Members of His Family* makes one wonder about G's correspondence with Roberts and Wells. This volume is so censored that it adds very little to what we know of G. *Born in Exile* and *New Grub Street* are certainly among G's best novels.

**864** Roberts, Morley. "Introduction," *The Nether World* (Lond: Nash & Grayson; NY: Dutton, 1927), pp. v–x.
It is necessary for mankind to be reminded that "we all live in the nether world"; G brings us to such a hideous world, a narrow world, that none of us wants to recognize it. G also despised the deprived humanity of *The Nether World,* yet he never understood the occupants of this intolerable region. His novel renounces such a world, "especially the economic world as some few of those outside its greatest bitterness and squalor may perhaps understand it." The result is a work that is "undoubtedly as painful as anything written by Zola."

**865** Roberts, Morley. "Introduction," *New Grub Street* (Lond: Nash & Grayson, 1927), pp. v–x.
Reardon represents G's main theme, "the life of those who find weakness the true misery." To write objectively was not within G's power. What he resented in the writer who sought only popularity is evident in Jasper Milvain. Part of man's exile is to lose not only money or strength, but his wife as well. G's "real genius was narrow," and he had but one subject: himself.

**866** *"A Victim of Circumstances,"* TIMES LITERARY SUPPLEMENT (Lond), 14 July 1927, p. 486.
The short story was not G's medium because "it showed up his strange

quality of conscientious flatness in narration." One gets the feeling that G "was looking down, in quivering disgust, on things to which he devoutly wished he could shut his eyes."

**867** Woolf, Virginia. "George Gissing," NATION (Lond), XL (26 Feb 1927), 722–23; rptd as "The Letters of George Gissing," NEW REPUBLIC, L (2 March 1927), 49–50; as "George Gissing," THE COMMON READER (Second Series) (NY: Harcourt Brace, 1932), pp. 238–44; as "George Gissing," COLLECTED ESSAYS (Lond: Hogarth P, 1966), I, 297–301.

G was "an imperfect novelist, but a highly educated man" who wrote his own problems into his fiction. He reverenced facts and idolized the intellect, but he had little imagination. G was self-centered and solitary; he was "one of those sharp lights beyond whose edges all is vapour and phantom." So close is he to his novels that when we read his stories we get neither a character nor an incident but "the comment of a thoughtful man upon life as it seemed to him." Gradually, G realized that Rome and Athens were more congenial to him than London.

## 1928

**868** Follett, Helen T., and Wilson Follett. "George Gissing," SOME MODERN NOVELISTS (NY: Holt, 1928), pp. 50–71.

Undervalued before his death, G is now interesting to us for his themes. Unlike Besant, who offered solutions to sociological problems that he never understood, G presses upon the reader stores of details documented in lower levels of society without volunteering a solution. G is a conscious craftsman, hard at work synopsizing long passages of undramatized episodes. Too frequently he fails to dramatize scenes of great emotional intensity. G is superior to his fellow novelists in the presentation of the daily outward lives of his fictional characters. Poverty degrades his creatures; it also makes them sickeningly alive. If G's characters have one thing in common, it is the desire to improve their condition; never beaten, they constantly strive. James was right in noting that G's characters are not often shown in conversation.

**869** Frierson, William C. "The English Controversy Over Realism in Fiction," PMLA, XLIII (June 1928), 533–50.

Once G gained the public ear with *A Life's Morning* (influenced by Meredith), he returned to the more realistic novel with *The Nether World* and *Born in Exile*.

**870** Roberts, Morley. "Introduction," *Demos* (Lond: Nash & Grayson; NY: Dutton, 1928), pp. v–ix.

For anyone who wishes to understand *Demos,* and particularly Richard Mutimer, it would be helpful to know G's feelings about labor. Actually, G "might understand working men as individuals," though he had no real knowledge of them as a class. "He feared them prodigiously," partly because they seemed to him threats against culture. In *Demos* the clergyman Wyvern "is very often but Gissing in disguise." The success of *Demos* is in large part attributable to the Trafalgar Square riots, and the urgency of completing the manuscript to catch the public attention undoubtedly prodded G. He caught "the whole feeling of unrest" even before the riots. *Demos* is certainly not G's best novel, though it is sufficiently characteristic of him that I knew he wrote it even when it was published anonymously, and I had bought my first copy in California.

**871** Roberts, Morley. "Introduction," *A Life's Morning* (Lond: Nash & Grayson, 1928), pp. v–ix.

Before agreeing to publish *A Life's Morning,* James Payn obliged G to revise a tragic ending and have Emily Hood marry. The novel is a "very beautiful and very quiet piece of work," showing G to advantage as a prose stylist. If he intrudes too much in his own personality when perhaps he need not, "I would not willingly part with any passage which is pure Gissing."

**872** Roberts, Morley. "Introduction," *Thyrza* (Lond: Nash & Grayson; NY: Dutton, 1928), pp. v–ix.

With a kindly portrait, G states his "theme of a girl, or of many girls, 'in exile.' " In *Thyrza,* G's literary debt is not as much to Dickens or Zola as to the Russians, although he could not represent the spirit of his country as they could. Yet he provides real representatives of England, and these living portraits assure G a place in literature.

**873** Wild, Friedrich. Die Englische Literatur der Gegenwart seit 1870: Drama und Roman (English Literature from 1870 to the Present: Drama and Fiction) (Wiesbaden: Dioskuren-Verlag, 1928), pp. 6, 17, 159, 188, 201–4, 233, 289, 324–25, 328.

G writes about London, the milieu he knows best but loves least. In his best works he deals with the lower classes, expressing a certain hatred of destiny as symbolized by poverty. He has been influenced by the French novelists and by Turgenev and Dostoevsky (whom he read in German translation). *Demos* is a study of the masses from the point of view of a hopeless naturalism. In *New Grub Street* G demands an absolute realism and, in this, goes beyond Dickens and Zola. *The Odd Women* resembles Moore's DRAMA IN MUSLIN. [In German.]

## 1929

**874** Delatte, F. "Comptes Rendus" (Reports), REVUE BELGE DE PHILOLOGIE ET D'HISTOIRE, VIII (April–June 1929), 595–96. *The Immortal Dickens* consists of the introductions G wrote for the "Rochester Edition" of Dickens's works. They are sound, logical, straightforward, honest criticism. G steers a middle course between unbridled enthusiasm and systematic condemnation. [An abstract of the introduction to OLIVER TWIST is given as an example.] [In French.]

**875** Gissing, Alfred C. "George Gissing: Some Aspects of His Life and Work," NATIONAL REVIEW, XCIII (Aug 1929), 932–41. My father attacked the evils of society "because of the bitterness they brought into his own life." The characters in G's novels did not know what aspiration was and could not possibly be heroic. Many of his novels "partake of the nature of essays, in which the evils of the world" are shown to be disgusting.

**876** Gissing, Alfred C. "Preface," *Selections Autobiographical and Imaginative from the Works of George Gissing,* ed by A.C. Gissing (Lond: Cape, 1929), pp. 17–24. While no novelist has used autobiography in his fiction more than my father has, one must still distinguish the autobiographical from the imaginative. Ancient history "stirred his imagination" more than any other object. *The Nether World* is his masterpiece in the treatment of the London worker. In his later years, his own circumstances allowed him to view "things in a more general light." *By the Ionian Sea* and *Our Friend the Charlatan* show this relief.

**877** Gissing, Ellen. "Some Personal Recollections of George Gissing," BLACKWOOD'S MAGAZINE, CCXXV (May 1929), 653–60. Between 1876 and 1883, my brother was in actual poverty. He was driven to be an artist by a great desire, determined as he was to gain a footing in literature. Our holidays together were always happy, his letters "full of fun." He took my sister and me to Paris for a visit and hoped we might someday go to Rome together. When he visited us in Wakefield, his appearance became a matter of curiosity; his hair was long, his clothes loose fitting. For years his lungs troubled him, and this weakness led to his fatal illness.

**878** Knickerbocker, Frances W. "Some Victorian Novelists," SEWANEE REVIEW, XXXVII (Jan 1929), 118–19.

The correspondence in *The Letters of George Gissing to Members of His Family,* ed by Algernon and Ellen Gissing (1927) does not contain much biographical fact or literary interpretation. Because G wished to "wallow and describe," he belongs with the French and Russian naturalists. G's grimness no longer shocks us; his works cannot be popular with "a generation that sits at the feet of Proust and Dostoevski."

**879** Miles, Hamish. "Gissing," NEW STATESMAN, XXXIII (13 April 1929), 12–13.

The collection entitled *Selections Autobiographical and Imaginative,* ed by A.C. Gissing (1929) is larded with quotations from G's letters, diary, and essays. His writing is the result of industry rather than inspiration. The true G exists in his novels rather than in *The Private Papers of Henry Ryecroft.* The selections of the present publication display the variety and scope of G's writing. All of his work is deeply colored by the "sociological preoccupations which the misfortunes of his life had forced him to observe more closely than most of his literary contemporaries."

**880** Muir, Edwin. "Reviews: George Gissing," NATION & ATHENAEUM, XLV (4 May 1929), 163.

The G that we find in *Selections Autobiographical and Imaginative,* ed by A. C. Gissing (1929) "appears most thoroughly old-fashioned." The subjects that interested G and the other rationalists at the end of the last century have greatly changed. Reading G provides a sense of continuity in literature. Miss Gertrude Stein is inconceivable to us, and G is "almost incomprehensible." What especially dates G is his "peculiar kind of pessimism," marked as it is by "almost anxious respectability."

**881** Rotter, Anton. DER ARBEITERROMAN IN ENGLAND SEIT 1880. EIN BEITRAG ZUR GESCHICHTE DES SOZIALEN ROMANS IN ENGLAND (The Labor Novel in England Since 1880. A Contribution to the History of the Social Novel in England) (Reichenberg: Gebruder Stiepel, 1929), pp. 25–44, 47–51, 58–59, 67–68, 83, 90–91, 105–6, 118–19.

Although Dickens is one of G's favorite writers, G is chiefly influenced by Besant and Kingsley. The influence of French naturalism can be seen in his treatment of milieu and of hopeless situations. *The Nether World* is G's most realistic study of slum life. G is less interested in social reform than in psychological analysis. In contrast to Besant, G dislikes the proletariat because his aesthetic sensibility is hurt by ugliness and radicalism. [In German.]

**882** Waugh, Arthur. "George Gissing," BOOKMAN (Lond), LXXVI (April 1929), 9–10.

*Selections Autobiographical and Imaginative,* ed by A. C. Gissing (1929) convinces one that G's imagination always came to life in Greece and Italy. But the quintessence of G appears in *New Grub Street,* because G's intelligence was enough to serve him in describing London. G's name is wearing wonderfully well. Younger readers respond to his fiction for its "mild imagination against the tenor of its age, and for its persistent and astringently intellectual effort towards the amelioration of social justice." As long as individual misery persists, G's novels showing man's injustice will claim our sympathy.

**883** Welby, T. Earle. "Reviews: Grub Street," SATURDAY REVIEW (Lond), CXLVII (9 Feb 1929), 181.

The book *Selections Autobiographical and Imaginative,* ed by A. C. Gissing (1929) proves once more that G's gifts were of a high order, but his personal grievances reduce his rank as a writer. Unable to be disinterested, G became petty. His anger was motivated more by his own personal lot than by the suffering of London's poor. Even G's fictional writers are no more than men of talent. It is ironic that "the chief realistic novelist of the later Victorian period was a man enamoured of the classical past." *The Private Papers of Henry Ryecroft* and *Veranilda* lead one to think that G ought to have been an historian. G's appeal is that he is "the fellow of all who under disabilities live the life of the intellect."

# 1930

**884** Brewster, Dorothy, and Angus Burrell. "George Gissing: Release Through Fiction?" ADVENTURE OR EXPERIENCE: FOUR ESSAYS (NY: Columbia UP, 1930), pp. 7–36; rptd in MODERN FICTION (NY: Columbia UP, 1934), pp. 18–39.

G's novels contain recurring themes: "the vicissitudes of young men with good minds and no money"; a sentimental over-evaluation or an unfair under-evaluation of women; the sexual adjustments, often disastrous, of the hero. G is incapable of being objective in treating his heroes. His early fiction shows a sense of revenge against society, a sense that is lost in his last books when he wrote about what he loved. Too often he wrote to prevent starvation, and then he commonly thought too much about himself. In his last years, granted some leisure, he produced *By the Ionian Sea, The Private Papers of Henry Ryecroft,* and *Veranilda.*

**885** Bryan, J[ohn] Ingram. THE PHILOSOPHY OF ENGLISH LITERATURE (Tokyo: Maruzen, 1930), pp. 228–29.

G represented the turning away from Victorian sentimentalism. His interest in Schopenhauer "tinctured all his work with doubt and gloom." He was inclined to idealize women; but he "fell into the slough of despond where sin and sorrow come to doubt the integrity of the universe."

**886** "Memorabilia," NOTES AND QUERIES, CLVIII (5 April 1930), 235.

George E. Hastings has informed us that, in cooperation with Vincent Starrett and Thomas Olive Mabbott, he has found G's "Brownie," as well as other stories not included in *Sins of the Fathers.* The tales originally appeared in the Chicago TRIBUNE.

**887** Phelps, Gilbert. "Russian Realism and English Fiction," CAMBRIDGE JOURNAL, III (Feb 1930), 277–91.

Because French realism was too drastic for English tastes, novelists turned more comfortably to the Russians. G admittedly was influenced by Dostoevski in *Workers in the Dawn* and *Thyrza,* and by Turgenev in *Isabel Clarendon.*

**888** Reid, Forrest. "Minor Fiction in the Eighties," THE EIGHTEEN–EIGHTIES, ed by Walter de la Mare (Cambridge: Cambridge UP, 1930), pp. 112–13.

G was an early experimenter in naturalism.

**889** Roberts, Morley. "George Gissing," QUEEN'S QUARTERLY, XXXVII (Autumn 1930), 617–32.

G's novels lack construction. Not "even under the evil influence of James Payn" could G write a story with a plot. Payn decided to print *Demos* only because the book came to him just after the Trafalgar Square riots. Zangwill complained that G's characters are shown not as they appeared to themselves but as they appeared to G. *The Nether World* is just short of being a masterpiece. It suffers because G had to suffer "the horrible old three-volume system" and because it lacks "that objectivity in the sense of high artistic detachment and suppression of the writer's personality." G thought of the episode in fiction as necessary "to lighten the gloomy course of the main story."

**890** Rotter, Anton. FRANK SWINNERTON UND GEORGE GISSING:

EINE KRITISCHE STUDIE (Frank Swinnerton and George Gissing: A Critical Study) (Prague: Rudolf M. Rohrer, 1930).
Swinnerton's fiction shows a debt to English realistic novelists from Dickens to G, especially to *Thyrza*. This debt is evident in matters of theme, point of view, characterization, and even style. [Reviewed by F. Delatte, "Comptes Rendus," REVUE BELGE DE PHILOLOGIE ET D'HISTOIRE, XII (Jan–June 1933), 213; Paul Meissner, BEIBLATT ZUR ANGLIA, XLII (1931), 308–11; "New Foreign Books," TIMES LITERARY SUPPLEMENT (Lond), 19 March 1931, p. 235; E. Rosenbuch, "Buchesprechungen," NEUREN SPRACHEN, XLI (Nov–Dec 1933), 473; Anton Weber, ENGLISCHE STUDIEN, LXVIII (1933), 142–47, 158–60. (Weber's review includes a letter addressed to him from Frank Swinnerton claiming that Swinnerton did not believe that his own fiction was influenced by his work on G.)] [In German.]

**891** Steinhardt, Maxwell. "A Devon Idyll," QUARTO CLUB PAPERS: 1928–1929 (NY: Quarto Club [ptd for the members], 1930), pp. 3–13.
*The Private Papers of Henry Ryecroft* is "at least a minor classic in English literature," containing the thoughts of a happy recluse who learns that "the contented philosopher is a more worthy citizen than the blustering and noisy man of affairs." In a style that "is rich though easily digested," G reflects the respite from the anxieties of life that allowed him the quiet of spiritual peace, idealized in a small, remote Devon cottage. Neither man nor woman disturbed this escape; he relished only the companionship of books. *Ryecroft* is certainly G's finest book.

**892** West, Geoffrey Harry [pseud of Geoffrey Harry Wells]. H. G. WELLS (NY: W. W. Norton, 1930), pp. 103ff, 120, 122ff, 133–34.
Wells persuaded G to learn to ride a bicycle. G introduced Wells to Rome, where "Wells invented the story of 'Miss Winchelsea's Heart'—so Gissing-like in conception, so utterly Wellsian in narration." From his experience at G's death, Wells described Edward Ponderevo's death in TONO-BUNGAY.

# 1931

**893** Eichler, A. "Sprache und Literatur" (Language and Literature), BEIBLATT ZUR ANGLIA, XLII (Jan 1931), 25–26.
*Veranilda: An Unfinished Romance* reveals G's interest in Roman history. Its structure is loose; some of the effective scenes are, however, held to-

gether by means of suspense and the colorful background. This fragmentary work cannot compare with Felix Dahn's KAMPF UM ROM, but its pleasing style and the skillful blend of original and historical matters make it a remarkable achievement. [In German.]

**894** Eichler, A. "I. Sprache und Literatur" (Language and Literature), BEIBLATT ZUR ANGLIA, XLII (Jan 1931), 26–27.

*Will Warburton* is not characteristic of G the realist. Although he deals with the artists, the bourgeois desire for money and social prestige, he no longer views class differences and the character of the artist (Künstlernatur) as hard and fast realities. The weaknesses of the middle class are touched upon, but the honest will to work and the inner decency of the hero triumph over bourgeois materialism. The novel is entertaining; the dialogues are brilliant; the presentation is ironic. The scenes in St. Jean de Luz border on a Dickensian kind of sentimentality. [In German.]

**895** Hastings, George Everett, Vincent Starrett, and Thomas Olive Mabbott. "Introductions," *Brownie* (NY: Columbia UP, 1931), pp. 7–22.

Impressed by Whelpdale's remarks in *New Grub Street* we were led to search the Chicago newspaper files of 1877 for additional stories by G. Singly, and in combination, we identified seven stories, originally published in Chicago papers, the TRIBUNE, JOURNAL, and POST, as either certainly or probably authored by G.

**896** Roberts, Morley. "The Letters of George Gissing," VIRGINIA QUARTERLY REVIEW, VII (July 1931), 409–26.

The real G came alive in Naples, where his simplest desires were satisfied. His letters—fifty-two of them I seem to have lost—described his enthusiasm for the joyous South, in Italy and Greece. G was a good letter writer. His subtle humor was consistent with his response to life. The melancholy of his novels contrasts with his zest for life. James Payn would not have published *Demos* if the manuscript had not appeared when there were riots in London. G was always in financial difficulties.

# 1932

**897** French, Yvonne. "Belles-Lettres-I," MERCURY (Lond), XXVI (Sept 1932), 462.

The short stories in *Brownie* do not have G's usual "drabness of description." The collection contains almost a "Brontëian touch of elemental fantasy in its imagination and slightly morbid idea."

**898** "Gissing in Chicago," TIMES LITERARY SUPPLEMENT (Lond), 26 May 1932, p. 384.

G's *Brownie,* a collection of tales gathered by George Everett Hastings, Vincent Starrett, and Thomas Olive Mabbott (NY: Columbia UP; Lond: Milford, 1932) is of bibliographic rather than literary interest. The title story is "commonplace countryside melodrama" by an unformed writer. The collection is a tribute to the efforts of the editors; they make G out as "the veriest amateur of his craft."

**899** Greenbaum, Elizabeth. "George Gissing," THE HISTORY OF THE NOVEL IN ENGLAND, ed by Robert Morss Lovett and Helen Sard Hughes (Boston: Houghton Mifflin, 1932), pp. 362–69.

G was an "importer of realistic elements from abroad, and a harbinger of developments to come." His chief characters were the "exceptional rather than the normal members of the proletariat." While his novels move readers to tears, G never achieves "that depersonalization which makes great tragedy universal." In his early novels, he repeated the theme of a mediator, set between two levels of society, using his wealth to help the people. G resembles Proust in suggesting the relationship between love and jealousy.

**900** Henriot, Émile. "Introduction," *Né en exil (Born in Exile),* (Paris: Editions du Siècle, Catalogne et Cie, 1932), pp. vii–xvi; rptd as "Un Julien Sorel Anglais," REVUE BLEUE, LXXI (7 Jan 1933), 16–20.

True literature is always fifty years ahead of its time, though not recognized until fifty years after its time. Translated by Marie Canavaggia, G's *Born in Exile* brings to us an autobiographical and pessimistic novel, a true story of human sentiment. G engages in social and psychological conflicts, providing robust and sincere portraits that come largely from his own sad life. G's contemporaries were not interested in his books because they threatened the status quo. Godwin Peak is a true brother of Julien Sorel, although the independence that Stendhal demanded of his characters was not easy for him. [In French.]

**901** Mabbott, Thomas Olive. "Correspondence: A Tale By Gissing Identified," TIMES LITERARY SUPPLEMENT (Lond), 7 July 1932, p. 499.

"An English Coast-Picture," a story that appeared in APPLETON'S JOURNAL (III [July 1877], 73–78) must be the work mentioned by G in a letter to his family. While signed by G. R. Gresham, the initials and the style encourage this assumption.

**902** Morley, Christopher. Ex Libris Clarissimis (Phila: University of Pennsylvania P, 1932), pp. 33–41.

G's name often occurs in my own fiction. Written after a bitter struggle in life, *The Private Papers of Henry Ryecroft* proves that "happier conditions made it possible to trace the presentation copies of G's books that were loaned by Morley Roberts to American friends."

**903** Morley, Christopher. "Pebbles from Gissing Pond," Atlantic Monthly, CXLIX (Feb 1932), 143–52.

One finds enormous pleasure in collecting books, particularly those by G. My dog, Mr. Gissing, "once mistook for the ocean itself" a pond in suburban Long Island. So the pond too was named after G. [Personal reminiscence.]

**904** Neugebauer, Paul. "George Gissing," in "Schopenhauer in England mit Besonderer Berucksich-Tigung seines Einfluss auf die Englische Literatur" (Schopenhauer in England with Special Attention to his Influence in English Literature). Unpublished thesis, University of Berlin, 1932, pp. 39–44.

To a certain extent G adopts Schopenhauer's thought. He emphasizes the fact that man is determined by a capricious destiny, that man's character does not change, and that the individual will is never satisfied. In contrast to Schopenhauer, G regards suicide as the end of suffering. [In German.]

**905** Rothenstein, William. Men and Memories. 2 vols (NY: Tudor, 1932), I, 60, 302–4, 328; II, 40–41, 261.

G was "a man of fastidious tastes"; he was "obsessed by the melancholy side of life." After G's death, Algernon Gissing came to tell me how much he valued his brother's portrait drawn about six years earlier. Possessing a tender sense of beauty, G had "a wistful, sensitive nature."

**906** Shafer, Robert. "Limited Editions and Scholarship," Bookman (NY), LXXIV (March 1932), 676–77.

The publication of *Brownie* is a monumental "example of misguided zeal," a travesty of scholarship unworthy of the Columbia University Press. Morley Roberts had years ago persuaded Christopher Hagerup not to publish these stories now brought out by George Hastings, Vincent Starrett, and Thomas Mabbott. Both Hagerup and Starrett followed references in *New Grub Street* to track down G's stories in Chicago newspapers.

**907** Weber, Anton. George Gissing und die Sociale Frage (George Gissing and the Social Question) (Leipzig: Bernhard Tauchnitz, 1932) (Beiträg zur englischen Philologie, XX).

A transitional figure, G broke with Victorian sentimentality to advocate an individualistic criticism of life. The pessimism and misery of his novels originated in his own life and readings. He synthesized various literary reform movements; his biting criticism of society is based upon both the materialistic west-European and the more idealistic east-European attitudes. His characters show the effects of social determinism. Circumstances combine with heredity and some fatal flaw in temperament to make the individual a passive being. His workers face problems in education, housing, and working conditions. Influenced by Ruskin and Morris, G thought of the arts as valuable means for humanizing the multitudes. He concluded that reforms are based on a refinement of cultural conditions, that any striving after culture is incompatable with poverty, and that only a few are able to respond to education. G argued for the dignity of the individual in his discussions of the emancipation of women and the divorce laws. It would seem that G's notions of determinism contradict his esteem of the individual. The paradox is resolved when we realize that his social realism was not his essential artistic impulse. He was a romantic who was devoted to the past and to beauty; he hated the ugliness of modern life. [Probably the best German work on G, though marred by somewhat hazy terminology.] [Weber's book was reviewed by Ernest A. Baker, "Reviews," MODERN LANGUAGE REVIEW, XXVIII (Oct 1933), 535–36; J. W. Beach, "Reviews," MODERN LANGUAGE NOTES, XLIX (March 1934), 200–201; "New Foreign Books," TIMES LITERARY SUPPLEMENT (Lond), 13 June 1935, p. 380; Anton Rotter, "Sprache und Literatur" (Language and Literature), BEIBLATT ZUR ANGLIA, XLIV (1933), 379–82.] [In German.]

## 1933

**908** Gissing, Alfred C. "Correspondence: Gissing's *By the Ionian Sea*," TIMES LITERARY SUPPLEMENT (Lond), 13 April 1933, p. 261.

I "disclaim all responsibility" for the introduction recently attached to the Jonathan Cape reprint of *By the Ionian Sea*.

**909** Gissing, Alfred C. "Correspondence: Gissing's *By the Ionian Sea*," TIMES LITERARY SUPPLEMENT (Lond), 27 April 1933, p. 295.

Let me itemize some of the errors contained in Virginia Woolf's introduction to the Jonathan Cape reprint of *By the Ionian Sea:* she misquotes G's letters; she claims G's education suffered because of family need; she says that he visited Sicily when he never did go there; and she claims that

G purchased Gibbon one volume at a time, whereas he made two purchases three volumes at a time. [For previous entries in this controversy, see the TLS for 13 April 1933 and 20 April 1933, and subsequently for 4 May 1933.]

**910** Jaloux, Edmond. "L'esprit des Livres" (The Feeling of Books), LES NOUVELLES LITTÉRAIRES, 4 March 1933, p. 3.

*Born in Exile,* translated by Marie Canavaggia (Editions du Siècle), possesses a severe beauty that comes from the sort of fatality that hangs over the hero. In this respect it resembles Hardy's JUDE THE OBSCURE. *Exile* is tragic and true to life, closer to the French novel after Balzac than to British fiction between Dickens and Woolf. But the pathetic side of the book, its serious discussions as well as the tragedy of the moral conflict, is typically English. [In French.]

**911** Lewis, Leslie L. "George Gissing." Unpublished dissertation, Cornell University, 1933.

[Listed in Lawrence F. McNamee, DISSERTATIONS IN ENGLISH AND AMERICAN LITERATURE (NY & Lond: Bowker, 1968).]

**912** Oda, Masanobu. GEORGE GISSING (Tokyo: Kenkyusha, 1933).

[This biographical and critical study of G was the first to be published in Japan. Though based on inadequate materials, it is both sympathetic and conscientious.]

**913** Stadler, Konrad F. "Die Rolle der Antike bei George Gissing" (The Role of Antiquity in George Gissing). Unpublished dissertation, University of Freiburg, 1933.

[Listed in Lawrence F. McNamee, DISSERTATIONS IN ENGLISH AND AMERICAN LITERATURE (NY & Lond: Bowker, 1968).] G's lifelong interest in antiquity and his extensive reading of the classics significantly influenced his handling of mythology, history, literature, and art in his novels. An enthusiastic student of antiquity in his youth, G's scholarly career was spoiled by a sad and unfortunate experience. The misery he found in the cities, he depicted in his fiction. Though his work was not done against the grain, he wished always to be able to escape into his dreamland in order to recover from the demands of the present. Owing to his scholarly approach and his pessimism, his interest in the classics was antiquarian in kind. Unlike Browning or Swinburne, G did not create any work entirely permeated by the ancients. His reading of the classics, however, is reflected in his characterizations, his comparisons, his diction, and in the high respect always assigned the classics. *The Private Papers of Henry Ryecroft* and *By the Ionian Sea,* though not his most characteristic works, are doubtless his most enduring. [In German.]

**914** Van Maanen, W. "George Gissing's Life from his Letters," NEOPHILOLOGUS, XVIII (Jan 1933), pp. 115–30.

Rather than approach G troubled by an academic background—as May Yates—or inflict their own personalities on him—as Morley Roberts and Frank Swinnerton—one should approach G "in a spirit of awe and humility," by reading his letters. [Van Maanen thereafter reconstructs G's life out of passages of his letters, those to members of his family as well as to Clement Shorter and Edward Clodd.]

**915** Washburne, R. B. "Remembering George Gissing," in Christopher Morley's column "The Bowling Green," SATURDAY REVIEW OF LITERATURE, X (30 Dec 1933), 383.

Readers still wait for Morley to carry out his promise to tell us about George Matthew Adams's copy of a notebook that G had with him in America. [Correspondent calls himself a devotee of G.]

**916** Woolf, Virginia. "Correspondence: Gissing's *By the Ionian Sea,*" TIMES LITERARY SUPPLEMENT (Lond), 20 April 1933, p. 276.

The introduction to Jonathan Cape's edition of *By the Ionian Sea* is mine, and I signed it. Alfred C. Gissing failed to mention this fact in his letter. [For the origin of this controversy see Alfred C. Gissing's letter to the TLS, 13 April 1933; for the continuation of the controversy see the TLS entries for 27 April 1933 and 4 May 1933.]

**917** Woolf, Virginia. "Correspondence: Gissing's *By the Ionian Sea,*" TIMES LITERARY SUPPLEMENT (Lond), 4 May 1933, p. 312.

I regret "that I may have led the reader to suppose that Gissing dined off lentils a year after he had given up eating them," that he took six journeys to a bookseller, not two; that I ought to have said "two days before he died" instead of "as he died." But such mistakes do not seem to be of a serious nature. I do apologize for saying that G had to "scrape together" what education he could, when there "was no shortage of money for educational purposes." [For the three previous letters in this controversy, see the TLS for 13 April 1933, 20 April 1933, and 27 April 1933, previously cited.]

## 1934

**918** Adams, George Matthew. "How and Why I Collect George Gissing," COLOPHON, Part 18 (Sept 1934).
I have gathered first editions and manuscripts of G with such addiction that on occasion I have failed to pay the interest on my home's mortgage. One of the most valuable items of my collection [reproduced in article] is a chart showing the income G received from his individual writings.

**919** Cowley, Malcolm. EXILE'S RETURN (NY: Viking, 1934; rvd ed, 1951), p. 20.
During our youth, members of the Lost Generation read enormously, seeking literary guidance. In the search, we found in *The Private Papers of Henry Ryecroft* G's hostility with the world. Like G, we were no longer members of society.

**920** Cunliffe, John W. "Late Victorian Novelists: George Gissing," LEADERS OF THE VICTORIAN REVOLUTION (NY: D. Appleton-Century, 1934), pp. 267–77.
While G was never a bestseller during his own life, he has secured a place in literary history as a "conscientious artist" who chronicled the lives of the humble poor. *New Grub Street,* which contains "the bitterness of his personal life as an author," will probably prove his best remembered book. He refused to gain popularity at the price of writing about romantic love or sensational realism.

**921** Gapp, Samuel Vogt. "George Gissing: Classicist." University of Pennsylvania dissertation, 1934. [Listed in Lawrence F. McNamee, DISSERTATIONS IN ENGLISH AND AMERICAN LITERATURE (NY & Lond: Bowker, 1968)]; pub as GEORGE GISSING: CLASSICIST (Phila: University of Pennsylvania P; Lond: Oxford UP, 1936); pp. 158–77 of original study rptd as "Influence of the Classics on Gissing's Novels of Modern Life," COLLECTED ARTICLES ON GEORGE GISSING, ed by Pierre Coustillas (Lond: Frank Cass, 1968), pp. 83–98.
G's enthusiasm for classical literature constantly appears in all his books, in his letters, and in his travels. It is both an emotional and intellectual enthusiasm documented repeatedly by allusions, by stylistic phrasing, and by narrative scheme. This enthusiasm is based upon his education in the classics and continued throughout his life by constant readings in the classics. References to ancient literature appear no less frequently in his most realistic novels, although the spirit of *By the Ionian Sea* most con-

spicuously catches the tone of his devotion and the depth of his knowledge. [Reviews include: E. A. Baker, "Short Notices," MODERN LANGUAGE REVIEW, XXXIII (Jan 1938), 123; "Gissing and the Classics," TIMES LITERARY SUPPLEMENT (Lond), 29 Aug 1936, p. 692; A. Rotter, BEIBLATT ZUR ANGLIA, XLVIII (1937), 376–78.]

**922** Legouis, Emile. "The Novel: Gissing," A STORY HISTORY OF ENGLISH LITERATURE (Oxford: Clarendon P, 1934), pp. 367–68.
G's novels have neither Dickens's humor nor Hardy's nature; they are characterized by bitterness and the horror of London. His writing seeks complete objectivity without lyrical efforts. G's "bare, unaffected, sober, and lucid prose is among the best of the period."

**923** Swinnerton, Frank. THE GEORGIAN SCENE: A LITERARY PANORAMA (NY: Farrar & Rinehart, 1934), pp. 10, 11, 49, 146, 156, 178, 186, 188, 193, 203, 233, 285, 442.
Among all the writers of the late nineteenth century, Moore and G "were trying in the published novel to tell the world something of the world at first hand." Moore recorded what he saw; G was detached but added his personal comment. Together, they gave rise "to a new school of naturalistic writers, Edwin Pugh, Arthur Morrison, Somerset Maugham, and others."

**924** Wells, H. G. EXPERIMENT IN AUTOBIOGRAPHY (Lond: Gollancz, 1934), II, 563, 567–81, 634.
G "was a strange tragic figure, a figure of internal tragedy." When we first met, he was "an extremely good-looking, well-built, slightly on the lean side" man whose appearance betrayed "little then of the poison that had crept into his blood to distress, depress and undermine his vitality and at last to destroy him." His "pseudo-marriage" to a French woman came as the outgrowth of the beginning of his Continental recognition. [Wells recalls in some detail his days discovering Rome with G as his guide.]

# 1935

**925** Conrad, Jessie. JOSEPH CONRAD AND HIS CIRCLE (Lond: Jarrolds, 1935), p. 75.
"It was to the Pent that H. G. Wells came, bringing G. B. Shaw, George Gissing, and many other men, and not a few ladies." [Information repeated by Jocelyn Baines, JOSEPH CONRAD: A CRITICAL BIOGRAPHY (NY: McGraw-Hill, 1959), p. 234; Gérard Jean-Aubry, JOSEPH CONRAD: THE SEA DREAMER (NY: Doubleday, 1957), p. 235. Jean-Aubry refers to G as "the naturalistic novelist."]

**926** Cowley, Malcolm. "What the Revolutionary Movement Can Do for a Writer," NEW MASSES, XV (7 May 1935), 20–22; rptd in THINK BACK ON US, ed by Henry Dan Piper (Carbondale: Southern Illinois UP, 1967), pp. 87–94.

Between 1880 and 1930, many serious novelists tended to occupy themselves with "the conflict between the individual and society, between the Artist and the World." One of the best statements of this alienation is G's *New Grub Street*.

**927** Neuschäffer, Walter. "Dostojewskij und der realistiche Roman um die Jahrhundertwende: George Gissing" (Dostoevski and the Realistic Novel at the Turn of the Century: George Gissing), DOSTOJEWSKIJS EINFLUSS AUF DEN ENGLISCHEN ROMAN (Dostoevski's Influence on the English Novel), (Anglistiche Forschungen) (Heidelberg: C. Winter, 1935), LXXXI, 16–22.

The political-social conditions of some G figures resemble those of some Dostoevski characters. Reardon and Thyrza are among those creatures whose plight is examined with great realism to show the effects of society in the batle for existence. It is useful to trace the influence of Dostoevski on English novelists, beginning with G and then continuing in Conrad and Maugham. [In German.]

**928** Shafer, Robert. "Introduction," *Workers in the Dawn* (NY: Doubleday, Doran, 1935), I, vii–lv.

*Workers in the Dawn* reveals G "in full possession of his imaginative powers, attacking personal and social problems," and learning how best to employ his literary powers. It gained for him the friendship of Frederic Harrison, who "placed Gissing on his feet." *Workers in the Dawn* brought G "before the public as a constructive and informed critic of contemporary life." Among the writers who influenced him, "Dickens had entered organically into" his very being, but there were differences between the novelists in both their methods and their aims. G treated the psychological qualities of his characters, without special preference to virtues or deserts. And while G was also influenced by Continental authors, he was never merely a disciple. His vitality rests in his "comment upon life and its problems," in the tracts or records of observation that form "living pictures of humanity caught in the toils of crushing circumstance." [Reviewed by R(aymond) D. H(avens), "Brief Mention," MODERN LANGUAGE NOTES, LII (Jan 1937), 76. Shafer's introduction to G's "powerful and almost unprocurable first novel" has provided an essay "important for its facts as well as its comments."] [A valuable and reliable study.]

**929** Shafer, Robert. "The Vitality of George Gissing," AMERICAN REVIEW, V (Sept 1935), 459–87.

G was a more important writer than Thomas Hardy, "though far below him as an artist." The serenity of *The Private Papers of Henry Ryecroft* is the book's dominant quality and explains its vitality. Regardless of the opinions of Morley Roberts, Frank Swinnerton, and H. G. Wells, *Ryecroft* gives us "the full quality of the mature man." G's importance as a writer is increasing for several reasons: his unpretentiousness, his cultivation and restrained independence, his sweetness, his simple decency, and his disillusioned yet not unfeeling serenity.

# 1936

**930** Hone, Joseph. THE LIFE OF GEORGE MOORE (Lond: Gollancz; NY: Macmillan, 1936), p. 107.
Moore was the first English novelist to apply the French naturalistic methods; G "would never have written of Kate Ede vomiting over her dress and the red velvet seat of her four-wheeler," as Moore did in A MUMMER'S WIFE.

**931** Mason, Walt. "Famous Too Late," in Christopher Morley's column "The Bowling Green," SATURDAY REVIEW OF LITERATURE, XIII (28 March 1936), 13.
G led a sad life, with little acclaim; now his books are in demand and getting firm prices.

**932** Swinnerton, Frank. AN AUTOBIOGRAPHY (NY: Doubleday Doran, 1936), pp. 31, 109, 111, 117–19, 136.
Martin Secker asked me to write a critical study of G. Before writing it, I read all of G's books, drew upon Thomas Seccombe, and (at Bennett's suggestion) called upon Wells for help. When it appeared, the book brought simultaneous reviews alongside Morley Roberts's THE PRIVATE LIFE OF HENRY MAITLAND. Moreover, Secker was so pleased with the success of the study that he asked for a similar study of Stevenson; it appeared in 1914. G is the model for one of the main characters in my ON THE STAIRCASE (1914).

# 1937

**933** Gissing, Alfred C. "Gissing's Unfinished Romance," NATIONAL REVIEW, CVIII (Jan 1937), 82–91.
G intended *Veranilda* "to produce a picture of great historical events." The

public was astonished to find so much distance between *Veranilda* and the books that built his reputation, like *Demos* and *The Nether World*. But ancient Rome was always a real world to G.

**934** Muller, Herbert J. MODERN FICTION: A STUDY OF VALUES (NY: Funk & Wagnalls, 1937), pp. 186–94.

A sociological novelist in the tradition of Mrs. Gaskell, Kingsley, and Reade, G sees the large implications of the social condition, documents it thoroughly, and provides a more accurate record. Physical suffering is made real in his fiction: hunger, cold, jealousy, hatred are made concrete. Misery characterizes his chief figures; they are ignoble and commonplace, but ambitious. Even in *New Grub Street,* G cannot imaginatively identify with his impoverished writers. G is squeamish and feminine in his painful observation of filth and pain, so that he is insufficiently vital and excessively detached in describing what he himself experienced.

# 1938

**935** Baker, E. A. "George Gissing," THE HISTORY OF THE ENGLISH NOVEL (Lond: Witherby, 1938), IX, 122–60.

G's novels "were composed out of his own personal experiences." G's philosophy was both austere and radical; he told the depressing repulsiveness of the slums. *Demos,* his first mature novel, gives a practical scheme for regenerating society. Reardon, of *New Grub Street,* "gives the history of his own martyrdom." Sidwell Warricombe, of *Born in Exile,* is G's most elaborate portrait of a "proper mate for his intellectuals," while Godwin Peak is as close as G ever came to a complete representation of his personal attitude. *The Private Papers of Henry Ryecroft* proves again that most of all G lacked a zest for life. Misery, his principal theme, overwhelmed him, so that pessimism dominated his art.

**936** Church, Richard. "Gleanings from Gissing," MERCURY (Lond), XXXVII (March 1938), 546–47.

The short pieces in *Stories and Sketches* remind us that almost everything G wrote "was sociological in interest." They are distinguished by G's scholarship, by his "mellifluous prose style, with its rich sonorous paragraphs," and by the sense of a broken spirit.

**937** Cruse, Amy. AFTER THE VICTORIANS (Lond: Allen & Unwin, 1938), pp. 23, 101.

Leslie Stephen's agnostic writings appealed to a considerable portion of the reading public; G's Godwin Peak of *Born in Exile* expressed the rationalistic position of agnosticism in fiction.

**938** Gissing, Alfred C. "Preface," *Stories and Sketches* (Lond: Michael Joseph, 1938), pp. 5–7.

G's stories might be regarded "as sketches of characterization and temperament." My father, like Trollope, "always maintained that plot without character in a story was like a vehicle without passengers." [This preface also contains a very slight comment on the source of each piece in the collection.]

**939** Haasler, Gerhard. "Die Darstellung der Frau bei George Gissing" (The Representation of Women by George Gissing), Unpublished dissertation, University of Greifswald, 1938.

[Listed in Lawrence F. McNamee, DISSERTATIONS IN ENGLISH AND AMERICAN LITERATURE (NY & Lond: Bowker, 1968).]

**940** Leavis, Q. D. "Gissing and the English Novel," SCRUTINY, VII (June 1938), 73–81.

The appearance of G's *Stories and Sketches* reminds us that G's vogue "had faded even out of literary history," but we are encouraged just the same to hope that *New Grub Street* might be reprinted. Marian Yule's "delicacy and fineness" are represented with complete success. The entire novel sustains the tone of "irony weighted with disgust."

**941** Mackenzie, Compton. LITERATURE IN MY TIME (Lond: Rich & Cowan, 1938), pp. 130, 180.

G had nothing to tell my generation because he did not provide the falsification we sought. *By the Ionian Sea* is an "overpraised piece of impressionism."

---

# 1939

---

**942** Hicks, Granville. "The Changing Novel: Gissing as Realist," FIGURES IN TRANSITION (NY: Macmillan, 1939), pp. 194–203.

G helped give "British literature a new direction." Rejecting Dickens's sentimentality, G sought to depict the truth of slum life to perform a literary task more than to assist social reform. He also discarded the Victorian complicated plot and manipulated incident, intending to deal with the commonplace in its bestiality. Tollady of *Workers in the Dawn* states G's purpose: "Paint a faithful picture of this crowd we have watched, be a successor of Hogarth, and give us the true image of *our* social dress, as he did of his own day." G brings the reader directly into the lives of the impoverished masses and impresses us with his seriousness in their representation. By 1895, G could recognize a new freedom for novelists because "public opinion no longer constrains a novelist to be false to himself." G had one great advantage over Moore: saturated in the commonplace, he knew the world at first hand and had strong beliefs about that world.

**943** Muchnic, Helen. DOSTOEVSKY'S ENGLISH REPUTATION: 1881–1936 (Smith College Studies in Modern Languages) (Northhampton, Mass., 1939), XX, 28, 41.

G was among the first British novelists to record his impressions of the stage version of CRIME AND PUNISHMENT, which he saw in Paris. G's study of Dickens called attention to the similarities between Dickens and Dostoevski.

**944** Philip, Brother C., F.S.C. "Gissing as a Prophet," in "Letters to the Editor," SATURDAY REVIEW OF LITERATURE, XIX (22 April 1939), 9.

Judging from this quotation in *The Private Papers of Henry Ryecroft,* we can surmise what G would have thought of European civilization and democracy today.

## 1940

**945** Henkin, Leo J. DARWINISM IN THE ENGLISH NOVEL: 1860–1910 (NY: Corporate P, 1940), pp. 123–25, 158–60, 224, 230–32.

Though G himself "detested the sciences," *Workers in the Dawn* shows that he had studied evolution and reached conclusions. Godwin Peak of *Born in Exile* satirized the quasi-scientific who would make peace between the Bible and evolution. In *New Grub Street*, natural selection is the villain, setting aside the conscientious Reardon to favor the opportunist Milvain. *The Private Papers of Henry Ryecroft* questions the idea that man is a product of the evolutionary law.

## 1941

**946** Gettmann, R. A. TURGENEV IN ENGLAND AND AMERICA (Illinois Studies in Language and Literature) (Urbana: University of Illinois P, 1941), 144–48.

Realism, for G, was "not simply a matter of documentation of the sensible world" but increasingly stressed the subjective element. G's letters do not once mention Flaubert, the Goncourts, de Maupassant, or Zola. But Turgenev "aroused G's special sympathy and admiration." In aims and artistic interests, "there was an unquestioned compatability" between them.

**947** House, Humphrey. THE DICKENS WORLD (Lond: Oxford UP, 1941; 2nd ed, 1942; rptd, 1950; Oxford Paperbacks, 1950), pp. 10, 145.

G is in error when he says that Dickens could not describe railroads with the same gusto and vision as that with which he described stage coaches.

## 1942

**948** Daley, Norma L. Schank. "Some Reflections on the Scholarship of Gissing," CLASSICAL JOURNAL, XXXVIII (Oct 1942), 21–30.

G's training in the classical languages and literature led to a genuine enthusiasm that is repeatedly evidenced in his books. In addition to countless classical allusions, his style ("cold, clear, even pellucid") reveals how deep his debt to the classics was. This debt is affectionately recorded in *The Private Papers of Henry Ryecroft* and *By the Ionian Sea.*

**949** Frierson, William C. "The Reaction Against Dickens," THE ENGLISH NOVEL IN TRANSITION (Norman, Okla: University of Oklahoma P, 1942), pp. 101–6.

Like Dickens, G focuses on characters whose inherent good qualities contrast with "prevailing sordidness"; unlike Dickens, he doubts the soundness of the social order and the "integrity of the universe." Lacking a remedy, he still voices a protest. No lover of the masses, whose plight he portrayed, he described with more loathing than any other author the "irremediable squalor" of slum life. G's vision—hatred of grossness, vulgarity, and poverty—is diffuse. G "altered the naturalistic novel to provide for social philosophizing, and he influenced Wells, George, Onions, Beresford, and Monkhouse.

**950** Niebling, Richard F. "The Adams-Gissing Collection," YALE UNIVERSITY LIBRARY GAZETTE, XVI (Jan 1942), 47–50.

In securing the G collection of George Matthew Adams, the Yale Library has acquired the finest and most complete set of first editions and manuscript material available. The collection includes about fifty letters dating from 1885 to 1901.

## 1943

**951** Bates, Herbert E. THE MODERN SHORT STORY: A CRITICAL STUDY (Lond: Thomas Nelson, 1943; Boston: Writer, 1949), p. 118.

Among short story writers of the 1890s, only Wells "is going anywhere."
"G is a minor echo of Dickens."

**952** Henkin, Leo. "Problems and Digressions in the Victorian
Novel," BULLETIN OF BIBLIOGRAPHY, XVIII–XX (Sept–Dec
1943 to Jan–April 1950).
[Work consists of listings of Victorian writings under numerous headings.
G's novels are listed in XVIII (Sept–Dec 1943), 41: *Born in Exile* and
*Workers in the Dawn* for the religious doubts of their central figures; in
XIX (Sept–Dec 1946), 8, 41, 56: *Demos* treats socialism, *The Nether
World* describes London's poor, and *Born in Exile* presents science as
the religion of its hero.] [Slight]

**953** "Menander's Mirror: Henry Ryecroft's Question," TIMES
LITERARY SUPPLEMENT (Lond), 16 Jan 1943, p. 27.
Published just forty years ago, *The Private Papers of Henry Ryecroft* deeply
impressed young readers at the time, advising them to depend entirely
upon themselves to secure quiet, to reject envy and ambition. To his contemporaries, G was an escapist, a scholar, and a craftsman. If he rarely
tried to provide answers to social dilemmas—except in the largest sense
that he opposed poverty—he did recognize the responsibility shared by
all serious and educated men to press for universal good. To equalize
the conditions of men, G proposed not a violent leveling but a rededica-
tion to the spirit. This answer came principally from G's classical training. The closest he ever came to suggesting a solution to society's troubles
was to recommend tolerance and charity.

**954** Orwell, George [pseud of Eric Blair]. "Not Enough Money:
A Sketch of George Gissing," TRIBUNE (Lond), 2 April 1943,
p. 15; rptd in GISSING NEWSLETTER, V (July 1969), 1–4.
G is "perhaps the best novelist England has produced," for while Dickens,
Fielding, and a dozen others had more natural talent, G "is a 'pure'
novelist, a thing that few gifted English writers have been." G's real master-
pieces are *The Odd Women* ("his most perfect and also most depressing
novel"), *Demos* (it shows a "rather surprising knowledge of the inner
workings of the socialist movement"), *New Grub Street*, and his book
on Dickens. He thought of London's poor as "savages who must on no
account be allowed political power."

**955** Purdy, Richard L. "George Gissing at Max Gate," YALE
UNIVERSITY LIBRARY GAZETTE, XVII (Jan 1943), 51–52.
G's account of his visit to Hardy at Max Gate shows how imperceptive G's
impression of his fellow writer actually was.

**956** Wagenknecht, Edward. "Towards a New Century: George Gissing, a Scholar in Grub Street," CAVALCADE OF THE ENGLISH NOVEL (NY: Holt, 1943), pp. 406–11.

G, a classical scholar, was fated to write about the wretchedness that he knew best, collecting the phenomena of the slums. Yet he despised the proletariat and had no faith in their ability to better their condition. His first novels were in the Victorian form, but with *Born in Exile* and *The Odd Women* he moved to treat the personal problems of the middle class. Since his critical studies of Dickens are among the best that we have, it is not surprising that his novels show Dickens's influence, particularly in techniques. He shows his transitional qualities in his materials, "unromantic, frank, skeptical in religion and politics alike." His characters survive now for their independence and integrity; his novels, while not popular, refuse to die.

# 1944

**957** Baldensberger, Fernand. "English 'Artistic Prose' and Its Debt to French Writers," MODERN LANGUAGE FORUM, XXIX (Dec 1944), 139–50.

A disciplined writer himself, G deplored careless expression in fiction. He derived "more pleasure from the imagery of things than from reality." He scorned the writing of popular fiction. Like Gautier, G tried to be "a careful student of etymology."

**958** Wing, Donald. "The Adams-Gissing Collection," YALE UNIVERSITY LIBRARY GAZETTE, XVIII (Jan 1944), 49.

Further gifts to the George Matthew Adams collection include fourteen of G's school and university certificates. One document certifies that G merited a "good conduct" award at Owens College for the period 1872–1875; there is no mention of his disgrace.

# 1945

[No entries for this year.]

# 1946

**959** Paterson, James. "Letters to the Editor: George Gissing," TIMES LITERARY SUPPLEMENT (Lond), 19 Oct 1946, p. 507.

To complete a book that I am writing on G, I would appreciate receiving letters written by him.

**960** Webster, H. T. "Possible Influence of George Gissing's *Workers in the Dawn* on Maugham's OF HUMAN BONDAGE," MODERN LANGUAGE QUARTERLY, VII (Sept 1946), 315.
In addition to specific similarities in characters and plot (e.g. Golding's marriage to Carrie and Philip's association with Mildred), the greater affinity of the shaping of the novels and their narrative values forces us to recognize parallels between *Workers in the Dawn* and OF HUMAN BONDAGE.

# 1947

**961** Niebling, Richard F. "The Early Career of George Gissing." Unpublished dissertation, Yale University, 1947.
[Listed in Lawrence F. McNamee, DISSERTATIONS IN ENGLISH AND AMERICAN LITERATURE (NY & Lond: Bowker, 1968).]

**962** "Notes on Recent Acquisitions," YALE UNIVERSITY LIBRARY GAZETTE, XXI (April 1947), 62.
Louis Rabinowitz has given the Adams-Gissing Collection twenty letters that G wrote his brother between 1880 and 1894.

**963** Plomer, William. *"In the Year of Jubilee,"* PENGUIN NEW WRITING 29, ed by John Lehmann (Lond: Penguin, 1947), pp. 116–22; slightly reworked and rptd as "Introduction," *In the Year of Jubilee* (Lond: Watergate Classics, 1947), pp. v–viii.
Among G's many enthusiasts are readers who ignore his prejudices and give him a fair reading. But because G writes about unattractive subjects, there is no chance for a G revival. His style lacks gusto; he provides little entertainment value. But G's novels sustain themselves by recording "the materialism and social injustice of his late-Victorian day." [The reprint of *Jubilee* was partly responsible for these two articles: V. S. Pritchett, "Books in General," NEW STATESMAN AND NATION, XXXIV (8 Nov 1947), 372; "The Permanent Stranger," TIMES LITERARY SUPPLEMENT (Lond), 14 Feb 1948, p. 92.]

**964** Plomer, William. "Introduction," *A Life's Morning* (Lond: Home & Van Thal, 1947), pp. 5–21.
G's novels constitute a thoughtful collection of sad books that illuminate the social conditions of his England and provide his personal protest. His works indict "the period in which he lived," particularly its economic struc-

ture that G thought "too often thwarted the growth of the finer man and woman." While G's "sentences are properly formed and free from extravagance," they do not have the "piercing precision, the intensity, the touch of strangeness to be found in writers, even prose-writers, with a poetic inventiveness or epigrammatic skill." Nevertheless, "he has caught and fixed in countless forms the vulgarity, the materialism, and the social injustice of his late-Victorian days in a manner and on a scale attempted by nobody else." [This reprint was the partial occasion for an article by V. S. Pritchett, "Books in General," NEW STATESMAN AND NATION, XXXIV (8 Nov 1947), 372.]

> **965** Pritchett, V. S. "Books in General," NEW STATESMAN AND NATION, XXXIV (8 Nov 1947), 372; rptd as "Poor Gissing," in BOOKS IN GENERAL (NY: Harcourt, Brace; Lond: Butler & Tanner, 1953), pp. 209–15.

[Originally occasioned by the reprint of *In the Year of Jubilee,* with an introduction by William Plomer in the Penguin New Writing Series, 1947; and *A Life's Morning,* also introduced by William Plomer (Lond: Home & Van Thal, 1947).] G was a man born out of his own time, but his failure is the source of his persistent fame. His reputation "drags its heavy-footed way in a kind of perpetual purgatory." But people still read G because "he speaks seriously about matters which no other novelist has taken so seriously. Instructed by his reading of the French and Russian novelists he is bleakly aware of the situation of his time." Historically he foreshadows a type of hero, "the uprooted intellectual of a later generation, cut off by education from his own class and by economic and social conditions from any other place in society."

> **966** Steiner, Jacqueline. "George Gissing to his Sister," BULLETIN OF THE BOSTON PUBLIC LIBRARY, XXII (Nov 1947), 324–36; (Dec 1947), 376–86.

The Boston Public Library has acquired seventeen letters written by G to his sister Ellen between 1885 and 1902. They reveal how much the family edited the volume of G's letters, and how solicitous G was of his sisters. [The letters acquired by the Library are printed after this brief introduction.]

# 1948

> **967** Evans, Myfanwy. "Introduction," *The Whirlpool* (Lond: Watergate Classics, 1948), pp. v–xi.

One would be wise to read *The Whirlpool* in a relatively egocentric state of mind. In this novel, G showed some sign of accepting life as it is, even as he placed less stress on the necessity for universal culture. *Whirlpool* is a cry of despair, suggesting "that the intelligent man might hold in himself, rather than in his situation, the seeds of his downfall." G further hints here that "a denial of the primitive in man's and woman's nature is not a virtue, but a failure to face up to reality."

**968** Hutton, Edward. "Letters to the Editor: George Gissing," TIMES LITERARY SUPPLEMENT (Lond), 21 Feb 1948, p. 107.
The author of "The Permanent Stranger" (ibid, 14 Feb 1948, p. 92) is incorrect in stating that G's fame rests upon his fiction, for as a man outside his time G will survive for *By the Ionian Sea*. [For a reply to Hutton, see V. de S. Pinto, "Letters to the Editor: George Gissing," ibid, 6 March 1948, p. 135.]

**969** Marchand, Leslie A. "The Symington Collection," JOURNAL OF THE RUTGERS UNIVERSITY LIBRARY, XII (Dec 1948), 1–15.
A survey of the letters written by Watts-Dunton from "The Pines" reveals that he corresponded with many authors between 1889 and 1907. G was among them.

**970** "The Permanent Stranger," TIMES LITERARY SUPPLEMENT (Lond), 14 Feb 1948, p. 92, rptd in COLLECTED ARTICLES ON GEORGE GISSING, ed by Pierre Coustillas (Lond: Frank Cass, 1968), pp. 43–49.
G's endurance depends on his fiction, not upon his reputation as "poor Gissing," the scholar-recluse of *The Private Papers of Henry Ryecroft*. Like D. H. Lawrence, G was chiefly preoccupied with class, with the struggle to prove himself in competition with other disadvantaged men. He sought to express his zest for life, but his novels scarcely yield any such quality, giving instead his anguish and horror. Now we are impressed with his rare ability to render "with such passionate intensity" the special quality of his age, however distasteful his contemporaries found that rendering. Between *Workers in the Dawn* and *The Unclassed* he moved from a socialist to an anti-socialist position; he despised the slums and cared for only those exceptional characters whose talents were destroyed by circumstance, crippled by poverty. The naturally superior men are "almost invariably manifestations" of himself, like Godwin Peak of *Born in Exile*. *New Grub Street* contains two of G's finest women characters, Amy Reardon and Marian Yule. G had a greater "sympathy and compassion" for rendering women than men. No novelist has surpassed G in portraying the "miseries of matrimony as they arise from woman's jealousy, shrewishness or sluttishness." G's best novels, *The Odd Women* and *In the Year of Jubilee,* are not "marred by special pleading and self-pity."

Concerned with surplus women, those lacking economic security, *Women* is G's "most objective novel, the nearest to the work of the French naturalists that he wrote, a most impressive study of loneliness" among respectable middle-class London women. *Jubilee* is G's most controlled expression of disgust, exposing the vulgarity of the age. All in all, G provided a "unique picture of the England of his time" as felt by a permanent exile, isolated and uprooted. It is a state of life also prevalent even now. [This long and important article was occasioned by the reprinting of two novels by G: *A Life's Morning* (Lond: Home & Van Thal, 1947) and *In the Year of Jubilee* (Lond: Watergate Classics, 1947), both with introductory essays by William Plomer.]

**971** Pinto, V. de S. "Letters to the Editor: George Gissing," TIMES LITERARY SUPPLEMENT (Lond), 6 March 1948, p. 135. Edward Hutton ("Letters to the Editor: George Gissing," ibid, 21 Feb 1948, p. 107) misjudges G's reputation; a pleasant travel book like *By the Ionian Sea* is not as memorable as the image we get from G's fiction, the novels of a thoughtful man's comments on life.

## 1949

**972** Innes, Michael. "The Arts and Entertainment: Radio Notes," NEW STATESMAN AND NATION, XXXVIII (31 Dec 1949), 779. The CONCISE DNB closes out G's biography by saying that he "re-visited Italy with Mr. H.G. Wells." This is the "final touch of the macabre" because Wells was scarcely the one to accompany G to the well spring of our culture. The "elderly and ill and disappointed and defeated and morbidly shy and sensitive" G could not possibly have been at ease with the cocky and impertinent Wells. [The article reviews a radio program by Kingsley Martin, "New Judgment." See Anthony West, "Correspondence: Gissing and Wells," ibid, XXXIX (14 Jan 1950), 37–38.]

**973** Zabel, Morton Dauwen. "Dickens: The Reputation," NA-TION, CLXIX (7 Sept 1949), 279–81. G is one of Dickens's three greatest critics: "Taine sensed the fact" of the actual Dickens; "Gissing got hold of it though with some uncertainty, Wilson has traced its lines through the novels."

## 1950

**974** Batho, Edith C., and Bonamy Dobrée. THE VICTORIANS AND AFTER: 1830–1914, rvd ed (Lond: Cresset, 1950), pp. 76, 95, 140, 267, 295, 327.

G gave impetus to the slice-of-life novel; in "pitiless prosaic prose" he reveals "the physical and cultural impoverishment of the lower middle classes." No social reformer, G was "purely a presenter."

**975** Donnelly, Mabel W. C. "Convention and Invention from Dickens to Gissing." Unpublished dissertation, Radcliff College, 1950.
[Listed in Lawrence F. McNamee, DISSERTATIONS IN ENGLISH AND AMERICAN LITERATURE (NY & Lond: Bowker, 1968).]

**976** Guidi, Augusto. "Borgian Cheese," NOTES AND QUERIES, CXCV (18 Feb 1950), 80.
In *By the Ionian Sea* G misunderstands the nature of *cacio cavallo;* it is not really butter, but part of a sphere of cheese at the soft core. G does not ordinarily make such mistakes.

**977** Hempel, Adolf. "George Gissing als Naturalist in seinen Jugendwerken" (George Gissing as a Naturalist in his Early Novels). Unpublished dissertation, University of Freiburg, 1950.
[Listed in Lawrence F. McNamee, DISSERTATIONS IN ENGLISH AND AMERICAN LITERATURE (NY & Lond: Bowker, 1968).] G's early novels, *The Unclassed, Thyrza,* and *The Nether World,* are "naturalistic" in the sense given the term in Zola's LE ROMAN EXPERIMENTAL. They reveal heredity, milieu, and coincidence as powers determining man's life. G derived this point of view not only from his own experience in life but also from his knowledge of the natural sciences, positivism, socialism, and Schopenhauerian pessimism. He had little in common with Dickens and was probably not directly influenced by any of the French and Russian novelists of his time. G's social determinism corresponds with Zola's, even if G is less outspoken and presents more individualized characters since he concentrates on the conflict between man and his environment. In the main, his narrative techniques are objective. Authorial comments are reduced to a minimum by the use of dialogue, indirect interior monologue, and impressionistic description. [In German.]

**978** Kirk, Russell. "Who Knows George Gissing?" WESTERN HUMANITIES REVIEW, IV (Summer 1950), 213–22; rptd in COLLECTED ARTICLES ON GEORGE GISSING, ed by Pierre Coustillas (Lond: Frank Cass, 1968), pp. 3–13.
G himself knew the sadness of life. In his best novels, G portrayed select characters by gradually revealing their minds. One finds G's hero in solitude, loving books, suffering the whims of life. To get G's stylistic best, read *The Private Papers of Henry Ryecroft.*

**979** Korg, Jacob. "George Gissing's Outcast Intellectuals," AMERICAN SCHOLAR, XIX (Spring 1950), 194–202.

G, "the most neglected of the substantial Victorian novelists," specialized in representing "the disinherited intellectual as the victim of social injustice." Using naturalistic methods, G wrote long novels "dense with minor incidents of illustrative rather than dramatic value." Like Zola and Moore, G believed that one depicted real life by copying it. The condition of the exiled intellectual is principally recorded in Waymark of *The Unclassed,* Reardon of *New Grub Street,* and Peak in *Born in Exile.* In these figures, G was really writing about himself, ruling out personal commentary "as a naturalist should." By scrupulous detachment, G masked his "intense moral indignation."

**980** West, Anthony. "Correspondence: Gissing and Wells," NEW STATESMAN AND NATION, XXXIX (14 Jan 1950), 37–38.

Michael Innes errs when he calls G's joy in Rome macabre. G enjoyed Rome both because it was the well spring of our culture and because he could introduce Wells to its antiquity. [See Michael Innes, "The Arts and Entertainment: Radio Notes," ibid, XXXVIII (31 Dec 1949), 779.]

## 1951

**981** Buckley, Jerome H. THE VICTORIAN TEMPER (Cambridge, Mass.: Harvard UP, 1951), pp. 210–12.

G's novels show how concerned he was with the crucial issues of his times. "As the major English novelist to begin publishing in the eighties, George Gissing understood both the purposes of the new socialism and the conditions that made necessary its work." But the British reading public was not prepared to accept the Reardons, Waymarks, and Goldings of G's books.

**982** Church, Richard. THE GROWTH OF THE ENGLISH NOVEL (Lond: Methuen, 1951), pp. 195–99.

A pioneer in fiction for his "psychological attack on his theme," G was the "first English novelist to explore the methods used by Dostoevski." In gloomy studies of middle-class life, G "dived deep into the privacies of self-contemplation."

**983** Lloyd, Michael. "Italy and the Nostalgia of George Gissing," ENGLISH MISCELLANY, II (1951), 171–98.

These quotations from G's writings demonstrate how enthusiastic he was about Italy, her sunlight, and her glorious past. His writings are full of the joy, sounds, and sights of antiquity. He loathed the ugly, and London gave him no delight; but he relished the careless life of the Mediterranean, particularly Naples. *Veranilda,* with its image of Rome threatened by barbarian hordes, is a warning to his own declining world; it catches the "sense of vertigo suffered when a civilization topples into space."

**984** Swinnerton, Frank. THE BOOKMAN'S LONDON (Lond: Allan Wingate, 1951; NY: Doubleday, 1952), pp. 13, 44, 132, 134–35, 149.

Among novelists, G best creates the London of the 1880s. He resided at several London addresses over the years, but he could find no comfort until he moved to the continent. James was right in calling G a misfit because as much as G watched the great city, he never penetrated it. He was "incurably middle-class (what he called 'aristocratic') in outlook."

**985** Takami, Jun [pseud of Takama, Yoshio]. "An Antipolitical Monologue," TOKYO SHIBUN, Nos. 3032, 3033 (4, 5 Feb 1951).

*The Private Papers of Henry Ryecroft* represents "an epicurean life in the truest sense of the word." [Includes quotations from *Ryecroft.*]

# 1952

**986** "Books to Come," TIMES LITERARY SUPPLEMENT (Lond), 5 Dec 1952, p. 804.

On the fiftieth anniversary of G's death, Phoenix House will publish a new edition of *The Private Papers of Henry Ryecroft* with a forward by Cecil Chisholm.

**987** Brooks, Van Wyck. THE CONFIDENT YEARS: 1885–1915 (NY: Dutton, 1952), pp. 174, 194, 391.

The techniques of Hamlin Garland and Robert Herrick sometimes remind one of G. If Paul Elmer More was attracted to G, perhaps enthusiasm for the classics was what they most shared.

**988** Gordan, John D. *"The Ghost* at Brede Place," BULLETIN OF THE NEW YORK PUBLIC LIBRARY, LVI (Dec 1952), 591–95.

G was one of twelve collaborators in a play principally written by Stephen Crane and performed on 28 Dec 1899 at Brede Place in East Sussex where Crane was living. [A facsimile of the program is printed.]

**989** Korg, Jacob. "George Gissing: A Study in Conflicts." Unpublished dissertation, Columbia University, 1952.

[Listed in Lawrence F. McNamee, DISSERTATIONS IN ENGLISH AND AMERICAN LITERATURE (NY & Lond: Bowker, 1968).]

**990** Neill, S. Diana. A SHORT HISTORY OF THE ENGLISH NOVEL (NY: Macmillan, 1952), pp. 197–203.

A "bridge between the old and the new schools of novelists," G represents "a new phenomenon in English life—the *déraciné* intellectual." He grew up at a time when education became a burden to material advancement. His novels are drab, showing no joy of life; they are addressed to social problems. Yet he is "not sympathetic to radicalism or a friend of democracy"; rather he remained a "Renaissance humanist venerating intellectual aristocracy." In *The Private Papers of Henry Ryecroft,* the real G emerges. The literary historian and the admirer of G will remember him most for those novels which "penetate into the mental hell reserved for the intellectual misfit in modern society." [One of the more perceptive surveys of G's fiction.]

**991** Nur, Sherif. "The Art and Thought of George Gissing, A Critical Study of his Development in his Works." Unpublished dissertation, London University, 1952.

[Listed in Lawrence F. McNamee, DISSERTATIONS IN ENGLISH AND AMERICAN LITERATURE (NY & Lond: Bowker, 1968).]

**992** "Recent Acquisitions," YALE UNIVERSITY LIBRARY GAZETTE, XXVII (July 1952), 52.

Louis Rabinowitz has given the Yale Library's Adams-Gissing collection eighty-seven autographed letters and many postal cards dating from 1880 to 1902.

---

# 1953

**993** Allen, Walter. "Books in General," NEW STATESMAN AND NATION, XLV (7 Feb 1953), 152–53.

Reading *The Private Papers of Henry Ryecroft* ["Foreword" by Cecil Chisholm (Lond: Phoenix House; Toronto: Dent, 1953)] makes one think of the death of Ponderevo in TONO-BUNGAY by H. G. Wells. If G "evokes one dominant image," it is of walking through a world of Ponderevos "holding his nose in shuddering and peevish revulsion." How did Wells ever find in G such a capacity for laughter and relish of the absurd? Reading G inevitably brings us back to the writer himself. *Ryecroft* is an "autobiographical fantasia," revealing the G hero, always at odds with society. The typical G hero, passionately felt, "approaches the intensity and power of the Russian novelists" that G so admired. Aside from *Ryecroft,* G's most successful characters are women—not ladies—like the working girls of *Thyrza* and *The Nether World,* or the lower, middle-class suburbanites of *In the Year of Jubilee.* G's distinctive contribution to English fiction comes in *The Odd Women, Jubilee, Born in Exile,* and *New Grub Street.* [Much of the material of this article reappeared in Allen's THE ENGLISH NOVEL (Lond: Phoenix House, 1954; NY: Dutton, 1955).]

> **994** Chisholm, Cecil. "Foreword," *The Private Papers of Henry Ryecroft* (Lond: Phoenix House; Toronto: Dent, 1953), pp. 7–15.

G himself was a curious figure, full of self-torture and self-pity. *The Private Papers of Henry Ryecroft* is more than a self-portrait, representing rather what G would aspire to become. G has always found devoted readers. T.P. O'Connor, "late Father of the House of Commons," took from the offices of his T.P. WEEKLY a copy of *Ryecroft* meant for review. He was enchanted by it and thereafter championed G. Others admire G for a variety of reasons: "his beautifully phrased and tranquil prose"; his rebellious ideas; his pioneering for the emancipation of women; his intellectual independence; his hatred of militarism; and, later, his "fascinating portrait of a frustrated artist." *Ryecroft* effectively asserts G's personal antagonism with the outside world. *New Grub Street* and *Born in Exile* assure G a place in the history of English literature, a "bridge between the old ample three volume novel of plot and grandiloquence of Bulwer Lytton, and the freshly observed, loosely constructed psychological novels of our own time." He prepared the way for Arthur Morrison, Somerset Maugham, Arnold Bennett, and H.G. Wells. [Announced in "Books to Come," TIMES LITERARY SUPPLEMENT (Lond), 5 Dec 1952, p. 804, this reprinting of *Ryecroft* and the accompanying "Foreword" received the following reviews: Walter Allen, "Books in General," NEW STATESMAN AND NATION, XLV (7 Feb 1953), 152–53; Cyril Connolly, "The Legacy of Gissing," LONDON SUNDAY TIMES, 25 Jan 1953, p. 5; "The Gissing Legend," TIMES LITERARY SUPPLEMENT (Lond), 30 Jan 1953, p. 74; and John O'London [Frank Swinnerton], "Letters to Gog and Magog: Author at Grass," JOHN O'LONDON'S WEEKLY, LXII (23 Jan 1953), 71.]

> **995** Connolly, Cyril. "The Legacy of Gissing," SUNDAY TIMES (Lond), 25 Jan 1953, p. 5.

*The Private Papers of Henry Ryecroft* (Lond: Phoenix House, 1953) is a "marvelous book," a legacy, "a daydream, a puritan's self-forgiveness on the edge of the grave, releasing the vision of an ideal life as seen by a tired, ill, impoverished, and unhappily married Londoner whose imaginative intensity gives an almost eerie quality to the daily round which he so realistically depicts." *Ryecroft* portrays a man who knows that peace is achieved only by those who are alienated by the world. G captures the English countryside; his writing contains a vein of satire and a touch of epigram.

**996** Gilmartin, Roger T. "The Social Attitudes of George Gissing." Unpublished dissertation, New York University, 1953.

[Listed in Lawrence F. McNamee, DISSERTATIONS IN ENGLISH AND AMERICAN LITERATURE (NY & Lond: Bowker, 1968).]

**997** "The Gissing Legend," TIMES LITERARY SUPPLEMENT (Lond), 30 Jan 1953, p. 74.

The reprinting of *The Private Papers of Henry Ryecroft,* with a foreword by Cecil Chisholm (Lond: Phoenix House; Toronto: Dent, 1953) reminds us of the legendary G. G himself helped foster the legend that he was a frustrated artist who was never able to achieve the peace he described in *Ryecroft.* This is a remarkable work, composed in great haste, almost like RASSELAS. It stresses the limitations of a scholarly mind—but that is only one side of his personality. Some of G's novels, notably *Isabel Clarendon* and *A Life's Morning,* show considerable feeling for character; and *New Grub Street* evidences his ear for dialogue. But *Ryecroft* is G's "masterpiece in the Ryecroft line."

**998** Himmelmann, Ilse. "Der Naturalistisch-Romantische Dualismus im Romanwerk von George Robert Gissing" (The Naturalistic-Romantic Dualism in the Novels of George Robert Gissing). Unpublished dissertation, University of Freiburg, 1953.

[Listed in Lawrence F. McNamee, DISSERTATIONS IN ENGLISH AND AMERICAN LITERATURE (NY & Lond: Bowker, 1968).] There are four periods in G's development. The short stories written for the Chicago TRIBUNE mark G's apprenticeship; the novels of the 1880s prove him a naturalist. In the 1890s G allowed more room for the romantic elements that characterized his work after 1900. G's development betrays two contradictory tendencies originating in his temperament and personal experiences. On the one hand, G was only too well aware of the social situation, viewing it with bitterness and describing it with naturalistic doctrines and techniques. On the other hand, he sought to escape from a world uncongenial to him. The romantic elements introduced into his writings include: (1) a nostalgia for Italy and the Mediterranean, (2) a longing for antiquity, (3) the discovery of the native landscape as an escape from the miseries of slum life, (4) the experience of the beauty of the arts, especially of music, (5) the idealization of women. [In German.]

**999** Kirk, Russell. THE CONSERVATIVE MIND (Chicago: Regnery, 1953), pp. 331–37.

To understand English society in the times of Salisbury and Balfour, G's novels are a great help. A "connoisseur of misery," G sensed the errors that "progress" brought to England. His representation of such clergymen as Wyvern in *Demos* disclosed "his longing after vanished certitudes." For though he was strongly influenced by Frederic Harrison and John Morley, G "was not born to be a radical." *Workers in the Dawn, Demos, Thyrza,* and *The Nether World* show that the suffering masses are unable to rule over their own passions and unfit to rule society. His later novels "are a prolonged protest against the frustrations" of modern life. Indeed, G's "whole endeavor is a work of moral conservatism." His novels and letters frequently repeat this theme, e.g. "Every instinct of my being is anti-democratic."

**1000** Koike, Shigeru. "Gissing in Japan," COMPARATIVE LITERA-TURE, ed by Kinji Shimada (Tokyo: Yajima Shobo, 1953); trans and rvd, BULLETIN OF THE NEW YORK PUBLIC LIBRARY, LXVII (Nov 1963), 565–73; rptd in GISSING EAST AND WEST (Lond: Enitharmon P, 1970), pp. 1–10.

The history of G in Japan is that of *The Private Papers of Henry Ryecroft.* G was first mentioned in Japan in THE SHUMI (Taste) in January 1908 by Tokoboku (Kuchi Hirata), who had come across G's work in England; he cited *Ryecroft* as his favorite book. The rural passages of *Ryecroft* were translated for publication in Japan in 1909; their interest in nature corresponded with the classical tradition of Japanese literature and made G "comprehensible" and "congenial" for Hirata. In 1924 the entire work appeared in a translation by Shigeru Fujino, introduced by the philosopher Yoshishge Abe. While G first attracted attention for his literary value, later his philosophical and social themes were also acclaimed. But the "rising storm of nationalism and militarism" led to the banning of *Ryecroft* in 1928. "It was a sign of the times that aspects of the book other than love of nature and solitude had attracted more attention." G's popularity is now on the wane in Japan.

**1001** O'London, John [pseud of Frank Swinnerton]. "Letters to Gog and Magog: Author at Grass," JOHN O'LONDON'S WEEKLY, LXII (23 Jan 1953), 71.

The reprinting of *The Private Papers of Henry Ryecroft* with a foreword by Cecil Chisholm (Lond: Phoenix House; Toronto: Dent, 1953), comes on the occasion of the fiftieth anniversary of that book's first publication. G was never fitted for life; in *Ryecroft* he dreams of tranquillity as though he had escaped a life sentence in prison to live peacefully in a Devon cottage. *Ryecroft* contains G's inmost thoughts, his happiest afterthoughts. Did the impulse to write *Ryecroft* originate with the reading of C.F. Keary's THE WANDERER (1901)? Chisholm's introduction contains information about G that I never knew before.

**1002** Price, J.B. "George Robert Gissing," CONTEMPORARY REVIEW, CLXXXIV (Aug 1953), 105–10.

G's writings on Dickens constitute the best criticism of that great Victorian. Although himself given to a deliberate and ironic treatment of the seamy side of life, G read Dickens thoroughly and sympathetically. "Yet he could not, like Dickens, recognize gladly the humour as well as the misery of the under-world." Perhaps the reason for this was G's inability to believe in the integrity of the universe; G "was moved only to despairing wrath."

**1003** Thomas, J.D. "The Public Purposes of George Gissing," NINETEENTH CENTURY FICTION, VIII (Sept 1953), 118–23.

G's novels do not state their theme within only one character; rather, one must discover what G approves and detests in each figure. He did not despise human nature, nor did he put forth any plan for reconstructing society. He distrusted science and socialism, and named the universal cause poverty.

**1004** Wolff, Joseph J. "Gissing's Revision of *The Unclassed*," NINETEENTH CENTURY FICTION, VIII (June 1953), 42–52.

In preparing *The Unclassed* (1886) for reissue by Lawrence and Bullen (1895), G revised and abridged the text. Revisions usually involved the elimination of lesser characters and minor subplots, the removal of his own intrusive remarks and intrusions as author, and the rewriting of awkward or wordy passages of narration, dialogue, or description. Hence the later version is closer in style to G's more mature fiction.

# 1954

**1005** Allen, Walter. THE ENGLISH NOVEL: A SHORT CRITICAL HISTORY (Lond: Phoenix House, 1954), pp. 274–81; (NY: Dutton, 1955), pp. 342–50.

G's most popular book, *The Private Papers of Henry Ryecroft,* represents a dream of irresponsibility, "a deliberate opting out of life." G's fictional heroes assume his own beliefs, and he expects us to share these beliefs. He is the first and perhaps the best delineator of the "proleterian intellectual." The G hero reappears in all the major novels, a man who lives in "self-created isolation," like Grail in *Thyrza,* Reardon in *New Grub Street,* Kingcote in *Isabel Clarendon. Born in Exile* represents the one exception to G's concentration, for Godwin Peak, an "arrogant Rationalist," sells himself out to gain the company of the upper class. His is the case of "intellectual dissimulation." Artistically, G's best novels are *The Odd Women*—though Rhoda Nunn is "badly dated"—and *In the Year of Jubilee.* Nancy Lord is perhaps G's "most successful heroine." [Allen originally wrote much of this criticism of G for his review of *The Private Papers of Henry Ryecroft;* see "Books in General," NEW STATESMAN AND NATION, XLV (7 Feb 1953), 152–53.]

**1006** Donnelly, Mabel Collins. GEORGE GISSING: GRAVE COMEDIAN (Cambridge: Harvard UP; Toronto: Saunders, 1954).

G is sustained by a variety of audiences: he attracts readers for his social themes, his classicism, his humanism, his importance in the history of the English novel. His life is crowded into his books, and a knowledge of his biography—his education, his poverty, his unfortunate marriages, his enthusiasm for Greece and Rome, his intimate familiarity with London life— is invaluable to those who would understand and appreciate his books. It is now possible to relate his novels to his life, thanks to the substantial holdings of the Yale University Library and the Berg Collection of the New York Public Library.

As he developed as a novelist, G came to prefer the "clean" story line to the complexity of the Victorian novel. By design, his novels concentrated on one solitary figure—a person not significantly unlike himself— who was "a little more than life-size, forced into a succession of relationships consisting usually of a central intimate relationship and a multiplicity of ephemeral relationships." G's novels "are essentially domestic novels of narrow range." His most skilled works—*New Grub Street, Born in Exile, The Whirlpool,* and *Our Friend the Charlatan*—are all simply constructed and indisputably focused. In *Thyrza* and *The Nether World,* the "subplots get out of hand," but the books survive for their brute passion rather than for their skill. *Eve's Ransom* best shows G's variations, as "the chief characters and the reader can look back into the past and forward into the future" rather than treat a stretch of years in leisurely fashion. For G, language itself "was a constant problem"; it is "often heavy and dull." His "ear for dialogue was true," especially in rendering the "muscular vernacular" of the lower classes. For belles-lettres, *The Private Papers of Henry Ryecroft* assures G a safe position; his studies of Dickens are repeatedly and deservedly praised as among the finest appreciations of the Victorian novelist. The self-deception that G often attributes to his fictional characters reflects his own circumstances: he was misanthropic, solitary, and greatly in need of love. Dazzled by society, particularly early in his career when he was befriended by Mrs. Gaussen and Frederic Harrison, G determined to endure humiliation and hardship to protect his artistic integrity. His own artistic code that fiction must be sincere and craftsman-like guided his best writing and dominated his life. Among earlier writers, Dickens, Tennyson, and Thackeray most gained G's admiration; he instantly recognized Conrad as an artistic genius.

[This study provides extensive and authentic materials about G's life; it is therefore immensely important in providing scholars with the first reliable and detailed biographical information about G. While reviewers were not unanimously generous in their praise, the usefulness and significance of Dr. Donnelly's book greatly advanced G scholarship not only because it documented his life and literary reputation but also it occasioned numerous reviews and articles in important publications. It was, after all, the prestigious Harvard UP that was advancing G's cause. The following represents a sampling of the response and testifies to a fresh revival for G: Carlos Baker, "World Within a World," NEW YORK TIMES BOOK REVIEW, 28 March 1954, p. 4 (This short but thorough critical biography shows G "as primarily a realist in search of a public." G himself "could neither fashion domestic quietude nor refashion the society in which he found himself."); "Biography and Memoirs," U. S. QUARTERLY BOOK REVIEW, X (Sept 1954), 292–93 (While not the definitive biography of G, this is the first book to use much unpublished material in the Yale and New York Public Libraries.); John L. Bradley, "Books in English," BOOKS ABROAD, XXVIII (Autumn 1954), 479 (Mabel Collins Donnelly's book directs our attention to G, a pioneer in naturalism, but Swinnerton's study remains superior to this more recent work.); "Briefly Noted," NEW YORKER, XXX (11 Sept 1954), 143–44 (GEORGE GISSING: GRAVE COMEDIAN is an "earnest, naive, and pretty uncritical book."); M. L. Cazamian, "Comptes Rendus," ETUDES ANGLAISES, X (Jan–March 1957), 66–67 (Dr. Donnelly pays homage to G as a painter of the slums in *Demos* and *The Nether World,* for his dramatic power in *New Grub Street* and *Born in Exile.*); D. R. Cherry, "New Books," DALHOUSIE REVIEW, XXXIV (Summer 1954), 201, 203 (This new study will concentrate our attention on G's contribution to English fiction, his break from the Dickens tradition, and his "very real success . . . in achieving brevity, focus, and objectivity."); Clifford Collins, "Other Recent Books," SPECTATOR, CXCIV (18 March 1955), 337 (This study suffers from being written by an American, a person out of touch with G's world. G deserves to be read because no other British writer—except perhaps Orwell—"combined artistic honesty with clinical exactness to portray the intellectual exile, who is also the feeling victim of his own neurosis and his gifts."); Oliver Edwards, "George Gissing," TIMES (Lond), 30 June 1955, p. 13 (G will be remembered chiefly for his record of escape from misery in *The Private Papers of Henry Ryecroft*. What is common to all G books is the "quirked character" of a "self-destroying but essentially likeable writer of thwarted talents."); R. Fauconnier, "Literary Biography," QUEEN'S QUARTERLY, LXI (Summer 1954), 278–80 (Here is a "rather indifferent biography"; Roberts had at least made G live. G himself lacked the character necessary to press for better publication conditions. G's life demands more research than this study provides.); Robert C. Gordon, "Book Reviews," COMPARATIVE LITERATURE, VII (Winter 1955), 67–68 (The "first reliable full-length" critical biography of G, this study includes excellent analyses of the novels. Donnelly provides "impressive evidence" of G's interest in many European writers, such as Zola, Turgenev, and Dostoevski.); Jacob Korg, "GEORGE GISSING: GRAVE COMEDIAN," NINETEENTH CENTURY FICTION, IX (Sept 1954), 146–49 (This work ignores G's ideas while concentrating on his techniques With so much material at hand, too little is accomplished.); "New Books in Brief: Victorian Rebel," NATION (NY), CLXXVIII (3 April 1954), 285 (G was an important social novelist who attacked the superficial reforming ideas of his day as vigorously as he attacked the abuses they were intended to reform.); "A Portrait of Gissing," TIMES LITERARY SUPPLEMENT (Lond), 5 Nov 1954, p. 699 (When criticism is demanded, Donnelly does not seem to grasp the issue, nor is she familiar with London or the nineteenth century. She fails to make use of George Moore in her comparisons; she picks the wrong novels for careful study, choosing *Eve's Ransom*, for example, instead of *Born in Exile, Thyrza,* or *The Odd Women*.); Gordon N. Ray, "Minor Victorian," SATURDAY REVIEW (NY), XXXVII (12 June 1954), 17 (While this work fills a "considerable gap in English literary annals," we still need a full scale biography. Her criticisms are strained to substantiate questionable theories about G's novels. She errs in not stressing *Thyrza, New Grub Street, The Nether World,* and *Born in Exile*.); W. B. Ready, "New Books Appraised," LIBRARY JOURNAL, LXXIX (15 March 1954), 543 (This is a necessary acquisition for college libraries; it is a "revealing and very readable biography.").]

**1007** Gordan, John D. GEORGE GISSING, 1857–1903: AN EXHIBITION FROM THE BERG COLLECTION (NY: NY Public Library, 1954); rptd from BULLETIN OF THE NEW YORK PUBLIC LIBRARY, LXVIII (Oct, Nov, Dec, 1954), 489–96, 551–55, 611–18; LXI (Jan 1955), 35–46.
[This forty-five page booklet, prepared for the New York Public Library's

exhibition marking the fiftieth anniversary of G's death, concentrates on the circumstances attending the publication of each work by G. Reliably extracted from materials in the Berg Collection, Gordan's informative and readable commentary became no less valuable to G scholars than to those attending the exhibition. A typical paragraph accompanying the display of a first edition copy of a novel would describe G's condition at the time of the writing, perhaps his own judgment of the book as expressed in his diary or letters, and often a comment on the significance of the book to G's career. This booklet is particularly useful for information about publication details: G's contract with the publisher, the costs involved, the public reception, including sales, and often an indication of the book's future success. Concentrated and informative, this publication remains invaluable in G research.]

**1008** Haymaker, Richard E. FROM PAMPAS TO HEDGEROWS AND DOWNS: A STUDY OF W. H. HUDSON (NY: Bookman, 1954), pp. 38, 96, 137, 149, 296, 329, 330.
The literary friendship between G and Hudson flourished through several meetings. The opening chapters of Hudson's FAN show G's influence both "in picturing the Chances of East End, and, especially, in the conception of Fan herself, who twice is made to declare her kinship to Thyrza."

**1009** Orel, Harold. "Victorians and the Russian Novel: A Bibliography," BULLETIN OF BIBLIOGRAPHY, XXI (Jan–April, May–Aug 1954), 61–63, 78–81.
In his novels, letters, and criticism, G showed his awareness of Turgenev and Dostoevski. [Items concerning G on pp. 63, 78, 79.]

**1010** Young, Arthur C. "The Letters of George Gissing to Eduard Bertz." Unpublished dissertation, Yale University, 1954.
[Listed in Lawrence F. McNamee, DISSERTATIONS IN ENGLISH AND AMERICAN LITERATURE (NY & Lond: Bowker, 1968).]

## 1955

**1011** Brown, Malcolm. GEORGE MOORE: A RECONSIDERATION (Seattle: University of Washington P, 1955), pp. 49, 197, 203.
Moore despised several of his fellow novelists; some others—including G, Butler, and Wells—he simply ignored. He never shared the Victorian admiration for *The Private Papers of Henry Ryecroft*.

**1012** Ford, George H. DICKENS AND HIS READERS (Princeton: Princeton UP for University of Cincinnati, 1955), pp. 8, 45, 61, 163, 171, 172, 194, 210, 224, 233, 245–49, 256.

G's two books on Dickens consist "essentially of fresh explorations of the problem of literary probability." While G scolded Dickens for extravagance and exaggeration, he came to realize that his own unpopularity was in part due to the fact that "few readers can enjoy the objective presentation of the dullness of life." G himself refused to be troubled by a reader's finding a novel repulsive or tedious. "An earnest, unexuberant scholar, G wrote the most reasonable and thoughtful appraisal of Dickens's achievement. The modest good sense of his argument does not make him a favorite with Dickensians, but many of the critical questions he raised are still with us."

**1013** Francis, C. J. "Aspects of Realism in the Novels of George Gissing." Unpublished dissertation, University of Manchester, 1955

[Listed in Lawrence F. McNamee, DISSERTATIONS IN ENGLISH AND AMERICAN LITERATURE (NY & Lond: Bowker, 1968).]

**1014** Korg, Jacob. "Division of Purpose in George Gissing," PMLA, LXX (June 1955), 323–36; rptd in COLLECTED ARTICLES ON GEORGE GISSING, ed by Pierre Coustillas (Lond: Frank Cass, 1968), pp. 64–79.

G's social consciousness opposed his artistic principles. From Shelley he adopted the idea that art should be free of propaganda, a belief influential in the pre-Raphaelites. But G's letters and stories repeatedly assert his social goals; particularly is this true in *Workers in the Dawn, The Unclassed,* and *Demos.* His travels heightened his own enthusiasm for beauty; however, his fictional characters, true to their working-class origins, were incapable of appreciating beauty, even if the opportunity did present itself. G's poor were devoid of imagination. While G insisted that art was incompatible with preaching, his novels violated that rule as he advocated social reform and demonstrated the bestial conditions of slum life. Thus, in several novels G's purpose was divided between his "professed 'worship' of 'pure art'" and his "hope of accomplishing a moral mission through his novels."

**1015** Pettoello, Decio. "Introduzione" (Introduction), *Nato in Esilio (Born in Exile)* (Torino: UTET, 1955), pp. 5–18.

While the various spiritual currents of the century were contending for supremacy, G showed the cruelty and ugliness of his time with bitter and powerful objectivity. His moral protest was raised in the name of aesthetics and refinement. In *Born in Exile* G's taste for introspection and accuracy was often detrimental to the dramatic power of the story. The minor characters were well-fitted into the whole fabric. In the development of characters, Hardy was less complex and coherent than G. [In Italian.]

## 1956

**1016** Adams, Ruth M. "George Gissing and Clara Collet," NINETEENTH CENTURY FICTION, XI (June 1956), 72–77.
G shared with Clara Collet an interest in the working classes and their problems. She "was one of the first women to deal sympathetically with the phenomenon of working women" near the end of the nineteenth century. ·She was enormously helpful both in providing G with personal stability and in assisting his wife and sons at critical times. Her own circumstances perhaps guided G in the creation of Miss Barfoot in *The Odd Women.*

**1017** "Gissing's Heroines," TIMES LITERARY SUPPLEMENT (Lond), 28 Dec 1956, p. 780; rptd in COLLECTED ARTICLES ON GEORGE GISSING, ed by Pierre Coustillas (Lond: Frank Cass, 1968), pp. 58–63.
[Occasioned by the reprinting of G's *By the Ionian Sea,* with a biographical foreword by Frank Swinnerton (Lond: Richards, 1956).] G repeatedly inquires into the nature of an effective morality, and he seems to find the answer in the love necessary for man to contend against the facts of existence. Life's struggle is less successfully represented in G's men than in his women, so that "the insufficiency or shadowiness of his men and the reality of his women points to a peculiar bias" of G's imagination. This bias, most clearly evident in *The Emancipated, New Grub Street,* and *Isabel Clarendon,* originates in G's "own miserable experience of two utterly disastrous marriages." Once his own life was less tortured, his power to feel the intensity manifestly present in his best work thinned, with the result that after *Eve's Ransom* his novels no longer compel our emotional engagement. A writer by nature, G was perhaps a better critic than novelist. His Dickens study is "still the best criticism of Dickens extant." But probably because of changes in his personal life, G's novels wavered in quality and changed in character and setting. He returned to familiar environments, as in *Demos, Thyrza,* and *The Nether World,* but his heroines were his strength whatever their social status. *Emancipated* best showed this fact. His failures are efforts at suburban comedy, like *The Paying Guest.* His fame comes as a thinking novelist rather than as a reflective essayist.

**1018** "Gissing's Period Piece," TIMES LITERARY SUPPLEMENT (Lond), 24 Feb 1956, p. 120.

*The Town Traveller,* G's novel just reprinted by Methuen, helps remind us that *The Private Papers of Henry Ryecroft* and *Veranilda,* for all their beauties, are not the authentic G. The real man is to be found in his city novels. G was a link "in that chain of novelists that stretched from Defoe to Joyce—those who communicate a full, still vision of the living, transient city." Insofar as G condescended, "it is the condescension of a creative comedian thoroughly at home with his characters." The novel is full of life, easy gaiety and irony.

**1019** M., O. *"The Town Traveller,"* PUNCH, CCXXX (7 March 1956), 302.

*The Town Traveller,* appearing in a Methuen reprint, is an unusual G novel because it is cheerful and entertaining. The book has "the smell of gas-lamps, fog and cheap eating-houses" that now seems part of the charm of late-Victorian days.

**1020** Phelps, Gilbert. THE RUSSIAN NOVEL IN ENGLISH FICTION (Lond: Hutchinson's University Library, 1956), pp. 88–94, 104, 108, 144, 163, 174, 179; portions from this book rptd as "Gissing, Turgenev, and Dostoyevsky" in COLLECTED ARTICLES ON GEORGE GISSING, ed by Pierre Coustillas (Lond: Frank Cass, 1968), pp. 99–105.

While G's "studies of 'minds maddened by hunger,' " to quote G on Dickens, "are Dostoyevskyan in their intensity," his approach is on the whole closer to Turgenev's. It is ethical and moral rather than psychological and mystical. In both Egremont of *Thyrza* and in the heroine of *Isabel Clarendon,* we have Turgenev types. G was among the very first critics of Dickens to discover the latter's similarity to Dostoevski.

**1021** Swinnerton, Frank. BACKGROUND WITH CHORUS (Lond: Hutchinson, 1956), pp. 130–35.

Martin Secker engaged me to write a study of G, although Secker's "literary taste did not embrace Gissing." What I wrote was mostly derived from a close reading of G's novels and from Thomas Seccombe. My efforts also led to meeting Wells and Roberts.

**1022** Swinnerton, Frank. "Biographical Foreword," *By the Ionian Sea* (Lond: Richards, 1956), pp. 7–14.

G's early years as a writer were troubled by poverty; through the help of Frederic Harrison, he secured students for private tutoring. After 1891 he was comparatively successful and was able to travel to the lands he loved. [The appearance of this reprint occasioned an important article on

"Gissing's Heroines" (TIMES LITERARY SUPPLEMENT [Lond], 28 Dec 1956, p. 780, q.v.), as well as reviews by Pierre Coustillas, "Book Reviews," GISSING NEWSLETTER, I (April 1965), 2–3; Patrick Leigh-Fermor, SUNDAY TIMES (Lond), 6 April 1956, p. 206; and Sylvère Monod, "Comptes Rendus," ETUDES ANGLAISES, X (July-Sept 1957), 268. The Richards reprint of *Ionian Sea* was originally anounced as having an introduction by Patrick Leigh-Fermor (TIMES LITERARY SUPPLEMENT [Lond], 3 Feb 1957, p. 6.).]

**1023** Thompson, Patricia. THE VICTORIAN HEROINE: A CHANGING IDEAL, 1837–1873 (Lond: Oxford UP, 1956), p. 119.
Despite the hope that celibacy was better than marriage, emancipated Victorian writers did not advocate spinsterhood for women. By G's time, however, "the intelligent, charming unmarried woman had come to have definite possibilities for the novelist that the old maid stock character never possessed."

**1024** "Traveller in Paradise," TIMES (Lond), 16 Feb 1956, p. 11.
*The Town Traveller,* issued by Methuen in a reprint, was written by G from 9 June to 14 July 1897, at a time when his contributions were sought after and his novel *The Whirlpool* was selling well. *Traveller* is a "completely happy book." The setting, story, and temper of the book—even the high spirits—are all G's own. Except for Lord Polperro, the characters are lifelike and well-observed. The strength of the book lies in its universality and the richness of the crowd that moves through the city.

## 1957

**1025** Clark, Jeanne Gabriel. "London in English Literature, 1880–1955," DISSERTATION ABSTRACTS, XVII (1957), 1761. Unpublished dissertation, Columbia University, 1957.

**1026** Cope, Jackson I. "Definition as Structure in Gissing's 'Ryecroft Papers,'" MODERN FICTION STUDIES, III (Summer 1957), 127–40; rptd as "Definition as Structure in *The Ryecroft Papers,*" in COLLECTED ARTICLES ON GEORGE GISSING, ed by Pierre Coustillas (Lond: Frank Cass, 1968), pp. 152–67.
Although *The Private Papers of Henry Ryecroft* is commonly looked upon as little more than autobiography, it really belongs to "those borderlands of genres when More's UTOPIA and Butler's EREWHON house

the marriage of philosophy and fiction." The theme of *Ryecroft* is the "cry of the human soul struggling to escape extinction amidst the grinding wheels of the mechanical world and the new industrialized, vulgarized England." External nature permeates the book, forming a symbol of the naturalness which G hopes to capture; this nature conflicts with the city as well as with man's perpetual violence. The "I" of *Ryecroft* is not G himself, but the "we of modern England's intellectual and ethical aristocracy." The rightness or fitness of England is best judged by the quality of its monarch and food; to judge in such matters is the patrician's virtue. In either consideration, the judge must have sufficient money to be independent, this independence guaranteeing him the virtue of sociability that is centered in a love of order. The ideal comes in tranquillity, calm, and moderation.

**1027** Gettmann, Royal A. "Bentley and Gissing," NINETEENTH CENTURY FICTION, XI (March 1957), 306–14; materials reworked in A VICTORIAN PUBLISHER (Cambridge: Cambridge UP, 1960), pp. 120, 123, 128, 196–97, 199, 215–22, 251, 253–56, 263.

The relations between G and Bentley were not "so unsympathetic and arbitrary as has generally been thought." Bentley thought well of G and hoped to publish his books, telling his staff: "I am glad to hear that Gissing's book is to be printed. It has great merits, however melancholy it may be." In 1882 Bentley agreed to publish G's "Mrs. Grundy's Enemies"; however, early in 1883, when reading proofs, Bentley asked G to soften certain passages. G balked, and Bentley asked Evelyn Abbott, fellow of Balliol and a classical scholar, to mark those passages of the novel which were "likely to keep the book out of the libraries." Abbott, while "genuinely solicitous about the novel," recommended numerous alterations, including the removal of two whole chapters. Bentley hesitated further, then decided not to publish the book. Nor did he choose to accept G's next book, *The Unclassed*. G's career spanned the period when the three-decker novel was giving way; his longer novels have some Victorian trappings, like multiple plots, while his shorter novels demonstrate how awkward he found the transfer to the one volume work. [Reviews: H. E. Gerber, "Reviews," ENGLISH FICTION IN TRANSITION, IV: 3 (1961), 62–64; "The House of Bentley," TIMES LITERARY SUPPLEMENT (Lond), 17 February 1961, p. 112.]

**1028** Guidacci, Margherita. "Introduzione" (Introduction), *Sulla Riva Della Junio* (*By the Ionian Sea*), (Cappelli, 1957), pp. 5–18.

Although it does not occupy a central position among G's books, *By the*

*Ionian Sea* is one of the most notable books G ever wrote. Moreover, it is certainly one of the most remarkable books about southern Italy ever written by a foreigner. [Sketches G's life, drawing upon Swinnerton, Baker, and James.] [In Italian.]

**1029** M[onod], S[ylvère]. "Comptes Rendus," ETUDES AN-GLAISES, X (April–June 1957), 186.

The reprint of *The Town Traveller* by Methuen is welcome. Its alert style, its fanciful and mysterious plot, remind one of Arnold Bennett's THE GREAT BABYLON HOTEL. The Dickens-like scenes of low life are most likely to interest the contemporary reader. [In French.]

**1030** "Propos de la quinzaine" (Subject Matter of a Fortnight), REVUE DES DEUX MONDES, 15 Nov 1957, p. 375.

The English press and the B. B. C. have been observing the anniversary of G's birth. Originally, G aspired to write in the tradition of Zola and Dickens. His work has generally been received more favorably in England than in France. [Outlines G's life, lists several of his more famous works, and mentions his happy years in France with Gabrielle Fleury.] [In French.]

**1031** Starrett, Vincent. "Books Alive," CHICAGO TRIBUNE MAG-AZINE OF BOOKS, 10 Nov 1957, p. 13.

On the 100th anniversary of G's birth, Chicago ought to recall the novelist's visit here and the story of his adventures as narrated in *The Private Papers of Henry Ryecroft* and *New Grub Street*.

**1032** Young, Arthur. "Gissing's *Veranilda*," NOTES AND QUER-IES, n.s. IV, (Aug 1957), 359.

In a letter to Eduard Bertz, Gabrielle Gissing cleared up a confusion over one word in Chap 30 of *Veranilda*, a word which neither Frederic Harrison nor Algernon Gissing could decipher.

# 1958

**1033** Amis, Kingsley. "The Hateful Profession," SPECTATOR, CCI (4 July 1958), p. 19.

G expected novelists to starve themselves, even as Reardon did in *New Grub Street* or as Maitland did in THE PRIVATE LIFE OF HENRY MAITLAND by Morley Roberts. MAITLAND is a "clear and full" presentation, telling how Roberts and G shared an "evil smelling Bohemia." G's life enters both books, particularly as the record of a "soul trapped in a network of agonies —poverty, self-doubt, sexual-discomfort." Fortunately, not all the characters are analogues of G; there is Jasper Milvain, that "liveliest sketch" of an "egotist who chisels his way to success" in such a way that even contemporary Grub Street would be hard pressed to find his parallel. [This article was occasioned by reprints of *New Grub Street,* with an introduction by G. W. Stonier (Lond: Oxford UP, 1958), and of THE PRIVATE LIFE OF HENRY MAITLAND by Morley Roberts, with an introduction by Morchard Bishop (Lond: Richards, 1958).]

**1034** Bergonzi, Bernard. "The Novelist as Hero," TWENTIETH CENTURY, CLXIV (Nov 1958), 444–55.

We get a picture of G in Morley Roberts's THE PRIVATE LIFE OF HENRY MAITLAND, and we learn from the Harrisons that G refused to "serve" as journalist. But the best portrait of G's ideals is Reardon of *New Grub Street.* Not really a novelist by temperament, but a scholar, Reardon not only stands as a foil to Jasper Milvain but personifies G, especially in his refusal to support himself by journalism. Like G too, Reardon represents the *fin de siècle* outcast hero. If compared to Arnold Bennett's hero in A MAN FROM THE NORTH, Richard Larch, another autobiographical story of a failure, we find that "Bennett is far more detached from Larch than Gissing is from Reardon."

**1035** Bishop, Morchard. "Introduction," THE PRIVATE LIFE OF HENRY MAITLAND by Morley Roberts (Lond: Richards P, 1958), pp. 1–18.

The friendship of Roberts and G started about 1873 when they were fellow students at Owens College, Manchester, and continued to G's death. Their association, disrupted during the extended absences of Roberts from England (to Australia and America), forms the principal material for THE PRIVATE LIFE OF HENRY MAITLAND. Written "in a state near to madness," MAITLAND was composed at the very time that Swinnerton was working on his critical biography of G, and both books appeared in 1912 —often enjoying reviews in combination. Morley Roberts himself is probably the model for several characters in G's novels, such as Malkin (*Born in Exile*) and Whelpdale (*New Grub Street*). This edition of MAITLAND is based on the revised text prepared by Roberts himself and includes many identifications of pseudonymous figures (e.g. Rawson is really W. H. Hudson). Roberts's papers—including presentation volumes from G—are now in the Leeds University Library as part of the Roberts Collection. [Reviewed by Madeleine L. Cazamian, "Comptes Rendus," ETUDES ANGLAISES, XIII (Jan–March 1960), 65–66.]

**1036** Brooks, Van Wyck. FROM A WRITER'S NOTEBOOK (NY: Dutton, 1958), pp. 24, 99–100.

Despite his hatred for the city, all but one of G's twenty-two novels "deal, at least largely, with London." Thus, "his instinct of artistic self-preservation was at war with his normal tastes."

**1037** Churchill, R. C. "Three Autobiographical Novelists," FROM DICKENS TO HARDY, ed by Boris Ford (Harmondsworth, Middlesex: Penguin, 1958), pp. 338–48.

G's world is almost a prose parallel to CITY OF DREADFUL NIGHT. G's best works—*Isabel Clarendon, A Life's Morning, New Grub Street, The Town Traveller*—show characteristic ironic detachment. Aside from *The Private Papers of Henry Ryecroft, Grub Street* is the most autobiographic of his books. Reardon is a self-portrait; Milvain expresses the author's own bitter comment. The novel is perhaps too "professional" to attain a wide popularity.

**1038** [Conrad, Joseph]. JOSEPH CONRAD: LETTERS TO WILLIAM BLACKWOOD AND DAVID S. MELDRUM, ed by William Blackburn (Durham, N. C.: Duke UP, 1958), p. 173.

Conrad told Blackwood that G wrote Clodd praising "Youth" and other Conrad tales for their "imaginative vigour, and such wonderful command of language." Conrad found G's suggestion that Clodd "talk about the book to every man and woman he knows" as "showing a practical interest."

**1039** Curtis, Anthony. "Gissing's Book-Mask," BOOKS AND BOOKMEN, III (Jan 1958), 10.

In *The Private Papers of Henry Ryecroft,* G "presented himself at one remove, and revealed as much as possible without seeming to violate the national code of reticence." In anticipation of the centenary of G's birth, one contributor has been engaged to prepare a biography of G for the B.B.C.

**1040** Kejzlarová, Inge. "Gissinguv román *Demos* a Anglický Socialismus" (Gissing's Novel *Demos* and English Socialism), ČASOPIS PRO MODERNÍ FILOLOGII (Prague), (1958), pp. 136–45. [Not seen.] [In Czech.]

**1041** Maurois, André. "George Gissing," LA REVUE DE PARIS (Feb 1958), 3–13.

[Maurois repeats much biographical information on G drawn particularly from the writings of Donnelly, Swinnerton, and Wells. He stresses G's ambiguous social position, comparing it to Wells's.] [In French.]

**1042** Pritchett, V. S. "A Chip the Size of a Block," NEW STATESMEN AND NATION, LV (14 June 1958), 781; rptd as "Grub Street," in THE WORKING NOVELIST (Lond: Chatto & Windus,

1965), pp. 62–67; rptd in COLLECTED ARTICLES ON GEORGE GISSING, ed by Pierre Coustillas (Lond: Frank Cass, 1968), pp. 126–30.

Critics often argue that as a native G knew London and the misery of its poor; in fact he was an alien living in London, exiled from the lands of classical Greece and Rome, dwelling among people he despised. No previous novelist ever carried so large a chip—he wrote grudgingly, not sympathetically, of the problems facing educated men in mean surroundings. *New Grub Street* concentrates that grudge in Reardon, who lacked merely the will to succeed. Milvain, on the other hand, "climbs boldly, cleverly, even engagingly." Amy marries him "with her eyes open and with a delicate lack of scruple." For G all this is comic and ironic, as he is "detached enough to see she has a right to drift with her self-esteem." But he fails to see that class differences are also matter for comedy, and in this failure he was not English, "but a foreigner or an exile."

**1043** Stonier, G. W. "Introduction," *New Grub Street* (Lond: Oxford UP, 1958), pp. vii–xii.

G's success is in failure: *New Grub Street* states that failure is the agony of novel writing. But our impression of G, both his life and his books, is one of starvation, disgrace, poverty, hopelessness: "humanity's dull ache, flatness and ignominy, the cruel ugliness taken for granted, the boredom we turn away from." However painful his subject, G never left it. His literary masters were the Goncourts, Zola, and Flaubert. But G stands "apart [from], rather than above or below his fellow novelists." He has won few advocates; Orwell offers the greatest praise but provides no reasons. Others read G grudgingly, "shamed into not neglecting him." G is "the moralist of a rainy day." [This introduction, though stimulating, might have been more thorough. The novel is unequal but powerful. Reviewed by S[ylvère] M[onod], "Comptes Rendus," ETUDES ANGLAISES, XIII (Jan–March 1960), 89.]

**1044** Wells, H. G. HENRY JAMES AND H. G. WELLS: A RECORD OF THEIR FRIENDSHIP, THEIR DEBATE ON THE ART OF FICTION, AND THEIR QUARREL, ed by Leon Edel and Gordon N. Ray (Urbana: University of Illinois P; Lond: Rupert Hart-Davis, 1958), pp. 17, 71, 72, 74, 77, 95.

In June 1901, James thanked Wells for some information relayed about G's health; James asked: "Why *will* he do these things?" The following month, still worried about G, James wrote: "He rather haunts me." When G died, James commended Wells for his "admirable effort for poor Gissing *in extremis*." In still another letter, James wrote his famous inquiry about "poor Gissing."

**1045** Wolff, Joseph J. "The Literary Reputation of George Gissing in England and America." Unpublished dissertation, University of Chicago, 1958.
[Listed in Lawrence F. McNamee, DISSERTATIONS IN ENGLISH AND AMER-
ICAN LITERATURE (NY & Lond: Bowker, 1968).]

**1046** Young, Arthur C. "A Note on George Gissing," JOURNAL
OF THE RUTGERS UNIVERSITY LIBRARY, XXII (Dec 1958), 23–24.
When G left England in May 1899 to "marry" Gabrielle Fleury he wrote
a postal card to F. G. Kitton, his collaborator in a new edition of
Dickens's works. [The postal card message is reprinted to show "the
equilibrium of Gissing's mind" and Kitton's respect for him.]

# 1959

**1047** Bruny, Simone. "George Gissing: Peintre des bas-fonds
Londoniens et humaniste accompli" (George Gissing: Portrayer
of Lower-Class Londoners and Accomplished Humanist), SYN-
THÈSES, XIV (July–Aug 1959), 445–55.
A man clearly ahead of his own time, G refused to sacrifice his beliefs for
popularity; he remains essentially unpopular today. His novels show no religious beliefs but a devotion to peace and a hatred of all war. Even in the
worst outbursts of nationalism in the late nineteenth century, G thought as
a European, a citizen of the world. [A sound biographical and critical
study of G, this article gives a summary of G's main ideas; Bruny's essay
is based on Donnelly's GEORGE GISSING: GRAVE COMEDIAN (1954), on the
letters published in 1927, on a careful reading of several of G's best
novels, and on information supplied by G's family.] [In French.]

**1048** Ellmann, Richard. JAMES JOYCE (NY: Oxford UP, 1959),
p. 242.
Joyce never took kindly to G. Of *Demos* he asked: "Why are English
novels so terribly boring?" Joyce thought *The Crown of Life* was out-
rageously written, the conversations in it reminding him of a noodle and
bean soup.

**1049** Kocmanová, Jessie. "The Revolt of Workers in the Novels
of Gissing, James, and Conrad," BRNO STUDIES IN ENGLISH, I
(1959), 119–35.
*Demos, Thyrza,* and *The Nether World* give us valuable insights into G's
attitudes toward socialism. G failed to understand the class-conscious attitude of William Morris. In *Demos,* which is technically old-fashioned, G

shrewdly exposed the weaknesses of the socialist movement. Mutimer forms a powerful picture of a socialist leader, though Mutimer is not socialism. If G failed to identify himself with the working class, he at least brought it to the foreground in the main novels of the 1880s.

**1050** Korg, Jacob. "The Spiritual Theme of George Gissing's *Born in Exile*," in FROM JANE AUSTEN TO JOSEPH CONRAD, ed by R. C. Rathburn and Martin Steinmann (Minneapolis: University of Minnesota P, 1959), pp. 246–56; rptd in COLLECTED ARTICLES ON GEORGE GISSING, ed by Pierre Coustillas (Lond: Frank Cass, 1968), pp. 131–41.

G's early novels frequently investigate the theme of a poor young intellectual blocked from taking advantage of his talents or his superior education by a lack of money. *Born in Exile* best shows that this "judgment of society was not merely a choice of abstract alternatives, but a moral problem involving fundamental problems of right and wrong." G's attitude certainly originated in his own personal experience and was stated earlier in *Workers in the Dawn, The Unclassed,* and *New Grub Street.* Though disguised, Godwin Peak of *Exile* parallels G in the problems facing an exceptional young man seeking the refined life for which his education and deep sensitivity have prepared him. Peak's ambition is frustrated by his own pretense: he fakes a religious conversion to win Sidwell Warricombe. But his "deception is due, not to lack of moral responsibility, but to uncompromising intellectual honesty." He concludes that any intellectual conviction is impossible; agnosticism is dishonest and deceptive no less than any other belief. Peak's conclusion is a candid confession that matches G's own position, "one phase of myself," as he told Bertz. G was probably influenced by his readings in Turgenev, Jacobsen, and Bourget; his nihilistic ideas seem echoes of their writings. But Peak seems even more clearly related to Raskolnikov of CRIME AND PUNISHMENT, in the tradition of spiritual exiles who "protest against the characteristic materialism of the nineteenth century."

**1051** Murry, J. Middleton. "George Gissing," KATHERINE MANSFIELD AND OTHER LITERARY STUDIES (Lond: Constable, 1959), pp. 3–68.

There is an important relationship between G's life and his novels. G's characters are "convincingly human"; his success derives "from the fact that his subjects were not congenial to him." What one remembers best of G's work includes his critical study of Dickens, his representation of women in his novels, and his understanding of the lower and middle classes. [Essay emphasizes G's life, particularly his youth and his memory of guilt. No new information is provided. Reviewed by André Crépin,

"Comptes Rendus," ETUDES ANGLAISES, XII (July–Sept 1959), 267–68; F. Léaud, "Bibliographie," LES LANGUES MODERNES, LIV (May–June 1960), 78.]

**1052** Ward, A. C. GISSING (Lond: Longmans, Green, 1959). A sincere and solid novelist, G was "animated by strict purposes." Perhaps the prejudices that dominated critics and reviewers during G's lifetime have passed so that now he can receive an honest judgment. Desiring to be the Balzac of England, G attempted to record the life of Londoners, even though only London natives can possibly hope to catch the courage, humor, and capacity for kindliness of the inhabitants. G had no desire to sympathize with any slum occupant if it meant that he might thereby lower himself to their conditions. G stood aloof, an aristocrat no less than Godwin Peak. His prose syle was unpretentious, often drab. *The Private Papers of Henry Ryecroft* deserves affection, even love; it is his best expression of the whole man, viewed from many sides. Among his novels, four books carry G's hopes for future fame: *Demos, New Grub Street, Born in Exile,* and *The Odd Women.* G's *Charles Dickens: A Critical Study* is not a scholarly book but "something more valuable—an illuminating one." [In addition to a biographical sketch, this booklet contains a select bibliography. It was published as No. 111 in the "Writers and Their Work" series for The British Council and The National Book League.]

---

# 1960

---

**1053** Ausubel, Herman. IN HARD TIMES (NY: Columbia UP, 1960), pp. 11, 22, 29, 30, 32, 34, 43, 47, 48, 54, 65, 66, 69, 87, 89, 95–96, 104, 110, 134–35, 148, 153, 164, 173, 174, 176, 181, 182, 186, 188, 196, 263, 323. [This thoroughly documented study of late nineteenth-century English reformers frequently cites G's life, letters, and fiction in examining the social, political, religious, and financial conditions.]

**1054** Boll, T. E. M. "A Forgotten Poem of George Gissing," NOTES AND QUERIES, VII (Dec 1960), 465. [Reproduces three-stanza "Song" from TEMPLE BAR for Nov 1883.]

**1055** Francis, C. J. "Gissing and Schopenhauer," NINETEENTH CENTURY FICTION, XV (June 1960), 53–63; rptd in COLLECTED ARTICLES ON GEORGE GISSING, ed by Pierre Coustillas (Lond: Frank Cass, 1968), pp. 106–16.

In 1883 G denied any commitment to a philosophy articulated in his fiction. Nevertheless, he had read Schopenhauer, who, like the realists, "conceives of art as an attempt to apprehend the essential Idea, to represent the Truth itself, to reproduce and clarify the thing outside the artist rather than his view of it." Whether he wished to suppress the personal element, consciously or unconsciously, G's novels were influenced by Schopenhauer, in content and form. In *The Nether World,* the futility of life turns towards resignation, not defiance; *New Grub Street* is an even better illustration of this attitude. Biffen and Reardon exemplify this futility by their rejection of the will-to-live; this corresponds to Schopenhauer's definition of passivity. Happiness for these men becomes impossible. G's tendency to pessimism is also present in the writings of several of his contemporaries.

**1056** Gettmann, Royal A. A VICTORIAN PUBLISHER (Cambridge: Cambridge UP, 1960), pp. 120, 123, 128, 196–97, 199, 215–22, 251, 253–56, 263.
[Some of this material already appeared in Gettmann's "Bentley and Gissing," NINETEENTH CENTURY FICTION, XI (March 1957), 306–14. For a review of the book, see Helmut E. Gerber, "Reviews," ENGLISH FICTION IN TRANSITION, IV:3 (1961), 62–64.]

**1057** "Gissing, George Robert," DIZIONARIO UNIVERSALE DELLA LITTERATURA CONTEMPORANEA (Universal Dictionary of Contemporary Literature) (1960), pp. 491–92.
G is at his best in describing autobiographical experiences and in denouncing evils and contradictions in society. His writing was influenced by Dickens and by the French Naturalists. [Contains biographical and bibliographical information, usually reliable.] [In Italian.]

**1058** Hodgins, James Raymond. "A Study of the Periodical Reception of the Novels of Thomas Hardy, George Gissing, and George Moore," DISSERTATION ABSTRACTS, XXI (1960), 196–97. Unpublished dissertation, Michigan State University, 1960.

**1059** Malbone, Raymond G. "George Gissing, Novelist," DISSERTATION ABSTRACTS, XX (1960), 4113. Unpublished dissertation, University of Minnesota, 1959.

**1060** Mansley, E. F. "A Critical Biography of the Novelist George Gissing." Unpublished dissertation, University of Nottingham, 1960.
[Listed in Lawrence F. McNamee, DISSERTATIONS IN ENGLISH AND AMERICAN LITERATURE (NY & Lond: Bowker, 1968).]

**1061** Nur, Sherif. "The Victorian Sunday in LITTLE DORRIT and *Thyrza,*" CAIRO STUDIES IN ENGLISH (1960), pp. 155–65.

The "Victorian Sunday" is perfectly merged into the structure of LITTLE DORRIT. In *Thyrza,* Sunday is more a part of G than of England. "The aesthete proves less skillful than the reformer at handling his material."

**1062** Orwell, George [pseud of Eric Blair]. "George Gissing," LONDON MAGAZINE, VII (June 1960), 36–43; rptd in COLLECTED ARTICLES ON GEORGE GISSING, ed by Pierre Coustillas (Lond: Frank Cass, 1968), pp. 50–57; COLLECTED ESSAYS, JOURNALISM, AND LETTERS OF GEORGE ORWELL, ed by Sonia Orwell and Ian Angus (Lond: Secker & Warburg, 1968), IV, 428–36.

Though G never described the very lowest conditions of human life, he did tell us enough of London at the end of the nineteenth century to convince us that we have progressed from a far uglier time. Though *New Grub Street* (G's masterpiece) and *The Odd Women* are out of print, we welcome the new editions of *The Whirlpool,* with an introduction by Miss Myfanwy Evans, and of *In the Year of Jubilee,* with an introduction by William Plomer. All G's novels "protest the form of self-torture that goes by the name of respectability." Remnants of Puritanism structured society with senseless taboos that destroyed all hope of happiness except for those who had at least £300 a year. The "average" worker did not preoccupy G; he spoke "not for the multitude, but for the exceptional man, the sensitive man, isolated among barbarians." *Grub Street,* G's most impressive book, deals with "that much-dreaded occupational disease, sterility," the dried-up writer powerless to write. For Reardon, G sought a wife; she ought to be "intelligent *and* pretty," but for G such a wife could be found only in the socially superior class. This idea also dates G's similar generalization that women, foolish or not, are all "miserably limited in outlook"; even the "clever and spirited ones" cannot escape "ready-made standards." G was an exceptional novelist for England because, like the best continental writers, he "was interested in individual human beings," could handle them sympathetically, and could "make a credible story" of their collisions. His 'faults' however, exist. His prose is "often disgusting," and his "range of experience" is narrow. But much of this is attributable to his own circumstances. Like Mark Rutherford, G was deficient in humor. While some novelists get laughs from grotesque lesser characters, G remained impartial in his treatment of the low and common. In his own life, G sought sufficient means to live comfortably and to read the ancient classics. We are fortunate that he never became a scholar, for then he would not have become "the chronicler of vulgarity, squalor and failure."

**1063** Starkie, Enid. FROM GAUTIER TO ELIOT (Lond: Hutchinson, 1960), pp. 79–80.

The influence of French naturalism can be found in the "slice of life" techniques employed by G in *The Nether World, Born in Exile,* and especially *The Odd Women.* [The reviewer for the TIMES LITERARY SUPPLEMENT (Lond) ("A Charm Against Francophobia," 8 April 1960, p. 224) suggests that it was apparently with ironic intent that Starkie finds "the vital and original English fiction of the late nineteenth century comprised the works of George Moore and Henry James, together with George Gissing, Hubert Crackanthorpe, Mr. Somerset Maugham and Arnold Bennett." Why does she neglect Conrad and Lawrence in outlining her claim for an English debt to France?]

**1064** Stevenson, Lionel. THE ENGLISH NOVEL: A PANORAMA (Boston: Houghton Mifflin, 1960), pp. 399–410, 414–24.

Along with Hardy, G "has defied the taboos of refinement by telling distasteful truths about cruelty and poverty, both rural and urban"; however, G was not convincing in the "treatment of sex, in spite of his pose of frankness. Partly this may have been due to his fear of antagonizing the critics and libraries, but also it must be attributed to the ineptness of his own relations with women."

**1065** Wells, H. G. ARNOLD BENNETT AND H. G. WELLS: A RECORD OF A PERSONAL AND LITERARY FRIENDSHIP, ed by Harris Wilson (Urbana: University of Illinois P; Lond: Hart-Davis, 1960), pp. 56, 62, 85.

In their correspondence, Wells wrote Bennett that G and Moore belonged to another school of novelists, an impersonal school. Wells resented the fact that Bennett devoted sections of FAME AND FORTUNE to G and Moore, but none to Wells. When G was very ill in June 1901, Wells told Bennett how much he admired G's *Charles Dickens: A Critical Study* and *By the Ionian Sea:* "I would be glad indeed if for once Gissing could have a shout." [In a review of the book, Helmut E. Gerber called Wells the "most diverse *writer,* Bennett the greatest *novelist,* and Gissing the greatest *artist."* ("Reviews," ENGLISH FICTION IN TRANSITION, IV: 2 [1961] 68–69.)]

**1066** Young, Arthur C. "The Death of Gissing: A Fourth Report," ESSAYS IN LITERARY HISTORY, ed by Rudolph Kirk and C. F. Main (New Brunswick, NJ: Rutgers UP, 1960), pp. 217–28.

Beyond the conflicting information of G's death provided by Wells, Cooper, and Roberts, we now have a "fourth report" from Gabrielle Fleury. She wrote Bertz in 1904 telling about G's vision of "l'autre monde, l'enfer et les diables" during his last night, expressing virulent anger at Wells's

"Impression" of G in the MONTHLY REVIEW ("George Gissing: An Impression," XVI [Aug 1904], 160–72). She said that Wells forced champagne, coffee, tea and milk, "coup sur coup," on G during her brief absence from the sickroom, with the doctor's subsequent reaction—"Il l'a tué!"

---

# 1961

---

**1067** Gettmann, Royal A. "Introduction," *George Gissing and H. G. Wells: A Record of Their Friendship and Correspondence,* ed by Royal A. Gettmann (Urbana: University of Illinois P, 1961), pp. 11–31.

Despite the many similarities between their experience and attitudes, G's temperament prevented his attaining the financial success which Wells won. It appears clear now that G was more charming than has generally been thought, that he often tested male characters by their response to a woman, that he had a talent for journalism but was too proud to produce it, that he lacked confidence, and that he could only write of things that interested him. G was a novelist, whereas Wells was a writer; but despite his dedication to his art, G never wrote a "thoroughly good novel." G's lack of success was partly due to "a failure to concentrate and dramatise." G lacked "sympathetic imagination" and "could not wholly lose himself in his characters." G was closer to Wells than to James. G "was a mediator between the Victorians . . . and the innovators of the 1920's." [Among the reviews that noted this important work are the following: Ruth M. Adams, "Reviews," VICTORIAN STUDIES, V (March 1962), 271–72 (In these letters G shows an "endless capacity for self-pity," though it is based on "real reasons for despair and depression." G's self-pity overflowed into three areas: "he could not find or mingle with his intellectual equals," "he could not rise higher on the social scale than the level of a hack writer," and "his books did not command an audience or bring in money."); D. R. Cherry, "New Books," QUEEN'S QUARTERLY, LXVIII (Winter 1962), 696 (From these letters we learn that G was a blend of "reporter, preacher, and malcontent." Only in his last years did G's circumstances allow him to become sufficiently detached and to be artistically effective.); Pierre Coustillas, "George Gissing et H. G. Wells," ETUDES ANGLAISES, XV (April–June, 1962), 156–66 (These letters are particularly valuable when read with the corresponding letters that G addressed to Gabrielle Fleury and Clara Collet for these years.); Helmut E. Gerber, "Reviews," ENGLISH FICTION IN TRANSITION, IV: 2 (1961), 68–89 (Prof. Gettmann's introduction and notes "provide a context for the letters"; his work has been done with "commendable thoroughness and scholarly care."); A. G. Hill, "Reviews and Comment," CRITICAL QUARTERLY, III (Winter 1961), 373 (It is unfortunate that these letters give so little of G's background, starting as they do well along in G's career. The more detached G is—as *The Odd Women* and *In the Year of Jubilee* show—the better his fiction.); V. S. Pritchett, "Casualties," NEW STATESMAN, LXI (26 May 1961), 841 (This correspondence tells us very little we did not already know about G. The "bumptious style of the new realism" of Wells and Bennett constituted the pose of the period, and G can hardly match this style. "The odd thing is that Gissing's feeling for failure in life and his almost wilful practice of it in writing have been his distinctive contribution to the English novel." G's characters are as passive and isolated as the novelist himself. "Only Gissing's women impress."); Sherif Nur, "Reviews," CAIRO STUDIES IN ENGLISH (1961–1962), 253–60 (G and Wells remained friends because of G's tolerance and generosity of spirit; Wells proved a reliable, though not always sympathetic and understanding, friend.); Norman Shrapnel, "Writing for Revenge," MANCHESTER GUARDIAN, 26 May 1961, p. 6 (G needed his suffering to write novels His "terrible attachment to anguish" became a powerful creative force.); Martin Shuttleworth, "Grubby Giant," SPECTATOR, CCVI (23 June 1961), 926–28 (G was a great writer "because the greatness of his intention survives." His achievement never reached the measure of his intention, however. His characters, when compared to Dickens's bright baubles, are merely beads; but "the London they move against is one of the greatest characters in English fiction."); "An Unequal Friendship," TIMES LITERARY SUPPLEMENT (Lond), 7 July 1961, p. 416 (The lengthy correspondence between G and Wells reveals their differences in fictional ideals. More often than not, Wells misunderstood G, although at the same time he provided encouragement and confidence. Wells failed to appreciate the depths of G's capacity for suffering frustration.); Joseph J. Wolff, "Book Reviews," JOURNAL OF ENGLISH AND GERMANIC PHILOLOGY, LXII (Oct 1963), 816–17 (These letters clarify the differences in the two novelists: Wells dedicated to the practical, G to the artistic. Probably the greatest merit of the volume is Prof. Gettmann's sensitive appraisal of G's literary achievement.); Christopher Wordsworth, "Lazarus and Friend," OBSERVER REVIEW (Lond), 1 Jan 1967, p. 25 (Temperamentally G and Wells were "oddly assorted, the pushing scrannel-voiced little Wells and Gissing with his classics, self-pity, and ruined-Viking physique." Was G the hair-shirt of Wells's artistic conscience?"); Arthur C. Young, "Gettmann's *George Gissing and H. G. Wells,*" NINETEENTH CENTURY FICTION, XVI (March 1962), 369–72 (G's relationship with Wells was not entirely unmarred; on the whole Wells was warmly sympathetic during G's lifetime. Gettmann might have identified more of the people referred to in the correspondence.).]

**1068** Jameson, Storm. MORLEY ROBERTS: THE LAST EMINENT VICTORIAN (Lond: Unicorn P, 1961), pp. 10, 11, 14–17, 32–33, 49, 60.

Roberts's first and closest friend, G, forms the subject of THE PRIVATE LIFE OF HENRY MAITLAND, "one of the classic biographies," a book that catches the tone and truth of G's life. MAITLAND is "profoundly honest, compassionate, and lively," though it contains "some slips, out of haste and a characteristic disdain for chronology." [Among the reviews of this book that mention G: Pierre Coustillas, "Comptes Rendus," ETUDES ANGLAISES, XV (April–June 1962), 197–98; Pierre Coustillas, "Reviews," ENGLISH FICTION IN TRANSITION, V: i (1962), 63–64; "Writer and Friend," TIMES LITERARY SUPPLEMENT (Lond), 27 Oct 1961, p. 767 (Roberts will be remembered "as the friend of men more famous than himself," men such as G and W. H. Hudson. MAITLAND is one of the best literary biographies in the language.).]

**1069** Korg, Jacob. "George Gissing's Commonplace Book: A Manuscript from the Berg Collection of the New York Public Library," BULLETIN OF THE NEW YORK PUBLIC LIBRARY, LXV (Sept, Oct, Nov 1961), 417–34, 534–46, 588–614; rptd with an intro by Jacob Korg, GEORGE GISSING'S COMMONPLACE BOOK (NY: New York Public Library, 1962), pp. 7–18; "Introduction" rptd as "The Main Source of *The Ryecroft Papers*," in COLLECTED ARTICLES ON GEORGE GISSING (Lond: Frank Cass, 1968), pp. 168–78.

From 1887 until his death, G kept a commonplace book, a collection of "reflections of a contemplative, lingering sensibility, equally responsive to beauty and incongruity, which is capable of energetic protest when its calm is disturbed by some encounter with stupidity, vulgarity, or injustice." Although G himself is the exact counterpart of Ryecroft, there is sufficient similarity between these jottings and *The Private Papers of Henry Ryecroft* that "they harmonize very well." Passages from the commonplace book echo in *Ryecroft,* so that specific parallels are identifiable. On the other hand, differences do exist, such as the contrasting attitudes between G and Ryecroft concerning common people. And since most of these brief observations were written before 1890, many of G's ideas had changed before he wrote *Ryecroft,* his best known work, published in 1903. [Reviews: Pierre Coustillas, "Comptes Rendus," ETUDES ANGLAISES, XVI (Jan–March 1963), 89–90; "Reviews," ENGLISH FICTION IN TRANSITION, V: 4 (1962), 49–50; "The Face Behind the Mask," TIMES LITERARY SUPPLEMENT (Lond), 13 April 1962, p. 250.]

**1070** Nur, Sherif. "The Friendship Between George Gissing and

Eduard Bertz as Revealed in Gissing's Letters," CAIRO STUDIES IN ENGLISH (1961–1962), 95–110.
G found in Bertz qualities that were absent in Morley Roberts. The Bertz friendship was of a distinctly intellectual order, involving little about G's relations with women. Bertz's weakness in ordinary life and his professional failure stimulated G, who thereby came out the stronger of the two.

**1071** Preble, Harry E. "Gissing's Contributions to VYESTNIK EVROPY," DISSERTATION ABSTRACTS, XXI (1961), 1571. Unpublished dissertation, University of Illinois, 1960.

**1072** Pritchett, V. S. "Foreword," *The Private Papers of Henry Ryecroft* (NY: New American Library, 1961), pp. vii–xvi.
G's failure is "the source of his persistent fame." His subject is the struggle of class forces—the workers in the lower and middle classes, or the members of the upper classes, in continual conflict. In addition to this struggle, the testing of the human character preoccupied G. "In essence what he looked for in his favored characters was their solitude." While G is the "most class-conscious of our novelists," he is really "not fundamentally interested in class at all," so detached is his observation. He views characters both "as they are and as what they might become." [Reviewed by Vincent Starrett, "Books Alive," CHICAGO TRIBUNE MAGAZINE OF BOOKS, 25 March 1962, p. 7.]

**1073** Ray, Gordon N. "H. G. Wells's Contributions to the SATURDAY REVIEW," LIBRARY, 5th ser, XVI (March 1961), 29–36.
[Identifies unsigned articles and reviews contributed to the SATURDAY REVIEW as the work of Wells.]

**1074** Ward, A. C. "Introduction," TONO-BUNGAY by H. G. Wells (Lond: Longmans, 1961), xxxv.
Wells's description of the death of Uncle Ponderevo is based in part upon his own experience "when he went across to France in 1903 to be with his friend the novelist George Gissing, who would otherwise have died attended by such strangers as hovered round Uncle Ponderevo."

**1075** Young, Arthur C. "Introduction," *The Letters of George Gissing to Eduard Bertz,* ed by Arthur C. Young (New Brunswick, NJ: Rutgers UP; Lond: Constable, 1961), pp. ix–xl.
This collection of 189 letters, dating from April 1887 to October 1903, was discovered in the Berlin house where Bertz had lived until his death in 1931. Now a valuable part of the Yale University G collection, the letters contain significant information about G's life, statements of his artistic creed, and expressions of his feelings and opinions about his own writing.

G and Bertz "were in accord on politics, literature, economic theories, and philosophy; they shared similar resentments and prejudices; they exalted knowledge and manners." During their long separation G valued his correspondence with Bertz and confided much to him that we scarcely find in his letters to his own family. [Prof. Young has carefully and admirably documented the text; what he provides is informative and economical, drawing repeatedly from G's diary and letters. Reviews of the collection include the following: Ruth M. Adams, "Reviews," VICTORIAN STUDIES, V (March 1962), 271–72 (G's letters never show him to be a "particularly intellectual individual" who might deserve more attention from his social and intellectual betters. He constantly complains in a "querulous, petulant tone."); Bernard Bergonzi, "Shabby Genteel," SPECTATOR, CCVIII (26 Jan 1962), 115–16 (It is amazing that G's fame continues to hold despite the fact that he remains "poor, isolated and misunderstood." In these letters G appears more interested in the mechanics of authorship—publishers, costs, contracts—than with his art.); Pierre Coustillas, "Comptes Rendus," ETUDES ANGLAISES, XVI (Jan–March 1963), 88–89 (For the first time since Roberts's book we have fresh information about G at Manchester.); Pierre Coustillas, "George Gissing et Eduard Bertz: Une Amitie Litteraire" (George Gissing and Eduard Bertz: A Literary Friendship), REVUE DE LITTERATURE COMPARÉE, XXXVII (July–Sept 1963), 394–405 (These letters help us understand G's life and place him in the literary history of England and all Europe.); Frederic E. Faverty, "When He Rose Above His Surroundings," CHICAGO TRIBUNE MAGAZINE OF BOOKS, 24 Dec 1961, p. 4 (The correspondence of G and Bertz is "particularly valuable as a record of countries visited, . . . books read, people met, impressions formed." Those interested in G will approve Young's scholarship and his introduction to the letters.); "Grub Street to Glory," TIMES LITERARY SUPPLEMENT (Lond), 12 Jan 1962, p. 27 (One merit of these letters is that they contain very little of the hysteria and self-pity that mar most of G's other writings. As in his previously published letters and in *By the Ionian Sea,* G excels in describing the beauties of Greece and Rome. Young's research has been diligent; his notes are informative and economical; if anything, he has been over-zealous.); V. S. Pritchett, "Artists on Oath," NEW STATESMAN, LXIII (2 Feb 1962), 164–65 (These letters are interesting "for the precise check they give to what is meant by Gissing's failure to earn his living as a novelist with a respectful but small public." They are the letters of a "tired man" and are almost totally "lacking in intimacy." G is a little patronizing towards Bertz.); David Williams, "Foreign Correspondent," PUNCH, CCXLII (10 Jan 1962), 117 (G deserved a better correspondent than Bertz; his best letters originated in Greece and Rome. This book is "scrupulously annotated."); Joseph J. Wolff, "Reviews," ENGLISH FICTION IN TRANSITION, V: 2 (1962), 36–38

(More than in his other letters, G here makes literary judgments. Young's introduction and notes are excellent; they escape the factual level to provide insights and relationships uncommon in such editions.).]

# 1962

**1076** Coustillas, Pierre. "Les femmes dans l'oeuvre de George Gissing" (Women in the Works of George Gissing), ETUDES ANGLAISES, XV (Oct–Dec 1962), 412–13; trans and rvd as "Gissing's Feminine Portraiture," ENGLISH LITERATURE IN TRANSITION, VI: 3 (1963), 130–41.

While G's critics and reviewers have repeatedly pointed out the autobiographical nature of his novels, they have not carefully related the women in the novels to G's mother, his sisters, and his wives. In doing so it is possible to see the parallels in his frustration and his relationships with women who degraded him. Nor have previous scholars given G sufficient credit for the detachment of these representations. There is a close relationship also between G's feminine characters and his evolving ideas about women. [Originally prepared for a talk in Lyons, France, 27 April 1962, for the second Congress of the "Société des Anglicistes de l'Enseignement Supérieur."]

**1077** Coustillas, Pierre. "Une lettre inédite de Gabrielle Fleury à Clara Collet" (A Letter written by Gabrielle Fleury to Clara Collet), ETUDES ANGLAISES, XV (April–June 1962), 167–71.

On 1 Jan 1913 Gabrielle Fleury wrote a spirited letter to Clara Collet about Morley Roberts's THE PRIVATE LIFE OF HENRY MAITLAND. [Editorial comments about the content of MAITLAND are included.] [In French.]

**1078** Francis, C. J. "Gissing's Characterization: Heredity and Environment," LITERARY HALF-YEARLY (Mysore, India), III (July 1962), 28–37; rptd in GISSING NEWSLETTER, III (April, June, Sept 1967), 1–4; 3–7; 1–6.

Though not absolutely objective in rendering character, G resembled other realists in his notions of inherited characteristics. His characters are often the result of heredity since, like Schopenhauer, G believed "that a man was born with a fixed inherited character, and that the only development of character was the growth of knowledge." Environment cannot affect man's basic characteristics. But, aided by her strength of will, a character like Miriam Baske can assert herself and in part deny her past. G sees that his characters are not separate entities but figures of circumstance. As for temperament, "the action of the physical upon the mental constitution," G tried at times to deliberately shock his readers. The animality of characters affects their decisions, as can be seen in the development of Clem Peckover in *The Nether World* or Waymark in *The Whirlpool*. G also attends to nervous sensitivity as an aspect of character.

> **1079** Howe, Irving. "Introduction," *New Grub Street* (NY: Houghton Mifflin, 1962), pp. v–xxi; rptd as "George Gissing: Poet of Fatigue," in Irving Howe's A WORLD MORE ATTRACTIVE: A VIEW OF MODERN LITERATURE AND POLITICS (NY: Horizon P, 1963), pp. 169–91; partly rptd as "George Gissing: Poet of Fatigue," COLLECTED ARTICLES ON GEORGE GISSING, ed by Pierre Coustillas (Lond: Frank Cass, 1968), pp. 119–25.

G is a novelist of experiences, rather than ideas, who dealt with the "physically displaced," telling his story from their alienated point of view. While G succeeds in representing women, his treatment of character is, on the whole, conventional. G's dominant perception is "the vision of human waste." [Reviewing this introduction, Pierre Coustillas ("Comptes Rendus," ETUDES ANGLAISES, XVII [July–Sept 1964], 294) suggests that it would have been profitable to have examined *New Grub Street* in the light of G's life. Coustillas claims that Howe's best passages deal with G's hero and with the heroine's fight for the emancipation of women.]

> **1080** Mitchell, J. M. "Notes on George Gissing's Stories," STUDIES IN ENGLISH LITERATURE (Tokyo), XXXVIII (March 1962), 195–205.

G's short stories are practically a virgin ground for critics and constitute a new aspect of G's genius. His stories of the 1890s resemble French and Russian models. They testify to G's power of succinct characterization and contain a wide and memorable range of characters and a great variety of themes. While deficient in dramatic power, G's stories are technically skillful.

> **1081** Pritchett, V. S. LONDON PERCEIVED (NY: Harcourt, Brace & World, 1962), pp. 90–91.

G's world of the genteel life, one notch above that of misery, aches "for refinement and education." G's view is unique because his London is "outside the conventional view of all the English novelists." G despises "the Class Game and attempts a psychological penetration."

## 1963

> **1082** Briggs, Asa. VICTORIAN CITIES (NY: Harper & Row, 1963), pp. 361–68, 392.

G's novels link the London of Dickens with that of Edwardian Fabianism. His association with Wells seems less pronounced than with Baudelaire in feeling "that the city kept the artist free and yet enslaved him." G observed London life meticulously. The symbols of progress there were actually symbols of decay; crowds both horrified and fascinated him. Thus far social historians have neglected to learn about the social texture of London from G.

**1083** Coustillas, Pierre. "George Gissing à Manchester," Etudes Anglaises, XVI (July–Sept 1963), 255–61.

Four previously unpublished letters that G received from John George Black [printed here], dating from February to April 1876, shed light on G's circumstances at Owens College and his efforts for Nell, the prostitute he later married. The official records of Owens College show that G was caught with the marked money he had stolen from an overcoat in the college's cloakroom. For his crime, G was sentenced to a month in prison; his friend Black was expelled from the school for his complicity, and then later readmitted because while he knew of the affair, he was not a participant in it.

**1084** Dial, Robert L. "George Gissing's Theory of the Novel." Unpublished dissertation, University of Kansas City, 1963.

[Listed in Lawrence F. McNamee, Dissertations in English and American Literature (NY & Lond: Bowker, 1968).]

**1085** Korg, Jacob. George Gissing: A Critical Biography (Seattle: University of Washington P, 1963).

G's dominant theme is "the destruction of human character in the crushing mill of social evils." His methods derive less from Dickens than is usually claimed; his resemblance is rather to George Eliot. Early in his career G believed that novels should describe ordinary activities, emphasizing in detail the texture of day-to-day existence, even using the essentially uninteresting for materials. Later, in an effort to secure a larger reading public, G attempted shorter, fast-moving novels. But his serious work, like *The Odd Women, In the Year of Jubilee,* and *The Whirlpool,* remained in the tradition of social criticism. He chose to minimize the amount of didactic comment, to give details, and to provide the reader with oblique direction. To give his works meaning, he intended to stress the relationship between beauty in life and social reform. So strong was his social motivation that G had a very difficult time in gaining objectivity. Essentially, G was a Victorian who loved good manners and pleasant conversations but who was committed to render the horrors of lower-class existence. As an artist, he believed in his responsibility to use his special powers of perception. By the time he wrote *A Life's Morning,* G matured in writing a "plausible study of the thought processes of a complicated and principled mind." In *Demos,* G insists that education alone cannot rescue the poor from their misery; poverty debases one so that self-rule is impossible. The theme is repeated in *Thyrza.* In *The Nether World,* G contrasts the rich and poor on a broad, static canvas; it demonstrates his habit of reporting from actuality by drawing upon his notes. As a result, G gains greater reserve and authenticity by giving the impression of animality in treating the creatures of poverty. Thereafter, G transferred his characters to a higher level of social existence to examine those who exploited the poor. He found middle-class life paralyzed by the desire for comfort; industrial society was impoverished spiritually. *The Emancipated* posseses a "perceptive irony" and a "curious symmetry of design" hitherto absent in G's novels.

G was fully aware of the effects of the industrial revolution on both the lower and the middle classes, and was familiar with the principal writings on the subject by continental and English authors. *New Grub Street,* "more authentic, more cogent, and clearer in construction than G's earlier novels," used the materials of failure even while G controlled his indignation with the "objectivity necessary for genuine realism." The success of *Grub Street* allowed G to write *Born in Exile,* recording the ideals of young scientists. He was interested in the compromise made by gifted young people, even as he thought he had compromised himself. The effects of marriage practices affecting women formed the chief theme of *Odd Women,* though the novel's remarkable subject is marred by the book's structural weaknesses. Marriage is again the issue in *Whirlpool;* now the distressing conditions of his own unhappiness with his second wife made all life appear a malevolent fate inflicted by society. G's studies of Dickens show both the strengths and weaknesses of his subject as well as G's own fictional ideals. Written in Italy, they strengthened G's reputation and assisted him financially. The continent, which had given G occasional relief, finally gave him Gabrielle Fleury, the sort of woman he "always admired from afar but he could never hope to marry." This attachment gave G the peace and happiness reflected in his most successful book, *The Private Papers of Henry Ryecroft.* By this time, the stern ideals that G had formed in his youth had softened, for just as he had formulated a reconciliation of science and religion as "the dominant fallacy" of *Exile,* so in *Our Friend the Charlatan* he devised the dominant fallacy of organizing society on scientific principles. That G was "never able to make up his mind about social issues" became, paradoxically, an advantage. His novels lack "a vision of life as a well-ordered whole," though his characters are "well realized both as spiritual and sociological beings." G's novels present "genuinely controversial moral issues" and are thereby a "turning from

motives of entertainment and propaganda." Ultimately, for G, the "novelist's supreme morality was the principle of truth to his own knowledge of
life, however limited it might be." [Korg's study gained considerable attention, as the following sampling of reviews and articles testifies: Ruth M.
Adams, "Book Reviews," SOUTH ATLANTIC QUARTERLY, LXIII (Spring
1964), 254 (No other novelist has focused so precisely as G "the phenomenon of the changing middle class, invaded from below by the ambitious half-educated proletariat and augmented from above by the
economically dispossessed of the gentry and the genteel—the 'unclassed'
new society."); R. F. Anderson, "Book Reviews," DALHOUSIE REVIEW,
XLIV (Spring 1964), 103-4 (This study provides the biographical information long needed for a better appreciation of G's novels.); Bernard
Bergonzi, "Reviews," REVIEW OF ENGLISH STUDIES, XV (Nov 1964),
441-42 (G has received considerable biographical attention, as though
his life formed "an archetype of the doomed and self-destroying late
nineteenth-century artist." His works demand more careful study.); Pierre
Coustillas, "Bibliographie," LES LANGUES MODERNES, LVII (Nov-Dec
1963), 594-95 (Time is confirming G's own death-bed statement that his
work would not soon be forgotten. Using the primary sources available
at the New York Public Library, the Yale University, and the Carl H.
Pforzheimer Library, Korg has prepared the best biography now available on G.); Pierre Coustillas, "Comptes Rendus," ETUDES ANGLAISES,
XVII (Jan-March 1964), 86-87 (There are only slight errors of fact to
mar Korg's life of G.); Francis Fytton, "Selected Books," LONDON MAG-
AZINE, V (July 1965), 101-3 (As a result of the pressures of his personal life, G's novels "were fabricated rather than inspired." Korg tries to
"explain away Gissing's socialism without realising that Gissing was a
social realist."); Gordon S. Haight, "A Self-Punishing Victorian," YALE
REVIEW, LIII (Autumn 1963), 107-9 (While Korg's study is a "careful
and critical analysis of all Gissing's work," there is still some important
information to be uncovered about G's family, his social and religious an-
cestry.); Norman Kelvin, "Books," WESTERN HUMANITIES REVIEW, XVIII
(Spring 1964), 184-85 (In addition to his talent in writing, G had "a
grim compulsion to create for himself degradations and denials."); Francis
King, "Book Reviews," LISTENER, LXXIII (25 Feb 1965), 305 (G's
novels about the poor are depressing because he thinks that their "plight is
irredeemable." "It is a pity that he never saw the Welfare State."); Leslie
L. Lewis, "Reviews," ENGLISH LANGUAGE NOTES, I (Dec 1963), 152-
54 (Korg has given a continuous record of G's life, although G the man
"becomes somewhat submerged under the weight of intellectual and literary
criticism."); Maghanita Laski, "The Wet Bird," LONDON OBSERVER, 7
March 1965, p. 27 (G lacked capacity for greatness not only in literature
but also in life. At social gatherings G sat in a corner, "crouched to-

gether like a wet bird"; that is how Harrison's son remembered him. Korg's study tells us how much G's books owe to his own resentment and hatred.); D[arshan] S[ingh] M[aini], "A Lonely Victorian," ILLUSTRATED WEEK-LY OF INDIA, LXXXVII (22 May 1966), 53 (G does not belong among "the great and the elect" novelists; he wrote despite the destitution that marked his hapless existence.); J[ames] B[oyer] M[ay], "Gissing: Pre-view of Modern Individualism," TRACE, No. 51 (Winter 1964), 341 (Korg's study of G presents a writer who, while not an "informed analyst of economics and large-scale causes," commented on various "isms" in the light of "ethical results and probabilities." His vision was limited; his principal novels concentrated on "fictionalized personal tribulations and observations."); William Kean Seymour, "A Victorian Realist," CON-TEMPORARY REVIEW, CCVI (June 1965), 333–34 (G failed to achieve greatness because he performed only on one string, viewing life "as a state remorseless and overpowering."); "Victorian Outsider," TIMES LITERARY SUPPLEMENT (Lond), 5 July 1963, p. 494 (G "would have been sur-prised and displeased to learn that the primary interest in his work, sixty years after his death, rests in his attempt to make artistic sense out of his personal confusions." Korg's book is "so good that one wishes he would undertake the definitive biography," so blurred is the image that we get from THE PRIVATE LIFE OF HENRY MAITLAND. While this study has much of value gained from the Yale, Berg, and Pforzheimer collections, there remain important unanswered questions, e.g., were G's early disastrous marriages the cause of his best novels; did he come to the "increased smoothness and certainty of style" in *Ryecroft* and *By the Ionian Sea* with his happiness in Gabrielle Fleury's companionship?); Joseph J. Wolff, "The Life and the Works: Jacob Korg's GEORGE GISSING," ENGLISH LITERATURE IN TRANSITION, VI: 4 (1963), 246–48 (Korg's work is basic to any serious study of G's achievements, particularly because it places G historically and draws upon his fellow novelists.); Frederick T. Wood, Current Literature, 1963," ENGLISH STUDIES (Amsterdam), XLV (Aug 1964), 344–45 (G had little sympathy with other liberal thinkers; he was skeptical of agnosticism, education, democracy, and science.); Arthur C. Young, "Jacob Korg, GEORGE GISSING," NINETEENTH CEN-TURY FICTION, XVIII (March 1964), 399–402 (Rather than a "critical biography," as the subtitle suggests, Korg's book is a "study of Gissing's thoughts as illustrated in his novels, and a comparison of his thinking with that of other Victorians such as Ruskin, Hardy, Eliot, H. G. Wells, and Sir Walter Besant." If the book makes meticulous use of recent scholar-ship, it gives few new insights and little of the "sense of life, of personal-ity: of humanity in either Gissing or the people concerned with his exis-tence." G vacillated "on questions of reform, politics, and aesthetics," while firmly adhering to agnosticism and adamantly refusing to supply the "pablum for the popular taste.").]

**1086** Preble, Harry E. "Gissing's Articles for VYESTNIK EVROPY," VICTORIAN NEWSLETTER, No. 23 (Spring 1963), 12–15.
G drew heavily upon London newspapers and magazines for the eight articles he prepared for the VYESTNIK EVROPY in 1881–1882. G repeatedly showed his liberalism in reporting the Irish problem, parliamentary debates, and the threats of war. But these articles reported little of the life and times of the English people. What he wrote for his journal is helpful to those who would understand *Workers in the Dawn* and *The Unclassed*.

**1087** Swinnerton, Frank. "Foreword," *By the Ionian Sea* (Lond: Richards P, 1963), pp. 7–14.
G's early years as a writer were troubled by poverty; through the help of Frederic Harrison, he secured students for private tutoring. After 1891 he was comparatively successful and was able to travel to the lands he loved.

# 1964

**1088** Coustillas, Pierre. "The Letters of George Gissing to Gabrielle Fleury (A Selection: Parts I–III)," BULLETIN OF THE NEW YORK PUBLIC LIBRARY, LXVIII (Sept, Oct, Nov 1964), 433–61, 525–48, 602–17; "Introduction" rptd in *The Letters of George Gissing to Gabrielle Fleury,* ed by Pierre Coustillas (NY: New York Public Library, 1964), pp. 7–20.
[The BULLETIN printed the same "Introduction," as well as about forty of the hundred letters contained in the book.] In 1898, Gabrielle Fleury wrote G to ask permission to translate *New Grub Street* into French. A correspondence followed; their friendship quickened into love, and marrige, within a year in Rouen. Though G's second wife survived, G told Gabrielle that she was his real wife. Life with Gabrielle brought him great happiness, dignity, and intelligent companionship. During the periods of their separation, when G was in England or when she was attending her aging and sick mother, they corresponded faithfully, as the letters here provided so abundantly reveal. These letters are valuable not only for what they say about G's personal life but also for the amplification they provide about G's ideas on women—as so much has been written about the question of G's knowledge of women. The letters printed here are in the Berg Collection of the New York Public Library. [Coustillas has exercised great care in editing these letters, as well as identifying the people and places mentioned in the exchange. Reviews of the volume include: H. E. Gerber,

"Gissing and Gabrielle: Private Lives," ENGLISH LITERATURE IN TRANSITION, VIII: 5 (1965), 311–12; "Mrs. Gissing II," TIMES LITERARY SUPPLEMENT (Lond), 5 Aug 1965, p. 680 (see also a letter correcting the title to Mrs. Gissing III, Sidney Blackmore, "Letters to the Editor: Gissing's Wives," TIMES LITERARY SUPPLEMENT [Lond], 19 Aug 1965, p. 722); Arthur C. Young, "Book Review," GISSING NEWSLETTER, I (Oct 1965), 1–2, 6–7; A. C. Young, "Comptes rendus critiques," REVUE DE LITTERATURE COMPARÉE, XLI (April–June 1967), 313–15.]

**1089** Fernando, L. "Feminism and the Novelist's Imagination in Eliot, Meredith, Hardy, Gissing, and Moore." Unpublished dissertation, Leeds University, 1964.

[Listed in Lawrence F. McNamee, DISSERTATIONS IN ENGLISH AND AMERICAN LITERATURE, SUPP I (NY & Lond: Bowker, 1969).]

**1090** Gordan, John D. "New in the Berg Collection: 1959–1961 (Part II)," BULLETIN OF THE NEW YORK PUBLIC LIBRARY, LXVIII (Jan 1964), 6–12; rptd as NEW IN THE BERG COLLECTION: 1959–1961 (NY: NY Public Library, 1964), pp. 20–21.

[Describes the first published stories in the author's file copies; first published novel, *Workers in the Dawn,* in crimson cloth; copies of thirteen contracts with various publishers and some sales reports; letters from Gabrielle Fleury.]

**1091** Haight, Gordon S. "Gissing: Some Biographical Details," NOTES AND QUERIES, XI (June 1964), 235–36.

What can we learn about G's London relatives, and particularly their social status? Were they working-class people? When G married Edith Underwood, he spoke of her as a "decent work-girl." Was her father a "plasterer's labourer," or was Roberts correct in calling him a "bootmake in Camden Town"? The answers might be significant because G himself was so conscious of social implications.

**1092** Karl, Frederick. "Five Victorian Novelists," AN AGE OF FICTION: THE NINETEENTH CENTURY BRITISH NOVEL (NY: Farrar, Strauss & Giroux, 1964), pp. 343–48.

G does not have Hardy's "sense of heightened tragedy" because he was not in sympathy with "those he wrote about." He creates "little life outside of his own sense of misery." Waymark's contrasting Christ and Prometheus, or Pessimism and Optimism, suggests G's beliefs. Like John Davidson, G "rebelled against acquiescence." *New Grub Street* "is rarely a novel of Life. It is more a fiction of ideas." Of most interest is what a G novel "suggests about his world." "The chief element is disgust," a "sense of nausea."

**1093** Korg, Jacob. "George Gissing," VICTORIAN FICTION: A GUIDE TO RESEARCH, ed by Lionel Stevenson (Cambridge: Harvard UP, 1964), pp. 401–13.

G research has been hampered by the fact that his life was for so many years known only through the excised letters, the misleading account of Morley Roberts, and the writings of Thomas Seccombe and Frank Swinnerton. More recently, Mabel Collins Donnelly, Arthur C. Young, and Jacob Korg have provided accurate and more detailed studies of both his life and career. Future scholarship should seek to discover missing manuscripts and letters, examine his contributions to periodicals, and critically analyze his fiction.

**1094** Lenehan, William T. "Techniques and Themes in the Early English and American Naturalistic Novels," DISSERTATION ABSTRACTS, XXV (1964), 452–53. Unpublished dissertation, University of Oklahoma, 1964.

# 1965

**1095** Coustillas, Pierre. "Gissing's Writings on Dickens: A Bio-Bibliographical Survey," DICKENSIAN, LXI (Autumn 1965), 168–79; rptd with revisions as GISSING'S WRITINGS ON DICKENS (Lond: Enitharmon P, 1969).

It is possible to document the details of G's work on Dickens, the circumstances of these writings, G's negotiations with publishers, his earnings, etc. They have appeared in book form, *Charles Dickens: A Critical Study* (1898), and in an abridgement and revision of John Forster's LIFE OF DICKENS (1903), G's *Critical Studies of the Works of Charles Dickens* (1924) and *The Immortal Dickens* (1925).

**1096** Coustillas, Pierre. "In Gissing's Footsteps," GISSING NEWS-LETTER, I (Jan, April 1965), 1–3; 1.

One can trace with relish the places where G lived or stayed briefly, both in England and France. In London, some of the buildings still stand; others have given way, destroyed by the war or by progress. In France, at the Chateau de Chasney, the very room where G stayed has both his picture and some of his books.

**1097** Coustillas, Pierre. "Some Unrecorded Editions," GISSING NEWSLETTER, I (June 1965), 6–7.

A list of G's books in various editions and reprintings is far from complete. [Itemizes certain editions, describing publisher, binding, etc.]

**1098** Daniels, Earl. "Gissing Autograph Material in the Collection of Earl Daniels," GISSING NEWSLETTER, I (June, Oct 1965), 2–3; 3–4.
[Prints contents of notes, postcards, and letters from G in his collection; itemizes related letters of G's friends and relatives.]

**1099** Graham, Kenneth. ENGLISH CRITICISM OF THE NOVEL: 1865–1900 (Oxford: Clarendon P, 1965), pp. 8–9, 16, 30, 32, 37, 41, 47–48, 73, 87–88, 123.
However much G's artistic conscience told him to disseminate ideas in his fiction, particularly to advance social and moral reform, he still denied that his works advocated any theory. G's realism was strongly criticized by reviewers.

**1100** Harris, W. V. "An Approach to Gissing's Short Stories," STUDIES IN SHORT FICTION, II (Winter 1965), 137–44.
An examination of the short stories G wrote for Chicago newspapers, and the tales in *Human Odds and Ends* and *The House of Cobwebs* shows that G was not as concerned with plot-line as he was with "warmth of characterization, the avoidance of dire misfortune, and the inclusion of instances of the minor joys of life." G's sensational climaxes in the Chicago newspaper stories are improved upon in the placid, ironic telling of the narrative in *Odds and Ends*. With the warmer tone of *Cobwebs,* G achieves mastery in his own realm of the short story; each story justifies its existence by the delicacy of characterization. G's stories celebrate the ideal of "quietly pushing on" in the face of adversity.

**1101** Koike, Shigeru. "Some Recent Gissing Publications in Japan," GISSING NEWSLETTER, I (Jan, June 1965), 3–4; 5–6.
G's writings appear as selections in English language textbooks in Japan.

**1102** Lansdowne, Arthur. "Where Gissing Lived," GISSING NEWSLETTER, I (Oct 1965), 4; II (Jan 1966), 6–7.
[A description of two G residences: 76, Burton Road, Brixton, London; 55, Wornington Road, South Kensington, London.]

**1103** Rogers, James A. "George Gissing: Poet of Fatigue or Fortitude?" GISSING NEWSLETTER, I (June, Oct 1965), 1–2; 5–6.
Irving Howe and Morley Roberts have given us the image of G as a man of excessive self-pity. But an author ought to be judged "in terms of a workable criteria." Such novels as *Born in Exile* are "first class psychology and writing." G's letters to Gabrielle show that his attitudes towards sex "were wonderfully fresh" and "unspoiled." G's workers assert man's dignity; he was not a hater of the working classes.

**1104** Selig, Robert Livingston. "George Gissing's Major Period: Novels of the Middle Class, 1891–1894," DISSERTATION ABSTRACTS, XXVI (1965), 2192. Unpublished dissertation, Columbia University, 1965.

# 1966

**1105** Birkenhead, Earl of. "Record of a Surprising Friendship," DAILY TELEGRAPH (Lond), 15 Dec 1966, p. 18.

The letters collected in Royal A. Gettmann's edition (Lond: Hart-Davis; Urbana: University of Illinois P, 1961) at first appear unbelievably flat and trivial, but gradually they provide a fascinating picture of Wells. G became, as Wells surmised, a novelist stored in dusty places known only by "professional men of letters and the more intellectual critics." [A. H. T. Midlane replied to this article, "Letters to the Editor: George Gissing," DAILY TELEGRAPH, 20 Dec 1966, p. 10.]

**1106** Blackmore, Sidney. "George Gissing and Clevedon," GISSING NEWSLETTER, II (Jan 1966), 1–2.

It is interesting to trace G's travels in Somerset, particularly in Clevedon on the Bristol Channel. *The Odd Women* is, in part, set in this region.

**1107** Coustillas, Helene. "Our Italian Journey," GISSING NEWSLETTER, II (April, Sept, Dec 1966), 3–5; 4–5; 6–7; III (Dec 1967), 7–8.

In August and September 1965, we toured Italy to visit the many places mentioned by G in his various writings. While the cities have changed considerably since his day, the countryside and the towns are remarkably untouched.

**1108** Coustillas, Pierre. "Gissing and Butler Clarke," GISSING NEWSLETTER, II (April 1966), 6–7.

In the last two years of his life, while living in St. Jean-de-Luz, in the lower Pyrenees, G met an English scholar of Spanish, Henry Butler Clarke. G probably consulted him about matters for his *Veranilda*.

**1109** Coustillas, Pierre. "Henry Hick's Recollections of George Gissing," HUNTINGTON LIBRARY QUARTERLY, XXXIX (Feb 1966), 161–70.

Henry Hick knew G from his early school days. Hick "jotted down his reminiscences of Gissing, which his daughter, D. Barbara J. Hick, has abstracted." They are valuable for showing how G became a man "who, outside the world of books, was often crippled by scruples and complexes." Hick's notes discuss G's relationship with his mother and his second wife, but the notes present a distorted picture of Gabrielle Fleury.

**1110** Coustillas, Pierre. "Introduction," *Les carnets d'Henry Ryecroft* (*The Private Papers of Henry Ryecroft*), ed by Pierre Coustillas. Collection bilingue. (Paris: Aubier-Montaigne, 1966), pp. 9–73, 497–542.

If one compares the two versions we have of *The Private Papers of Henry Ryecroft,* that held by the Carl H. Pforzheimer Library and that revised for publication in 1901, the superiority of the second is apparent: it is less aggressive in thought and better in balance. Besides the commonplace book, already examined by Jacob Korg (1962), G also drew from a memorandum book now in the Huntington Library. Most of the facts, with the major exception of the retired life in a Devonshire cottage, are auto-biographical. And Ryecroft's resignation remained G's aspiration. *Ryecroft* is in the tradition of a pseudo-journal and deserves to be assessed as a revelation of human character and as a journal. The work occupies a central place in G's career. [This bilingual text contains elaborate apparatus, including detailed notes to elucidate the writing. Wherever possible the source of the passage is suggested. In addition, the volume contains a survey of G's life and works as well as a study of the origin and genesis of this book. Reviews include: Mauricette Aussourd, "Book Review," GISSING NEWSLETTER, III (Sept 1967), 7–12; Jean Cazemajou, "Comptes Rendus," REVUE DE LITTERATURE COMPARÉE, XLIV (Jan-March 1970), 139; C. S. C[ollinson], "Comptes Rendus," ETUDES ANGLAISES, XX (Jan–March 1967), 96–98; Jacob Korg, "George Gissing: *Les carnets d'Henry Ryecroft,*" NINETEENTH CENTURY FICTION, XX (Sept 1967), 206–7; Jacob Korg, "Ryecroft in French," GISSING NEWSLETTER, II (Dec 1966), 5.]

**1111** Davis, Oswald H. GEORGE GISSING: A STUDY IN LITERARY LEANINGS (Lond: Johnson Publication, 1966).

The genius of G's novels compels admiration and produces a peculiar charm; readers of various circumstances and tastes are drawn to read him. G combines the realistic, poetic, and the idealistic. In *The Town Traveller,* G represents the people of Lambeth, the most sordid of London. G lampoons his subject through tragi-comic spectacles. G's short stories are "sober works in the genre of the artisan or lower middle classes." Perhaps the most interesting part of G's fiction concerns the implication of themes represented by the characters, in the documentation of conflicts between mutually antagonistic characters, such as Mutimer and Adela in *Demos.* The theme of *New Grub Street,* an objective representation of the opposing claims of idealism and mercenaries in literature, bears out a similar contrast. While G has his faults, e.g. his bias, his prejudice, his pessimism, he also has great attractions: his choice and expression of character, the articulate reflection of restless, diversified, and complex heroes and heroines. They are really idiosyncratic. G repels even when he attracts; we are drawn to his successful depiction of squalor and abnormality. [Reviews include: Pierre Coustillas, "Comptes Rendus," ETUDES ANGLAISES, XX (April–June 1967), 198–99 (This book is addressed to the initiated; it quietly ignores chronology. Davis belongs to the group of critics who place G's fiction above his other writings.); TIMES LITERARY SUPPLEMENT (Lond), 18 Aug 1966, p. 749.]

**1112** De Vooys, Sijna. "The Sociological Novel by George R. Gissing and Mrs. Humphrey Ward—A Contrast," THE PSYCHOLOGICAL ELEMENT IN THE ENGLISH SOCIOLOGICAL NOVEL IN THE NINETEENTH CENTURY (NY: Haskell House, 1966), pp. 75–116. With William Morris, G shared ideas about a spirit of democracy, the deep gulf separating the rich and poor, and a tone of despondence and a sense of failure. Barriers separating men, arising from social classes and education, are especially evident in *Demos, Thyrza, The Nether World,* and *New Grub Street.* In *Demos,* socialist interference comes to nothing; in *Thyrza* philanthropy is ineffective; the idealistic Walter Egremont is disillusioned. In *Nether World,* G aims to show that relief from poverty best comes from superior people who rise from the ranks of poor workers, and not from money or education. All of these books use contrasting characters to represent contrasting ideas, but this device is most effective in *Grub Street.* All in all, G was never really "one of the poor in their outlook on life," though he did at least live among them. Mrs. Humphrey Ward saw this life with "entirely different eyes" because "she never lived with them." "Whereas Gissing again and again emphasizes the thought that the gulf between rich and poor is wider than ever, and that nothing but a complete change is able to better the lives of the poor, Mrs. Humphrey Ward believes in political changes, in the old order made sound; and where Gissing points out the failure of philanthropy, Mrs. Humphrey Ward urges us to put our hand to the plough, and bring about what little changes are possible, relying on the Future to complete our works." [In every respect a dissertation, this book appears to be the printing of an older study. Not one reference is made to any work after 1924.]

**1113** Evans, Joyce. "Some Notes on *The Odd Women* and the Woman's Movement," GISSING NEWSLETTER, II (Sept 1966), 1–3.
Although *The Odd Women* seriously engages the reader with the problems

of the unmarried and unemployed woman, G appears not to have been acquainted with early organizations in the woman's movement.

**1114** Haydock, James Joseph. "The Woman Question in the Novels of George Gissing," DISSERTATION ABSTRACTS, XXVI (1966), 3923. Unpublished dissertation, University of North Carolina, 1965.

**1115** Koike, Shigeru. "The Education of George Gissing," STUDIES IN ENGLISH LITERATURE, English No., March 1966, pp. 15–39; rvd and rptd in ENGLISH CRITICISM IN JAPAN, ed by Earl Miner (Tokyo: University of Tokyo P, 1972; available through Princeton UP), pp. 233–58.

G's education, a long exercise in patience, can be traced both in his letters and in the exiled figures of his novels. The heroic outcasts all await the relief that Greece extended in promise to the youthful G. Like Godwin Peak of *Born in Exile,* Reardon of *New Grub Street,* Arthur Golding of *Workers in the Dawn,* or Miriam Baske of *The Emancipated,* G himself waited patiently for his escape. "Perseverance" was the key to all he lived by. But G also had something of Leonard Bast (HOWARDS END) in him; like E. M. Forster's aspiring youth, G suffered through a life of futility and alienation.

**1116** Kropholler, P. F. "The Character of Earwaker in *Born in Exile,"* GISSING NEWSLETTER, II (Dec 1966), 4.

Earwaker is a sympathetic character: charitable, methodical, and unashamed of his low birth. He perhaps derives his stoicism from Marcus Aurelius.

**1117** Kropholler, P. F. "On the Names of Gissing's Characters," GISSING NEWSLETTER, II (Sept 1966), 5–7.

In some respects G resembles his Victorian predecessors in picking names for his characters. Some give individuality; others are comic or symbolic.

**1118** Lelchuck, Alan. "George Gissing: The Man and the Novelist," DISSERTATION ABSTRACTS, XXVI (1966), 6716–17. Unpublished dissertation, Stanford University, 1965.

**1119** Midlane, A. H. T. "Letters to the Editor: George Gissing," DAILY TELEGRAPH (Lond), 20 Dec 1966, p. 10.

The Earl of Birkenhead wonders who reads G today, aside from "professional men of letters and the more intellectual critics" ["Record of a Surprising Friendship," DAILY TELEGRAPH, 15 Dec 1966, p. 18]. "Well, I do for one when I can get them," but unfortunately too few are in print. Like Trollope, G should be rescued by a reprinting of all his books.

**1120** Rosengarten, Herbert. "The Theme of Alienation in *Thyrza,"* GISSING NEWSLETTER, II (Dec 1966), 1–3.

Thyrza is "physically and temperamentally" unfitted for her life among the working class, alienated by "a natural refinement" and the "yearnings of a passionate imagination." While her "aristocratic nature transcends the artificial barriers of class, money, education," her hopes are denied satisfaction because her social superiors have been conditioned to reject her.

**1121** Woodcock, George. THE CRYSTAL SPIRIT: A STUDY OF GEORGE ORWELL (Boston: Little, Brown, 1966), pp. 239, 291, 303–7, 316, 324, 346, 358.

Orwell's criticism is "eminently sociological." The changing nature of society itself affects our reading and understanding of any book. "Even the class into which we are born can make a novel or a poem entirely different to us than to a man bred 'above' or 'below' us." Orwell realizes that G's tragic life "cannot be dissociated from either the peculiar dingy tone or the gloomy subject matter of his novels."

**1122** Young, Arthur C. "Poems by Thomas W. Gissing," JOURNAL OF THE RUTGERS UNIVERSITY LIBRARY, XXX (Dec 1966), 23–26.

G's father loved poetry and taught G to recite Tennyson when the boy was only four or five years old. Himself a writer of poetry, the father's love of literature "nourished the creativity and imagination of his son George."

**1123** Zucker, Jack. "Gissing's Tragic Thought," GISSING NEWSLETTER, II (April 1966), 1–3.

Perhaps we can classify G as "a tragic pessimist whose conservatism was founded on frustrated utopianism." He was an agnostic who believed in an almost strict determinism. His heroes are sensitive idealists who are crushed by society. G's nobility sometimes leads to fraternity inasmuch as he was an agnostic; sometimes it leads to passivity, "the abnegation of the will to live."

# 1967

**1124** Badolato, Francesco. "George Gissing and Calabria," GISSING NEWSLETTER, III (April 1967), 5–7.

Driven by his interests in the classical past, G traveled to Calabria, where he came to have a feeling for the residents, from both a sociological and an archaeological point of view. Above all he had a sensitive relationship with all poor people.

**1125** Badolato, Francesco. "Italian Translations of Gissing," GISSING NEWSLETTER, III (Dec 1967), 4–5.

Among G's books, the following have been printed in translation in Italy: *Thyrza, Born in Exile, By the Ionian Sea,* and *The Private Papers of Henry Ryecroft.*

**1126** Coustillas, Pierre. "George Gissing à Alderley Edge," ÉTUDES ANGLAISES, XX (April–June 1967), 174–78; rptd as GEORGE GISSING AT ALDERLEY EDGE (Lond: Enitharmon P, 1969).

Before entering Owens College, G was a student at Lindow Grove School, Alderley Edge, Cheshire, starting there in 1871, the year following his father's death. The Headmaster, James Wood, as well as the faculty and students, greatly impressed G, and passages of *The Private Papers of Henry Ryecroft* undoubtedly developed from his memory of these school days. In 1896, G revisited his boyhood town of Wakefield, and then traveled to Colwyn Bay to return to his school and visit Wood. At the request of the old headmaster's wife, G wrote a short essay, reminiscing about his school days; this piece, "The Old School," was printed in THE DINGLEWOOD MAGAZINE in December 1897. It is written in a style that anticipates the tone and rhythm of *Ryecroft.* When G died, his boyhood friends wrote to the local papers recalling G's achievements at Lindow Grove. [Coustillas provides considerable documented information about G's school days, incorporating in this booklet not only G's essay but several additional excerpts from THE DINGLEWOOD MAGAZINE, T. P.'s WEEKLY (22 Jan 1904, p. 100), THE CHESHIRE ECHO, and THE ALDERLEY AND WILMSLOW ADVERTISER. This material is further evidence of Coustillas's persistent research into G's life. See "The Resuscitation of George Gissing," TIMES LITERARY SUPPLEMENT (Lond), 11 June 1970 p. 630.] [Two pages of the original version of the introductory remarks are in French.]

**1127** Coustillas, Pierre. "George Gissing: Textes Inédits. Edition Critique" (George Gissing: Unpublished texts. Critical edition). A thèse de doctorat d'université, Paris, 1967.

[This work consists of previously unpublished materials from the Pforzheimer Library with an introduction, pp. 3–82. Included texts: "The Hope of Pessimism," "Along Shore," "All for Love," "The Last Half-Crown," "The Quarry on the Heath," "The Lady of the Dedication," "Mutimer's Choice," and "Their Pretty Way." All except "Their Pretty Way" (1894) appear to have been written between 1880 and 1884.] [In French.]

**1128** Coustillas, Pierre. "On the Authorship of 'Some Recollections of George Gissing,' " GISSING NEWSLETTER, III (Dec 1967), 1–3.

An article in GENTLEMAN'S MAGAZINE (CCC [Jan 1906], 11–18) is usually attributed to Arthur Henry Bullen, though that is most unlikely. Rather, the article was probably written by Noel Ainslie because its phrasing so strikingly resembles that of a piece on G published a few months later and signed by Ainslie.

**1129** Goode, John. "George Gissing's *The Nether World,*" in TRADITION AND TOLERANCE IN NINETEENTH-CENTURY FICTION, by David Howard, John Lucas, and John Goode (Lond: Routledge & Kegan Paul; NY: Barnes & Noble, 1967), pp. 207–41.

Oppositions formed the subject of G's early novels, oppositions representing beliefs personified by characters. *Demos* was "the battle between the conservative aristocrat and the socialist artisan-turned-industrialist," or between "a theological and metaphysical polity." The hostility also took the form of a conflict between fate and man's intelligence, the basic conflagration of G's major works. By the time he wrote *The Nether World,* G had become disillusioned with positivism and convinced that life was a series of personal battles in which every character, isolated and fighting to survive, struggled in a futile war against poverty. This novel concentrates on that fight, predetermined by economic situations. We attend to the psychology of characters whose lives are all fixed by the economy. If anyone is released from the urgent need for money—the controlling force of the nether world—he is turned over to a higher living standard where other kinds of misery operate. Or one might escape poverty by thinking. "The central irony of the novel is that, in a world dominated by scarcity, talent is either misdirected or superfluous, and that it is precisely the scarcity which creates waste." The employed are engaged in making money by manufacturing useless articles for people of means. A "superfluity of aspirants" competes for each job; the competition engages all the occupants of the nether world, each against all, dominated by individual greed. "Like Morris, Gissing sees industrial progress partly and importantly as a matter of diminished opportunities for the skilled worker." There is no hope for the fighting multitudes, and all the novelist can do is present individual human lives. Industrial capitalism is the enemy of the worker; it is impersonal, abstract, a controlling principle rather than a human element. For G, therefore, "Victorian standards of personal conduct" are irrelevant; money is omnipotent. [Admirers of G have for years said that his biography must be filled in before meaningful criticism and significant historical data could be written. This essay is both an extended examination of one novel with biographical and historical perspective and a lucid appreciation of G's art of fiction. Reviewed by Jacob Korg, "Book Review," GISSING NEWSLETTER, IV (April 1968), 4–8, in one of the finest articles ever to appear in this publication.]

**1130** Gross, John. "Introduction," *New Grub Street* (Lond: Bodley Head, 1967), pp. v–xii.

Despite the plaudits of admirers, G never won the fame he deserves, perhaps because he represented himself as a scholar *manqué*. The "most soundly constructed" of his longer novels, *New Grub Street* is built around the contrast between Reardon the idealist and Milvain the careerist. G reproduces material features and human types which had their counterparts in real life. He excelled in conveying "the sheer sweat of writing, the frayed nerves"; he is unsurpassed in revealing how "poverty eats into the spirit." G specializes in the "convolutions of wounded pride." Like their creator, the characters who fail are animated by a masochistic tendency to go under. G himself was scarcely normal: he exaggerated the disgrace of his expulsion from Owens College, clinging to the image of the outcast. "Gissing's novels are as much a record of his disturbed emotional life as Lawrence's." *Grub Street* is more than a period piece; it still "throbs with the resentment of men and women who know that they are not being allowed to live the lives they deserve." [A valuable introduction because it explores G's literary importance without restricting itself to one novel. The reviews of this edition include: "Book and Bookmen," TIMES LITERARY SUPPLEMENT (Lond), 29 June 1967, p. 573 (A reasonably successful author himself, G judged success in others by the degree of their corruption. Reardon's "solution for his problems is a purely emotional one. Like Gissing he demands the healing power of love, and when practical Amy suggests that he should go away alone to the sea and try to write, he regards this as one more proof that she does not love him." G's "deep serious tenderness" makes his novels worthwhile. "In his own way he is one of the great English novelists." In the "Letters to the Editor" column of this publication for 27 July 1967, p. 573, Pierre Coustillas and Louis Mione call attention to some factual errors in Gross's introduction.); C. B. Cox, "Intellectual Masochist," SPECTATOR, CCXVIII (2 June 1967), 647–48 (G was a masochist who intellectualized suffering and took a perverse pleasure in it because he thought it good for the spirit.); Angus Wilson, "Lower Depths of Literature," OBSERVER REVIEW (Lond), 21 May 1967, p. 27 (*Grub Street* is "the most unbearably poignant of our nineteenth-century novels. More unbearable, I think, than Zola's L'ASSOMOIR because Gissing's novels have only an occasional rather forced poetry and scarcely any humour at all." *Grub Street* is the crown of all G's uneven fiction.).]

**1131** Haydock, James J. *"Denzil Quarrier* and the Woman Question," GISSING NEWSLETTER, III (June 1967), 1–3.

Like *The Odd Women, Denzil Quarrier* argues that more intelligent women must train the others, the hero repeating some of the ideas of Rhoda Nunn and other feminists. But Ada Peachy of *In the Year of Jubilee* had some contrary ideas on the subject.

**1132** Kamo, Giichi. "Gissing and I," ASAHI SINBUN (Tokyo), 16 Sept 1967; rptd in GISSING EAST AND WEST (Lond: Enitharmon P, 1970), pp. 11–13.

Early in this century, when I was a school boy, I purchased a copy of *The Private Papers of Henry Ryecroft* and translated it from the English with considerable difficulty. Its plain, beautiful style and meditative vein remind us of the Japanese classic Hojoki. Since then I have sought copies of G's works in Osaka, Tokyo, and other Japanese cities. Nor has my enthusiasm thinned, for "few writers were purer in heart and better educated than Gissing." G's "purity of soul" forced him to rebuild the lower classes in elements of human decency.

**1133** Kropholler, P. F. "George Gissing and Hugh Walpole," GISSING NEWSLETTER, III (April 1967), 7.

In Hugh Walpole's THE KILLER AND THE SLAIN, the principal character is significantly affected by his readings in G. In his journal, Walpole compared himself to G as worthy of small footnotes in history.

**1134** Kropholler, P. F. "Some Notes on Gissing's Style in *Born in Exile,"* GISSING NEWSLETTER, III (Dec 1967), 6–7.

G's style is marked by a fairly heavy classical element, the frequent use of the negative to "express a somewhat diffident statement," and by refined and aristocratic qualities.

**1135** Mattheisen, Paul F., and Arthur C. Young. "Gissing, Gosse, and the Civil List," VICTORIAN NEWSLETTER, XXXII (Fall 1967), 11–16.

At the time of G's death, Wells encouraged Gosse to attempt to secure a pension for G's two surviving sons. There was some difficulty in persuading the prime minister to award the financial aid, because of G's reputation as a realistic novelist and because of the gossip about his marriages. Ultimately, Gosse's good offices secured for Walter and Alfred G £37 each, anually, for the period of their minority. Wells reluctantly accepted the idea of sharing the trusteeship; to share this job Clara Collett's name was put forth, but Wells rejected her, preferring instead G's old friend, an attorney named George Whale.

**1136** Migdal, Seymour. "The Social Novel in Victorian England," DISSERTATION ABSTRACTS, XXVII (1967), 2536A. Unpublished dissertation, University of California (Davis), 1966.

**1137** Pritchett, V. S. "Moral Gymnasium," NEW STATESMAN, LXXIII (5 May 1967), 619.
Like Dorothy Richardson, G rejected the traditional English character; instead, he showed people "flatly in their situation and their minds." Both writers achieved "a deeply felt and intimate picture of London" in their novels.

**1138** Robey, Cora. "Matthew Arnold's Concept of Culture on the Late Victorian Novel, the Operation of this Idea in the Novels of George Eliot, George Meredith, Thomas Hardy, and George Gissing," DISSERTATION ABSTRACTS, XXVII (1967), 3061A. Unpublished dissertation, University of Tennessee, 1966.

**1139** Sporn, Paul. "The Transgressed Woman: A Critical Description of the Heroine in the Works of George Gissing, Thomas Hardy, and George Moore," DISSERTATION ABSTRACTS, XXVIII (1967), 645A. Unpublished dissertation, State University of New York at Buffalo, 1967.

# 1968

**1140** Bergonzi, Bernard. "Introduction," *New Grub Street* (Harmondsworth, England: Penguin; Magnolia, Mass.: Peter Smith, 1968), pp. 10–26.
*New Grub Street* is about the dull routine of unremitting toil, depicting a society where literature is a commodity and where the writing of fiction is comparable to industrial or commercial labor. In Chap 8, Marian Yule sits in the Reading Room of the British Museum; the imagery compares the room to a spider's web, to a circular prison. In this world, one may accept the standards and succeed, as does Milvain, or else struggle against these standards in the interests of noble literature, like Reardon. Using Reardon, G develops the theme of masculine aspiration versus feminine materialism. Like G, Reardon has a "marked self destructive streak." G's life was "dominated by the myth of the artist who must subject himself to intense suffering if he is to produce anything of value." [This Penguin reprint brought comment in the TIMES LITERARY SUPPLEMENT (Lond), in a catch-all review of four books called "Going into Gissing," 27 June 1968,

p. 680. Also, V. S. Pritchett, "Gissing: Our Only Russian," NEW STATESMAN, LXXV (14 June 1968), pp. 795–96 (G is "paralysed" by the contradictions in his mind, so that his voice falls off into "a lonely impartial and personal bleat." G's book owes much to the continent, particularly to the Russians and French.); Dennis Nigel, "Gissing the Truthful," SUNDAY TELEGRAPH (Lond), 18 Aug 1968, p. 8.]

**1141** Cohen, Morton N. "KIM at an American College," KIPLING JOURNAL, XXXV (June 1968), 10–12.

G's *New Grub Street* is among eleven novels read by undergraduates in a course on nineteenth-century English fiction at the City College of New York. Students rated MIDDLEMARCH the most popular, THE EGOIST least popular. *Grub Street* placed fourth above novels by Austen, Wilde, Kipling, Trollope, Dickens, Thackeray, and Meredith.

**1142** Coustillas, Pierre (ed). COLLECTED ARTICLES ON GEORGE GISSING (Lond: Frank Cass, 1968).

Contents, abstracted under date of first publication: Pierre Coustillas, "Introduction" (1968); Russell Kirk, "Who Knows George Gissing?" WESTERN HUMANITIES REVIEW (1950); Stanley Alden, "George Gissing, Humanist," NORTH AMERICAN REVIEW (1922); Ruth Capers McKay, ["Gissing as a Portrayer of Society"], from GEORGE GISSING AND HIS CRITIC FRANK SWINNERTON (1933); "The Permanent Stranger," TIMES LITERARY SUPPLEMENT (Lond) (1948); George Orwell, "George Gissing," LONDON MAGAZINE (1960); "Gissing's Heroines," TIMES LITERARY SUPPLEMENT (Lond) (1956); Jacob Korg, "Division of Purpose in George Gissing," PMLA (1955); Samuel Vogt Gapp, ["Influence of the Classics on George Gissing's Novels of Modern Life"], from GEORGE GISSING: CLASSICIST (1936); Gilbert Phelps, ["Gissing, Turgenev and Dostoyevsky"], from THE RUSSIAN NOVEL IN ENGLISH FICTION (1956); C. J. Francis, "Gissing and Schopenhauer," NINETEENTH CENTURY FICTION (1960); Irving Howe, ["Gissing: Poet of Fatigue"], from "Introduction," *New Grub Street* (1962); V. S. Pritchett, ["Grub Street"], from "A Chip the Size of a Block," NEW STATESMAN AND NATION (1958); Jacob Korg, "The Spiritual Theme of *Born in Exile*," from FROM JANE AUSTEN TO JOSEPH CONRAD, ed by Robert C. Rathburn and Martin Steinmann, Jr. (1959); Greenough White, "A Novelist of the Hour," SEWANEE REVIEW (1898); Jackson I. Cope, "Definition as Structure in *The Ryecroft Papers*," MODERN FICTION STUDIES (1957); Jacob Korg, ["The Main Source of *The Ryecroft Papers*"], from "George Gissing's Commonplace Book: A Manuscript from the Berg Collection of the New York Public Library," BULLETIN OF THE NEW YORK PUBLIC LIBRARY (1961). [Reviewed by James Haydock, "Book Review: Once More Into Gissing,"

GISSING NEWSLETTER, IV (Nov 1968), 1–7; Dennis Nigel, "Gissing the Truthful," SUNDAY TELEGRAPH (Lond), 18 Aug 1968, p. 8.]

**1143** Coustillas, Pierre. "Collecting George Gissing," BOOK COLLECTING AND LIBRARY MONTHLY, No. 1 (May 1968), 9–13; rvd and rptd in GISSING EAST AND WEST (Lond: Enitharmon P, 1970), pp. 21–30.

I first learned about G from reading Legouis and Cazamian's writings as a student. Copies of G's books were hard to come by in France. But I have been collecting eagerly, so that by 1967 I had gathered 324 editions, and by 1970, 400 editions. Part of my zeal comes from the relish of the collector, the delight of possession; part also comes from sheer admiration: "In many a domain, political, intellectual, social, spiritual, I share his opinions."

**1144** Coustillas, Pierre. "Introduction," COLLECTED ARTICLES ON GEORGE GISSING, ed by Pierre Coustillas (Lond: Frank Cass, 1968), pp. vii–xii.

An important figure at the end of the nineteenth century, G was often ill-served by contemporary reviewers and critics. Time now serves his cause, as considerable attention and praise has been awarded him in recent work. Biographical and critical studies far superior to those by Morley Roberts and Frank Swinnerton have been published; more are in various stages of completion. This anthology contains a sampling of sixteen pieces, some concentrating on major works, some more general in scope. [This introduction also contains a brief resume of G's life and a bibliography of his works.]

**1145** Coustillas, Pierre. "Letters to the Editor: Going Into Gissing," TIMES LITERARY SUPPLEMENT (Lond), 25 July 1968, pp. 788–89; rptd in GISSING NEWSLETTER, IV (Oct 1968), 8–9.

Very few who have actually read G ever depreciated his work, so that he has had "numerous and sympathetic interpreters." [This is contrary to the opinion expressed by Dachine Rainer, "Letters to the Editor: Going Into Gissing," TIMES LITERARY SUPPLEMENT (Lond), 4 July 1968, p. 705; 22 Aug 1968, p. 905]. Furthermore, G's revival is clearly in evidence; his letters and his books are now available. G not only lived down the scandal of his youth, he gained the praise of Orwell, Murry, and Woolf. His significance is not exclusively Yorkshire in origin; G must be related to all Europe, as he merits. [See Herbert Van Thal's reply in ibid, 5 Sept 1968, p. 945.]

**1146** Coustillas, Pierre. "Negotiating Gissing Manuscripts," GISSING NEWSLETTER, IV (April 1968), 1–3.

As executor of G's estate, his brother Algernon began selling several manuscripts in 1912. Unfortunately some of G's papers disappeared after Gabrielle's death in France in 1954. Algernon was not able to raise any substantial amounts of money by selling manuscripts.

**1147** Coustillas, Pierre. "Two Letters to a Fellow Invalid," GISSING NEWSLETTER, IV (Nov 1968), 9–12.
[Reproduces two letters of 8 Dec 1901 and 2 Jan 1902 written by G in Archachon to Miss Rachel Evelyn White, whom he had met in the summer of 1901 at the East Anglian Sanitorium.]

**1148** Foote, Janet V. "Gissing and Schopenhauer: A Study of Literary Influence," DISSERTATION ABSTRACTS, XXIX (1968), 596A. Unpublished dissertation, Indiana University, 1968.

**1149** "Going Into Gissing," TIMES LITERARY SUPPLEMENT (Lond), 27 June 1968, p. 680; rptd in GISSING NEWSLETTER, IV (Oct 1968), 4–6.
"The wind seems to set fair for a Gissing revival." The reprinting of *New Grub Street* (Penguin), *The Odd Women* (Blond), GISSING: "NEW GRUB STREET," by P. J. Keating (Arnold), and COLLECTED ARTICLES ON GEORGE GISSING, ed by Pierre Coustillas (Cass) lead us to reassess his significance. Did Woolf, Murry, and Orwell praise G for his interesting reflections on their own concerns? Should G still be linked to continental authors? Or does he belong to the Home Counties, Dickens, and E. M. Forster? "His heroes look back on the one hand to Copperfield and forward on the other to Leonard Bast." [This article set off a flurry of letters to the editor of the TIMES LITERARY SUPPLEMENT, from Dachine Rainer (4 July 1968, p. 705); from Pierre Coustillas (25 July 1968, pp. 788–89); from Andrew Mylett (8 Aug 1968, p. 857); from Dachine Rainer (22 Aug 1968, p. 905); and from Herbert Van Thal (5 Sept 1968, p. 945).]

**1150** Keating, P. J. GEORGE GISSING: "NEW GRUB STREET" (Lond: Edward Arnold, 1968).
*New Grub Street* grew out of the three volume tradition, hence its unwieldy form. Its symbols are usually obvious. G's writing is uneven because it "is at times ponderous and artificially literary." The subject of the novel has to do with the troubles of a writer who must support himself; we experience his troubles with publishers and journalists. *Grub Street* remains a "profoundly disturbing book," and its analysis of the writing profession is shot through with brilliant insight and perception. [This critical study was intended for students in the sixth forms and universities. The

content approaches the novel under such headings as "Tradesmen," "Artists," and "Men of Letters."]

**1151** Kohler, C. C. "Gissing From a Bookseller's Point of View," BOOK COLLECTING AND LIBRARY MONTHLY (Dec 1968); rptd in GISSING EAST AND WEST (Lond: Enitharmon P, 1970), pp. 15–19.

Booksellers occasionally have inquiries about *The Private Papers of Henry Ryecroft* or *New Grub Street,* perhaps even *By the Ionian Sea.* My enthusiasm for G was stimulated in 1965 by Pierre Coustillas. Since then I have found G's works to possess a strong market value; my own private library has prospered. It now includes collector's items of rare and curious value. My interest extends to the personal effects of G, his autographs, letters, but especially rare first editions in excellent quality.

**1152** Korg, Jacob. "Gissing and Orwell," GISSING NEWSLETTER, IV (Nov 1968), 8.

Orwell, long an admirer of G, was approached by Home and Van Thal to write G's biography, but Orwell declined saying that he would not be able to do the necessary research.

**1153** Korg, Jacob. "Introduction," *Notes on Social Democracy* (Lond: Enitharmon P, 1968), pp. i–x.

In 1880, at the time that *Workers in the Dawn* was published, G was approached by John Morley to prepare three articles on socialism for the PALL MALL GAZETTE; G's articles appeared in Sept. Though primarily factual, they reflect G's attitudes on political and social matters "during the period of his intellectual enrichment." G got some of his information on socialism from his German friend Eduard Bertz and from his readings in positivist literature. That his ideas continued to mature can be gauged from changing attitudes expressed in both *The Unclassed* and *Demos. Workers* had set forth G's pessimistic ideas about the "possibilities of social reform." Four years later, in *Unclassed,* Waymark represents how far G had dissociated himself from the socialist attitudes. [Announced in the GISSING NEWSLETTER, IV (Nov 1968), 7, this booklet was later reviewed by Pierre Coustillas in the same publication, VI (April 1970), 15–19. Also, "The Resuscitation of George Gissing," TIMES LITERARY SUPPLEMENT (Lond), 11 June 1970, p. 630.]

**1154** Kropholler, P. F. "Some Notes on the Titles of Gissing's Novels," GISSING NEWSLETTER, IV (April 1968), 12.

More than once G rejected a title chosen for a book before or during the time he wrote it; five of his novels bear the name of the central character.

**1155** Le Mallier, Denise. "Gissing Scenes and People," GISSING NEWSLETTER, IV (April 1968), 9–10.

In Nov 1900, Gabrielle and G were the guests of her cousins, the Eustaches, at "Le Chesnay," a country home near Fourchambault. He seems to have felt little sympathy for the place that had memories for her of childhood.

**1156** Lester, John A., Jr. JOURNEY THROUGH DESPAIR: 1880– 1914 (Princeton: Princeton UP, 1968), pp. 30, 50, 62, 63, 74, 97, 111, 164.

The inspiriting disillusionment that G so often expressed in his novels foreshadowed the defeat that time has since brought us.

**1157** Mylett, Andrew. "Letters to the Editor: Going Into Gissing," TIMES LITERARY SUPPLEMENT (Lond), 8 Aug 1968, p. 857

In response to the wish that more G works were in print, let me say that the AMS Press has reprinted not only *Born in Exile* but seventeen other G titles as well. [The appearance of four G titles reviewed in the TIMES LITERARY SUPPLEMENT (Lond) under "Going Into Gissing," (27 June 1968, p. 680), led to the printing of four other "Letters to the Editor": Dachine Rainer (4 July 1968, p. 705; 22 Aug 1968, p. 905); Pierre Coustillas (25 July 1968, pp. 788–89); and Herbert Van Thal (5 Sept 1968, p. 945).]

**1158** Rainer, Dachine. "Letters to the Editor: Going Into Gissing," TIMES LITERARY SUPPLEMENT (Lond), 4 July 1968, p. 705; rptd in GISSING NEWSLETTER, IV (Oct 1968), 6–8.

The patronizing reviews of G's books [see "Going Into Gissing," TIMES LITERARY SUPPLEMENT (Lond), 27 June 1968, p. 680] fail to recognize what compelling reading G often is. If some of his work is "hastily and amateurishly written," *By the Ionian Sea* and *The Private Papers of Henry Ryecroft* help make G "one of the greatest writers of the nineteenth century." All his books deserve to be reprinted. [Under the same heading, three further letters appeared in the TIMES LITERARY SUPPLEMENT (Lond), one from Pierre Coustillas (25 July 1968, pp. 788–89); one from Andrew Mylett (8 Aug 1968, p. 857); another from Dachine Rainer (22 Aug 1968, p. 905); the last from Herbert Van Thal (5 Sept 1968, p. 945).]

**1159** Rainer, Dachine. "Letters to the Editor: Going Into Gissing," TIMES LITERARY SUPPLEMENT (Lond), 22 Aug 1968, p. 905; rptd in GISSING NEWSLETTER, IV (Oct 1968), 9–10.

As soon as my letter regretting that G's novels were not in print appeared in your columns (4 July 1968, p. 705), I was deluged with announcements and brochures, including one from the AMS Press offering to sell me eighteen works by G, for prices ranging from eight to thirty dollars each. The public certainly cannot afford such prices; they are only possible for American libraries with easy-going attitudes about money. [Occasioned by a review article in the TIMES LITERARY SUPPLEMENT (Lond) ("Going Into Gissing," 27 June 1968, p. 680), several letters to the editor were printed, including: Dachine Rainer (4 July 1968, p. 705); Pierre Coustillas (25 July 1968, pp. 788–89); Andrew Mylett (8 Aug 1968, p. 857); and Herbert Van Thal (5 Sept 1968, p. 945).]

**1160** Swinnerton, Frank. "Introduction," *The Odd Women* (Lond: Anthony Blond; NY: Stein & Day, 1968), pp. vii–x.

*The Odd Women* is about women such as really lived. "How he knew them it is impossible to say; but their circumstances were as he described them to be." The novel shows G's "remarkable narrative gift," although it is "less than his finest work." G's life was a constant struggle. His private life was oppressive. His literary efforts were not welcomed by the public because G refused to amuse while describing the variety of London's world. [Short introductory outline of G's biography with no new information or insights. Reviewed by Dennis Nigel, "Gissing the Truthful," SUNDAY TELEGRAPH (Lond), 18 Aug 1968, p. 8; Robert Pitman, "Share a Leaky Umbrella with This Sad Victorian," SUNDAY EXPRESS (Lond), 19 May 1968, p. 8.]

**1161** Van Thal, Herbert. "Letters to the Editor: Going Into Gissing," TIMES LITERARY SUPPLEMENT (Lond), 5 Sept 1968, p. 945.

I have attempted to promote G by publishing his novels, both *A Life's Morning* and *The Odd Women*. Unfortunately, though I am prepared to publish a reprint of *Born in Exile,* G's books simply do not sell. [Started by a review article on four G books, "Going into Gissing," the TIMES LITERARY SUPPLEMENT (Lond) printed four other "Letters to the Editor," two from Dachine Rainer (4 July 1968, p. 705; 22 Aug 1968, p. 905), one from Pierre Coustillas (25 July 1968, pp. 788–89), and one from Andrew Mylett (8 Aug 1968, p. 857).]

**1162** Walzer, Judith B. "Class and Character in the Work of George Gissing," DISSERTATION ABSTRACTS, XXVIII (1968), 2700A. Unpublished dissertation, Brandeis University, 1967.

**1163** Weber, Carl J. "Hardy and James," HARVARD LIBRARY BULLETIN, XVI (Jan 1968), 18–25.

The artist William Rothenstein wanted Hardy's help in finding some illustrative matter to print along with his sketch of G. Hardy replied that he did not have the "requisite knowledge" of G's work and enclosed James's article on G ("The English Novel and the Work of George Gissing," HARPER'S WEEKLY, XLI [31 July 1897], 754) and then recommended James for the task. Hardy said, "He could do it in a few minutes if he were willing, and certainly nobody else could do it so well."

**1164** Yenter, Charles E. "Checklist of Gissing's Periodical Contributions, 1872–1877," GISSING NEWSLETTER, IV (Dec 1968), 7.

[Lists G's publications at school in England and then in America before he wrote his first novel.]

**1165** Young, Arthur C. *"Henry Ryecroft* and Professor A. W. Ward," NOTES AND QUERIES, XV (May 1968), 186–87.

G sent A. W. Ward, who had once been his professor at Manchester, a copy of *The Private Papers of Henry Ryecroft.* Calling attention to a passage from Goethe in the "Autumn" section, Ward advised G that it ought to have been interpreted as ironical rather than optimistic. Ward liked Ryecroft's philosophy and called the book "powerful."

# 1969

**1166** Coustillas, Pierre. GISSING'S WRITINGS ON DICKENS (Lond: Enitharmon P, 1969); essentially the same as Coustillas's "Gissing's Writings On Dickens: A Bio-Bibliographical Survey," DICKENSIAN, LXI (Autumn 1965), 168–79.

Approached by John Holland Rose to prepare a volume of critical essays on Charles Dickens for the Victorian Era Series (Blackie & Sons), G went to Siena in 1897 and wrote what has ever since been considered one of the finest studies of Dickens's fiction (*Charles Dickens: A Critical Study,* 1898). The success of this volume led to further opportunities to write introductions for Methuen reprints of several novels by Dickens for the Rochester Edition, although only six appeared before G's death. The prefaces were gathered for publication years later (*Critical Studies of the Works of Charles Dickens* [NY: Greenberg, 1924], with an introduction by Temple Scott, and *The Immortal Dickens* [Lond: Cecil Palmer, 1925], with an introduction by B. W. Matz). In addition to subsequent articles on Dickens for magazines, G also abridged and revised John Forster's LIFE OF DICKENS for Chapman & Hall in the year before his death. [Appendix reprints two reviews that G wrote for the TIMES LITERARY SUPPLEMENT (Lond), July and August 1902, one concerning "Swinburne on

Dickens," the other "Mr. Kitton's Life of Dickens." Also see, "The Resuscitation of George Gissing," TIMES LITERARY SUPPLEMENT (Lond), 11 June 1970, p. 630.]

**1167** Coustillas, Pierre. "Introduction," *Isabel Clarendon,* (Brighton, Sussex: Harvester P, 1969), pp. xv–lxii.

To understand and appreciate a G novel it is valuable to consider his biography. *Isabel Clarendon* was written fairly early in G's career when G was introduced by the Frederic Harrisons to their friend Mrs. Gaussen and thereby also to her family. Through Mrs. Gaussen G learned quickly to enjoy the pleasant atmosphere of a society far removed from the world of *Workers in the Dawn* and *The Unclassed.* Mrs. Gaussen became the Lady of Knightswell in the new book he promptly started, and G used his newly acquired information of the West End of London. Soon finished, the novel went to Chapman & Hall, and exceptionally good fortune brought the book to their reader, Meredith. G was happy to cooperate in revising the book according to Meredith's advice, and since then readers and critics have frequently noticed Meredith's influence in the novel. Isabel herself certainly resembles Mrs. Gaussen, and countless reasons lead one to see G himself in Kingcote. Since G's death, critics have also seen Turgenev's influence in *Clarendon,* and there are passages that echo the ideas of Schopenhauer. In 1895 Lawrence & Bullen invited G to revise the novel for a reprinting, but G chose not to do so. Since then the book has not been easy to obtain, and this printing therefore revives for us "a novel that deserves to live." [The introductory essay and various accompanying notes give not only G's biography and a survey of the novel's reception when it first appeared, but also explanatory notes and identifications of key words and expressions in the novel. Review of this volume: "The Resuscitation of George Gissing," TIMES LITERARY SUPPLEMENT (Lond), 11 June 1970, p. 630.]

**1168** Haydock, James. "Miss White a Source for Miss Rodney?" GISSING NEWSLETTER, V (Jan 1969), 7–11.

Coustillas has provided the letters G wrote to Rachel Evelyn White, a fellow patient at the East Anglia Sanitorium in 1901. She matches in all important respects the title figure of "Miss Rodney's Leisure," a short story that G wrote early in 1902. Both are intelligent, modern, advanced young women; witty, opinionated, and forceful.

**1169** Korg, Jacob. "Some Unpublished Letters by Gabrielle Gissing," GISSING NEWSLETTER, V (Oct 1969), 1–8.

The Berg Collection of the New York Public Library contains several letters written by Gabrielle Gissing after G's death, especially to Wells and

Roberts. They protest the false impressions given at the time of G's death and reveal something of her own movements on the continent.

**1170** Kropholler, P. F. "Gissing's Characters and their Books," GISSING NEWSLETTER, V (April 1969), 12–16.
Books are important to numerous characters in G's novels, and we are led to judge people by the works they choose. Sympathetic characters usually find consolation in books.

**1171** Kropholler, P. F. "The Speech of Characters in *The Town Traveller*," GISSING NEWSLETTER, V (July 1969), 4–10.
Aware of class differences, G made his characters speak "in character." Cockney illiteracies, colloquialisms, and vulgarisms help distinguish one figure's speech from another's.

**1172** Lees, Francis Noel. "George Gissing at College," GISSING NEWSLETTER, V (April 1969), 1–11.
From G's letters, the OWENS COLLEGE MAGAZINE, and various records and papers of the institution, we can reconstruct the atmosphere and the circumstances of G's education at Owens College. [In an editor's note, Coustillas verifies and corrects certain items of fact in the article.]

**1173** Matthiason, E. F. "Gissing's Veiled Period: An Imaginary Reconstruction," GISSING NEWSLETTER, V (Jan 1969), 1–7.
Discovered for his theft from fellows students at Owens College, G spent a month in prison before he went to America. What miseries did he suffer during those days! But both G himself and his family have been so reticent about the facts of the imprisonment that we have only our imaginations to detail the dreadful stay.

**1174** Rogers, James A. "The Art and Challenge of George Gissing," DISSERTATION ABSTRACTS, XXIX (1969), 4501A. Unpublished dissertation, New York University, 1968.

**1175** Selig, Robert L. "A Sad Heart at the Late Victorian Culture Market: George Gissing's *In the Year of Jubilee*," STUDIES IN ENGLISH LITERATURE: 1500–1900, IX (Autumn 1969), 703–20.
*In the Year of Jubilee* deals with the relationship of culture and society, stressing mass culture and consumers. Concerned with the insufficient education of women and their unsatisfactory marriages, G frequently refers to popular songs and advertising to reveal the discrepancy between sentimental idealizations of love and the brutal realities of sexual relationships. G himself was certainly not pleased when Nancy submitted to her husband because of his greater cultivation.

**1176** Sporn, Paul. "Gissing's *Demos:* Late Victorian Values and the Displacement of Conjugal Love," STUDIES IN THE NOVEL, I (Fall 1969), 334–46.

How the economics, the class divisions, and the values of late-Victorian England affect women and marriage is one of G's central themes in fiction. In *Demos,* G shows, through his portrayal of three women (Emma, a working-class girl; Alice, a bourgeoise *arriviste;* and the heroine, Adela, a young lady with close connections to the landed gentry) that women from all classes are victimized by a basically corrective society. The novel is additionally interesting because it suggests that the heroine, urged into marrying a man she does not love, mainly for reasons of money, is driven to a disturbed erotic experience.

# 1970

**1177** Adams, Elsie B. "Gissing's Allegorical 'House of Cobwebs,'" STUDIES IN SHORT FICTION, VII (Spring 1970), 324–26.

Reduced to live in a dilapidated house, decaying and void of intellectual life, Goldthorpe produces a book which defies the tenets of archaic literary taste. His book symbolizes G's own efforts, in a stifling society, to write fiction for a new school of novelists; his efforts signal the collapse of the inartistic middle-class norm.

**1178** Allen, Walter. "Introduction," *Born in Exile* (Lond: Gollanz, 1970), pp. 5–12.

*Born in Exile* deserves to stand next to *New Grub Street* among G's novels. "It is a novel of great intellectual power and a fierce intransigence." A "disturbing and uncomfortable book," *Exile* is principally the novel of Godwin Peak, "a figure of an intellectual arrogance and fanatical ambition unmatched in English fiction except by Joyce's Stephen Dedalus." Nor is Peak all autobiography; he evidences the strength of G's imagination, a member of G's assembly of displaced persons. "A most striking piece of characterization." Peak is distinguished by intellectual honesty. In losing his Christian faith, he maintained his Christian ethic, living that ethic more intensely than "believers." Peak has "true affinity" to Dostoevski's Raskolnikov and Turgenev's Bazarov. [Reviews include: "Books of the Day," GLASGOW HERALD, 10 June 1970, p. 15; Austin Clarke, "A Good Apprentice," IRISH TIMES, 4 July 1970, p. 10 (G wrote about squalid conditions in London; he remains a neglected Victorian novelist. But this reprint "will hardly attract attention."); J. G. Farrell, "Old Wives' Tale," SPECTATOR, CCXXIV (20 June 1970), 822 (G's life hardly promised the achievement his books attained, nor did his reviewers welcome his social realism.); "Fiction: *Born in Exile*," BRITISH BOOK NEWS, Aug 1970, p. 658; "The Resuscitation of George Gissing," TIMES LITERARY SUPPLE-MENT (Lond), 11 June 1970, p. 630; Derek Stanford, "Fiction," SCOTS-MAN, 1 Aug 1970, p. 3 (Because *Exile* is better than the vastly overrated *Private Papers of Henry Ryecroft*, the reprinting of this novel will help us assemble "a fuller portrait of this gloomy social cartographer.").]

**1179** Bolton, Glorney. ROMAN CENTURY (NY: Viking, 1970), pp. 137–39, 145–47.

Among the "outcasts and sinners" who found relief in Rome, G gloried in the antiquity of this city. He wrote frequently and eloquently of walking in the ways known to him only through the classics. He led Wells through churches and galleries little frequented by the tourists.

**1180** Chapple, J. A. V. DOCUMENTARY AND IMAGINATIVE LIT-ERATURE: 1880–1920 (Lond: Blandford; NY: Barnes & Noble, 1970), pp. 95, 96–99, 100, 120, 133, 141, 221, 238, 278, 367, 373.

Mad Jack of G's *The Nether World* exemplifies the Satanic slum dweller "of the period when industrial civilisation is the topic." The entire novel stresses the squalid and horrible circumstances of G's London; it comes from the novelist's own firsthand knowledge of the slums. But G thought that reforming the poor—whatever the remedy—was beyond hope.

**1181** Coustillas, Pierre. "Introduction," "MY FIRST REHEAR-SAL" AND "MY CLERICAL RIVAL" (Lond: Enitharmon P, 1970), pp. 1–11.

"My First Rehearsal" and "My Clerical Rival" were written in the earliest years of G's career as a novelist, about the time of his return to England from America. They have not been readily available to the public or to scholars. Compared to other tales by G, such as those published in *Brownie* (1931), these are "sentimental, mildly adventurous tales written in a much lighter vein" and can be profitably compared to G's "An Heiress on Condition." These tales can be profitably read in relationship to G's youth in Wakefield and Alderley Edge.

**1182** Crowley, John W. "George Gissing and George Cabot Lodge," GISSING NEWSLETTER, VI (Oct 1970), 7–9.

After he met G in Paris in May 1901, George Cabot Lodge was inspired to model a novel on *New Grub Street*. Called "Mediocracy," the book was never published.

**1183** Doi, Osamu. "The Banishment of Ryecroft," GISSING NEWSLETTER, VI (Oct 1970), 10–11.

During World War II, *The Private Papers of Henry Ryecroft* was banished in Japan, for its celebration of quiet and solitude contrasted with the national mood of militarism. Now the work is again used in the schools as a model of refined and grammatically dignified English.

**1184** Fernando, Lloyd. "Gissing's Studies in 'Vulgarisms': Aspects of His Anti-feminism," SOUTHERN REVIEW (Adelaide), IV: 1 (1970), 43–52.

While we ordinarily hear that G was ahead of his time in being sympathetic to feminist causes, he was in fact convinced that "emancipationist ideas gave direct rise to the social vulgarity he detested." In his private life, domestic turmoil haunted G until Gabrielle Fleury brought him peace. His novels contain numerous heroines who, "with their author's approval, patronise their women, assuming a natural superiority in all important matters." Waymark, Quarrier, Barfoot, Tarrant, Hilliard, and Rolfe "all smugly accept the premise that, on the whole, women fall short of men" intellectually. Educating women would only widen the gap between the few and the majority, these latter forming a multitude of shrews, sluts, and wantons. Among the novels, *The Whirlpool* (his "most skilful novel in every respect") and *In the Year of Jubilee* most successfully embody "the attitudes of reasoned opponents to female emancipation." For most of his life G judged everyone by intelligence; only in his last years did he learn the importance of the heart.

**1185** Fielding, K. J. "1870–1900: Forster and Reaction," DICKENSIAN, LXVI (May 1970), 85–100.

"It was left to Gissing to write the single book on Dickens (1898) that deserves serious attention since the LIFE he admired by John Forster." Dickens raised G's spirits. "As a novelist himself he had moments of genius and was always intelligent, but he could be cranky, wooden in conception of character, and repetitive." G's book is never condescending.

**1186** Griffing, A. H. "Henry Ryecroft's Trick," GISSING NEWSLETTER, VI (Jan 1970), 1–7.

In *The Private Papers of Henry Ryecroft,* G frequently uses the device of allowing his title figure to be mentally transported in time and space, a form of association discussed by Bergson in MATTER AND MEMORY (1896). In this "trick," the hero's reflective memory is triggered to recall distant phenomena, moments recalled from the classics, perhaps, or from his own earlier years. Did G know of Bergson, possibly through Gabrielle Fleury? [Francis Noel Lees raises the question of whether this "trick" is an "actual phenomenon of life which would be noticed by anyone of alert consciousness." Did G get the idea from Pater's "A Child in the

House"? See "Concerning Henry Ryecroft's Trick," GISSING NEWSLETTER, VI (July 1970), 17–18.]

**1187** Keech, James M. "Gissing's *New Grub Street* and the 'Triple-Headed Monster,'" SERIF, VII (March 1970), 20–24.
Jasper Milvain realized that the three-volume novel was "a triple-headed monster, sucking the blood of English novelists." Biffen and Reardon, also of *New Grub Street,* both fall to the tyranny of this method. G's novel foreshadows the death of the three-decker system, and like George Moore he learned to write the one volume work. *Grub Street* makes clear to us how novelists had to pad out their stories to fit the format.

**1188** Kropholler, P. F. "Marriage and Class in Gissing's Novels," GISSING NEWSLETTER, VI (Jan 1970), 11–14.
Like G himself, the characters in his novels are conscious of whether their marriages will raise or lower them in the scale of social classes.

**1189** Lees, Francis Noel. "Addendum to 'George Gissing at College,'" GISSING NEWSLETTER, VI (April 1970), 12–15.
Was the Rev. S. A. Steinthal, a Unitarian minister identified by Pierre Coustillas as the friend who helped gather funds to send G to America, the same person that Morley Roberts identifies in THE PRIVATE LIFE OF HENRY MAITLAND? [See Francis Noel Lees, "George Gissing at College," GISSING NEWSLETTER, V (April 1969), 1–11.]

**1190** Monod, Sylvère. "Dickens and Fame, 1900–1920: The Age of Chesterton," DICKENSIAN, LXVI (May 1970), 101–20.
Because of his fiction and his health, G was unable to write more than he did about Dickens. Pierre Coustillas has called attention to the precise details of G's work on Dickens.

**1191** Parlati, Sister Mary Aurelia. "A Critical, Sociological, and Technical Analysis of George Gissing's Short Stories and Sketches," DISSERTATION ABSTRACTS INTERNATIONAL, XXXI (1970), 5371–72A. Unpublished dissertation, Fordham University, 1970.

**1192** "Resuscitation of George Gissing," TIMES LITERARY SUPPLEMENT (Lond), 11 June 1970, p. 630.
While we are happy to salute the publication, for the first time in volumes and pamphlets, of several G essays, G's reputation nevertheless depends not upon his journalism but on his novels. Coustillas and Korg present accurate and sympathetic introductions, and they edit carefully. Allen's introduction to *Born in Exile* repeats biographical errors. The new facsimile

edition of *Isabel Clarendon* prompts comparison to Moore's A MODERN
LOVER: G is superior in insights and profundities, Moore is less sentimental
and writes better. Coustillas clearly "intends not just to idolize Gissing but
to Edelize him." [This article led P. Collins to write "Letters to the Editor:
Gissing in Russia," TIMES LITERARY SUPPLEMENT (Lond), 2 July 1970,
p. 726. Turgenev had arranged for G to write for the Russian publication
VYSTNIK EVROPY, not for LE MESSAGER DE L'EUROPE. Turgenev recruited
G through Professor Edward Beesly of University College, London.
Pierre Coustillas added to this information (TIMES LITERARY SUPPLE-
MENT [Lond], 4 Sept 1970, p. 974) by providing copies of two letters
G had written to Turgenev. He noted also that six of G's novels had ap-
peared in Russian periodicals: *A Life's Morning, Demos, Thyrza, New
Grub Street, Eve's Ransom,* and *The Nether World.* This article constitutes
an omnibus review of the following publications: *Notes on Social Democ-
racy,* ed by Jacob Korg (Lond: Enitharmon P, 1968); GISSING'S WRITINGS
ON DICKENS, ed by Pierre Coustillas (Lond: Enitharmon P, 1969);
GEORGE GISSING AT ALDERLEY EDGE, ed by Pierre Coustillas (Lond:
Enitharmon P, 1969); *Born in Exile,* intro by Walter Allen (Lond:
Gollanz, 1970); *Isabel Clarendon,* intro by Pierre Coustillas (Brighton,
Sussex: Harvester P, 1969).]

**1193** Rogers, James A. "George Gissing and Christopher Morley," GISSING NEWSLETTER, VI (April 1970), 1–12.

G's name was a byword for Christopher Morley, appearing with affectionate, even sentimental, associations in numerous essays and books. Streets,
ponds, dogs are christened Gissing; haunted bookshops treasure G's works,
especially *The House of Cobwebs.* Morley would like to be remembered
as another G. JOHN MISTLETOE, PIPEFULS, and THE HAUNTED BOOKSHOP
frequently evoke G's name.

**1194** Selig, Robert L. " 'The Valley of the Shadow of Books':
Alienation in Gissing's *New Grub Street,"* NINETEENTH CENTURY
FICTION, XXV (Sept 1970), 188–98.

The theme of isolation in G's fiction becomes clear in historical perspective in a way that was never available to G himself. Both in symbol and in
action, the writers of *New Grub Street* arc cstranged from commercial
civilization; in a world of mechanical progress, the horse has significant
symbolic value. G's constant allusions to classical authors contrast his remoteness in time and his distance from his own contemporaries, secluded
as he is in a museum reading room. But money actually dominates G's
thinking, so that Milvain's cynical effort to write exclusively for cash iso-
lates him from other literary men. One is estranged in either case, the
writer immersed in the present or lost in the past.

**1195** Williams, Raymond. THE ENGLISH NOVEL: FROM DICKENS TO LAWRENCE (Lond & NY: Oxford UP, 1970), pp. 156–63.

After Dickens, the setting of the English novel moved from the city, as Eliot and Hardy kept apart from London in their novels. But G returned it to the city where the crowd compelled his attention. The despair of the city was one of alienation, a "drawing back, do-not-touch-me kind of exile." G's "authentic and powerful note" consisted of the indignation of the "separated frustrated life-carrying individual."

**1196** Zucker, Jack. "To George Gissing," GISSING NEWSLETTER, VI (Jan 1970), 7–8.

[An original poem addressed to G.]

# Index

## AUTHORS

Included here are authors of articles and books on Gissing, editors and compilers of works in which criticism on Gissing appears. Editors and translators are identified parenthetically: (ed), (trans). Numbers after each name refer to the item(s) in the bibliography where the name occurs.

# Index

## TITLES OF SECONDARY WORKS

Titles of articles in periodicals and chapters in books are in quotation marks; book titles are in upper case; translations of article titles originally appearing in a foreign language are in parentheses, without quotation marks and in lower case; translations of book titles originally appearing in a foreign language are in parentheses and in upper case. Numbers after each title refer to the item in the bibliography where the title appears.

# Index

## PERIODICALS AND NEWSPAPERS

Included here are periodicals and newspapers for which entries occur in the bibliography. Numbers after each title refer to the number(s) of the item in the bibliography where the title appears.

# Index

## FOREIGN LANGUAGES

Included here are the languages in which articles and books listed in the bibliography originally appeared. Numbers under each language refer to items in the bibliography where the foreign-language title is given. English language items are not listed.

# Index

## PRIMARY TITLES

Included here are all titles by Gissing which occur in titles of articles or books or in the abstracts. Numbers after each title refer to the item in the bibliography where the title appears.